P9-DVP-850

PROCEDURES
in the
JUSTICE
SYSTEM

Third Edition

GILBERT B. STUCKEY

Charles E. Merrill Publishing Company
A Bell & Howell Company
Columbus   Toronto   London   Sydney

Published by Charles E. Merrill Publishing Co.
A Bell & Howell Company
Columbus, Ohio 43216

This book was set in Optima
Production Coordinator: Molly Kyle
Cover Designer: Cathy Watterson

Library of Congress Catalog Card Number: 85–61838
International Standard Book Number: 0–675–20360–0
Printed in the United States of America
1 2 3 4 5 6 7 8 9 10—91 90 89 88 87 86

This third edition of *Procedures in the Justice System,* as did the first and second editions, provides the reader with a thorough understanding of our justice system from the time of arrest through sentencing of a criminal offender. It presents legal rules of procedure in language that is easy to understand. This edition explains changes in procedural rules that have occurred, as the result of new legislation and court decisions, since the earlier editions.

Today's increasing crime rate is a major problem not only in the United States but throughout the world. It is the primary responsibility of those directly connected with the justice system, that is, members of law enforcement agencies, the courts, and correctional officers, to fight crime. Yet, to effectively curb crime, society needs the assistance of every law-abiding person.

By studying history we often see the mistakes of the past and can make efforts not to repeat those mistakes in the future. One mistake in the past was the failure to recognize that the members of the justice system are a team who must work together. Yet, to work as a team, it is necessary for each member to understand his own responsibility as well as those of the other members.

This third edition emphasizes more fully the role of the law enforcement officer, enumerates the various federal and state agencies responsible for curbing crime, and explains their functions. I have explained the importance of the correctional officer and described the types of correctional facilities now being considered for construction. The problem of sufficient probable cause to make a legal arrest has been expanded in this third edition.

This book was written for those interested in our justice system, and particularly for police and correctional science students. It explains duties and responsibilities of the law enforcement agencies, courts, and correctional departments, in relation to law violators, from the time of accusation until completion of sentence. The police and correctional science student should, however, study more than just judicial procedures. The student should have some knowledge of why we have laws and why those laws are broken, be cognizant of the constitutional rights of an accused, and have a better understanding of the philosophy of correctional endeavors. Thus, material on these subjects is incorporated into this text. I hope the information in this text will help the student of police and correctional science, as well as others, attain a more thorough knowledge of our justice system and of the role each member must play to achieve, through teamwork, law and order for all.

Although I am keenly aware of the key positions women hold throughout our justice system, for purposes of simplication *only,* I have used the term "he" more frequently

iii

than "he or she" or "she." I hope no reader is offended by this compromise.

To help the instructor present the material in this edition, a complete Instructor's Manual contains objectives, chapter outlines, teaching aids, interesting appellate court decisions, and examination questions and answers, including true-false, multiple choice, and fill-in questions.

I wish to again express my deep appreciation to La Velle Anderson, Department Chairperson, Speech Communication and Drama Department, Mt. San Antonio College, for her valuable assistance in the manuscript preparation for all three editions of this book. Among the many users of the earlier editions whose suggestions for improvement have made this a better book, I especially want to thank the reviewers of the latest edition: Richard F. McGrath of Cerritos College; Linda R. Feinberg of Trenton State College; and Lionel J. Neiman of Ball State University.

Gilbert B. Stuckey

contents

CONTENTS

viii

one

HISTORICAL DEVELOPMENT OF LAWS AND CRIME CAUSATION

The Early Development of Laws

From birth until death, everyone is affected either directly or indirectly by the criminal. A person may be directly affected by being the victim of a violent criminal act. Others may be only indirectly affected by the mere fear of going out after dark.

The annual cost of crime affects us all. It is difficult to estimate the total cost, but statisticians have set the figure at $100 billion annually. This figure staggers the imagination, yet it may be too low. There are certain costs that can be determined to the penny because of the budget money that must be allocated for the maintenance of law enforcement agencies, courts, and correctional institutions. A fair estimate can be made of the property taken by the law violator and the damage inflicted by vandalism, but there are a number of hidden costs that cannot be estimated with any degree of accuracy. These include such costs as the loss of time from work and medical expenses suffered by the victim of a violent crime. The loss of wages experienced by persons who must appear as witnesses in criminal trials must be considered. It is impossible to determine the cost that is being suffered by many legitimate businesses that are forced to close because of organized crime having taken over in that particular field. The amount of money that goes out of the country for the purchase of illegal drugs affects our economy and us indirectly. In addition, each protection device installed to prevent an attack from the criminal or to prevent thefts must be estimated in the cost of crime because if there were no law violators, there would be no need for locks on cars, homes, and businesses. There would also be no necessity for the elaborate burglar alarm systems installed in business establishments or for the many privately employed security guards. So the figure of $100 billion annually could probably be *doubled* and still not be too high.

Thus with the physical and mental anguishes suffered and the property losses inflicted upon the people of this nation, there is little wonder that there is concern over the high crime rate and that demands are being made to do something about it. As was stated in the preface, curbing crime is actually everyone's business, but those primarily responsible are those comprising the justice system, that is, the law enforcement agencies, the courts, and the correctional departments. It is their function to properly administer justice in this country. In so doing, they must take the necessary action against the criminal offender so that our society will be protected. Therefore, when a criminal law is broken, the justice system must begin to operate. An arrest must be made by the appropriate law enforcement agency. The accused is entitled to a speedy trial, so the courts must function, and if the accused is convicted and sentenced, the correctional officer comes into the scene. In the administration of justice many judicial procedures must take place between the time of the arrest and the sentencing, each of which will be explained in detail throughout this text.

Since the entire administration of justice begins with the breaking of a criminal law, it may be well to digress momentarily from the study of the legal procedures and determine what a law is and whether laws are necessary in our form of society. A law in its simplest form is merely a *guideline for human behavior.* Its purpose is to encourage a person to do what is right and discourage him from doing wrong. It has been described as a social tool to mold and regulate human conduct. Legally a law is defined as an act of a legislative body written and recorded in some public repository informing people of what is right and wrong. In the case of *Koenig* v. *Flynn,* 258 NY 292 (1932) it was stated as: "that which must be obeyed and followed by citizens, subject to sanctions or legal consequences, is a law."

The next question to be answered is: are laws necessary today? It has been stated frequently that laws are made to be broken. Also it has been alleged that if there were no laws, they would not be broken. In fairness to the declarant of this statement, it is only logical to assume that if there were nothing to break, nothing would be broken. So we return to the question: are laws necessary? Before answering, it may be well to consider the origin of laws and why they came into being.

A human being comes into the world with certain basic needs which remain throughout his or her life. These are the needs for food, shelter, companionship, and sexual gratification. If untrained and uncontrolled, a person may attempt to satisfy these needs in a most animalistic manner. If one were completely isolated from all other human beings, the fashion in which he might try to accomplish satisfaction of personal needs would be relatively unimportant. However, the moment one comes in contact with another person, the needs of each individual must be considered, and each must respect the desires of the other. Each person must learn to realize that his liberties cease where the other's begin. Certain restraints upon activity must be imposed. Thus there is a necessity for some guidelines about satisfying personal needs without infringing upon the rights of others. They may agree upon a division of territory, and each will confine his activities to that territory. If this takes place there is little reason for other guidelines, but if they should agree to combine their efforts, further regulations must be made. It must be decided who will do what and how they will share. As more and more persons enter the picture, the necessity for more rules becomes apparent. Eventually it will be necessary to choose a leader or chief to see that the rules are followed and to keep order within the tribe or society.

Undoubtedly many of the early established guidelines came about through trial and error. When it was recognized that a tribal member committed an act that threatened the existence of the tribe, a restraint against that act was created, and a violation of that restraint was what we now know as a crime. It probably did not take long for members of a primitive tribe to learn that they could not go about killing each other and have the tribe continue to exist. Therefore rules against murder were established. To satisfy man's need for food and shelter, he devised certain tools that became his property. The taking of these tools by another, depriving the owner of their use, was a serious act, so a rule against theft was enacted. People took mates to satisfy their needs for companionship and sexual gratification. The mate was also their personal property and to violate that property right was an offense, so rules against adultery were formed.

As tribes, or societies, grew in number and became somewhat more sophisticated, so did their regulations. As time passed people developed belief in a deity. Regulations respecting these beliefs were also established, and the violation of these rules was a serious offense against the society. Biblical historians tell us that when Moses led the Israelites out of Egypt some thirteen hundred years before Christ, he quickly realized that these people must have some guidelines to follow if they were to exist. Through an inspiration from God, ten basic rules known as the Ten Commandments were established. Included were not only those laws that earlier tribes found necessary for existence, that is, rules against murder, theft, and adultery, but also more sophisticated rules that pertained to admonitions against not respecting God. In addition were admonitions against certain thoughts that man may conceive which might lead him into greed. Thus he should not covet his neighbor's property. When Moses gave these guidelines to the people of Israel, he commanded that they obey them, as they would insure life and entrance into the possession of the land. He further indicated that these laws were not to be tampered with in the interest of human weakness. There was no mention that these laws were made to be broken. Nor has there been any such suggestion by anyone in authority since that time that laws are made to be broken.

Because of the effect of ecclesiastical law on the nations of Europe, most of these Commandments were incorporated into their laws and, in turn, were brought to this country by the colonists. Our early criminal laws included rules against murder, theft, adultery, working on Sunday ("blue laws"), profanity, perjury, and those describing family responsibilities. Although we have become a more permissive society and take some of the earlier guidelines less seriously, there are a few of the Commandments still found in the criminal laws of all the states of this nation because they are necessary for the existence of any society. These are the laws against murder, theft, perjury, and adultery; and other laws are added to these from time to time. As societies become more complex so do their laws. New restraints are placed upon their activities. These laws are designed with the hope that people can and will live more peacefully and pleasantly with their fellow human beings. Again we see, from a sociological standpoint, that laws are necessary for mankind's existence. From a legal standpoint, laws are necessary to inform people what is right and what is wrong. They must be made aware of the acts for which, if committed, they may be prosecuted. In our form of government each criminal law must be spelled out in detail so a person may know the exact act which, if committed, is a violation of the law. If a law is considered too vague, it will be declared null and void.

The Common Law

Much of the basic criminal law of this country originated from the common law of England. Originally, the common law of England was nothing more than a set of unwritten regulations and customs which acted as guidelines in settling disputes, determining the inheritance of property, and dealing with persons who committed misdeeds of a serious antisocial nature. As time passed, court decisions were made a part of the common law. Thereafter, the common law was further enlarged by legislative enactments, and was brought to this country by the colonists to act as guidelines for conduct.

Modern Criminal Law

Today the criminal law of the various states is a written set of regulations that is largely the result of legislative action. These regulations are recorded in some official record within the states, and are often referred to as the *penal code*. Criminal laws vary somewhat between the states. In some states there is no reliance upon the common law to determine what is right and wrong. The statutes spell out specifically the act that is made a crime and the punishment that may be inflicted for the commission of such an act. For example, the code may state that *manslaughter* is the unlawful killing of a human being without malice. This definition will be followed by a statement that one convicted of manslaughter may be imprisoned for a period not to exceed four years. The statutes of other states provide that "manslaughter" is punishable by imprisonment not to exceed a prescribed number of years. But this statute does not define what act constitutes manslaughter. The courts must then look to the common law to determine the interpretation of manslaughter.

Classification of Crimes and Punishment

In our present form of jurisprudence, not only do we tell people what a criminal act is, but we also tell them the punishment they may be subjected to if they commit the act. The following definition is generally found in the statutes of the states. A crime or public offense is an act committed or omitted in violation of a law forbidding or commanding it, and to which is annexed, upon conviction, one or more of several punishments. The basic forms of punishment are death, imprisonment, fines, removal from office, or disqualification to hold and enjoy any office of honor, trust, or profit. We have classified criminal laws in accordance with their seriousness to society and stated the punishment that could be inflicted upon conviction. Earlier in our history we classified criminal laws as *treason, felonies, and misdemeanors.* Most states eliminated treason as a category of crime and listed it merely as another felony violation. Thus two classifications remained: felonies and misdemeanors. However in recent years a few states have added a third classification, that of an *infraction.*

With the felony being the most serious crime, the violator is subjected to the most severe punishment—either by death, imprisonment in a state prison, or carrying a sentence of more than one year. The misdemeanor, being a less serious threat to the existence of a society, carries a lesser punishment, the most severe of which is usually not more than a year in jail. The infraction is the least serious crime, carrying a fine or probation but no imprisonment.

The procedure by which one accused of a crime is brought to trial and punished is known as a *criminal action,* and the one prosecuted is known as the *defendant.* All criminal actions are commenced with the filing of a formal written document with the appropriate court. This document is referred to as an accusatory pleading. In most felony prosecutions, the document will be an indictment or an information, both of which will be explained in detail in chapter 5. In misdemeanor prosecutions, the accusatory pleading is generally a complaint, as explained in chapter 4. When a criminal law is broken, it is against society as a whole, so the prosecutive action is brought in the name of the people; thus, the action is generally entitled "People versus the defendant," stating the defendant's name.

Civil Laws

Although we are primarily concerned with criminal laws as they relate to our study of the administration of justice, we must not overlook other laws that regulate conduct between individuals. These we know as civil laws. Civil laws cover many subjects, including rules against negligent or careless actions, defamation of reputation, and trespass onto property. These laws impose both the duty to perform contracts entered into voluntarily and the responsibility to pay debts. When one of these laws is broken, court action can be taken against the offender in an effort to get some redress in the form of damages. The violation is considered as being against the individual or victim. Therefore, the victim must take the necessary action against the wrongdoer, and the suit is filed in the name of the victim, known as the *plaintiff,* versus the wrongdoer, known as the defendant.

Crime Causation

To better understand the judicial processes involved in the administration of justice, and particularly the correctional philosophy, it may be well to consider both the causes and the extent of crime in the United States.

Crime in the United States

It has been alleged that the United States is the most crime-ridden nation in the world. This is a debatable statement as undoubtedly there are other nations which are equally crime-ridden. However, one could easily get the impression that the United States has the most serious rate of crime for three major reasons: freedom of the press, which devotes much space and time to coverage of criminal activities; maintaining outstanding records and statistics on crime; and efficient law enforcement agencies, making many arrests which, in turn, are recorded in files and publicized in the news media.

Whether or not we are the most crime-ridden nation in the world, we definitely have too much crime. There are many reasons why this is true. These reasons should not operate as an excuse for lawlessness, but as explanations with which we must work to control crime in the future. One reason for the United States' high crime rate is that our society contains mixed emotions concerning law and order. Perhaps there is no place on earth where people wish to live more comfortably and peacefully with others than in the United States, yet no group of people resent more than we do being told what we can and cannot do. We want to be protected by the authority vested in our government, particularly in law enforcement, and at the same time we do not hold authority in particularly high esteem. Too many of our citizens want their families to be safe from the hoodlum but do not want their favorite bookie arrested. They want their streams stocked with fish at all times, but they like to brag about "bagging" more than the limit. Americans want Junior to grow up as a wholesome law abiding citizen, but while on the Sunday drive they station him in the back seat to be the lookout for "cops" while Dad speeds. Too many want the law to control the "other guy" but want complete freedom of movement for themselves. These same people expect to be aided in an emergency but do not want to become involved in others' problems. In summary, as a nation our people love freedom and individuality—without restraint.

8

Another reason for our high crime rate is that the United States is a nation made up of an extremely heterogeneous people, from different nations, and of varied races and ethnic backgrounds. Such people tend to gather in cliques in certain sections of a city often isolating themselves from other nationalities. Many are belittled and discriminated against, and they find becoming part of a community is a frustrating experience. This frustration frequently leads to resentment and hostility and a striking-out against society.

The constant urge to acquire material possessions contributes to the high American crime rate. We enjoy the luxuries of life—the comforts of a nice home, the joy of good transportation, the pride of nice clothes, and the pleasures that the radio, television, and other entertainment can give us. Since we live in an affluent society, there are many material things to be had. The fact that one cannot always afford these luxuries does not make the desire for them any less. When these luxuries cannot be obtained legitimately, there is always the temptation to get them by various devious means, such as prostitution, pushing narcotics, stealing, or buying items at a low price from a questionable source without asking any questions.

An additional reason for the high crime rate is that the United States is a highly mobile society. We enjoy the right to move to any place at any time without restrictions. As a result many are constantly on the move from one community to another. Therefore they establish no roots and do not become a part of any community. They care little about what takes place in the community as long as it does not affect them directly. Thus, general social disapproval of criminal acts, once a factor in curbing crime in a stable community, is unknown in a mobile society. With the weakening of the family, neighborhood, and community, the potential offender is more ready to challenge authority as his identity is more easily lost, thereby making discovery more difficult. And the offender, if caught, may feel that the punishment will be reduced because of the lack of local emotional involvement in the criminal act.

Individual Crime Causation

Up to this point in the discussion of crime rates, we have been concerned with the population as a whole. But our high national crime rate is the result of many individuals committing crimes within our society. Thus, our study must now turn to why individuals commit crimes. As stated, laws are established so that society may exist and so that people may live more peacefully together. Why then are these humanitarian rules broken? In recent years more has been written about this subject than about almost any other, but we still have no concrete answer as to why people commit crimes or how to cure them. In view of the volumes of material that have been written on the subject of crime causation, it is impractical to indulge in a lengthy discussion of the subject. But a general discussion of some of the alleged more prevalent causes of crime will be presented.

It is interesting to note that in spite of our scientific accomplishments during the past half century, no definite answers to crime causation or its cure have been determined. Scientists have been able to transport humans from one end of the country to the other in a matter of hours; have made it possible for persons to sit in their living rooms and watch the events of the world take place by merely beaming a light ray through space; and have placed astronauts on the moon and returned them to earth within a few hundred yards of their designated landing spot. Medical science has all but wiped out epidemics and has extended the life span of humans by many years. Yet the cause of crime and its cure still remain riddles to humanity. Why should this be so when we have been able to perform other miraculous feats? The answer to this question is not an easy one to attain. However, there may be some plausible explanations.

In the past humans have devoted much time and study to the development of material objects that would make life easier and more pleasant. They did not concern themselves too seriously with crime as that was something that only involved the "other fellow." Besides, they felt that it was the responsibility of the church and religion to mold human conduct. If those who committed crimes were not caught and punished on earth, God would see that they received some divine punishment after death.

As the emphasis on religion as a motivating factor in community life began to wane, people turned to the school and education as a solution to all of their problems, including the regulation of human behavior. But as time passed people realized that crime was beginning to affect them indirectly, if not directly, and that neither church nor school had been the solution in curing crime. Therefore, a direct study of crime causation and its cure was begun. But this study is only a little over a century and one half old, and the beginning studies left much to be desired. It is only during the past fifty years that any concentrated study has taken place.

Type theory of crime causation.   When the first study of crime causation was made, it was believed that the criminals fell into physical types. For example, it was believed that if all of those who committed a particular type of crime were placed together, certain basic physical similarities would be detected, such as same height, weight, or facial characteristics. In other words, robbers would be of a different physique than burglars. Based on this theory, it was concluded that if a person possessed physical characteristics of a criminal group or type, that person was doomed to a life of crime.

Phrenology.   Following the "type theory" of crime causation and deviating somewhat from it was the approach known as "phrenology." This approach also took into account the physical makeup of humans, that is, the anthropometrical aspects, but the concentration was on the head and particularly on the skull. Although not the originator of this theory, Dr. Cesare Lombroso (1836–1909), an Italian physician, was a strong advocate of this theory and fostered much study concerning it as a cause of crime. He first became interested in man's conduct while acting as a medical doctor for the Italian Army. He noted that the more troublesome soldiers seemed to have similar physical characteristics whereas the less troublesome soldiers did not possess any outstanding characteristics. He also noted that the more hardened soldier practiced tattooing his body with crude and indecent types of tattoos, whereas the reliable soldier had inoffensive and simple types of tattoos. As a result of these observations Dr. Lombroso became interested in human behavior. He began to question if any of these characteristics could be a crime causation. To further his study, he visited prisons in Italy where he noted that a number of the inmates had peculiarly shaped heads or odd facial features. He concluded that if one's cranium were of a specific shape, that person was born a criminal and there was little control over his destiny. Although a number of criminologists accepted Dr. Lombroso's theory, it finally fell by the wayside early in the twentieth century. This was bound to happen, as his theory had one major weakness, and that was the fact that there were just as many persons with misshaped heads who did not commit crimes as there were who did. While the Lombroso theory has been the subject of criticism, Dr. Lombroso is given credit for concentrating on the individual as a possible cause of crime, rather than trying to fit the violator into a type of crime. Thus his name goes down in history for his contribution in this respect.

Endocrinology.   Another theory based upon the physical aspects of humans followed the phrenology approach. It was called the "endocrinology" approach, and was based upon the science of the endocrine, or ductless, glands. The advocates of this theory concluded that because of the malfunctioning of one or more of man's ductless glands he was compelled to behave in a certain way and that way was often in an antisocial manner. As other theories have been propounded in recent years, the endocrinology approach has received less and less acceptance. However it has not been entirely discarded. Medical and psychological studies have established that people do react in certain ways as the result of physiological weaknesses. It is well known that a glandular imbalance can cause tensions and that many children are hyperactive because of neurological impairment. As a result they act impulsively, but with proper medication they are able to control themselves and adjust to their surroundings and others. If this control were not achieved, their continued hyperactivity could develop into real social problems. Studies are being made on human chromosomes in order to determine their effect, if any, as they relate to criminal tendencies. So the physical makeup of humans should not be overlooked as having some effect on the causes of crime.

Behavior is Caused Approach

Contemporary studies on crime causation approach the subject more from the psychological aspects than from the physiological. These studies have led to the belief that all behavior is caused from environmental experiences and not from some physiological weakness or peculiarity. This approach has been referred to as the *orthopsychiatric* theory. It emphasizes the fact that in early childhood certain traumas are experienced which often lead to emotional and social maladjustment in later life.

In order to more thoroughly understand this approach, consideration may be given to human mental makeup. We come into the world with the basic instincts necessary to satisfy our needs for survival, but all other things must be learned, including adjusting properly to the demands of the society in which we live. Our first introduction to society begins in the home. If we experience feelings of acceptance, love, security, and controlled discipline from the beginning, adjusting to society will be an easy task and the chances of becoming wholesome citizens are good. On the other hand, if we are met as children with rejection, cruelty, and insecurity, we may find that conforming to the demands of society is difficult, if not impossible, to attain. Also it is very likely that one may develop a hostility toward society that will cause the reaction of striking out violently against it. Frequently the victims of this violence have no relationship to the aggressor, but are merely members of the society with which he is endeavoring to get even. Thus we see that the home environment and parental guidance, or lack of it, are major contributing factors in the future behavior of each individual.

Most parents do a satisfactory job rearing their children, which accounts for the fact that most people are law abiding citizens. There are some parents who have a sincere desire to raise their children properly, but fail in many aspects because of a lack of knowledge of human behavior. Parents often unintentionally cause heartaches, frustrations, and insecurities in a child. These reactions do not always result in the child becoming a criminal offender. For many, these feelings make adjustment to society difficult, and the more sensitive child could de-

12

velop into a behavioral problem. The following are a few examples of mistakes that parents make in their treatment of children.

Parents often hold up the academic accomplishments of one child to another by saying, "Why don't you get good grades like your brother?" There may be reasons other than laziness why one child does not achieve as well as another. Not all children within a family have the same mental capacity for learning. Also some undetected physical impairment, such as a sight or hearing problem, may handicap a child in learning. Such a comparison may cause the child to develop a feeling of insecurity and rejection. No two persons, not even identical twins, come into the world with exactly the same mental, physical, and temperamental attributes. This explains why one child in a family may become an offender while the other children adapt well to society.

In many homes the evening meal is the only time when the entire family is together. Instead of this being a happy social gathering, it sometimes becomes a court session. Dad becomes the judge and metes out the sentencing, including promising Junior a beating after dinner for scratching the new car with his bicycle. In vivid anticipation of what is to come, he loses his appetite, whereupon Dad tells him to sit up and eat. When Junior cannot do so, Dad "belts" him one then and there, not realizing that Junior's stomach is in no more condition to receive food than Dad's would be if he had just learned that the tax bill had doubled. Parents often severely punish a child for wetting the bed at the age of eight or nine, thinking that he is too lazy to go to the bathroom, not knowing that because of some physical or emotional disturbance he has no control over the ailment and that the punishment only creates greater anxiety and less control.

On the other hand the permissive parent feels that the only proper way to raise a child is to grant him complete freedom and to deny him nothing. Little does that parent realize that he is doing both the child and society a disservice. Our earlier study has revealed that members of a society must be regulated and controlled in order to exist. The child who has never been controlled or denied a desire finds adjustment to society most frustrating, and too many times he is unable to cope with the situations and may strike out violently to release his frustrations. To fit into our society, a child must be taught control, discipline, and the need to share with others at an early age.

Our real behavioral problems come from those families who do not raise their children properly. This failure by parents may be the result of one or a combination of reasons. Many parents are completely ignorant concerning the raising of children. Perhaps no career is more important to the existence of society than parenthood, yet in no other occupation do we send into the world individuals less equipped to handle the job than in many instances of parenthood. Also, there are many parents who have no moral or social values, so they impart none to their children. Parents are often hostile toward society and frequently release that hostility by acts of cruelty upon their children. The responsibilities of parenthood are too much for some parents to handle, so children are abandoned, leaving them with feelings of rejection and insecurity. Children of such parents often develop behavior problems at early ages, causing them to lead a life of crime.

Poverty

Poverty has been considered by some to be a cause of crime. It cannot be denied that it is miserable to be poor. The child who experiences the discomforts of the elements because of improper shelter, the pains of hunger from the lack of food, and the piercing cold from inadequate clothing may find it difficult to overcome the temptation to rid himself of these miseries by committing a crime. If there is no other way out, he may continue to satisfy his desires by a life of crime.

Broken Homes

Also alleged to be a contributing factor in causing crime is the broken home. Many criminal offenders are from broken homes. This is understandable because the parent raising a child in a broken home must do double duty. He or she must be both father and mother, and often must also be the family breadwinner. Frequently this leaves insufficient time to devote to the child and his needs. Many times he is left to his own resources, which are inadequate in meeting his needs, and he often gets into trouble.

Slum Areas

Like poverty and broken homes, slums do not condemn one to a life of crime. Yet many criminals come from slum areas. This is understandable since slums are the gathering places of many persons of little or no income. Many are unemployed, and some have no incentive to be employed. They may have a hopeless outlook on life, as the future presents little in the way of relief for their miseries. Yet they desire some of the common material things that make for a better life as well as some of the pleasures that luxuries can bring. When these things cannot be acquired legitimately, many see crime as the only solution. In addition, slums are a haven for the criminal since few questions are asked about one's background, character, or identity, and the criminal is generally accepted.

14

Narcotics

Narcotic addiction undoubtedly is a cause of crime. If ever gainfully employed, the addict soon becomes unemployed because of his inability to function normally. It is not necessary to discuss here what causes narcotic addiction, other than to state that most addicts get started in an effort to escape the frustrations of reality. The addict's narcotic need becomes increasingly expensive as his system develops more and more of a tolerance for the drug. Being unemployable, the addict turns to crime as a source of income to satisfy his addiction. The female addict often turns to shoplifting or prostitution, and, along with the male, may commit robberies, burglaries, and thefts.

Gangs

Not all gangs or gang members are prone to crime, but many are. It is well to consider why someone joins a gang. It is normal to belong to a group, and most people at some time are part of a group, such as a social or hobby club, or a service organization. Such groups provide companionship, common interests, and recognition. The boy or girl who does not belong to a family, school, or community group may turn to the gang to satisfy these desires. The gang supplies to the member a common bond with others who may be in conflict with family, school, and, too often, the police. The gang provides security in a dangerous world and protection from rival gangs. The gang enables the member to commit acts of vandalism, destructiveness, and crime without the social disapproval of his peer group.

Many Causes of Crime

Additional causes of crime could be listed, but those already set forth should give the reader some idea of the magnitude of crime causation. There may be not just one factor that causes an individual to commit crime, but a combination of factors. If it was necessary to establish a single cause, lack of proper parental guidance probably would be the choice. It must be remembered, however, that the child who is reared in poverty or who is the product of a broken home is not committed to a life of crime. Many people have overcome these conditions to become outstanding citizens.

Review Questions

1. What is the annual estimated cost of crime in the United States?
2. Define a law from the standpoint of the sociologist.
3. Why are laws necessary?
4. How do criminal and civil laws differ?
5. Name three reasons for considering the United States the most crime-ridden nation in the world.
6. Explain the phrenology, endocrinology, and ortho-psychiatric theories of crime causation.
7. What may be considered to be the chief single cause of crime?

HISTORICAL DEVELOPMENT OF THE JUSTICE SYSTEM

As we study the procedure that is followed from the arrest of the offender to his conviction, we will find that many technical rules and procedures must be followed or the conviction may be reversed upon appeal. These procedures are the result of a long evolutionary process. This process is interesting, particularly the development of the right of an accused to a trial by jury. The trial by jury is regarded as one of the greatest achievements of the justice system.

Upon mentioning the trial by jury, we immediately visualize a comfortable courtroom with a judge sitting behind a desk on a raised platform and presiding over the trial proceedings in a dignified and formal manner. We see the jury sitting in the jury box listening to the testimony of witnesses who have some knowledge about the facts of the case, and the prosecuting attorney presenting evidence in an effort to prove the defendant guilty beyond a reasonable doubt. We may also picture the defendant conferring with the attorney throughout the trial. At the conclusion of the trial we visualize the jury deliberating on the evidence that has been presented, and their returning a verdict of guilt or innocence. This scene is substantially what takes place in a jury trial.

However guilt or innocence has not always been decided by a jury trial. In fact the jury system as we know it today is of comparatively recent origin, coming into being around the beginning of the eighteenth century. Early in our history of jurisprudence efforts to determine guilt or innocence were primarily calls upon the supernatural or for signs from God.

As we trace the development of the trial by jury, our concentration will center primarily on England, from which most of our judicial system came. Many blank spots are encountered in tracing the history of a jury trial because of the lack of records. But it is known that the Christian church played an important role in the development of much of the law and procedure of early England. Most of the early records available for study of the beginnings of the judicial system were prepared by the clergy and are mostly incomplete. They were not compiled as a history of the time, but were merely a documentation of certain customs and events of the era.

The Invasion of England

History tells us that Julius Caesar invaded England in 55 B.C. and that Christianity was taught there as early as A.D. 64. At that time Christianity was not accepted by the Romans, and any activity of the Church throughout the Roman Empire had to be underground. Yet in spite of the persecution of Christians, the Church continued to grow. Religious societies and new congregations were being formed. Rules, regulations, and laws were being established to be followed by the Christians, but they were unlawful in the eyes of the Romans. However these laws were soon to become the laws of the continent of Europe and England. By the year A.D. 200 Roman jurisprudence had reached its peak, and from that time on Roman law began to decline. Instead of looking forward, the Roman leaders were looking backward to what had been. The Roman persecution of Christians terminated in A.D. 303 and in A.D. 313 Christianity was established as a lawful religion. Almost immediately the bishops of the Church involved themselves in politics, and they soon became as powerful as the emperor. The Church law, also known as the canon or ecclesiastical law, began to dominate the lives of people throughout Europe.

There is little doubt that Julius Caesar took much of the Roman law to England, but the Romans did not have an easy life there because other peoples invaded England. The Saxons conducted raids on the coastal plains as early as the third century and continued to do so thereafter. The Romans are said to have abandoned England sometime before A.D. 429, and the Anglo-Saxon invasions began on a large scale in A.D. 449. The Anglo-Saxons are believed to have established laws since they were known to have existed on the continent of Europe at the time, but records of the Anglo-Saxon laws and procedures are mostly fragmentary. Those that are available shed little light upon the judicial procedures of that time. It is known that kings established themselves and ruled until they were overthrown or died. A king formulated his own laws which were known as the king's laws, laws of the land, temporal, or secular laws. The Anglo-Saxons held reign in England until the Norman Conquest in A.D. 1066. Prior to this time England was experiencing considerable strife. Much of the administration of justice was left to the bishops of the Church to be processed through the ecclesiastical courts, and the canon law continued to play a dominant role. But as kings began to establish themselves more securely, they continued to formulate more and more laws affecting the people. These laws were enforced through the king's courts, known as secular or temporal courts. The king's court was presided over by the king's justices. Although there was an effort made to separate the jurisdiction of the secular courts and the ecclesiastical courts, rivalry still arose, particularly as it related to appeals. The ecclesiastical courts had jurisdiction over all matters pertaining to man's soul and church-related matters, including violations by the clergy. All laymen were subject to both the ecclesiastical laws and the secular laws. The ecclesiastical laws regulated many affairs of the layman's life, such as marriage, divorce, and the distribution of property after death. Through the ecclesiastical courts the laymen could be tried and punished for various offenses, including such crimes as adultery, fornication, incest, bigamy, defamation, and blasphemy. Originally the ecclesiastical courts were presided over by the bishops of the Church, but as the case load increased charges were often heard by the bishops' assistants, known as archdeacons. Crimes of murder, theft, and attacks on property or persons were violations of the secular laws and the offender was tried and punished by the secular courts.

The Magna Charta

When the offender was convicted, his property was usually forfeited. This forfeiture became a source of great revenue to the church or king depending upon what law was broken. In order to increase their revenue, kings frequently made various acts a crime in order to confiscate the property of a landowner or merchant. How the people fared depended largely on the amount of compassion of the king at the time. In tracing our judicial procedure frequent mention is made of the Magna Charta (also spelled Magna Carta) and its influence on people's rights. This document is considered to be the forerunner of the right of due process of law as the Magna Charta granted to the people of England certain political and civil rights. The Magna Charta is the result of the king being unduly oppressive to the people of England, and was signed during the reign of King John, who has been referred to as the "cruel ruler."

King John took over the reign of England in A.D. 1199 after the death of his brother, King Richard, the "Lion Hearted." King John was described as being clever but greedy and tyrannical in ruling his people. Conditions under him became unbearable for both the nobleman and the commoner. In an effort to improve the situation the noblemen gathered together and prepared a document containing certain resolutions which were felt to be in the best interest of the people. King John was maneuvered onto the Plains of Runnymede on June 15, 1215, where he was forced to sign this document known as the Magna Charta (also referred to as the Great Charter). Among other resolutions in the Magna Charta was the guarantee which, stated briefly, held that no free man shall be seized and imprisoned except by judgment of his peers or by the law of the land. Contrary to the thoughts of many, this guarantee did not give to the people the right to a trial by jury. Trial by jury as we know it today did not come into existence until the latter part of the seventeenth century. It merely meant that when a criminal accusation was made against a person, he was entitled to have the charge reviewed by a council consisting of members of the community. If the council concluded that the charge was well founded, they would command that the accused be held to answer for trial. His guilt or innocence was decided by the procedures of the time—trial by ordeal or trial by battle. This council became known as a grand jury and was composed of a body of between sixteen and twenty-four persons.

The right of an accused to appeal his case was practically unknown in early judicial procedure. But as time passed, a limited right of appeal was granted. Appeals in the ecclesiastical courts, in the twelfth century particularly, were taken to the bishop from the court presided over by an archdeacon, and from the bishop to the archbishop. The final appeal was to the pope in Rome. The final appeal from the king's court was to the king. Although the kings for the most part respected the jurisdiction of the ecclesiastical courts, this final appeal to the pope was upsetting to them. The inevitable result of this final appeal to the pope was to give recognition to the fact that the canon law was a world-wide system and was not limited to any national boundary. The kings were jealous of the pope's outside influence, over which the kings had little control, so they often tried to restrict this outside influence. King William I declared that no one was to receive a letter from the pope unless it was first shown to him. Later other kings declared that there should be no appeal to the pope without consent of the king. Yet it is interesting to note that with all the king's jealousy of the pope, King John, in his desperation, sought the assistance of Pope Innocent III after he was forced to sign the Magna Charta on June 15, 1215. King John requested that the pope annul the Magna Charta, which he did on August 25, 1215. The pope further forbade the king to enforce the Magna Charta upon the grounds that this charter was extorted from King John by force and that the terms of the charter were "dishonorable, unjust, unlawful, and derogatory" to the king. But after the death of King John in October, 1216, the Magna Charta was revised, and its provisions were again placed into operation. It was expected that kings thereafter would comply with these provisions.

Early Treatment of Offenders

With the Church playing the paramount role in the administration of justice in the early history of England, it is only natural that the deity was called upon to assist when efforts were made to determine the guilt or innocence of one accused of a crime. From the time of the invasion of England by the Romans until the Norman Conquest, one who was accused of breaking the law could be handled in one of four ways: the community could make war on the offender; the offender might be exposed to the vengeance of those he had offended; the offender might be permitted to make atonement for his crime; or the community might inflict upon the offender the penalty already established for the particular crime after his guilt had been determined.

Outlawry

Perhaps the earliest method of handling one who was accused of committing a crime was to wage war upon him. It was held that when one had gone to war with the community by committing a crime the community was not only entitled to, but bound to, make war upon the offender. He was declared "outlawed" or without the protection of the law. So the community was to pursue the offender and slay him, burn his house, ravage his land, and take his possessions. As time passed this form of punishment was inflicted upon only the man of lowest status, the slave.

The Blood Feud

If the accused was not outlawed, the community might leave him unprotected against those he had offended. Whereupon they might revenge themselves by taking whatever action they deemed appropriate in accordance with the crime committed, even to the slaying of the offender. Some of the offender's relatives may be slain also, since not all persons were of the same status in the early history of England. The lowest status was that of slave; next was the serf, who was bound to native soil instead of being the absolute property of a master such as the slave; then status continued up to the highest, that of king. In between were a number of other classes of persons, such as the barons and knights, who were referred to as "thegns"; the freeman workers were known as "ceorls." It was alleged that six ceorls were the equivalent of one thegn. So if a ceorl should slay a thegn, the slayer and five of his kinsmen also would have to be slain. However it might take time to locate the kinsmen in order to slay them, and other members of the family might inherit the responsibility of avenging the crime, thus the blood feud took place.

Atonement

There is no doubt that blood feuds were not the most popular method of settling a crime that had been committed, particularly when the blood feud reached a point when relatives of the offended or offender became involved in avenging the crime. It is only natural that the relatives would prefer to conduct some type of financial bargaining rather than engage in a lengthy hunt for the offender or his relatives and then become involved in a bloody entanglement to avenge a crime. Frequently a price of so many cows, horses, or a sum of money was agreed upon which the offender of his relatives could pay in order to bring about peace in the community. Thus the system of atonement was established. Each particular crime developed a designated price that had to be paid when that crime was committed. Even murder could be atoned under certain circumstances depending upon the status of the offender and the offended. Atonement was an accepted procedure in most instances not only by the offended but also by the Church and the king, as each would receive a portion of the atonement depending upon the crime. For example, if a couple were caught committing adultery, the man paid the king in order to regain his peace in the community. The woman would pay the Church for the sin she had committed. If the offender was without possessions, in order to make atonement, he might have to go into bondage or be subjected to a prescribed punishment. The system of atonement is the forerunner of the present procedures of fining persons for having committed certain crimes.

Trial by Ordeal

Not all persons were permitted to make an atonement, so other procedures had to be devised to bring those guilty of having committed a crime to justice. One of the most prevalent methods utilized in determining guilt or innocence of an accused was the trial by ordeal. The accused would be called upon to perform some physical feat. This procedure was a call to the deity for assistance in determining the guilt or innocence of the accused. The theory was that if the accused were innocent, God would enable him or her to perform the required ordeal. If guilty, the accused would fail in his performance. The accused would then be subjected to the prescribed punishment for the crime committed. When punishment was inflicted it was usually severe. The punishment may have been death by hanging, beheading, stoning, burning, or drowning. If the punishment did not amount to death, the guilty one might have one or both ears cut off; the nose or upper lip severed; a hand or foot cut off; be castrated; or be flogged, tarred, and feathered. If he falsely accused someone he might lose his tongue. In addition he might be banished from the land, which was later referred to as outlawry, or be sold into slavery.

The ordeal which the accused might be subjected to varied greatly in procedure, but whatever it may have been, it was preceded by an oath by the accused. It was an oath of innocence to God. If found guilty—by failing in the ordeal—the accused would not only suffer the punishment inflicted upon him but would receive divine punishment according to the belief of the time. Most of the ordeals were supervised by priests.

The most prevalent ordeal utilized was that of the "hot iron." The accused would appear before the altar, give his oath, and have his hand sprinkled with holy water. A red-hot iron would be laid across his hand, and he would take nine paces and drop the iron. The accused would return to the alter where a priest would bind his hand. Three days later the accused would return to the priest and have his hand unbound. If the wound had healed, the accused was found innocent; if it had not healed, the accused was adjudged guilty, and he would than be subjected to the prescribed punishment in accordance with the crime committed.

Another type of ordeal was that of the "boiling pot of water" from which the accused might be required to remove a large rock. The same binding procedure would be followed as in the instance of the hot iron. It would seem that under this system there would be few acquittals, but apparently many priests would take compassion upon those accused and would assist God in determining guilt or innocence. Records reveal that in one period of time there were eighty-three acquittals out of eighty-four trials by ordeal. Upon viewing the wound, the priest declared that the wound had healed. This record of acquittals caused the king much displeasure because of the loss of revenue.

The accused might be subjected to other types of ordeals in addition to the hot iron and boiling pot of water. For example, the accused might be required to walk barefoot and blindfolded over nine red–hot ploughshares laid lengthwise at unequal distances, or he might have his thumbs tied to his toes and be thrown into a lake or pond. If he sank, he was declared innocent. Also utilized was the "ordeal of the accursed morsel," where a piece of bread was prayed over. It was then given to the accused who was to swallow it. If he choked, he was found guilty. The "decision of the cross" involved the laying of two pieces of wood on an altar, one of which had been marked with a cross. After a prayer asking for a sign from God, a priest or young boy would pick up one of the pieces of wood without looking at it. If it bore the mark of a cross, the accused was deemed to be innocent.

Trial by Battle

Another method of determining guilt or innocence was trial by battle. In this method the accused and the accuser would go into actual combat with each other, usually using battle axes. Before the battle took place, each would swear to God that he was right. It is believed that the trial–by–battle procedure was brought to England by the Normans. It is known that trial by battle was used as a method of determining guilt on the continent before the Norman Conquest, and there is no record of its use in England before the Norman invasion. The Church displayed less favor to trial by battle than to trial by ordeal, because it involved a certain amount of pagan ceremony. However trial by battle was tolerated because it also involved a call to God, and the one who came forth the victor did so not from brute force but through the assistance of God.

Trial by Compurgation

The Church was always seeking ways to determine the guilt or innocence of an accused person without the tortures of the ordeal or the bloodshed of the battle, particularly when its own hierarchy was involved. It is believed that determining guilt by compurgation, through oath helpers or wager of the law, by which terms it was also known, originated within the Church, but the method was not confined to church personnel. For a time it was used for the layman as it related to violations of the secular and ecclesiastical laws. Trial by compurgation originated on the continent of Europe, but there are records indicating its existence in England before the Norman Conquest.

In the trial by compurgation both the accused and the accuser would take an oath to God. The accused would swear to his innocence, and the accuser would swear that the accusation was true. Each would be assisted by oath helpers, or compurgators. The compurgators of the accused would swear to God that the oath given by the accused was a true oath. The accuser would bring with him oath helpers who would swear to his truthfulness.

Initially the accused's oath helpers were often relatives, and if the accused should fail in the oath taking experience, the matter might turn into a blood feud. So the relatives were usually very willing to assist, although their assistance frequently led to perjury. Because of the unreliability of the relatives as oath helpers, the accused soon had to select oath helpers from persons in the community who were not relatives. If the accused had a bad reputation, he might experience difficulty in getting oath helpers. An oath helper might be compared with a character witness in our present judicial system. In some instances the accused had to select oath helpers from a list supplied to him by the accuser or by one of the priests or justices involved. Many times the accused would be unknown to these persons, so they were permitted to swear to the truthfulness of the accused's oath, to the best of their knowledge and belief. The number of oath helpers that were called to assist varied considerably. Any number between four and sixty-six were called, but most frequently the number was twelve.

Although trial by compurgation was used for a time, it did not replace the trial by ordeal or the trial by battle. As time passed the wording of the oath to be taken by the accused and the oath helpers became so complex that repeating it without error was almost impossible. If an error was made the accused was automatically declared guilty, and the prescribed punishment was inflicted. Thus with the technical language of the oath and the general unreliability of the oath helpers, trial by compurgation was somewhat of a farce. It soon fell into decay and disuse, and other methods were adopted to determine guilt or innocence.

The Establishment of Juries

As early as the ninth century Frankish kings on the European continent would summon, through a public officer, the most trustworthy people of a community. These people were then placed under oath to answer truthfully all questions directed at them during sessions with the king. These sessions did not necessarily arise out of criminal activity or litigation, but were often merely fact finding meetings in which the king could gather information about the community. These sessions were referred to as *inquests*. During the inquest the king might ask such questions as : what were the rights of the king in their particular community? Who were the land owners and how much land did they own? What were the customs of their area? Who had a better title to a piece of property, John or James? The number of people summoned to serve on this body varied from three to seventy-two, but twelve was the number most frequently called.

In addition to seeking the answers to the questions mentioned above, the king would also ask this body who they suspected of having committed murder, rape, or robbery. This body, later referred to as a jury, was the first crude form of an accusatory jury. But the Frankish kings did not always confine the use of the jury merely to accuse one of a crime; they often called upon the jury to render a verdict of guilt or innocence. In order to collect their revenue for crimes committed, these kings frequently preferred the verdict of this body of people over that of a trial by ordeal, battle, or compurgation. During the early use of the jury held by kings it is not inconceivable that a person may have found himself accused and convicted without even knowing that an accusation had been directed toward him.

To collect the wages of sin, the Frankish bishops were also known to have used the inquest to determine who had committed crimes against the Church. Records reflect that certain Frankish bishops selected a number of trustworthy men from an assembled laity, or congregation, who were administered an oath to tell the truth and conceal nothing for love or hate, reward or kinship, and to report their suspicions about their neighbors who might have sinned against the Church. These suspected sinners then would be put through the ordeal.

There is little record of the inquest being used in England until after the Norman Conquest. However Ethelred the Unready, King of England, is alleged to have decreed early in the eleventh century that a "moot" was to be held in every "wapentake," and that the twelve eldest "thegns" were to go out with the "reeve" and swear on a "relic" that they would accuse no innocent person nor conceal no guilty man. In our terminology, a meeting was to be held in every county subdivision where the eldest trustworthy members of that community were to go out with a local representative of the king and swear on some religious object that they would accuse no innocent person nor conceal one guilty of a crime.

Accusatory Juries

Hardly had England been conquered in A.D. 1066 when William the Conqueror summoned bodies of persons from all the communities to assist him in obtaining general as well as criminal information concerning their respective areas. In the mid–twelfth century King Henry II made great use of the juries to determine what cases his justices should hear as they rode their circuits through the kingdom. He would summon twelve of the most trustworthy noblemen of a hundred (or county) and four men from each township, who were sworn to hear accusations and determine if they were well founded. If so, the accused would be given an opportunity to prove his innocence by one of the various trial procedures.

King Henry II also suggested that the bishops of the ecclesiastical courts should not rely merely upon an accuser's unsworn suggestion that one had committed a crime before subjecting him to the ordeal, battle, or compurgation. Rather, they should have the sheriff summon twelve of the most lawful men of the neighborhood to hear an accusation to determine its reliability before the accused be put on trial.

The accusatory jury had become such an important part of justice by the beginning of the thirteenth century that when King John ignored its use and acted upon his own knowledge of accusations, the right to an accusatory jury was made a part of the Magna Charta. Included in the provisions of the Magna Charta was this guarantee: "No freeman shall be taken, or imprisoned, or disseized, or outlawed, or exiled, in any way harmed—nor will we go upon or send upon him—save by the lawful judgment of his peers or by the law of the land." It was expected that King John and all following kings would comply with this guarantee—the forerunner of our grand jury system.

The Development of Trial by Jury

As time passed greater use of the jury was made. It was called upon to decide not only whether an accusation was well founded, but, as in the case of some of the Frankish kings' juries, the same jury was to render a verdict of guilt or innocence. It was eventually believed that a jury should not be both an accusatory jury and a trial or verdict jury. Whereupon one jury would be summoned to hear the accusation. This jury was later referred to as the grand jury, and another jury was summoned to render a verdict of guilt or innocence, which was known as the petit jury. The petit jury usually consisted of twelve persons. Initially the trial, or petit, jury functioned entirely differently from the juries of today. These early trial juries assembled and stated what they knew about a particular crime, or they might be assembled and commanded to go forth into the countryside and ascertain facts about the alleged crime. Whereupon the jurors would talk to neighbors, pick up hearsay information and rumors, and would undoubtedly be contacted by the accused and the accuser. After gathering their evidence they would reassemble and draw a conclusion as to guilt or innocence. If the accused was found guilty, the prescribed punishment for the crime was inflicted upon him. Soon the jurors not only expressed what they had learned about the crime, but witnesses might even appear before the jury and relate what they knew about the accusation. The knowledge of the witnesses also was often no more than rumor or hearsay, and the jury might give little weight to the testimony of the witnesses and decide contrary to the general concensus of the witnesses. This was particularly true if the witnesses believed the accused to be innocent. The reason that the jury might decide contrary to the belief of the witnesses was that the jury was fearful of rendering a false verdict, thus denying the king his revenue. The jurors knew that the king's justices often had advance information about a crime because of reports from the sheriffs and the coroners. If the jurors made a false verdict in the eyes of the justices, they would be required to make atonement, and were even punished in some instances.

Because of the danger of conviction in a trial by jury, an accused would frequently revert to the trial by ordeal. However after the ordeal was abolished around A.D. 1215 and trial by compurgation had met with disfavor, the only procedure remaining was trial by battle. But if the accuser was a woman or a noncombatant, trial by battle was impossible, so it was unknown what should be done with the accused who refused a trial by jury, or put himself upon the country, as the jury trial was sometimes referred to. Occasionally under the circumstances the accused was hanged immediately. In other instances he was imprisoned for a year and given only a sip of water daily and a small morsel of bread. Sometimes he would be imprisoned and weights would be placed upon his chest in increasing amounts until he submitted to a trial by jury. Often the accused would prefer being crushed to death in an effort to save his possessions for his family, rather than having them confiscated by the king, should the jury pass a conviction.

As time passed and the king could no longer confiscate property as payment for crimes and jurors were no longer punished or required to make atonement for possible erroneous verdicts, greater reliability was placed on the testimony of witnesses. So we see the development of trial by jury as we know it today. But it still had a way to go even when the colonists settled in this country. The *Maryland Archives* reveal that on September 22, 1656, a judge in Patuxcut, Maryland, impaneled a jury of seven married women and four single women to determine the guilt of one Judith Catchpole, who was accused of murdering her child. She denied guilt and even denied having a child. Whereupon the judge commanded the jury to go forth and determine first if Judith had a child and, if so, whether she murdered it. It is interesting to note that even at this time in history, the jury was to "go forth into the countryside and seek information" rather than depend upon the sworn testimony of witnesses. It is also interesting that a jury of eleven instead of twelve was impaneled because long before that time a number of twelve for a trial jury was well established in England. By the thirteenth century, the usual number for a petit jury in England was twelve. By the fourteenth century a jury of twelve persons was firmly established, and thereafter twelve persons composing a trial jury seems to have developed some superstitious reverence. Why a jury of twelve evolved is lost in the annals of history, if it ever was known, but it is believed to have been based upon Christ having chosen twelve apostles. It has been alleged that twelve was a popular number at the time of Christ as witnessed by the twelve tribes of Israel, the twelve tablets, Solomon's twelve judges, and the twelve signs of the zodiac. Thus is is highly likely that the jury composed of twelve persons is based upon that fact, especially since the Church played a dominant role in the development of the judicial systems in both Europe and England. One of the ancient kings of Europe, Morgan of Gla-Morgan, is alleged to have adopted a form of trial by jury which he called the Apostolic Law and declared that as Christ and his twelve apostles were finally to judge the world, so human tribunals should be composed of the king and twelve wise men. Also at a later time, the following oath is alleged to have been required of a trial jury of twelve: "Hear this, ye justices, that I will speak of that which ye shall ask of me on the part of the king, and I will do faithfully to the best of my endeavor. So help me God, and these holy Apostles."

When the colonists came to North America they were well indoctrinated with the view that a trial jury should be composed of twelve persons, although it is known that one or two of the colonies permitted a jury to be composed of less than twelve. It is not entirely clear from historical data whether permitting less than twelve was a conscious effort to break from tradition; a defiance of the king and England; or whether it was because of the small number of people in the colonies involved, making it difficult to find twelve qualified jurors. This may have accounted for the fact that the judge in the *Catchpole* case impaneled only eleven women instead of twelve. It was also a break with tradition to impanel women instead of men on the jury as women were not generally considered to be qualified as jurors.

Historical Development of the Bill of Rights

As we approach the study of the judicial procedure followed today, it is well to review some of the rights and guarantees granted to one accused of a crime. These rights and guarantees are to be found either in the Constitution of the United States or in the constitutions and statutes of the various states. Some of these rights are based upon the common law of England. Others were developed over a period of time as a result of dealing with accused persons.

Returning now to the Magna Charta, we find that it created no panacea, but it did insure to the people certain liberties, which they had been denied previously, and made way for the establishment of due process of law. But the people of England continued to be subjected to many oppressive practices and many were persecuted because of their religious beliefs. To escape these practices a number of people left for North America to establish colonies. The king considered these colonies to be his possessions; the colonists were still under the rule of the king, and all too often that rule lay heavily upon them. They were taxed excessively and were generally oppressed. When they objected they were often taken to England for trial. As time passed more and more opposition was created by the members of the colonies. This became a source of irritation to the king who sent his armies to enforce his rule. Suspected objectors were frequently subjected to searches and seizures without cause and imprisoned without justification.

As a result of the extreme actions of the king, the colonists banded together and adopted a resolution declaring their political independence from England. This document is the Declaration of Independence. It announced to the world that the American people were serious in their aim to become an independent nation and it asked for understanding and compassion for other nations. The Declaration of Independence set forth the reasons for their actions and grievances against the king. Among the charges were that the king "has refused to assent to laws, the most wholesome and necessary for the public good; . . . has obstructed the administration of justice; . . . has kept among us, in times of peace, standing armies without the consent of our legislatures; . . . has deprived many the benefits of trial by jury; . . . has transported us beyond seas to be tried for pretended offenses." It is by a review of this Declaration of Independence that we are able to appreciate the conditions of the time and the conflicts experienced by the people of America, which became the basis of the guarantees later to be embodied in our Constitution.

The king did not take this Declaration of Independence lightly. He sent additional armies to subdue the colonies, resulting in the Revolutionary War. When peace was restored in 1783 the colonies became a nation—now governing itself. A governmental structure had to be formed. Laws had to be made for governing the people. Various efforts at governmental structures were attempted, but each developed weaknesses. In 1787 representatives of the colonies, now referred to as states, met in Philadelphia to again attempt to formulate an acceptable and workable governmental structure. The result of this conference, known as the Constitutional Convention, was the United States Constitution which was finally adopted in 1789. It established three branches of government: executive, legislative, and judicial. As the various state representatives reviewed this document, they felt that a vital weakness still remained in its structure. The people were not guaranteed protection against oppression should this central government become too strong and powerful. So it was agreed that certain additions should be made to the Constitution. Again representatives of the states met in Congress during 1789, at which time twelve amendments to the Constitution were proposed. Ten were adopted in 1791. These first ten amendments, known as our Bill of Rights, guaranteed certain rights to the people. The two amendments which were not adopted did not pertain to guarantees but were related to the legislative structure of the government. Because of the importance of these amendments to the administration of justice, they are being set forth for review at this time.

The Bill of Rights

Amendment I: Restriction on Powers of Congress.   Congress shall make no law respecting an establishment of religion, or prohibiting the free exercise thereof, or abridging the freedom of speech, or of the press; or the right of the people peaceably to assemble, and to petition the government for a redress of grievances.

Amendment II: Right to Bear Arms.   A well-regulated militia being necessary to the security of a free State, the right of the people to keep and bear arms shall not be infringed.

Amendment III: Billeting of Soldiers.   No soldier shall, in time of peace, be quartered in any house without the consent of the owner; nor in time of war, but in a manner to be prescribed by law.

Amendment IV: Seizures, Searches and Warrants.   The right of the people to be secure in their persons, houses, papers, and effects, against unreasonable searches and seizures shall not be violated, and no warrants shall issue but upon probable cause, supported by oath or affirmation, and particularly describing the place to be searched and the persons or things to be seized.

Amendment V: Criminal Proceedings, Condemnation of Property.   No person shall be held to answer for a capital or otherwise infamous crime, unless on a presentment or indictment of a grand jury, except in cases arising in the land or naval forces, or in the militia, when in actual service in time of war or public danger; nor shall any person be subject for the same offense to be twice put in jeopardy of life or limb; nor shall be compelled in any criminal case, to be a witness against himself; nor be deprived of life, liberty, or property, without due process of law, nor shall private property be taken for public use without just compensation.

Amendment VI: Mode of Trial in Criminal Proceedings.   In all criminal prosecutions the accused shall enjoy the right to a speedy and public trial, by an impartial jury of the State and district wherein the crime shall have been committed, which district shall have been previously ascertained by law, and to be informed of the nature and cause of the accusation; to be confronted with the witnesses against him; to have compulsory process for obtaining witnesses in his favor, and to have the assistance of counsel for his defense.

Amendment VII: Trial by Jury.   In suits at common law, where the value in controversy shall exceed twenty dollars, the right of trial by jury shall be preserved; and no fact tried by jury, shall be otherwise reexamined in any court of the United States than according to the rules of common law.

Amendment VIII: Involuntary Servitude.   Excessive bail shall not be required, nor excessive fines imposed, nor cruel and unusual punishment inflicted.

Amendment IX: Certain Rights Not Denied to the People.   The enumeration in the Constitution of certain rights shall not be construed to deny or disparage others retained by the people.

Amendment X: State Rights.   The powers not delegated to the United States by the Constitution, nor prohibited by it to the States, are reserved to the states, respectively, or to the people.

Due Process of Law

As we study these amendments we must remind ourselves that, when they were adopted, the oppressive conditions which brought them into being were still vivid in the memory of the people. Thus these guarantees were to protect the people against any action that might be attempted by the federal government and as such were only applicable to federal officers. The states, as provided in the Ninth and Tenth Amendments, were free to establish their own guarantees relating to the actions permitted by state and local officials. We will find that the Fourth, Fifth, Sixth,

The United States Supreme Court Building, Washington, D.C.
(Paul M. Schrock Photos.)

and Eighth Amendments are most significant in the administration of justice.

As time passed slavery and involuntary servitude, such as forcing men to build public roads and/or to serve in a state militia without pay, were permitted in some states. After the Civil War the Thirteenth Amendment, abolishing slavery, was added to the United States Constitution. To prohibit other oppressive and arbitrary actions by the states, the Fourteenth Amendment was adopted in 1868. This amendment held that:

> All persons born or naturalized in the United States, and subject to the jurisdiction thereof, are citizens of the United States and of the State wherein they reside.
>
> No State shall make or enforce any law which shall abridge the privileges or immunities of citizens of the United

States; nor shall any State deprive any person of life, liberty, or property, without due process of law; nor deny to any person within its jurisdiction the equal protection of the laws.

It should be emphasized that this amendment was directed to the states to prevent them from depriving any person of life, liberty, or property without due process of law. This created a question regarding the interpretation of the term "due process of law" as it related to the administration of justice. The courts later concluded that if an accused had his "day in court" with the right to appeal a conviction, the due process of law clause of the Fourteenth Amendment had been satisfied. We will find in our study of the judicial procedure throughout this text that the United States Supreme Court has since placed a different interpretation on the meaning of the due process of law clause of the Fourteenth Amendment. This Court, through case decisions, has stated that if this clause is to have any meaning whatsoever, the guarantees of the First, Fourth, Fifth, Sixth, and Eighth Amendments must be complied with by the states. Decisions making these guarantees applicable to the states will be discussed as the judicial procedure is further explained. For practical purposes, these amendments are as applicable to state and local officers as they are to federal officers.

In addition to the guarantees provided by the Bill of Rights, each state has furnished to the people within that state additional guarantees and rights. These additional rights are contained in statute or constitution. To insure that the guarantees of the Bill of Rights and the state statutes are properly afforded the people, court structures have been established.

Court Structures

After a person is arrested, unless the charge against him or her is dismissed, some prosecutive action must be taken. This action will occur in the appropriate court. In order for the student to have a clearer understanding of the judicial proceedings from the time of arrest through sentencing, a discussion of the court structure follows. Although the court structure may vary somewhat among the states, it is basically the same. The states are divided into territorial divisions known as counties, except in Louisiana where they are called parishes, and in Alaska which is divided into four judicial districts. Each county, parish, or district has its own trial court system. The chief trial court is known as the superior court, district court, or circuit court, depending upon the title which the court is given in a particular state. This court, in addition to trying civil matters, will hear trials involving felony cases and possibly some more serious, or high, misdemeanor charges. Generally this court holds forth in the county seat. Although these courts are technically county courts, they are referred to in many books on judicial procedure as "state courts" as distinguished from federal courts.

Coming to the county seat from outlying areas of the county has often presented hardship and expense to many of those involved in a trial. To accommodate these persons and to relieve part of the case load of the superior court, some counties have been divided into judicial districts, each containing a lower court. This lower court is often referred to as an inferior court, as opposed to the superior court, and is known in many places as the justice court. The judge is frequently called the justice of the peace. This court has limited jurisdiction, hearing certain misdemeanor charges and civil matters involving small amounts of money. Usually the judge is elected by the people within the district, and generally in the past there was no requirement that he have legal training. The reason for no such requirement was that in many outlying judicial districts there were no attorneys, but the people of those districts were entitled to some judicial assistance. Today, as more attorneys are available, many states have phased out the judges of the inferior courts who are not attorneys. However, the elimination of the non-law-trained judge has met with resistance. Some contend that the local inferior, or lower, court can provide a form of justice that is convenient both for the accused and the accuser and that the non-law-trained justice of the peace is part of the American heritage. Others contend that to subject an accused to possible imprisonment after a conviction in a trial presided over by a non-law-trained judge is denying the accused the right to due process of law. This matter was brought before the United States Supreme Court in the case of *North* v. *Russell,* 437 US 328 (1976), after North was convicted of drunk driving and sentenced to 30 days in jail by a non-law-trained police court judge. North contended that his conviction for drunk driving and sentencing to 30 days in jail was a violation of his right to due process of law as provided in the Fourteenth Amendment. The Court upheld the conviction upon the grounds that North could have taken his case to a higher court and had it completely tried again by a court presided over by an attorney judge. Therefore, North was not denied due process of law. The Court pointed out that there was an advantage to the accused in having the trial in a community near his residence rather than traveling to a distant court where a law-trained judge was provided. The decision did not rule out all non-law-trained judges as being a denial of due process of law, but it should be noted that the judicial structures of some states do not provide for a conviction in a lower court to be taken to a higher court and the case started anew. Where such a procedure is not available, courts could hold that an accused would be denied the right of due process of law in a proceeding before a non-law-trained judge.

In the judicial organization of some states another type of inferior court known as the municipal court has been created. This court will serve a city or a judicial district in much the same manner as the justice court, but the municipal court has increased jurisdictions in many states, and the judge in most areas must be an attorney with three to five years experience in the practice of law. Once this court is established in a judicial district, the justice court will be eliminated.

Since all prosecutive action must begin in either the superior court or the inferior court, these courts are sometimes referred to as courts of original jurisdictions.

Appellate Courts

Although the grounds and procedure for appeals will be discussed in chapter 14, the reader must now be made aware that if a defendant is convicted of a crime, he may appeal his case to a higher court for review. States differ in their appellate court structures. Some states have only one higher appellate court, which is usually known as the supreme court. Other states have district courts of appeal. These district courts of appeal hear cases brought up on appeal from the superior courts of the counties comprising their particular district. In addition to the district court of appeal, there is a state supreme court to which a defendant may appeal his case. In most instances, however, he will have to appeal first to the district court of appeal. The decision of this court will usually stand unless there is some important matter of procedure or law to be interpreted. In this case, the state supreme court may agree to hear an appeal from the district court of appeal. The supreme court in these instances hears the case and makes the decision in order that guidelines may be established to be followed in future cases that come before the trial courts and courts of appeal.

Depending on the appellate court structure of a state, appeals from an inferior court may be taken to the superior court or to an appellate court. If the case is taken to the superior court, the judge will act in the capacity of an appellate justice. A separate trial is not generally held because the decision will be made on the record of the lower court.

Federal Court System

Although we are primarily interested in the criminal procedure of the states and their court systems, it must be understood that there is also a federal court system created to handle cases involving violations of federal laws. The structure of the federal courts is much like that of the state system. The chief trial court is known as the United States District Court. States are divided into federal jurisdictional districts. In states that have a high concentration of people in a specific area, there may be more than one judicial district within the state. In the more sparsely populated states, the judicial district may consist of the entire state. The first appellate court in the structure is known as the Court of Appeals. The fifty states are divided into ten federal Courts of Appeal. Each district is known as a circuit. The District of Columbia is a separate circuit and is the eleventh circuit. Above the Court of Appeals is the United States Supreme Court, sometimes referred to as the "court of last resort" since there is no other court to which an appeal can be taken.

It is to be noted that in the federal structure there is no inferior court in the sense that we find it in the state court system, but there are United States magistrates who handle many of the pretrial procedures, such as arraignments and removal hearings. They also have the authority to handle certain federal misdemeanor matters.

Venue

Defined simply, venue is the geographical area in which a case may be heard. It is the place where a case is brought to trial and the area from which the jurors are selected. Usually venue will lie within the county in which a crime is committed. Venue may be waived by the defendant. There are times when a defendant may request that a trial be held in a county other than where the crime was committed.

Occasionally situations arise where it is difficult to determine in which county a crime was committed in order to have venue established. Many states have set forth guidelines to overcome this dilemma. They include such provisions as (1) when an offense is committed in part in one county and in part in another, the trial may be held in either county, and (2) when an offense is committed on the boundary of two or more counties, or within 500 yards (this distance may vary between states) of the boundary, the trial may be held in either jurisdiction. Prior to the passage of such provisions, there was a joke among old-time sheriffs and prosecutors about wearing out dead bodies by dragging them across county lines to avoid the responsibility of investigations and prosecutions. It has also been held that when a crime is committed within the state in a boat, motor vehicle, aircraft, or common carrier, the trial may be held in any county through which the trip passed or was terminated. Venue will be further discussed in chapter 6, under the heading "Place of the Trial."

Jurisdiction

The inherent power of a court to hear and decide a case is jurisdiction, whereas venue designates a particular *area* in which a case may be heard and decided. Unfortunately, the statutes of some states use the term jurisdiction when in fact the statute refers to venue, which leads to confusion to the layman. This dual use of the term "jurisdiction" stems from the fact that it is an all-encompassing word, embracing every kind of judicial action.

Federal Versus Local Jurisdiction

Since we have learned that there are two court systems, that is, the state system and the federal system, it may be well at this point to compare the jurisdiction of each. As has been previously stated, there are criminal laws enacted by the United States Congress which are known as federal criminal laws and enforced by federal officers. There are criminal laws passed by the state legislatures which are generally enforced by city police departments and/or sheriffs and their deputies, and assisted by state officers where they have the authority to do so. Although most of the criminal laws within a state are state–enacted, the violators are prosecuted in the county court or local system, as that is where the trial courts are located. So our discussion of the jurisdiction of the two systems is directly related to the trial jurisdiction of the federal and county courts.

When a crime is committed, the violator may have broken either a federal law or a state law depending upon the act. For example, a person may rob a liquor store which would be a violation of a state statute, as all states have laws making robbery a crime. Or a person may violate the Sherman Antitrust Law, which would be a federal violation. In the case of the robbery, the county court would have exclusive jurisdiction to try the case, and the federal government would have exclusive jurisdiction to try the antitrust violation. It is possible for a person to commit both a federal and a state violation with a series of acts arising out of a sequence of events. For example, a person may steal an automobile in one state and transport it to another state. Such an individual could be prosecuted in the local courts for the theft of the vehicle and prosecuted in the federal courts because it is a federal crime to transport a vehicle from one state to another knowing it has been stolen. In this example, the offender has actually committed two violations as a result of two different acts—one being the theft and the other the transportation of the vehicle while knowing it has been stolen. In these two examples each court has its own trial jurisdiction exclusive of the other.

As stated, it is possible for an individual to violate both a federal and state law by the same act. For example, an individual may kill a federal officer, which violates a federal statute, and the killing may also violate a state homicide statute. Under these circumstances, "concurrent" jurisdiction would exist. The question then would be whether the accused could be prosecuted in both the federal and state courts. This question can best be discussed in chapter 5, which deals with the plea of once in jeopardy.

Although most crimes committed on government reservations are also local or state violations, the federal courts have *exclusive* jurisdiction to try those matters because they were committed on a government reservation. It should be pointed out that government reservations are comparatively few in number. In order for a territorial area to be a government reservation the land must have always been United States property with the title still retained by the United States, or property acquired from a state for which all right and title was relinquished. Most military installations and national parks are government reservations; most post offices are not. Scattered throughout the United States are many national forests, but most of these are not government reservations and any crimes committed in these forests are within the jurisdiction of the local courts. However, any theft of the trees from these forests is a theft of government property which would be a federal violation.

In review, jurisdiction—as it relates to the administration of justice—refers to the right and the power of a particular court to try a case. It includes jurisdiction over the person and the subject matter of the issue to be tried. For example, inferior courts have jurisdiction or the right to hear misdemeanor matters. The superior court has jurisdiction or the right to hear felony cases. Jurisdiction is basic to the trial of a case and it cannot be waived. It is a right of the court—established by law.

Review Questions

1. What is meant by the ecclesiastical law?
2. At approximately what date in history did the ecclesiastical law begin to dominate the lives of people in Europe?
3. When was the Norman Conquest?
4. In what year was the Magna Charta signed?
5. What significant contribution did the Magna Charta make in reference to the administration of justice?
6. List four methods of action taken against an accused in England between the time of the Roman Invasion and the Norman Conquest.
7. How did the trial by ordeal and trial by battle differ?
8. Describe a trial by compurgation.
9. What use was made of early juries?
10. What was the accusatory jury?
11. The United States Bill of Rights is what part of what document?
12. What portions of the Bill of Rights are of particular significance to the administration of justice?

13. What amendment makes the Bill of Rights applicable to the states?
14. Define venue.
15. Define jurisdiction.
16. How do jurisdiction and venue differ?

Local Procedure

Since judicial procedure differs slightly from state to state, the reader may wish to consult the local prosecuting attorney for the procedure within his or her state.

1. By what names are trial courts known in this state?
2. What are the trial jurisdictions of the trial courts in this state?
3. What are the qualifications of the judges presiding over the trial courts?

THE ARREST

three

Arrest of the Law Violator

When a person violates a criminal law, society must take some action against that person. An arrest should be made. Originally, the members or citizens of society were responsible for taking the violator into custody. So much was it the responsibility of members of society to make the arrest that failure to do so was a violation. Even withholding information about a known crime from the authorities was a violation. In both instances the violation was known as a "misprision of a felony." As law enforcement agencies were created, the citizen was relieved of much of the responsibility for making arrests. Yet the citizen, or "private person," has not given up this right to make an arrest.

Private Person Arrest

The arrest by a private person is sometimes referred to as a "citizen's arrest," but the private person does not have to be a citizen to make an arrest. The private person may make arrests under certain conditions. These conditions are restrictive to discourage the private person from making arrests. Arrests should be made by the professional, the law enforcement officer. A private person arrest generally requires that the crime for which the arrest is made must have been committed, or attempted, in the presence of the arresting person. The statutes of some states provide for the arrest of a felon even though the crime occurred in the absence of the private party. A felony must have in fact been committed, and the private person had reasonable cause to believe that the person arrested committed the felony.

Although the powers of arrest and the procedure in making arrests will have been covered in other areas of study, a brief discussion of arrests is useful because of their importance in the prosecution of cases. If an arrest is not made lawfully, any information learned or physical evidence obtained will in most instances be inadmissible in court, and it is likely that the offender will never be brought to trial.

In *Legrand* v. *Bedinger*, 20 Ky 539, the court stated:

> The term 'arrest' is derived from the French, arreter, to stop or stay, and signifies a restraint of a man's person; depriving him of his own will and liberty, and binding him to become obedient to the will of the law. It is called the beginning of imprisonment.

Legally, an arrest has been defined as the taking of a person into custody in the manner authorized by law. The arrest is made by actual restraint of the person or by submission of the offender to the custody of an officer. The person arrested may be subjected to such restraint as is reasonable for the arrest and detention. There must be sufficient probable cause for the arrest to be made. Briefly, it has been held that probable, or reasonable, cause is shown if a person of ordinary prudence would be led to believe that a crime had been committed. Reasonable cause may exist even though there may be some room for doubt. But it must be more than a mere suspicion that a crime had been committed. It is difficult to set forth guidelines in determining probable cause. One might ask what facts would cause an ordinary prudent person to believe that a crime had been committed? The test for probable cause must be determined by the circumstances of each individual case based on the situation confronting the officer at the time that the arrest is made. The ordinary prudent person test has been criticized as being unrealistic because the officer, through training and experience, could recognize certain facts that would cause him or her to believe that a crime had been committed. Such facts may not be of a suspicious nature to the ordinary prudent person. Yet the courts have consistently adhered to this test. However most courts will consider the facts as seen by the officer before dismissing a charge due to lack of probable cause.

Arrest by Peace Officer

We should define the term "peace officer" before continuing this discussion. A peace officer is a person employed by some branch of the government and sworn to uphold the laws of the United States, the state, county, or city by which he or she is employed. The statutes of some states specifically spell out who are peace officers within that state, and if not listed in the statutes a person is not a peace officer within that state. Peace officers may be placed in four basic categories: Federal officers, employed by the United States government; State officers, employed by the state; the sheriff, employed by the county or parish; and city police officers, employed by their respective cities.

For an arrest by an officer to be lawful, the officer must have had the authority to have made the arrest. Peace officers have the authority to make an arrest in accordance with a warrant of arrest. In most instances the officer may make an arrest without a warrant under several conditions. An arrest may be made whenever there is reasonable cause to believe that the person to be arrested has committed a public offense in the officer's presence or when a person arrested has committed a felony, although not in his presence. The officer may also arrest upon reasonable cause to believe that the person to be arrested has committed a felony, whether or not a felony has in fact been committed. The power of arrest by a peace officer without a warrant is only slightly greater than that of a private person. The difference is that an officer has the right to make an arrest upon *reasonable cause to believe* a crime has been committed.

Territorial Jurisdiction to Make an Arrest

From a procedural standpoint it is important to determine if an officer has the authority to make an arrest, particularly when he has no warrant. If he does not have the authority, the arrest will be declared unlawful. One factor that becomes significant in determining the officer's authority is whether the officer was in his or her territorial jurisdiction. In most states the territorial jurisdiction of the city police is confined to the city limits. Any arrest without a warrant made beyond the city limits would have to be made as a private person and meet the restrictions of a private person arrest. Similarly the territorial authority of the sheriff of a county or parish is limited to the county or parish line. Some states limit the jurisdiction of the sheriff within the county, allowing arrests only in unincorporated areas. These states remove the sheriff's authority to make arrests within an incorporated city. However, in most states the sheriff is considered to be the chief law enforcement officer of the county and has authority to make arrests any place within the county. The sheriff, when within city limits, would have concurrent authority with the city police.

It was held for a long time that if an outlaw was able to out-distance a sheriff to the county line, the sheriff had to discontinue the pursuit since he had no authority to make an arrest in the adjoining county. To prevent the escape of an outlaw under these circumstances, the "hot pursuit" rule was developed. This rule provided that if an officer was in "hot" or "fresh" pursuit of an offender, the officer could follow him into another jurisdiction to make an arrest. The problem presented by this rule was: what would be interpreted as fresh pursuit? In early times when the local officer made his pursuit on horseback, it was concluded that if the officer could keep the outlaw in sight or still see the dust kicked up by his horse, he was in fresh pursuit. With the advent of the motor vehicle as a means of escape, as well as pursuit, the "in sight" theory became impractical. Therefore it is generally held today that if a pursuit is uninterrupted and continuous, it is a fresh pursuit. But even with this concept of fresh pursuit, the local officer had no authority to cross a state line to make an arrest. Thus, if the fleeing offender was able to reach the state line before apprehension, he or she had sanctuary in the next state. With rapid transportation available to criminals, new rules and regulations concerning the extent of pursuit had to be formulated.

Uniform Act of Fresh Pursuit

Today most states have adopted what is known as the Uniform Act of Fresh Pursuit. This act provides that a peace officer of one state may enter another state in fresh pursuit to arrest one who has committed a felony in the state from which the offender fled. It should be pointed out that in adopting the Uniform Act of Fresh Pursuit, a few states have not only made the act applicable to felonies, but to certain misdemeanors, usually those involving moral turpitude. Moral turpitude has been defined as conduct contrary to justice, honesty, modesty, or good morals. There is no specific distance set forth in the act that the officer may proceed within the state in order to make the arrest. The act does provide that after the arrest is made the officer must take the arrested person before a local magistrate, without unnecessary delay, for a hearing to determine the lawfulness of the arrest. If the magistrate concludes that the arrest was lawful, the magistrate will either commit the accused or release him on bail pending extradition proceedings. The procedure followed in the extradition of an offender will be discussed in chapter 17.

Limited Arrest Powers

A few states do grant local officers the right to make an arrest without a warrant anywhere in the state. This right is based on the theory that, when sworn as a peace officer within a city or county, the officer swears to uphold the constitution and laws of the state as well as local ordinances, thereby giving the officer statewide arrest powers. But as stated, in most states the local officer has authority to make arrests without a warrant only within the territorial jurisdiction in which he is employed, except in fresh pursuit instances. Some people in the justice system believe that this limited arrest power by local officers hampers law enforcement. As a result, statutes have been passed in some states extending the arrest power of local officers. Although the extended authority differs among states, the power to make arrests without a warrant beyond the territorial area in which an officer is employed is usually confined to any one of three situations. Authority has been granted in some states permitting an officer to make a lawful arrest beyond the officer's area if the officer has prior permission from the chief or sheriff of the area in which the arrest is to be made. This granted authority is based upon an old *posse comitatus* right of a sheriff. The posse comitatus right came into being early in the history of this country and particularly in the western part of the United States. The sheriff was often the only law enforcement officer within the county, and frequently needed assistance in locating and apprehending a criminal. To obtain this assistance, he was authorized by law to call on citizens of the county and deputize them to assist in the location and apprehension of a dangerous felon. These deputies were formed into a posse. Under posse comitatus, the officer making the arrest, in a sense, is a temporary officer of the jurisdiction in which the arrest is made. Also, the right to make an arrest beyond the officer's area of employment has been granted in instances when the offender is wanted for a crime committed in the officer's area of employment. In other instances, authority has been granted to an officer to make arrests beyond the officer's jurisdiction on an extended private person arrest power. This extended right permits the officer to arrest a person who has committed a crime, or where there is reasonable cause to believe that a crime was committed in the presence of the officer, and that lives may be in danger, property may be immediately damaged, or the offender may escape.

State Police Agencies

All states except Hawaii have some type of state police or law enforcement system. The state police agencies have state wide territorial jurisdiction, but states vary considerably as to the power of its state police to make arrests. In some states the state police have the power to enforce all state laws and have concurrent power throughout the state with local law enforcement agencies. In other states, the state police have limited jurisdiction that confines them to enforcing criminal laws only on state property. In addition to the state police, there are a number of investigative agencies in most states that have limited investigative authority and arrest power and are employed to perform specific duties. Examples of limited investigative authority and arrest powers are game wardens and drug administrations. In some states the state police not only enforce state laws generally but patrol the highways; other states have a separate agency for this purpose, a highway patrol. Although the territorial jurisdiction of state police is restricted to the state boundaries, the Uniform Act of Fresh Pursuit is applicable to these agencies as well as to local officers.

Federal Law Enforcement Agencies

Technically, the only peace officers of the United States government are the U.S. Marshals within the Department of Justice. But as with the states, there are a number of federal investigative agencies that have emergency arrest powers. All federal officers have territorial jurisdiction throughout the United States and possessions. Also within the U.S. Department of Justice is the Federal Bureau of Investigation (FBI) which was established in 1908 and has investigative jurisdiction over all federal violations not specifically assigned to some other federal agency. The FBI investigates a wide range of violations. Examples of FBI investigations include bank robberies, kidnappings when the victim has been, or is presumed to have been, transported across a state line, theft from interstate shipment, internal security matters, and interstate organized crime activities. The Federal Drug Enforcement Administration and the Immigration and Naturalization Service, of which the Border Patrol is a part, is within the Department of Justice.

Within the U.S. Treasury Department is the Secret Service, first created in 1865 to investigate and curtail counterfeiting of the United

States currency. After the assassination of President William McKinley in 1901, the Secret Service was charged with the duty of protecting the President of the United States. This duty has been expanded to include not only the President, but his immediate family, certain other high governmental officials, and some foreign dignitaries. Other agencies within the U.S. Treasury Department are the Customs Service, the Alcohol, Tobacco, and Firearms Service, and the Internal Revenue Service. Among the duties of the Customs Service are investigations of smuggling operations. The Alcohol, Tobacco, and Firearms Service investigates violations pertaining to the illegal manufacture of alcoholic beverages, illegal possession of certain firearms, and tobacco infractions. The Internal Revenue Service oversees the collection of federal income taxes and violations of federal income tax law.

U.S. Postal Service inspectors investigate violations pertaining to the mail, such as use of the mails to defraud and mail theft. There are a number of other investigative agencies of the federal government, but the foregoing are the ones most frequently encountered in law enforcement.

Force in Effecting an Arrest

The laws among the states are comparatively uniform as to the amount of force which may be used by a peace officer in making an arrest, but there seems to be some doubt as to the degree of force that may be used by a private person. The statutes of most states provide that any peace officer who has reasonable cause to believe that the person to be arrested has committed a public offense may use reasonable force to effect the arrest, to prevent escape, or to overcome resistance. It is also generally held that he may break open a door or window of a house in which the person to be arrested is, or is believed to be located. Unless there is a danger to the life of the officer or others, the officer must first demand admittance and explain the purpose for which the admittance is desired.

But what about the private person? How much force may he or she use to effect the arrest? The statutes of many states are silent on this issue. While it is generally conceded that a private person may also use that degree of force reasonably necessary to make the arrest and to overcome resistance, most states do not give this person the right to break into a dwelling to make an arrest for a misdemeanor violation.

Calling for Assistance

In making an arrest an officer or private person may call upon as many persons as is deemed necessary for assistance in making the arrest. In general, there is no prosecutive action that can be taken against anyone for refusing to assist the private person in making an arrest. However, the statute of one state provides that any person making an arrest may orally summon as many persons as he finds necessary to aid him, and that all persons failing to obey such a summons shall be guilty of a misdemeanor. This provision implies that one failing to assist a private person will be subject to prosecution. Most states make it a violation for certain persons to refuse to assist an officer in making an arrest when summoned to do so. As was the case with states who allow officers to arrest outside their jurisdiction, this provision is based upon the old posse comitatus policy that a sheriff had the authority to deputize members of a community and demand that they assist him in the location and apprehension of an outlaw. In modern practice it is not necessary in an emergency situation to deputize a person before requesting assistance. Many times an officer is confronted with circumstances where immediate help is needed in making an arrest. Under these circumstances, he may orally summon those present to assist him, and a failure to come to his aid may subject those persons to prosecution.

States differ considerably as to who must assist an officer in making an arrest or be subjected to prosecution. The statutes of several states provide that an officer making a lawful arrest may command the aid of every male person over 18 years of age to assist him, and a male person failing to obey the command for assistance shall be guilty of a misdemeanor. It is to be noted that this provision makes no mention of the male individual being "able-bodied." This provision was excluded purposely. When an officer is presented with an emergency situation, he should not have to spend time determining who is physically capable of assisting him before summoning assistance. It also prohibits an individual from using the excuse that he is not physically able to assist. Not all requests for assistance entail a physical encounter with the accused. The assistance may be only a request that the individual radio for other police units to come to the aid of an officer, which under the circumstances could be performed by a person in a wheelchair.

The statutes of some states provide that every able-bodied person over the age of 18 years who refuses to aid an officer in making the arrest after being commanded to do so is guilty of a misdemeanor. Such a provision makes both men and women subject to prosecution should they fail to assist in making an arrest after being summoned to do so by an officer. The problem created with the provision that the person be "able-bodied" is what criterion is to be used in determining if the person summoned was able-bodied. It has been held that the mere fact that there may be some danger involved in rendering assistance is not sufficient to refuse to assist. The statutes of a few states provide that every person who fails to obey a command by an officer to assist him in making an arrest shall be guilty of a misdemeanor. Such a provision is all encompassing as no mention is made of the person being able-bodied, male or female, or within a specific age designation.

The statute of one state provides that the officer requesting assistance must be in uniform for prosecutive action to be applicable. This again is to eliminate the possibility of an individual using the excuse that he did not know that the person requesting assistance was an officer. However, this restriction is not without complications. In view of the wording of the statute, even if an individual knows that the person summoning assistance is an officer, unless the officer is in uniform when he summons aid, the individual cannot be prosecuted if he fails to assist the officer. The provision also raises the question: what is a uniform? Some law enforcement agencies have adopted the sport coat or blazer and sport pants style of uniform, which gives the appearance of civilian clothing. Would this be considered a uniform within the meaning of the statute? Perhaps only a test case in the future will answer this question.

Resisting Arrest

Generally, it is a violation to willfully resist, delay, or obstruct a peace officer in the performance of his duty, including making an arrest. Yet may an individual who is being arrested by a private person resist that arrest without being subjected to prosecution for the resistance? Most state statutes are silent on this point. Since there is no provision that an individual can be charged with an act of resisting arrest by a private person, presumably one is not subject to any additional charge except the one for which the arrest is being made, and the only peril is in meeting the resistance of the private person.

In this discussion a question regarding the right of a person to resist an unlawful arrest must also arise. As previously stated, it is generally held that resisting an officer in the performance of his duty is a violation. But is he performing his duty if he makes an unlawful arrest? It was previously held at common law that a person could resist an unlawful arrest, and this view is followed in some of the states whether the arrest is being made by an officer or a private person. This results in many curbside court sessions and brawls between the accused and the arresting person, with each claiming to be right and violent resistance taking place. Other states have provided that if a person is being arrested or has reasonable cause to believe he is being arrested by an officer, he is under the duty to refrain from using force or any weapon to resist such arrest. By court interpretation, it has been held that this provision refers to unlawful arrests as well as lawful ones. It is to be noted, however, that the provisions pertains *only* to officers and is still silent as to resisting arrest by a private person.

Although a person may not resist an unlawful arrest in some states, he or she is not without recourse. One is entitled to seek immediate release from custody by a writ of habeas corpus proceeding, and may sue those responsible for the illegal arrest for damages in civil court.

Immunity from Arrest

There are classes of persons who are immune from arrest because of statutory regulations. These include certain representatives from foreign countries, legislators, and-out of-state witnesses.

Diplomatic Immunity

International law and various agreements between nations exchanging representatives are the bases for diplomatic immunity. For example, in the United States, as provided by international law, diplomatic officers, their staff, members of their families, and their servants are free from local jurisdiction and as such they should not be arrested or detained for any offense unless they are citizens of or permanent residents of the United States. (See 22 United States Code, section 252.) The diplomatic officers who enjoy this unlimited immunity are ambassadors, ministers, their assistants, and attachés. The purpose behind the doctrine of diplomatic immunity is to contribute to the development of friendly relations among nations and to ensure the efficient performance of the diplomatic missions.

Although these persons have complete immunity from arrest, detention, or prosecution, the immunity does not give them blanket authority to disregard the laws of the United States and of the individual states. As established by international law, it is the duty of all foreign representatives to respect the laws and regulations of the land. If a member of the diplomatic corps commits a crime, the offense should be brought to the attention of the United States Department of State, and if the crime is a serious one, the State Department may request that the member be recalled from the country.

Consular Immunity

Consuls and their deputies are also representatives of foreign nations but have only limited immunity. In all cases, however, they are to be treated with due respect. The consular officers are not liable for arrest or detention pending a trial except in cases of a serious felony having been committed. Since consular officers' immunity is limited to acts in performance of their duties, the immunity does not include members of their families or servants, but they too should be treated with proper respect. If a consular officer commits a traffic violation, the traffic officer may treat him the same as he does anyone else. The traffic officer may only warn the consular officer and let him go on his way, or he may issue a citation, as this is not considered in violation of the immunity of arrest and detention.

Most diplomatic corps are stationed in either Washington, District of Columbia, or with the United Nations in New York, but consular officers are assigned to stations in many large cities throughout the United States. Peace officers in the United States may encounter members of these groups anyplace, as many of them travel extensively. Each member of these groups should have official identification in his possession, whereby a peace officer may determine the official status of the member and the immunity to which he is entitled.

Legislative Immunity

Most states have some type of provision in their statutes granting immunity to legislative members, but this immunity is most limited in nature. Many of the states hold that the immunity relates only to arrest arising out of some civil matter and that there is no immunity from arrest on a criminal charge.

Out-of-State Witnesses

The *Uniform Act to Secure the Attendance of Witnesses from Without the State in Criminal Cases* has been adopted by most of the states. This act provides that if a person goes into a state in obedience of a subpoena to testify in that state, he shall not be subject to arrest in connection with any crime committed in the state prior to his entrance into the state to testify. He is also granted a reasonable time to leave the state after testifying without being subject to such an arrest. He is not, however, granted any immunity from arrest for a crime that he may commit while in the state to testify. A similar immunity is given to persons passing through a state to testify in another state in obedience of a subpoena. One might question this immunity from arrest given to a witness. The reason is that the testimony is more important to a particular case than is the prosecution of a witness for some past violation of the law. In addition, if the prosecution were significant, there is no reason why extradition proceedings could not be brought against the witness.

Booking

When people are arrested the usual procedure is to take them to the police station for booking. Booking consists of recording the arrest in official law enforcement records, fingerprinting, and photographing the accused. If the charge is a bailable offense, the accused is entitled to post bail at this time. If bail is not posted, the accused will be searched and placed in jail until he does post bail or until final prosecution takes place.

Right to Telephone Calls

Whether an arrest is made by a law enforcement officer or by a private person, the accused is entitled to certain rights. One of these rights is to be informed of the offense for which he is being arrested. Another right provided by the statutes of some states is the right to make telephone calls. This right has been incorporated into the laws to prohibit an individual from being held indefinitely without anyone knowing that he has been arrested, in other words, to prevent him from being held incommunicado.

In those states in which the arrested person is permitted to make telephone calls, there is a considerable difference in the rights afforded the arrested person. These rights differ as to the number of calls that may be made, to whom, how soon after the arrest, at whose expense, whether the calls can be monitored, and whether the arrested person must be advised of the right to make the calls. It is generally held that the arrested person is entitled to make the calls immediately after being booked, or, except where physically impossible, within a prescribed time, such as three hours, after the arrest. It is also generally provided that the arrested person is entitled to make at least one or more completed calls to an attorney, bail bondsman, relative or other person. The calls are to be made free of charge if to a local area and otherwise at the expense of the arrested person. Some jurisdictions require that the arrested person be advised of the right to make the calls; others merely require that the right be posted in a conspicuous place in the area of detention. This right is a continuing one and is not waived if the arrested person does not request to make the calls immediately after being booked. Some states also require that if the arrested person is physically unable to make the call, he is entitled to the assistance of an officer.

Issuance of a Citation

At one time in our history all criminal offenders were brought to court with force. Even in civil matters an arrest was frequently used to bring the defendant to court. Today the defendant in a civil matter is not forced to appear in court. If the defendant fails to appear as requested, the person bringing the suit, who is known as the *plaintiff,* is given the judgment by default. Even in criminal matters, particularly involving minor violations, efforts are made to persuade the accused to come to court with as little inconvenience to all as is possible. But when a warrant of arrest is issued, the person named in the warrant must be taken into custody, booked, and transported for arraignment unless he posts bail before his arraignment. This same procedure is followed in most arrests made without a warrant. Each of these steps is time consuming, and if the person does not post bail, he must be confined to jail pending the judicial proceedings. This detention often causes overcrowding of the jail facilities, and in some instances, an injustice to the accused. To alleviate this situation, many states have adopted legislation whereby an officer may issue a citation for a misdemeanor or infraction violation instead of taking the person into custody.

A *citation* (sometimes referred to as a summons) is a written notice issued to a violator to appear in court. The citation lists the violator's name, address, and the offense committed. It also sets forth the time, place, and date that the violator is to appear in court. If the arrested person signs the citation agreeing to appear in court as directed, he is entitled to be released without further action being taken at that time.

In most instances, a citation will be issued for an infraction and for a traffic violation. But it is generally within the discretion of the law enforcement officer whether a citation will be issued for a misdemeanor violation. Many law enforcement agencies have established guidelines as to which misdemeanor violations a citation may be issued in lieu of taking the offender into custody. One reason for the selective practice is that it may be felt that the violator would not appear in court, and that booking and confinement until he posts bail is the preferable procedure. Some law enforcement agencies have established a policy of taking an offender into custody, booking him, and then releasing him on a citation. In a sense this procedure defeats part of the purpose of issuing the citation in that the offender is taken into custody, transported to the station, and booked. Those following this process feel that the identifying data obtained from the booking justifies the time consumed, particularly if the violator does not appear as agreed and must be sought on a bench warrant. To discourage the booking-and-then-release practice, some jurisdictions require that the arresting agency conduct a background investigation to determine if the person should be released on a citation. The investigation should include the person's name, address, length of residence at that address, length of residence in the state, marital and family status, current employment, length of current employment, prior arrest record, and such other facts as would bear on the question of the release of the individual.

Even though the violator is released in the field by signing the citation, most jurisdictions permit the law enforcement agency involved to request that the violator be booked prior to commencement of final judicial proceedings in order to get identifying data for future reference.

Citation Court Procedure

In some jurisdictions a copy of the citation is filed with the appropriate court. This citation will become the accusatory document instead of the officer filing a complaint. In other jurisdictions a copy of the citation is furnished to the prosecuting attorney, and based upon this citation a complaint will be filed with the court which is to hear the case. After the citation has been issued and before the arraignment, the violator may post bail for his appearance. If he should fail to appear as agreed, the bail may be forfeited. The judge in his discretion may order that no further proceedings shall take place on the matter, or he may issue a bench warrant for the arrest of the violator. The judge will then proceed on the original charge for which the citation was issued, and in most jurisdictions the violator can be charged with a misdemeanor for failure to appear.

The Summons

Although a citation is sometimes referred to as a summons, technically a summons differs from a citation. The true summons is issued by a judge in lieu of a warrant of arrest. The summons commands the accused to appear in court at a specified time and eliminates the need of arresting the accused and bringing him before the court. The summons may be issued by a judge when he feels that the accused will appear as commanded without an arrest needing to be made. The summons, like the warrant of arrest, is based upon a complaint filed with the court. After the summons is issued it may be personally delivered or mailed to the accused. If the person named in the summons fails to appear as commanded, a warrant of arrest will be issued for him. A summons differs from a citation in that a summons is issued by a judge and either mailed to the accused or served upon him personally commanding his appearance; a citation is generally issued by an officer in the field to the accused.

Review Questions

1. Define an arrest.
2. Define probable cause for an arrest.
3. Who are peace officers?
4. What is meant by fresh pursuit?
5. What is meant by diplomatic immunity?
6. What officials fall within the diplomatic immunity provisions?
7. For what reason is an arrested person entitled to make telephone calls?

8. What is a citation?
9. How does the procedure followed in the issuing of a citation differ from executing a warrant of arrest?

Local Procedure

1. Do peace officers have state-wide arrest powers?
2. Who, if anyone, must come to the aid of an officer in making an arrest when called upon to do so or else be subject to prosecution?
3. Does an arrested person have the right to make telephone calls, and, if so, to whom and how many calls may he make? Must the person under arrest be advised of this right to make the calls?
4. Has the state adopted the *Uniform Act of Fresh Pursuit?* If so, does the act apply to felony violations only or has it been made applicable to misdemeanors? If applicable to misdemeanors, what types?

four

THE INITIAL APPEARANCE

Purpose of the Initial Appearance

Although there is no mention of the "initial appearance" in our Bill of Rights, it is a basic right of an arrested person to be taken before a magistrate without unnecessary delay. This right is included in the federal rules of procedure and in the laws of the states. The initial appearance consists of the accused appearing before a magistrate to be advised of certain rights to which he or she is entitled. A magistrate may be defined as anyone having the authority to issue a warrant of arrest. From a practical standpoint a magistrate generally is a judge of one of the inferior courts who spends much time conducting initial appearance hearings. The initial or "first" appearance is sometimes referred to as an "arraignment." The term *arraignment* is used in many areas, and even the U.S. Supreme Court in the landmark cases of *McNabb* v. *United States,* 318 US 332 (1943) and *Mallory* v. *United States,* 354 US 449 (1957) referred to the initial appearance as an "arraignment." In some states the accused is permitted to enter a plea at the initial appearance which adds to the tendency to call the initial appearance an arraignment.

At the initial appearance, the accused will be officially informed of the charge against him. Although the person is entitled to be informed of the charge at the time of the arrest, the charge is often changed between the time of the arrest and the initial appearance. For example, a person may be arrested on a charge of aggravated assault but between the time of the arrest on that charge and the initial appearance the victim dies. The charge is usually changed from aggravated assault to a homicide charge. Also, at the initial appearance, if the offense is one for which bail may be posted, the accused will be informed of the right to make bail if he is not already out on bail. If the accused is not represented by an attorney, the rights to the assistance of counsel and to remain silent will be explained to him. Each of these rights will be discussed in detail.

Time of the Initial Appearance

One of the more troublesome problems involved in an initial appearance concerns when it must be held once the arrest is made. For many years neither the courts nor law enforcement agencies were particularly concerned about the timing of the initial appearance. As a result many arrested persons were held incommunicado in jail for days and sometimes weeks before being taken before a magistrate. To overcome the injustice of this procedure, it is now provided that an arrested person must be taken before a magistrate without unnecessary delay. However this provision is not without its complications. What will the courts accept, if anything, as necessary or reasonable delay in taking the defendant before a magistrate, and what penalties will be attached if there is an unnecessary delay deemed in the initial appearance? To assist officers in determining time limits, most states have enacted provisions setting forth the time within which the initial appearance must take place. The time limit varies considerably among the states but the following is typical of the wording of such statutes:

> The arrested person must be taken before a magistrate without unnecessary delay, and in any event no longer than two days, Sundays and holidays excluded. If the two day period expires when the court is not in session, the time for the initial appearance will be extended until the next regular court session.

This provision implies that the two-day period is actually based on a forty-eight hour limit. It is pointed out that the forty-eight hour restriction is not a blanket authority to hold all arrested persons for that period of time without taking them before a magistrate. A delay in the initial appearance for a much shorter time could be interpreted as an unnecessary delay. Some states have a seventy-two hour limit instead of the forty-eight hour, and a few states merely provide that an arrested person must be taken before a magistrate without unnecessary delay. If an arrested person is not taken before a magistrate within the prescribed time, he must be released. Whether the person could be arrested again after the release is doubtful; much would depend on the facts of the particular case and the reason for the delay in the initial appearance. In some instances, the release of the accused will result in a dismissal of the charge and will bar further prosecutive action, particularly in misdemeanor cases.

The time within which an initial appearance must be held and the penalties that may be attached for the delay were placed in particular emphasis by the landmark decision handed down by the United States Supreme Court in 1943 in the case of *McNabb* v. *United States*. The facts of that case reveal that some of the defendants were held for six days after the arrest before being arraigned, during which time confessions were obtained from them. These confessions were introduced against the defendants in their trial for the murder of a federal officer. The conviction was appealed to the United States Supreme Court upon the grounds that the confessions had been involuntarily given. The Court concluded that there was an unnecessary delay in the arraignment, during which time these confessions were obtained. To discourage unnecessary delay in arraignments, the court held that any confession obtained during an unnecessary delay would be inadmissible as evidence in a court proceeding. This was an entirely new approach to the admissibility of confession. Prior to the *McNabb* decision the test of admissibility was voluntariness in the giving of the confession. So the Court, in that case, attached a very significant penalty to a delay in arraigning an arrested person.

Although this decision pertained only to federal officers, several states have adopted the rule as set forth in the *McNabb* decision by maintaining that confessions obtained by local officers during a delay in arraignment are inadmissible as evidence. It becomes important to determine what, if anything, might be considered as a necessary delay in arraigning an arrested person. Following the *McNabb* case the United States Supreme Court handed down other decisions relative to the time factor in arraignments. It was indicated in one case that the Court took into consideration that an arrested person should be booked before being arraigned. In another case it was held that some investigative activity to verify information furnished by the defendant before being arraigned would be tolerated. (See *Mallory* v. *United States.*)

The United States Supreme Court cases mentioned are of little assistance in furnishing guidelines for how long an accused may be held within the prescribed time limit before the initial appearance and still have the delay considered necessary. It has been held by the courts that if the delay is solely for the purpose of interrogating the accused, such delay is not considered necessary. Yet it is recognized that some questioning after an arrest may be in order, followed by a reasonable investigation to verify or refute information given by the arrested person. Such questioning could assist in the early release of an innocent person or act as a justification for the arrest. For example, in one case the delay in initial appearance for almost the entire prescribed time was upheld. In that case, the owner of an old model car took the car to a garage to be repaired. The mechanic told the owner that the car would be ready in three days. When the owner did not return for the car for over a week, the mechanic checked the car in an effort to locate some identification in order to notify the owner that the car was ready. The mechanic found no identification, but he did find $1500.00 cash in the glove compartment. He became suspicious and notified the local authorities. The officers were also unable to determine the owner and asked to be called if he should return for the car. Upon returning for the car a few days later, the owner was questioned by the officers but gave evasive answers. He was arrested for reasonable cause to believe that a crime had been committed, as it was thought that an ordinarily prudent person would hold such a belief under the circumstances. But what crime should he have been booked for? Had he committed robbery, burglary, grand theft, or some other crime? He was charged with grand theft, but there were no facts to verify such a crime in the area. He was further questioned by the officers but refused to reveal his identity or place of residence. The investigation revealed no damaging evidence. As the forty-eight hour limit approached the authorities realized that the accused would have to be released, yet they believed that he had been involved in some type of crime because an innocent person would have assisted in getting his own release much earlier. Just before the time limit was reached, the officers received a call from a woman reporting her husband as missing. The description of the missing husband fit that of the man in custody. It was learned that the accused had cashed a number of forged checks and the money in the glove compartment was from his check cashing activity. He had forgotten that it was in the glove compartment when he took the car to the garage. It is interesting to note that he stated that he was cashing the forged checks to get enough money to buy a small ranch where he could raise his children in a wholesome atmosphere.

Generally, a delay in an initial appearance or in an arraignment is not sufficient grounds for a reversal of a conviction on appeal unless it can be shown that the delay deprived the defendant of a fair trial. A few states have adopted the *McNabb* rule of excluding a confession obtained during a delay in arraignment. But there are other penalties besides the procedural one pertaining to the admissibility of confession that may be attached to a delayed arraignment. Many states hold that a public officer who willfully delays bringing a defendant before a magistrate for the arraignment is guilty of a misdemeanor. It has also been held that once the time limit has been reached wherein an arrested person must be taken before a magistrate, any detention beyond that period is illegal, and the officer responsible for such detention is subject to a civil suit for damages on a false imprisonment allegation.

Accepting the Accused for the Initial Appearance

Whether the accused was arrested by a private person or by an officer, he must be taken before a magistrate. The laws of many states provide that a private person who arrests another must take that person before a magistrate without unnecessary delay or deliver the arrested person to a peace officer who will in turn see that the accused is taken before a magistrate. The usual procedure is that the private person will deliver the arrested person to a peace officer rather than take the person before a magistrate himself. This creates the problem of how far the officer should go in determining the legality of the arrest before accepting the accused. There seems to be no uniformity in the answer to this problem. The courts of some states have held that if a competent private person informs the officer of the charge for which the arrest was made and demands that the officer take the accused, the officer has no right to refuse acceptance of the arrested person. This is reinforced by the further provision in some states that an officer who willfully refuses to accept one who has been charged with a crime is also subject to prosecution. Under the circumstances an officer is not civilly liable for false arrest by accepting one arrested by a private person. The officer in reality is only a transportation officer and not an arresting one. (See *Kinney* v. *County of Contra Costa,*

FIGURE 4-1 Sample of complaint

IN THE MUNICIPAL COURT OF _____, JUDICIAL DISTRICT _____,
COUNTY OF _____, STATE OF _____
THE PEOPLE OF THE STATE OF _____,

                                        Plaintiff,

                                                    COMPLAINT—Misdemeanor

                                            v.

JOHN DOE
111 Court Street
Walnut,

                                        Defendant.

    The undersigned declarant and complainant states that he is informed and believes and upon such information and belief declares that on or about September 24, 19____, at and in the above-entitled Judicial District, in the County of _____, State of _____, a misdemeanor, to wit, Section _____ of the Penal Code of the State of _____

was committed by John Doe

who did willfully and unlawfully resist, delay and obstruct a public officer of the County of _____, City of Walnut, State of _____, to wit, Henry P. Jones, in the discharge and the attempt to discharge a duty of his office, to wit, the arrest of a person, to wit, John Doe, whose true name to affiant is unknown for a violation of law.

    Said declarant and complainant therefore prays that a warrant may be issued for the arrest of said defendant who may then be dealt with according to law.

    Executed on September 24, 19____ in the County of _____, State of _____

    I declare under penalty of perjury that the foregoing is true and correct.

                                        _____
                                        Declarant and Complainant

ARRESTING AGENCY: _____ Walnut Police Department _____

                            WITNESSES
Officer A.B. Brown, #O, Walnut Police Department

87 Cal Rptr 638 [1970].) Other states permit the officer to make a determination concerning the legality of the arrest by the private citizen before accepting the accused. Such a ruling places a tremendous burden upon the officer. He is partially acting as a court in making a determination as to the legality of the arrest. If he incorrectly concludes that the arrest was legal, he could possibly be held civilly liable for accepting the accused.

The Complaint

Prior to the initial appearance a legal document must be filed with the court setting forth the charge against the accused, who will be referred to as the defendant hereinafter in relation to the judicial procedure. In most instances this legal document will be a complaint. The complaint is comparatively simple. It sets forth the name of the defendant, the date and place that the offense took place, and the nature of the offense. The complaint must contain enough facts to enable the judge to determine whether a crime has been committed and if there is reasonable cause to believe the defendant committed it. If the defendant is not in custody, a warrant of arrest will be issued based on this complaint. The complaint is sometimes referred to as an *accusatory pleading.* As we progress further into the judicial procedure, it will be determined that other accusatory pleadings follow the complaint in felony cases, but in misdemeanor matters it is usually the only accusatory pleading filed with the court. A sample of the typical complaint appears in Figure 4–1.

The Warrant of Arrest

A warrant of arrest is a legal document commanding a peace officer to arrest the person named in the warrant and to bring that person before the magistrate issuing the warrant. By law in some states the warrant of arrest may be directed to a specifically named person who is not necessarily a peace officer. This is seldom done. A warrant of arrest is executed by taking the person named into custody. In most states a warrant is good until executed or withdrawn by the court issuing it, and may be executed anywhere within the state. In a few states the warrant of arrest may be executed only within the county where issued unless specifically designated as being statewide. In most cases an arrest on a warrant is lawful even if the arresting officer does not have the warrant in his possession at the time of the arrest. Upon request by the arrested person, the warrant must be displayed to him as soon as practical. A warrant of arrest for a felony may be executed at any time of the day or night. But in most jurisdictions, a warrant of arrest for a misdemeanor may not be executed at night unless it is so designated by the issuing court. A few jurisdictions

FIGURE 4-2   Sample Warrant of Arrest

County of _____
The people of the State of _____ to any peace officer of said State:
Complaint on oath having this day been laid before me that the crime of _____ (designating it generally) has been committed and accusing _____ (naming defendant) thereof, you are therefore commanded forthwith to arrest the above named defendant and bring him before me at _____ (naming the place), or in case of my absence or inability to act, before the nearest or most accessible magistrate in this county.
Dated at _____ (place) this ____ day of _____, 19 ____

(Signature and full official title of magistrate.)

permit a misdemeanor warrant of arrest to be executed until 10:00 P.M. without a nighttime designation. After a warrant of arrest has been executed, the arresting officer must return a copy of the warrant to the court issuing it. A notation must be made on the copy indicating where and when the arrest was made. It is to be noted that if a warrant of arrest is directed to a peace officer, a private person has no authority to execute a warrant of arrest. Usually at the time the judge issues a warrant of arrest he will designate on the warrant the amount of bail he considers proper under the circumstances. A sample warrant of arrest appears in Figure 4-2.

John Doe Warrant

There are times when the true identity of a person committing a crime is not known. Through investigative action, facts have established that a crime was committed and by a particular person. But since the true identity of that person is not known, the court will permit a complaint to be filed in the name of John Doe, or some other fictitious name, and the warrant of arrest will carry the same name. There must be sufficient identifying data included in the warrant to enable the officer executing it to know whom to arrest. This data should include the accused's residence, or where the accused can be located, and as much personal descriptive information as it is possible to obtain.

Bail

The Right to Post Bail

The right of an arrested person to post bail to obtain release from custody is an inherent right. As stated in the case of Stack v. Boyle, 342 US 1 (1951): "This traditional right to freedom [by posting bail] before conviction permits the unhampered preparation of a defense, and serves to prevent the infliction of punishment prior to conviction. . . . Unless this right to bail before trial is preserved, the presumption of innocence, secured only after centuries of struggle, would lose its meaning." But the right to post bail is not a guarantee included in our Bill of Rights. The Eighth Amendment to the United States Constitution merely provides that "excessive bail shall not be required," implying that not all offenses are bailable. By constitutional provision or by statute, the right to post bail by one arrested under certain conditions is granted by all states. If the defendant has not been released on bail by the time of the initial appearance, his right to post bail will be explained to him at that time.

Historical Development of Bail

The origin of the term "bail" has been obscured by time. Some believe that the term is from the old French word "baillier" meaning to deliver. Others hold that it originated from the common law procedure of bailments. A bailment is the deposit of something of value with another for a particular purpose. In the case of bail, the deposit was for the release of one in custody. It could be argued that bailment also originated from the word baillier. The right to post bail is found in the early history of England. By the time of the Norman Conquest in A.D. 1066, the posting of a form of security to obtain the release of an accused was a common practice on the continent of Europe, and it became a part of the common law of England. It was developed as a humanitarian procedure. Previously, people accused of crimes were thrown into the dungeons of local noblemen to make sure that they would be available for trial when the judge made his circuit. This custom was important to the king. If the charge was serious and the accused was convicted, his property was confiscated, thus providing a lucrative source of revenue for the king.

Often by the time of the trial, the accused would have died from malnutrition and neglect. To prevent this from happening, relatives or friends of the accused would seek his release to their custody upon a promise that they would produce him for the trial. To make certain that the relatives or friends would fulfill their promise, they were required to post some security in the form of chattels or objects of value. If the accused was not produced for trial, these chattels would be confiscated by the king. In addition the persons posting the security had to suffer the punishment that the accused would have been subjected to had he been convicted. As time passed, the practice of punishing those who had posted security was discontinued, and they only lost the security.

Purpose of Bail

Today we continue to place persons who are arrested in jail. We do so not as a form of punishment because one cannot be punished or imprisoned until found guilty of a crime. We confine the arrested person to make sure that he or she will be available for trial. If we can obtain that surety by permitting him to post bail, he is entitled to be released from custody until found guilty of the accusation. So the only purpose of bail is to secure the release from custody of one who has been arrested upon his promise to appear at the various court proceedings related to the offense. These may include the arraignment, the preliminary hearing, the trial, and other such proceedings that the court may direct.

At common law it was felt that there was no way to insure the trial presence of one who was charged with a capital offense, so bail was denied to that type of offender. The statutes of many states have included similar provisions holding that one charged with a capital offense may be denied bail if the proof of guilt is great. Even in those states in which capital punishment has not been made a penalty, bail may be denied to one arrested for murder if the proof of guilt is evident.

Denial of Bail for Protective Reasons

A few jurisdictions have provided that bail may be denied to an arrested person if his release on bail would be a danger either to himself or to the public. This policy is based upon an interpretation of the Eighth Amendment to the United States Constitution by the United States Supreme Court in the case of *Carlson* v. *Landon*, 342 US 524 (1952). In review the Eighth Amendment guarantees that "excessive bail shall not be required. . . ." In the *Carlson* case the Court rested its interpretation of the Eighth Amendment on the common law, stating:

> The bail clause was lifted with slight changes from the English Bill of Rights Act. In England that clause has never been thought to accord a right to bail in all cases, but merely to provide that bail shall not be excessive in those cases where it is proper to grant bail. When this clause was carried over into our Bill of Rights, nothing was said that indicated any different concept. The Eighth Amendment has not prevented Congress from defining the classes of cases in which bail shall be allowed in this country. Thus in criminal cases bail is not compulsory where the punishment may be death. Indeed, the very language of the Amendment fails to say all arrests must be bailable.

Thus it was concluded that the Eighth Amendment does not grant the right to bail. The Eighth Amendment can be construed to mean only that bail shall not be excessive in those cases in which it is proper, and that the denial of bail in certain cases is permissible. In recognition of the Court's interpretation of the Eighth Amendment, Congress has enacted an elaborate plan of *preventive detention* which has been implemented in the District of Columbia. The District of Columbia Court Reform Act of 1970 has defined specific categories of defendants who are subject to pretrial detention, where their release would not adequately protect the public safety. Also several states have passed statutes permitting preventive detention, sometimes referred to as "protective detention." In a few states judges have adopted a practice of holding individuals in protective detention when the facts warrant such action. But in the absence of statutes permitting such action protective detention by a court could be interpreted as unlawful imprisonment. It has been stated by some judges that bail is not a means for punishing defendants nor for protecting the public safety.

Form of Bail

To post bail is to deposit an acceptable object of value with the appropriate court to insure the appearance of the accused in court. Generally the acceptable object of value is cash; United States or state bonds; or an equity in real property. If real property is pledged as security, most states require that the value of the property be twice that of the amount of bail. This requirement is made because of the possible fluctuation of real estate values and the difficulty involved in converting the real property into cash.

Inasmuch as most arrested persons do not have these forms of security, they must rely upon someone to post bail for them, which person is known as a *surety*. This person may be a friend or relative, but in most instances, the person depositing the security will be one in the business of posting bail—a bail bondsman. For a fee the bail bondsman will post the required security which is usually a surety bond issued by some reliable company. Should the accused fail to appear as promised, the surety bond guarantees the bail payment in cash to the appropriate court. The fee which the bail bondsman charges for this service is about ten percent of the amount of the bail. If the bail bondsman has some doubt as to whether the accused will appear if released on bail, he may request relatives of the accused to deposit collateral funds to reimburse him if the accused does not appear. If the risk of the accused not appearing is too great and no one will come to the aid of the accused by depositing collateral funds, the bail bondsman may refuse to post the bail, and the accused will be detained until the judicial proceedings are completed. But once bail has been deposited the accused is entitled to immediate release from custody. The law is silent in most jurisdictions on the extent of time that a defendant may be free on bail, but it is generally assumed that he is entitled to be free throughout all the proceedings up to conviction. However, at his discretion, a judge may commit a defendant during the trial. Also the defendant is not guaranteed the right to be free during an appeal time. Upon conviction, the defendant is no longer presumed to be innocent but is presumed to be guilty. But again a judge, in his discretion, may permit a defendant to post bail during the appeal proceedings.

Amount of Bail

The bail that is required to be posted is that amount which will insure the court appearance of the accused. Anything above that amount could be considered excessive. Determining this amount is not easily accomplished. The amount that would guarantee the appearance of one person may be entirely different for another. Also the amount that would insure the appearance on one charge may differ from another charge. In determining the amount of bail, a judge may consider the seriousness of the crime; the previous criminal record of the defendant; his employment record; his family ties; whether he was a fugitive at the time of his arrest; whether he is wanted in any other jurisdiction; how great the evidence of guilt may be; the financial burden that he may suffer if he does not appear; and whether he has more to gain than to lose by not appearing.

The amount of bail set by a judge will not necessarily remain the same throughout the proceedings. Circumstances may arise that justify an increase or decrease in the amount. If the defendant has been released on bail and the amount is increased, he must post the amount of the increase or be placed in custody again.

Excessive Bail

As has been stated, the Eighth Amendment to the United States Constitution provides that "excessive bail shall not be required," and what constitutes excessive bail is not easily determined. What is excessive for one defendant may not be excessive for another depending upon financial resources. Whether the wealth or poverty of a defendant should be considered in determining the amount of bail is a difficult question to answer. There is no doubt that a wealthy defendant could more readily post bail, flee the country, and live elsewhere in comfort. Whereas the poverty-stricken defendant may be unable to post even the smallest amount of bail. However, the mere fact that one cannot post bail does not mean that it is excessive. The courts have held that for bail to be excessive it must be unreasonably great and clearly disproportionate to the offense involved. If a defendant believes that his bail is excessive, he may make application to the court for a reduction, and if this fails, he may appeal the matter to an appellate court for review on a writ of habeas corpus.

Bail Schedule

Since the amount of bail required is largely dependent on judicial discretion, the amount varies extensively. To establish uniformity in the amounts required, many states have adopted a procedure whereby judges of a county agree upon the amount of bail that is considered to be equitable on each misdemeanor violation. These amounts are listed in a schedule and act as guidelines for judges of the county. The amounts may still vary between counties. It has been recommended that a similar schedule be prepared for felony charges. But as has been pointed out, it is difficult to determine the amount that will insure the appearance of a defendant in court, particularly in felony matters, so such a schedule could be most unrealistic. A few states, however, have adopted a schedule for felony charges.

Forfeiture of Bail

Once the defendant is released on bail, and if, without sufficient cause, he fails to appear when lawfully required to do so, the bail will be forfeited. Forfeiting bail means that the security posted by the defendant, or by someone in his behalf, is confiscated by the court and deposited in an official fund. The confiscation is justified on the grounds that the security will be used to pay additional court costs and costs involved in locating the defendant. In felony cases particularly, if the defendant does not appear as agreed, the court will issue a bench warrant for the immediate arrest of the accused. When arrested he will be tried on the original charge, and in some jurisdictions he can be charged with an additional violation of "failing to appear," or as it is more commonly known, "bail jumping." If a defendant does not appear on some minor misdemeanor charges or on most traffic violations, a judge, at his discretion, may forfeit the bail considering it the equivalent of the fine, dismiss the charge, and order that no further action be taken on the matter.

Surrender of Defendant by Surety

The surety who posted bail for a defendant may surrender him to the court having jurisdiction over the case any time before bail is forfeited. Upon surrendering the defendant, the surety is relieved of all responsibility, and he is entitled to have the security returned to him. For the purpose of surrendering the defendant, the surety may arrest the defendant. This arrest is an extension to the power of arrest by a private person. It is given upon the old theory that one posting bail has indirect custody of a defendant, and the surety may be relieved of that obligation by seizing the defendant and surrendering him to the court.

Exoneration of Bail

If the defendant appears in court at all times required, the bail has served its purpose, and the surety is entitled to have it returned to him. This return is known as exoneration of bail.

Release on Own Recognizance

In the past, judges developed a practice of releasing defendants charged with minor offenses without posting bail—merely upon their promise to appear. This procedure became known as releasing one on his own recognizance, or O.R. release. The statutes of most states have extended this practice to any bailable offense, including felony charges. The laws provide that a judge, at his own discretion, may release a defendant on his own recognizance if it appears that he will comply with the agreement to appear as directed. However these laws do not give the defendant the right to be released merely on his own recognizance. Even though a defendant is released on his own recognizance, a judge may later require the defendant to post bail or even to be committed to actual custody.

Prior to being released on his own recognizance, the defendant must agree in writing to appear at all times and places as ordered by the court, and that if he does not appear and is apprehended in another state, he waives extradition proceedings. In most states it is provided that if the defendant who is released on his own recognizance fails to appear as agreed, he can be charged with the failure to appear. If the original charge was a felony, then the defendant can be charged with a felony for failure to appear. If the original charge was a misdemeanor, he can be charged with a misdemeanor failure to appear. It has been recommended that greater use be made of O.R. releases, particularly in minor offenses, to obtain the release of those who are unable for financial reasons to post bail.

Bail for a Material Witness

The laws of most states permit a judge to demand that a material witness to a felony violation deposit security for his appearance at the trial if the judge believes that the witness will otherwise not appear. If the witness is unable to post the security (bail) for his appearance, he may be held in custody. The detention of a witness who is unable to post bail is unusual in our form of judicial procedure as it permits the incarceration of one not charged with a crime. For this reason it is not used extensively. To further overcome the inconvenience of a material witness being detained, many jurisdictions provide that if a material witness cannot deposit security to ensure his appearance at the trial, his testimony may be incorporated into a *deposition*. A deposition is a written statement of a witness, taken under oath before a magistrate, with both the prosecution and defense having the right to be present.

Review Questions

1. What is the purpose of the initial appearance?
2. Who may serve a warrant of arrest?
3. What is a "John Doe" warrant, and what information must it contain?
4. How soon after an arrest must the accused be furnished with an initial appearance?
5. What is the purpose of bail?
6. In what form may bail be posted?
7. What is meant by preventive detention?
8. How much bail is a defendant required to post?
9. What is forfeiture of bail?
10. What is the significance of the term "released on one's own recognizance"?

Local Procedure

1. Within what period of time must the initial appearance take place?
2. May an accused enter a plea at the initial appearance?
3. May a defendant be denied bail for protective detention?
4. Can a defendant be prosecuted for failure to appear after posting bail?

PLEAS, THE GRAND JURY, AND PRELIMINARY HEARINGS

Entering Pleas

As previously discussed, during an arraignment the defendant is given an opportunity to enter a plea to the charge alleged in the complaint. The defendant may either enter the plea at that time, or request time to consider the plea to be entered. Depending upon the jurisdiction the defendant may enter any one plea. The pleas of guilty, not guilty, nolo contendere, not guilty by reason of insanity, former jeopardy, or former judgment of acquittal or conviction may be entered. Generally the law provides that if a defendant does not plead "not guilty by reason of insanity," he or she shall be conclusively presumed to have been sane at the time the crime was committed.

Guilty Plea

At one time in our history defendants were not permitted to enter guilty pleas as it was thought that the only way justice could be accomplished was by a trial. A plea of guilty is an admission of every element of the offense charged, and no proof of the crime needs to be presented. "A plea of guilty is more than a confession which admits that the accused did various acts; it is itself a conviction; nothing remains but to give judgment and determine punishment." (See *Boykin* v. *Alabama,* 395 US 238 [1969].) Thus the plea of guilty cannot be accepted lightly by a judge.

Generally a plea of guilty must be made by the defendant in open court—either orally or in writing. The purpose behind the requirement that the defendant personally enter the plea is to ensure that it is his own plea. Most states provide that a judge may not accept a plea of guilty, particularly in felony cases, unless the defendant is informed of his right to the assistance of counsel. If the defendant understands this right to counsel and waives the right, the judge may then accept the plea of guilty. However some states will not permit a judge to accept a guilty plea to a capital offense charge, or one in which the punishment is life imprisonment, without the possibility of parole, unless the defendant is represented by counsel. A few states will not permit a defendant to enter a guilty plea to a capital offense even with the assistance of counsel.

In accordance with the *Boykin* decision, before a judge may accept a guilty plea to any charge, misdemeanor or felony, the judge must inform the defendant of the significance of the guilty plea. The defendant must be informed that by pleading guilty he waives his right against self-incrimination, his right to a jury trial, and his right to be confronted by his accusers. Even though the defendant is represented by counsel at the time of the guilty plea, the records of the case must reflect that the judge advised the defendant of the guarantees that would be waived by the plea

74

of guilty. The laws of some states provide that before the judge may accept a guilty plea an inquiry must be made to make certain that the accused has actually committed a crime serious enough to justify the guilty plea. The extent of the inquiry will depend largely upon the facts of each case. The judge may confine the inquiry to the facts in the transcript of the preliminary hearing or of the grand jury. Or the judge may use whatever procedure is best under the circumstances, including interrogating the attorneys involved in the case. The accused does not have to admit his guilt expressly at the time of the guilty plea. In some states a guilty plea may be accepted even though accompanied by a claim of innocence. (See *North Carolina* v. *Alford,* 400 US 25, [1970].) A judge does not have to accept a guilty plea, particularly if the judge feels that the defendant does not understand the significance of the plea or if there is some question as to the plea being voluntarily given. A few jurisdictions hold that if the defendant is not a citizen of the United States, he must be advised that if he pleads guilty he may be subject to deportation.

After a plea of guilty is accepted the next step is to sentence the defendant. If the charge is a misdemeanor, the judge of the inferior court has the authority to mete out the sentence, but if the charge is a felony, the case must be transferred to the superior court for sentencing. A judge of an inferior court has the authority to accept a guilty plea to a felony charge in most jurisdictions, and the plea will have the same effect as if it had been entered in the superior court. A few jurisdictions do not permit a defendant to enter a plea to a felony charge in the inferior court, and the case must be transferred to the superior court for both the acceptance of the plea and the sentencing.

Withdrawal of Guilty Plea

In most jurisdictions, a defendant, upon showing a good cause, may withdraw a guilty plea and enter a not guilty plea or one of the other pleas any time before the pronouncement of sentence. A few jurisdictions hold that if the defendant was not represented by counsel at the time the guilty plea was entered, the judge must permit the defendant to withdraw the guilty plea upon showing good cause. For this reason most judges are reluctant to accept a plea of guilty if the defendant was not represented by counsel, particularly in felony cases. The request of a defendant to withdraw a guilty plea is not taken lightly. If the withdrawal is permitted, it means that the defendant is entitled to a trial on one of the other pleas that may have been entered. This action could inconvenience witnesses, crowd court calendars, and cause additional expense. But if the defendant can show sufficiently good cause, the withdrawal should be permitted by the trial judge; otherwise, the denial of the withdrawal may be overturned by an appellate court. The problem created by this procedure is determining what would be considered good cause. It has been held that if the defendant did not understand the meaning or significance of the guilty plea, this allegation is sufficient showing of good cause. In *Henderson* v. *Morgan*, 426 US 637 (1976), the United States Supreme Court permitted the withdrawal of a guilty plea nine years later upon the grounds that the plea had been involuntarily given. In that case the trial court accepted a guilty plea to a charge of second degree murder. The defendant later attempted to withdraw the guilty plea on the grounds that he did not know that "intent" was a necessary element of second degree murder and, further, that he had not been sufficiently informed of the sentence he would receive if he pleaded guilty. The appellate courts of New York upheld the judge's denial of the withdrawal and the case was appealed to the United States Supreme Court upon the grounds that the defendant had been denied due process of law. The Supreme Court held that since the defendant had not been advised by either the judge or the attorneys involved that intent was a necessary element of the crime of second degree murder, his plea of guilty was "as a matter of law involuntary and must be set aside." It was stated that a plea could not have been voluntarily given unless the defendant had "received real notice of the true nature of the charge against him, the first and most universally recognized requirement of due process." But it was felt that the defendant had been sufficiently informed of the sentence that he might receive if the guilty plea was received. In most jurisdictions there is no requirement that a defendant be advised in advance of the sentence that may be imposed if a guilty plea is accepted. The acceptance of a guilty plea upon the basis of the sentence that may be imposed is discussed in chapter 9, under the heading "plea negotiation."

An additional reason why some states require a judge to make an inquiry concerning the facts surrounding a guilty plea is to prevent a defendant from later challenging the plea as being a free and voluntary act, as was successfully done by Morgan some nine years after his guilty plea in the *Henderson* v. *Morgan* case. It is interesting to note that the dissenting justices in that case felt that the withdrawal of the guilty plea should have been denied. It was their opinion that the trial judge had held a factual inquiry and that the inquiry revealed that the defendant had sufficient knowledge of the elements of the crime. Thus, these justices believed that the guilty plea had been voluntarily given. The facts in *Parker* v. *North Carolina*, 397 US 790, (1970), present an interesting attempt to withdraw a guilty plea. The defendant argued that his guilty plea was the product of a coerced confession. The court stated that even on the assumption that the confession had been coerced, the court could not believe that the alleged police conduct during the interrogation period was of such nature or had such enduring effect as to make involuntary a plea of guilty entered over a month later. According to the appellate court, the trial judge was within his rights to refuse the request for withdrawal of the guilty plea.

Not Guilty Plea

When a plea of not guilty is entered by the defendant, a trial must be held. If the plea is to a misdemeanor charge, the case will be set immediately for trial, which in most instances will take place in the inferior court. If the not guilty plea is to a felony charge, further proceedings must take place either by a grand jury hearing or by a preliminary hearing before the case can be set for trial in the superior court. This protects the accused from being held for trial without sufficient cause. The grand jury and preliminary hearings will be discussed later. Most jurisdictions permit a defendant to withdraw a not guilty plea and enter a plea of guilty any time during the trial. This eliminates much trial time, particularly if the change of plea takes place early in the trial proceedings.

Occasionally a defendant will refuse to enter any plea and stands mute before the court. History reveals that when this occurred in early common law the defendant was returned to the prison from which he had been brought and made to lie naked on his back on the floor. Great weights of iron were placed on him and he was fed only three "morsels of the worst bread" the first day, and three sips of stagnant water the next, with this diet alternating daily until the prisoner died or entered a plea. In later years a more humane procedure was followed. When the defendant stood mute before the court, the silence was treated as a guilty plea. Today, if the defendant refuses to plead, a plea of not guilty is entered for him followed by a trial.

Nolo Contendere Plea

A plea of nolo contendere, meaning "I will not contest it," or "no contest," is essentially equivalent to a plea of guilty. In some states the nolo contendere plea is known as "non vult contendere" and is sometimes abbreviated as "non vult." As with the plea of guilty, the judge must inform the defendant of those rights to which he is entitled and of those which he waives by such a plea. The most significant effect of the nolo contendere plea is that it may not be used against the defendant in a civil matter because the defendant has not admitted guilt. As pointed out, a plea of guilty is a formal type of confession of the act charged. Not all states permit a nolo contendere plea to be entered by a defendant. In those states in which the plea has been adopted there is a variance as to who must agree to accept the plea. In some states only the judge must agree to accept the plea; in others, the prosecuting attorney also must agree before the nolo contendere plea may be accepted.

This plea has been adopted to satisfy the thinking of two types of defendants charged with a violation. Some defendants will admit to committing a particular act but refuse to admit that the act was a crime, so they enter the "no contest" plea of nolo contendere. For example, a

78

person may be charged with speeding on a freeway. He may admit to excessive speed but allege that, since no one was injured or endangered, no crime was committed. So he merely enters the plea of nolo contendere.

Other defendants have committed acts which may subject them to civil suits for damages or restitution as well as to criminal prosecution. They feel that the evidence against them is so great that it would be useless to contest the criminal charges, but do not want to permit the guilty plea to be introduced against them in a civil trial. Under these circumstances, they may wish to enter the nolo contendere plea. As an example, this plea is frequently entered by a defendant who has been arrested for driving under the influence of alcohol after being involved in a serious accident in which persons were injured or killed. The defendant may know that the evidence against him is strong enough that a trial would result in a conviction. To save the expense of a trial and to prevent the conviction from being used against him in a civil suit, the defendant will attempt to enter a plea of nolo contendere. In this instance, the judge may refuse to allow the defendant to enter the nolo contendere as it could work an injustice to the victims of the accident. A defendant may not plead nolo contendere as a matter of right, but must have consent of the judge, its acceptance being entirely a matter of grace.

Not Guilty by Reason of Insanity Plea

By entering a plea of not guilty by reason of insanity the defendant is admitting the commission of the act for which he is charged, but he alleges that he cannot be held responsible for the crime because he was not sane at the time he committed it. The whole issue of the ensuing trial is whether the defendant was sane or insane at the time the crime was committed. His present sanity is not at stake because he cannot be tried if he is not sane at the time of the trial.

Most states provide that if the defendant enters this plea, he has the burden of proving that he was insane at the time he committed the offense, and the prosecution may endeavor to meet that allegation by introducing evidence to prove that the defendant was sane at the time of the offense. A few states hold that the burden of proving beyond a reasonable doubt that the defendant was sane at the time he committed the act still rests with the prosecution. The defendant has only to meet the prosecution's case by creating a doubt as to his sanity. If the defendant is found to have been sane at the time he committed the crime, the only procedure to follow is sentencing the defendant because he has already admitted his guilt by the plea of not guilty by reason of insanity. If he is found to have been insane at the time the offense was committed, technically he is entitled to be set free because his present sanity is not in question. However most jurisdictions provide that the judge hearing the case may demand that the defendant be confined for a period of time, usually not less than ninety days, for observation to determine that the defendant is not a danger to society. If, after the confinement period, it is determined that he is not a danger, he must be released from custody.

A few states permit a defendant to enter dual pleas. He may enter a plea of not guilty and at the same time enter a plea of not guilty by reason of insanity. This procedure has been criticized, as the pleas are actually inconsistent pleas. Upon entering the plea of not guilty, the defendant is denying his guilt. In the second plea he is confessing his guilt but alleging that he cannot be held responsible for the offense because of his insanity at the time. Where this procedure is permitted, the trial on the not guilty plea takes place first. If the defendant is found not guilty, he is entitled to be released without further action being taken. If he is found to be guilty, the trial on the plea of not guilty by reason of insanity must follow. If he is found to be sane at the time of committing the act, the sentencing procedure will take place. But if he is found to have been insane at the time he committed the offense, the same procedure for release or observation will be set in motion as was previously described.

Not all states permit a plea of not guilty by reason of insanity to be entered, but insanity may be raised as a defense to the crime charged. The insanity issue will be discussed further in chapter 12.

Plea of Once in Jeopardy

The guarantee against being placed twice in jeopardy, also referred to as the *right against double jeopardy,* is of ancient origin having been found in procedures of the early Greek and Roman jurisprudence. It was established in the common law of England and brought to this country by the colonists. The guarantee is embodied in the Fifth Amendment to the United States Constitution and the laws of all the states. Basically, the guarantee provides that no man shall be placed in jeopardy of his life or liberty more than once for the same offense. It prohibits undue harassment and oppression by those in authority. If it were not for this guarantee against double jeopardy, an accused could be tried and retried until found guilty. Likewise, he might be retried if it were felt that the sentence resulting from the first trial was not severe enough.

If an accused is charged with a crime, and he believes that he has been previously placed in jeopardy by court action on that same charge, he may enter the "plea of once in jeopardy." But there are many ramifications involved in this plea, such as what comprises jeopardy and under what conditions an accused may be placed twice in jeopardy. Many persons are under the impression that an accused cannot be tried twice for the same offense. This is not necessarily true. There are situations in which a defendant may be tried twice or more times for the same offense.

Generally, if a defendant is acquitted of a crime, he cannot be tried again for that particular offense. But if he is convicted, he may appeal his conviction to an appellate court. If the conviction is reversed upon appeal, the case may be retried. Upon appealing the conviction, the defendant is in a sense waiving his guarantee against double jeopardy. In the same manner, if the defendant requests a new trial after being convicted, he is waiving the double jeopardy guarantee. Also, it has been held that if the jury cannot arrive at a verdict, the case may be retried by a different jury without the second trial being a violation of the double jeopardy right.

When Jeopardy Sets In.   The determination of when an accused has been placed in jeopardy is not without its complications. The Fifth Amendment guarantee against double jeopardy is of little assistance, as it merely provides that an accused shall not "be subject for the same offense to be twice put in jeopardy of life or limb." As the courts began to grant the guarantee against double jeopardy, it became necessary to determine when jeopardy set in. In making this determination, the courts had to look to the common law of England. The common law rule at the time that the Fifth Amendment was adopted was comparatively simple, merely providing that a defendant had been placed in jeopardy only when there had been a conviction or an acquittal after a complete trial. Early English history of jurisprudence reveals that, once commenced, most trials were completed. It is stated that the traditional practice was to keep the jury together unfed and without drink until they could deliver a unanimous verdict. As late as 1866, an English Court stated that the rule seemed to command the confinement of the jury until death if it did not agree on a verdict. At the time of the enactment of the Fifth Amendment, most criminal prosecutions in this country proceeded until a verdict was reached. At that time, neither the defendant nor the prosecution had any right to appeal an adverse verdict. The verdict in such a case was unquestionably final, and barred further prosecution for the same offense.

But as time passed, this strict rule was relaxed through United States Supreme Court decisions. One of the first relaxations was the right granted to one convicted of a crime to be able to appeal the conviction if there was some error committed during the trial. If the conviction was reversed upon appeal because of some error during the trial, the prosecution could retry the case. As stated, the appeal by the defendant amounted to a waiver of the right against double jeopardy. However, the United States Supreme Court in *Burks* v. *United States,* 57 L Ed 2d 1 (1978), held that once a jury's verdict of acquittal is returned, that acquittal is a bar against further prosecutive action against the accused for the offense charged. The Court stated that the acquittal is an absolute bar "no matter how erroneous its [the jury's] decision" may be. In the past, some states have held that if the jury returned an erroneous verdict of acquittal, the defendant could be retried because jeopardy did not set in until a just verdict had been rendered. The *Burks* decision has eliminated such a contention.

Since it was believed that jeopardy did not set in until the verdict stage was reached, many trials were commenced but did not reach the verdict stage. A judge often would stop a trial if he believed that the defendant was guilty and that the jury selected would not return a guilty verdict. The judge would dismiss that particular jury and have the trial started over with a new jury. This procedure could be repeated until the judge and prosecution felt that the jury selected would return a guilty verdict. This procedure resulted in injustices. To prevent these injustices, rules were established that held that if a jury was dismissed without sufficient cause after the trial began, the defendant would have been placed in jeopardy and could not be retried.

The reason behind this rule was expressed by the United States Supreme Court in the *Burks* v. *United States* decision. The Court stated:

> The Double Jeopardy Clause forbids a second trial for the purpose of affording the prosecution another opportunity to supply evidence which it failed to muster in the first proceeding. This is central to the objective of the prohibition against successive trials. The Clause does not allow the state to make repeated attempts to convict an individual for an alleged offense since the constitutional prohibition against double jeopardy was designed to protect an individual from being subjected to the hazards of trial and possible conviction more than once for an alleged offense.

The Court further stated in the case of *Crist* v. *Bretz*, 57 L Ed 2d 24 (1978):

> The basic reason for holding that a defendant is put in jeopardy even though the criminal proceeding against him terminated before verdict was perhaps best stated in *Green* v. *United States,* 355 US 184: "the underlying idea, one that is deeply ingrained in at least the Anglo-American system of jurisprudence, is that the State with all its resources and power should not be allowed to make repeated attempts to convict an individual for an alleged offense, thereby subjecting him to embarrassment, expense and ordeal and compelling him to live in a continuing state of anxiety and insecurity, as well as enhancing the possibility that even though innocent he may be found guilty."

The ruling that held that a defendant had been placed in jeopardy once the jury trial began created the problem of determining at what point the jury trial commenced. The legislatures and courts of the various states tried to establish guidelines to solve this problem, but there was no uniformity among the states. Some states held that a jury trial began once the jury was selected and sworn to do its duty in arriving at a verdict. Other states held that a jury trial did not commence until after the jury was selected and the first witness was sworn. The United States Supreme Court settled the problem in *Crist* v. *Bretz* by holding that a jury trial commences once the jury is selected and sworn. The Court stated:

> . . . the federal rule that jeopardy attaches when the jury is empaneled and sworn is an integral part of the constitutional guarantee against double jeopardy. . . . The reason for holding that jeopardy attaches when the jury is empaneled and sworn lies in the need to protect the interest of an accused in retaining a chosen jury. That right was described in *Wade* v. *Hunter* as a defendant's valued right to have his trial completed by a particular tribunal. It is an interest with roots deep in the historic development of trial by jury in the Anglo–American system of criminal justice. Throughout that history there ran a strong tradition that once banded together a jury should not be discharged until it had completed its solemn task of announcing a verdict.

The rule provides that the defendant will have been placed in jeopardy if, once the trial begins, the jury is dismissed without sufficient cause before the verdict stage is reached.

There is no clear criterion concerning what is considered sufficient cause for a trial not to continue to the verdict stage. A sufficient cause may result from a mistrial having been declared by a judge. Often during a trial, a situation such as misconduct by a juror or some improper remark by a witness while testifying may cause a judge to believe that the defendant could not receive a fair trial if the trial was allowed to proceed. Even when a mistrial is declared primarily for the benefit of the defendant, the defendant usually must agree to the mistrial being declared; otherwise, an appellate court may conclude that jeopardy had set in and the defendant could not be retried.

The United States Supreme Court in *Crist* v. *Bretz* indicated that a court trial (that is, a trial by the judge without a jury) begins when the first witness is sworn. Unless the trial is continued to the verdict stage, the defendant will be placed in jeopardy. Remember that the defendant could be retried if the trial is discontinued for good cause.

Plea of Former Judgment of Conviction or Acquittal

This plea is not included in the statutes of all states. However, it has been held by some states that a defendant is not properly protected by the plea of double jeopardy in some instances. When a defendant commits an act and breaks both state and federal criminal laws, the defendant could be prosecuted by either the state or federal government. The question arises: may he be prosecuted by both without a violation of the double jeopardy guarantee? This question was answered by the United States Supreme Court in the case of *United States* v. *Lanza*, 260 US 377 (1922), and reiterated in *Abbate* v. *United States*, 359 US 187, (1959), in which cases the Court concluded that a defendant could be tried by *both* federal and state governments. The Court based its decisions upon the fact that a citizen of this nation owes a duty to both the federal and state governments. In committing an act which violates the laws of both sovereignties, both may prosecute. About half of the states have statutory provisions which hold that if a defendant is prosecuted by one government, prosecution by the local courts in that state for the same act is prohibited. The plea of former judgment of conviction or acquittal would be the proper plea under the circumstances.

This plea would be proper also if a defendant were acquitted of one charge and retried on a lesser charge arising out of the same act. However most states hold that the plea of once in jeopardy covers this situation and have not included the former judgment of conviction or acquittal plea in their statutes.

The Grand Jury

A grand jury is a group of persons representing a cross section of a community, usually a county, whose primary purpose is to hear certain types of criminal accusations in order to determine whether there are sufficient facts to hold the accused for trial. As was stated by the United States Supreme Court case of *Wood* v. *Georgia*, 370 US 375 (1962):

> Historically, this body (the grand jury) has been regarded as a primary security to the innocent against hasty, malicious and oppressive persecution; it serves the invaluable function in our society of standing between the accuser and the accused, whether the latter be an individual, minority group, or other, to determine whether a charge is founded upon reason or was dictated by an intimidating power or by malice and personal ill will.

The grand jury procedure came into being early in the common law of England. As was pointed out in chapter 2, the Magna Charta provided that no freeman was to be seized and imprisoned except by judgment of his peers. This provision established the procedure that before a person could be held for trial on a serious charge, the accusation had to be presented to a council composed of the accused's peers to determine if the charge was well founded. This council later became known as a grand jury as opposed to the petit or trial jury. This grand jury consisted of no less than sixteen persons and no more than twenty-three. There is really no logical reason for these numbers having been selected, except that it was thought that since a person was accused of a serious crime, a reasonable number of his peers should hear the accusation and make a determination as to whether the accused should be held for trial. Also to prevent the body from becoming too large and unwieldy, a maximum of twenty-three was selected.

The grand jury was created as a safeguard for the accused. It prevented him from being held on a serious charge without sufficient cause or justification. The idea of the grand jury was brought to this country from England, and it was embodied in the Fifth Amendment of the United States Constitution. This Amendment provides that "no person shall be held to answer for a capital or otherwise infamous crime, unless on presentment or indictment of a grand jury." A capital offense is one punishable by death; an infamous crime has been defined as one punishable by hard labor or imprisonment for over one year. For all practical purposes an infamous crime is any felony. This amendment was applicable only to federal charges and the states were free to establish their own safeguards. Approximately one half of the states hold that all felonies, and in some instances serious misdemeanors, must be presented to a grand jury. The remaining states provide that the accusation may be presented to a judge or magistrate in the form of a preliminary hearing in lieu of grand jury action.

Selection and Qualification of Grand Jurors

The selection of grand jurors varies greatly from state to state. In some states they are selected at random, often using the list of voters for the territorial jurisdiction. The clerk of the court will cut the names from the list and place them in a box from which the required number of names will be drawn. In other states the trial judge, or judges, of the county will furnish to the clerk of the court the names of prospective jurors. These names will be placed in a box from which the required number will be drawn. In some areas the grand jury is composed of persons who volunteer their services because it is considered to be a position of honor to serve on a grand jury.

Following the common law tradition, grand juries in this country vary in size from sixteen to twenty-three in number, but most grand juries consist of nineteen persons. They are usually selected at the beginning of the calendar year and generally serve for one year. The qualifications necessary to serve on the grand jury are very similar to those of a petit jury. Those qualifications demand that the individual be eighteen years of age or over; a citizen of the United States; a resident of the jurisdiction for at least one year; and have sufficient knowledge of the English language to properly communicate. After the grand jurors have been selected they are given an oath in which they promise to do their duty and to keep their proceedings secret and confidential. The oath is generally administered by a superior court judge. At this time the grand jury is considered to be impaneled. After the grand jury is impaneled, the judge will either appoint a member of the grand jury to act as foreman or the judge may instruct the grand jury to select one of their members to act as foreman. When the appointment of a foreman is completed, the grand jury is authorized to hear criminal charges to determine if an accused should be held for trial.

The Indictment

Prior to the grand jury hearings the prosecuting attorney will prepare a formal document setting forth the charge against the accused. This document is known as an indictment. It is also referred to as "true bill of indictment" in some jurisdictions. At one time in our history the indictment was a very technically worded document, and any failure to word it properly would give a judge the right to dismiss the charge. In fact the wording became ridiculously technical. For example, if the charge was for murder and if the indictment did not particularly designate the deceased as a human being the indictment was considered faulty. Or if the initials A.D. did not accompany the date, it was held that the indictment did not reflect that the charge had not been outlawed by a passage of time. Today, the indictment is a comparatively simply worded instrument. It is very similar in form to the complaint. The indictment sets forth the name of the accused, the crime which is alleged to have been committed, the date and place of the alleged crime, and a few pertinent facts about the crime.

The indictment serves several purposes. First, it informs the grand jury of the charge about which they will receive evidence during the hearing. Second, if the required number of grand jurors votes in favor of holding the accused for trial, they will so designate that fact by having the foreman sign the indictment, or as it is known, "endorsing the indictment." The indictment is then filed with the court in which the trial will take place. Third, if the accused is not in custody when the indictment is endorsed and filed with the court, the indictment will enable the judge to issue a warrant of arrest. The indictment is also an accusatory pleading and is the document that sets the trial in motion in the superior court. Finally, the indictment informs the defendant of the charge against which he must defend himself. If the accused is charged with more than one crime, these additional crimes may be included in the same indictment and they are referred to as *counts*.

Grand Jury Hearings

The frequency with which the grand jury meets depends upon the number of criminal charges that must be heard. In highly populated areas, the grand jury may meet daily, Monday through Friday. In other areas it may meet only when there is an occasion to do so, which could be only once a month or less frequently. Although the grand jury may call a hearing on its own, the members usually meet at the request of the prosecuting attorney. The grand jury meets in closed hearings, and the procedure is secret. In determining whether an accused should be held for trial, jury members will question witnesses and receive the evidence that is deemed pertinent by the prosecuting attorney. Before testifying, each witness takes an oath to tell the truth and not to reveal the proceedings that take place during his presence before the grand jury. During the examination of the witnesses, the prosecuting attorney is usually present to assist in questioning. Also, a court reporter who records the testimony of the witnesses is usually present.

After hearing all of the witnesses and receiving the evidence of the case, the grand jurors will deliberate on the facts of the matter among themselves. After deliberating on the facts, they will vote to determine if in their minds there are sufficient facts to believe that a crime has been committed and if the accused committed it. Their belief does not have to be to a point beyond a reasonable doubt as to guilt, but only sufficient probable cause to believe that the accused is guilty of the act. Only the grand jurors may be present during the deliberation and voting. Jurisdictions vary somewhat on the number that must vote to hold the accused for trial, or, "vote for the indictment." If the grand jury is composed of nineteen members, some states only require twelve to vote in favor of the indictment, whereas other states require fourteen. If the grand jury is composed of twenty-three persons, some states require fourteen to vote in favor of the indictment and others require sixteen. If the required number vote in favor of holding the accused for trial, the foreman of the grand jury will endorse the indictment indicating that the grand jury believes in the truthfulness of the charge. Thus we get the *true bill* as a name for an indictment that is returned by the grand jury holding an accused for trial. The foreman of the grand jury is either selected by the jurors themselves once they are impaneled or appointed by the presiding judge. In some states if a grand jury investigates a criminal charge which was not referred to them by the prosecuting attorney, the accusatory pleading is known as a *presentment* rather than an indictment.

If the required number do not vote in favor of holding the accused for trial, the foreman will so designate on the indictment. At one time in our history, the foreman would write the word "ignoramus" on the indictment indicating that the grand jury ignored the indictment. Today the foreman will usually write on the indictment that the grand jury does not believe in the charge, or in other words that there is no bill of indictment forth coming, or a *no bill.*

The defendant is not entitled to be present during a grand jury hearing, and there is some doubt as to whether he may demand to present evidence in his own behalf. If the grand jurors feel that other witnesses besides those presented by the prosecution would be helpful in determining the truth of the indictment, the grand jurors have the authority to call additional witnesses, including the accused. The accused does not have to answer any questions that might subject him to punishment.

If a grand jury fails to hold the accused for trial, the question which arises is whether the facts may be presented to a new grand jury. The answer to the question varies between states. Some states have statutory regulations prohibiting re-presenting the case to another grand jury. Other states are silent on the matter, which would indicate that there is no bar to re-presenting the case since a grand jury hearing is not an action in which jeopardy will set it.

Secret Indictment

If the defendant is not in custody at the time the indictment is returned, a warrant of arrest will be issued based upon this indictment. Under these circumstances no public record is made of the indictment and warrant in order that the defendant will not be alerted to the fact that he is wanted, thereby making his location and apprehension more difficult. The indictment in this case is referred to as a secret indictment.

Open Hearings

Frequently a grand jury is called on to investigate and hold hearings concerning alleged acts of misconduct by public officials. In these situations most jurisdictions permit the hearing to be open to the public when it is believed to be in the best interest of justice. To hold an open hearing usually requires that a request be made to the presiding judge by the prosecuting attorney and by the foreman of the grand jury.

Dismissal of Indictment

Prosecution does not necessarily follow, even though an indictment has been returned by a grand jury. The indictment may be dismissed. In many jurisdictions the prosecuting attorney is permitted to dismiss the indictment. This procedure is referred to as a *nolle prosequi* action, a formal entry on the record of the case stating that no further prosecutive action will be taken in the matter. Other jurisdictions hold that only the presiding judge may dismiss the indictment. He may dismiss the indictment on his own if he does not believe that the facts will support a conviction, or he may dismiss the indictment upon the recommendation of the prosecuting attorney. It may seem to be somewhat paradoxical for the prosecuting attorney to seek an indictment and then reverse himself by dismissing it. But he may take this action because a material witness may have become unavailable, or facts may have been developed which, in the best interest of justice, indicate that the case should not go to trial.

Additional Functions of the Grand Jury

In many states, the sole function of the grand jury is to hold hearings on criminal charges to determine if a crime has been committed and if the accused should be held for trial. But in a few states the grand jury performs other functions, such as investigating public expenditures. It may also inspect jails, prisons, and mental institutions within its territorial jurisdiction to determine if these facilities are complying with safety and health regulations.

Criticism of the Grand Jury System

Many legal scholars have severely criticized the grand jury system. It has been alleged that the grand jury is not a safeguard of the accused, but that it is merely a rubber stamp of the prosecuting attorney. Another allegation is that the grand jury is not representative of the peers of the accused as was indicated to be necessary by the Magna Charta. The term "peers" seems to weave its way into the legal language of criminal procedure, but the term is seldom found in the qualifications necessary for being a member of either a petit or grand jury. The dictionary definition of "peers" reflects that they are one's equals or associates. Under this definition a grand jury of one's peers could result in the impaneling of an odd group of persons, particularly if the accused had spent much of his life in prison. Generally it is held that if the grand jury is a representative group of citizens from throughout the county, or a cross section of the county, it is the equivalent of one's peers, and such a group will fulfill the due process of law provision. However greater emphasis is being placed on what determines a representative group when a member of a minority society is the accused. The cross section of the county provision has also been challenged by younger defendants, particularly since the age qualification for service on juries has been changed from twenty-one to eighteen.

As valid as the argument is that the grand jury does not represent a cross section of society, it is most difficult to obtain a truly representative group. Most grand jurors receive little or no compensation for their services. In those areas in which the grand jury holds frequent hearings, most persons cannot afford to serve on a grand jury. This results in many grand jurors being retired or wealthy individuals who can afford to give their services. It has also been alleged that the grand jury is a cumbersome system because it cannot do anything that a magistrate could not do more efficiently at less cost.

Those advocating the retention of the grand jury system in lieu of a preliminary hearing by a magistrate often quote Justice Harlan's dissenting opinion in the case of *Hurtado* v. *California,* 110 US 516 (1884). Justice Harlan stated:

> . . . nothing stands between the citizen and prosecution for his life, except the judgment of a justice of the peace [in a preliminary hearing]. Anglo-Saxon liberty would, perhaps, have perished long before the adoption of our Constitution, had it been in the power of government to put the subject on trial for his life whenever a justice of the peace, holding his office at the will of the crown, should certify that he had committed a capital crime. That such officers are, in some of the States, elected by the people, does not add to the protection of the citizen; for, one of the peculiar benefits of the grand jury system, as it exists in this country and England, [the grand jury system has since been abolished in England] is that it is composed, as a general rule, of a body of private persons, who do not hold office at the will of the government, or at the will of voters. In many if not in all of the States civil officers are disqualified to sit on grand juries. In the secrecy of the investigations by grand juries, the weak and helpless—proscribed perhaps, because of their race, or pursued by an unreasoning public clamor—have found, and will continue to find, security against official oppression, the cruelty of mobs, the machination of falsehood, and the malevolence of private persons who would use the machinery of the law to bring ruin upon their personal enemies.

Thus we find the grand jury system continuing to function in many states; however as time passes it is highly possible that more states will adopt the preliminary hearing procedure.

The Preliminary Hearing

In order to speed up the justice process, about one-half of the states have adopted another form of safeguard, in lieu of the grand jury hearing, for one accused of a serious crime. That safeguard is the preliminary hearing, also referred to as the *preliminary examination.* The preliminary hearing is very much like a junior trial. It is conducted before a magistrate. A magistrate has been described as any officer of the court who has the power to issue a warrant of arrest. From a practical standpoint the magistrate is a judge of the inferior court who acts in the capacity of a magistrate as well as a trial judge.

During the preliminary hearing the magistrate sits without a jury, and the prosecuting attorney presents the evidence against the accused. This evidence will consist of the testimony of witnesses and such physical evidence as the prosecuting attorney may deem pertinent. The defendant must be present, and may be represented by an attorney. There must be an opportunity for the defendant or his attorney to cross-examine the witnesses of the prosecution.

As previously pointed out, the Fifth Amendment of the United States Constitution, among other provisions, provides that all capital or otherwise infamous crimes be presented to a grand jury. Most of the provisions of this Amendment have been made applicable to the states through the due process of law clause of the Fourteenth Amendment of the United States Constitution. When the preliminary hearing procedure was first adopted, there was some doubt as to whether this procedure would fulfill the due process of law clause. But this doubt was resolved by the *Hurtado* case in which the United States Supreme Court upheld the preliminary hearing procedure. The Court stated that the preliminary hearing "carefully considers and guards the substantial interest of the prisoner. It is merely a preliminary proceeding, and can result in no final judgment, except as the consequence of a regular judicial trial, conducted precisely as in the cases of indictments." Therefore the safeguard of the preliminary hearing is as great as a grand jury action and fulfills the due process of law clause of the Fourteenth Amendment.

Even though the preliminary hearing procedure has been adopted by a number of states, the grand jury system has not been eliminated in most of those states. Instances may arise in which the prosecuting attorney will prefer to present a charge to the grand jury rather than holding a preliminary hearing. It is the prerogative of the prosecuting attorney to decide whether a preliminary hearing will be held or if the case will be presented to a grand jury. When the defendant is in custody and the felony charge is of a routine nature, a preliminary hearing will be held in most instances. If the defendant is not in custody and a secret indictment is desired, the charge will be presented to a grand jury.

Before a preliminary hearing may be held, the defendant must have been arrested and a complaint filed charging him with a felony or, in some jurisdictions, either a felony or a serious misdemeanor. If the defendant enters a plea of not guilty, the judge will set a date for the preliminary hearing, which is usually only a few days after the plea. The hearing is open to the public unless the defendant requests that the hearing be closed—which he has the right to do in most jurisdictions. Even if the hearing is not closed, the witnesses, at the request of either the prosecution or the defense, may be excluded from the courtroom until after they have testified. The judge may also exclude the witnesses on his own motion. During the hearing the prosecution must present enough evidence to convince the judge that there is sufficient cause to believe that a crime has been committed and that the defendant committed it, in order to hold the defendant for trial in the superior court. This is the same degree of proof that must be presented to the grand jury.

After the prosecution has presented its evidence, the defendant may enter evidence in his own behalf, if he so desires, in an effort to convince the judge that he should not be held for trial. If the judge is under the belief that a crime has been committed, and there is sufficient probable cause to believe that the defendant committed it, the judge will hold the defendant to answer for trial in the superior court. This is sometimes termed as being "bound over for trial." If the judge is not convinced that a crime was committed or that the defendant committed it, he will dismiss the charge, and the defendant is entitled to be released. Unless there is some statutory regulation against further presentation of the matter, the case could be presented to a grand jury to determine if an indictment was forthcoming, but usually the prosecuting attorney will not go this far to seek prosecution.

If the judge holds the defendant to answer for trial, the prosecuting attorney must prepare a legal document setting forth the charge against the defendant. This document is known as an *information*. It is very similar in form to the indictment returned by the grand jury, and the information serves the same purposes as the indictment. It is the accusatory pleading that sets the trial in motion in the superior court. The information must be filed in the superior court within a few days, usually fifteen, after the defendant is held to answer for trial. Failure to comply with this time regulation could be grounds for dismissal of the charge.

In some jurisdictions the complaint which is filed with the magistrate before the initial appearance is known as an information. If the defendant is held to answer for trial, then the information will be filed with the clerk in the court where the trial will be heard.

Waiver of Preliminary Hearing

Although the preliminary hearing is a safeguard established for the benefit of the defendant, he may waive it if he so desires. However in most jurisdictions the waiver must be agreed to by the prosecuting attorney and the judge. There are advantages and disadvantages to both the defendant and the prosecution in the waiver of the preliminary hearing. If the defendant is unable to make bail, a waiver of the hearing results in an earlier trial date being set. On the other hand, by demanding a preliminary hearing a defendant might bring about a dismissal of the charge and his release from custody. The judge might conclude as a result of the hearing that there was insufficient cause to hold the defendant for trial. Another advantage to the defendant in having a preliminary hearing is that he may discover evidence held by the prosecution as it is unfolded during the hearing. This is particularly true in those jurisdictions where the right of the defendant to examine the evidence held by the prosecution before the trial is not recognized. This right is known as the "right of discovery" or the "right of inspection." It is granted to a defendant in order that he may better prepare his defense.

As it relates to the prosecution, there may be advantages in holding a preliminary hearing because it gives the prosecuting attorney an opportunity to obtain the testimony of the witnesses on an official record or transcript at a time when the facts are fresh in their memories and they are less likely to falsify. This record can be used during the trial, should the witness become unavailable. In those states in which the right of discovery is not recognized, the prosecuting attorney may agree with the waiver so that he will not have to reveal his evidence to the defense. The waiver will also eliminate a dilemma for the prosecuting attorney. In a preliminary hearing the prosecuting attorney must present enough evidence to convince the judge that the accused should be held for trial, but the prosecuting attorney does not want to reveal any more evidence than is necessary in order to prevent the defense from endeavoring to obtain perjured testimony to meet the prosecution's case.

It is interesting to note that although the grand jury system was established to safeguard the accused, this system has been under attack by defendants. It has been alleged that the preliminary hearing more nearly fulfills the due process of law clause of the Fourteenth Amendment. The reasoning behind this allegation is the fact that the grand jury meets in secret, and the defendant is not permitted to be present nor can he demand that he be permitted to present evidence in his own behalf. Generally, the courts have held that either the grand jury hearing and/or preliminary hearing system may be adopted by the states, as they see fit, and both satisfy the due process of law requirement. As was stated by the Court in the *Hurtado* decision:

> It is said by the court [the United States Supreme Court] that the Constitution of the United States was made for an undefined and expanding future, and that its requirement of due process of law in proceedings involving life, liberty and property, must be interpreted as not to deny to the law the capacity of progress and improvement; that the greatest security for the fundamental principles of justice resides in the right of the people to make their own laws and alter them at pleasure.

As stated, the courts in most jurisdictions have held that an accused is protected from unwarranted prosecution by either a grand jury indictment or a preliminary hearing. The supreme court of one state recently held, however, that even though an accused had been indicted, he was still entitled to a preliminary hearing. That court held that only by granting the accused a post-indictment preliminary hearing were his fundamental rights of due process of law protected. These rights include the right of counsel, the right of confrontation, the right of cross-examination, and the right to present evidence in his own behalf.

This decision has been criticized by many legal scholars as being unnecessary to protect an accused as well as imposing an additional burden upon the prosecution. Whether other state courts will follow this precedent in granting an accused the right to a post-indictment preliminary hearing only time will tell.

The Arraignment

When an indictment is returned or an information is filed with the trial court, the accused will be arraigned upon that accusatory pleading. At the arraignment the accused will be permitted to enter a plea to the charge set forth in that accusatory pleading. If a plea of not guilty or not guilty by reason of insanity is entered, a trial must take place. If the accused was not arrested before the indictment was returned, this arraignment may be the first or initial appearance for the accused. At the arraignment the accused will again be advised of his constitutional rights. Even though the accused may have been taken before a magistrate after a complaint was filed, the accused is still entitled to be arraigned after the filing of the indictment or information. In a sense, the indictment or information is a separate formal charge. The arraignment under these circumstances is not to be confused with the initial appearance, even though in some areas, the initial appearance is referred to as an arraignment.

The Coroner

From a sequential standpoint in the study of the administration of justice, the next procedure to be considered includes the various ramifications of the trial. Before entering that phase of the procedure, however, it is well to consider the county coroner and the important part he plays in the judicial process. The primary function of the coroner is to investigate the cause of certain deaths which take place within the county.

The coroner came into being in England shortly after the Norman Conquest, being traced back as far as A.D. 1194. He was a direct representative of the king, or the crown or corona—thus coroner. The coroners were elected by the king's judges as they rode through the countryside. In the beginning each county had four coroners. Their responsibility was to keep records on all that went on in the county as it concerned the administration of justice and to guard the revenues which might come to the king if justice was done. In the early history of England, as previously pointed out, if a person was convicted of a felony, his property was confiscated by the king, which resulted in a sizeable revenue for the king. It was to the king's interest to see that those accused of felonies were brought to trial and that their property was not dissipated before conviction. Thus the office of the coroner was created. Around the beginning of the thirteenth century the coroners began to investigate all sudden deaths that took place in their jurisdiction to determine if they were brought about by criminal means. Although this investigation was primarily the duty of the sheriff, it was thought that since the sheriff was only responsible to the people of the county, he might be hesitant to bring the offender to trial. The sheriff knew that, if convicted, the accused would undoubtedly be put to death or banished from the country and his property confiscated.

Duties of the Coroner

As time passed and the king was no longer able to confiscate the property of a convicted felon, the coroner should have disappeared from the judicial picture. But by that time the coroner had so entrenched himself into the judicial process that he remained a public official, and his office was carried from England to the United States. The coroner is a part of most county governments throughout the United States, and his present duties deviate greatly from those first performed in this position.

The duties and power vary somewhat among the states, but the primary function is quite uniform among all the states. It is the duty and right of the coroner to inquire into and determine the circumstances, manner, and cause of all violent, sudden, and unusual deaths. In general these would be deaths believed to have been the result of hanging, suicide, burns, poisoning, cutting, stabbing, drowning, vehicular accidents, industrial accidents, explosion, gunshot, electrical shock, alcoholism, drug addiction, strangulation, suffocation, criminal means, illegal abortion, starvation, or contagious disease. In most jurisdictions he will also inquire into the cause of a death that occurs when no one else is present; when in a penal institution; when a physician has not been in attendance for ten days or some similar number of days depending upon the jurisdiction; or when the attending physician is unable to state the cause. It is the duty of any law enforcement officer, physician, funeral director, or other person knowing of such an aforementioned death to report same to the coroner.

Upon receiving such a report, the coroner's inquiry may be very informal if he determines that the death was the result of natural causes, or that no negligence by another, nor criminal means, was involved. If the cause of death cannot be readily determined, the coroner has the authority to take possession of the deceased body and to have an autopsy performed and conduct such other investigation as may be necessary to assist him in determining the cause of death. The coroner also may hold an inquest as a further aid. Most jurisdictions permit the coroner, at his discretion, to hold the inquest sitting alone or before a coroner's jury. During the inquest witnesses who have some knowledge concerning the cause and manner of the death will be questioned. Physical evidence, including the body of the deceased, may be viewed if deemed pertinent. If the coroner decides to use a jury, the members of the jury will be selected from persons in the community who could qualify as petit jurors. The number selected varies among the states, but between nine and fifteen will usually be called, from which at least six or more will serve on the jury.

The purpose of the inquest is to determine the name of the deceased; the time and place that the death took place; the medical cause of the death; and whether the death was by natural causes, suicide, accident, or at the hands of another. Some jurisdictions require that during the inquest it not only be determined if the death was at the hands of another, but, if so, at whose hands and if by criminal means. In those jurisdictions following this latter procedure, some permit the coroner to issue a warrant of arrest for the accused if it is determined that the death was caused by criminal means. This procedure stems from the fact that some states consider the primary purpose of a coroner's inquest as providing means for the prompt securing of information for the use of those charged with the detection and prosecution of crime. Other jurisdictions hold that the inquest merely determines if the death was brought about by the hands of another. Any arrest or prosecution that may follow will be at the discretion of the prosecuting attorney. Jurisdictions vary as to the admissibility of the information developed by the inquest.

Selection and Qualifications of Coroner

In some jurisdictions the coroner is appointed by the county governing body, and in other places he is elected by the people of the county. Generally there are no prescribed qualifications set forth. Even though his responsibility is to determine the medical cause of death, in most jurisdictions there is no requirement that the coroner be medically trained. When not, the coroner will have to rely upon a physician to perform the autopsies. In some jurisdictions the sheriff is permitted to act in the capacity of coroner as well as that of sheriff. By legislative action, other jurisdictions have authorized county governments to replace the coroner with a medical examiner.

The law sometimes provides that the coroner will act as the sheriff, should the sheriff become incapacitated or unable to perform his duties. In those jurisdictions where the sheriff and the coroner are the same individual, this dual capacity creates an awkward situation if the sheriff is unable to act. Most jurisdictions, however, provide that if the sheriff becomes incapacitated, the undersheriff or the next in line, will act until the sheriff can be replaced. Even though the coroner may not function as a sheriff, the coroner does have the status of a peace officer in many states.

The coroner is often required, in addition to his other duties, to take custody of the personal property in the immediate possession of the deceased. This usually includes the property on the person of the deceased, but it may also include taking the necessary precautions to see that the property in a residence is secured if no relative, or other responsible person, is available. The property is then released to the legal representative of the deceased when such person is determined.

Review Questions

1. What is a guilty plea?
2. Before a guilty plea may be accepted, of what must the defendant be advised?
3. What is the next procedural step after the acceptance of a guilty plea?
4. What is the significance of a nolo contendere plea?
5. Define double jeopardy.
6. What is a grand jury?
7. List the qualifications for being a grand juror.
8. What is an indictment?
9. Who may be present during a grand jury's deliberation on an indictment?
10. What is a no bill?
11. What is a secret indictment?
12. Explain a nolle prosequi action.
13. What criticisms have been made of the grand jury system?
14. What is the purpose of the preliminary hearing?
15. What is an information?
16. Describe the primary function of the coroner.

Local Procedure

1. What pleas may a defendant enter?
2. May a defendant enter a plea of guilty to a capital punishment charge? If so, under what circumstances?
3. How many members compose a grand jury?
4. May a defendant be brought to trial on a felony charge by an information or must he be indicted?
5. How are the grand jurors selected?
6. May the prosecuting attorney enter a nolle prosequi?
7. Is the accused entitled to a preliminary hearing even though indicted?

six

PLACE AND TIME OF THE TRIAL

Pretrial Action

Before the trial phase of the administration of justice occurs, many decisions must be made before the trial itself begins. It must be determined when and where the trial will take place; whether the trial will be by the judge alone or by a jury; whether the defendant will represent himself or be assisted by counsel; what witnesses will be called; what physical evidence will be presented; and whether a pretrial hearing will be held. In view of the importance of each of these processes, each will be discussed in some detail. These decisions and the trial procedure are basically the same whether the charge involved is a felony or a misdemeanor.

Place of the Trial

Venue

The Sixth Amendment to the United States Constitution guarantees to an accused the right to a "speedy and public trial by an impartial jury of the State and district wherein the crime shall have been committed. . . ." This guarantee was placed in the Sixth Amendment as a result of the colonists having been dragged from their homes to some secret place, often to England, and tried away from their peers. This guarantee applies to the states through the due process of law clause of the Fourteenth Amendment. Thus, the place of the trial, or *venue,* lies within the judicial district in which the crime occurred. The term "venue" is derived from the French word *visne* meaning neighborhood. If the charge is a felony, the judicial district is the county; if it is a misdemeanor, the judicial district would be that specific area of the county so designated and established by law. The burden is on the prosecution to present evidence during the trial to prove that the crime was committed within the judicial district in which the trial is being held. Proving venue may be accomplished merely by an investigating officer testifying as to the specific location where the crime was committed within the county. If venue is not established by the prosecution, a conviction may be reversed on appeal because it is the right of the defendant to have the jury chosen from the judicial district in which the crime was committed.

Motion to Change Venue. Although the defendant is entitled to have the trial in the district where the crime occurred, that right may be waived and a request made that the trial be held in some other district. This is particularly true in felony cases. The defendant often believes that a fair and impartial trial cannot be had in the county in which the crime was committed. This is usually based on a belief that adverse publicity, the nature of the crime, or community hostility make it impossible for him to obtain an impartial jury. Under these circumstances, the defendant will file with the trial court a written request, known as a "motion to change venue." The trial judge will hold a hearing on this request at which time the defendant will present evidence in an effort to convince the judge that a change of venue should be granted. It may be alleged that, because the defendant is an outsider and the victim of the crime was popular, there is adverse feeling toward the accused. Or it may be alleged that because of the widespread publicity given to the crime, most persons in the county already believe in the defendant's guilt. In most instances, the prosecuting attorney will oppose the change of venue because of the inconvenience to witnesses and staff, and because of the cost involved. However, the cost is not to be considered by the judge in granting or denying a change of venue because the accused is entitled to a fair and impartial trial, regardless of cost. The prosecuting attorney will oppose the change of venue on grounds other than cost in most instances. The prosecuting attorney may contend that even though many persons have formed opinions unfavorable to the defendant as a result of what was published, it does not follow that persons without such views could not be found within the county to act as jurors or that those who had adverse opinions could not set those opinions aside and try the case in a fair and impartial manner based on the evidence. Or the prosecuting attorney may contend that because of the widespread publicity given to the crime, it would be equally difficult to obtain an impartial jury in another county. Another contention may be that the emotional involvement with the crime has subsided sufficiently by the trial that an impartial jury could be selected.

If, from the evidence presented during the hearing, the judge feels that a change of venue should be granted, the trial will be held in a county in which it is believed that a fair trial can be had. In most instances, the trial will be moved to an adjoining county. The cost of the trial will be borne by the county where the crime occurred. If the rule were otherwise, a county could impose on an adjoining county a terrific cost burden for trials of crimes not taking place within that county. If the judge does not grant a change of venue, and the defendant is convicted, the refusal to grant a change of venue may be grounds for appeal. If the appellate court concludes that a change of venue should have been granted, the conviction will be reversed.

States differ on whether the prosecution may request a change in venue. Some states have adopted a strict rule holding that the only time the prosecution may be granted a change in venue is when the jury panel has been exhausted and a jury has not been selected. Other states permit by statute the prosecution to be granted a change of venue upon proper showing of cause. Proper showing of cause would be situations such as the prosecution being unable to receive a fair and impartial trial, a general state of lawlessness existing within the district where the crime was committed, the enforcement of law in the district having met with hostility, or prosecution witnesses or jurors having been intimidated. To date, these statutes permitting the prosecution a change of venue under these circumstances have not been declared unconstitutional as violating the Sixth Amendment guarantee.

Time of Request for Change of Venue.   Generally, a request for change of venue must take place before the date set for the commencement of the trial. A change may be made after the commencement date if the jury panel is exhausted without a jury being selected, or if there is danger of violence taking place within the district.

Time of the Trial

The Sixth Amendment to the United States Constitution provides that the "accused shall enjoy the right to a speedy . . . trial." This same guarantee is embodied in the laws of all the states. The right to a speedy trial is a fundamental right of an accused; otherwise many injustices may be suffered. The people, or society, also have an interest in the guarantee that an accused be brought to trial without unnecessary delay. This is the only way that society can be properly protected from the offender. These guarantees provide little in the way of guidelines as to exactly when a trial must be held in order to comply with the speedy trial regulation. So the decision of when to hold a trial becomes a troublesome and most difficult one to make. The right to a speedy trial does not permit the defendant to demand that a trial be held the same day as the arrest because the prosecution has the right to prepare its case against the defendant. But the prosecution may not take an indefinite period of time in its preparation. In setting the trial date many factors must be considered, such as what is a reasonable length of time to permit each side to prepare its case, and whether the accused is in jail or has posted bail. Also, the rules of procedure of most states require that criminal trials be set for those in jail ahead of those who have posted bail when other factors are equal. Even if a trial date is set, this does not mean that the trial will begin on that date since continuances may be granted that will cause delay.

Continuances

Although the right to a speedy trial is designed primarily for the benefit of the accused, this right, like others, may be waived by the defendant, and often is. Defendants make frequent requests for continuances in bringing the case to trial. Often months pass between the time that an arrest is made and the defendant is brought to trial, particularly in felony cases. Regardless of the hardships that may be suffered in not having a speedy trial, the defendant often will delay the trial date as long as possible. Delay often works to the advantage of the accused because, with the passage of time, witnesses for the prosecution are more likely to become unavailable and their memories are more likely to dull. In addition, physical evidence becomes difficult to identify and is likely to become lost or contaminated.

Although the defendant may suffer from continuances, there are others who also suffer, particularly witnesses who must return to court many times only to find that the case has been continued. These witnesses usually receive no notice that a continuance will be granted. A continuance often is not granted until the case is called for trial, so notice is not possible. As a result, many witnesses must take time off from work, thus losing pay and experiencing the expense and inconvenience of traveling to and from court many times. It is understandable that people become reluctant to admit witnessing a crime. Delays also cause overcrowding of the court calendar, and other trials must be delayed, particularly civil trials.

Although the statutes of most states provide that a continuance may be granted only upon sufficient grounds and with sufficient notice, in most instances no specific grounds or time for the notice is stated. The most frequent ground alleged for a continuance is adequate time to prepare the case. Other grounds include obtaining witnesses or physical evidence, securing adequate and effective counsel for the defense, and ensuring the sound physical condition of the defendant. There is no set procedure to be followed in making a request for a continuance. It may be made orally in open court, or by written request in advance of the trial date. Whether a continuance will be granted is at the discretion of the trial judge.

The United States Supreme Court in the case of *Barker* v. *Wingo*, 407 US 514 (1972), discussed may of the ramifications of a speedy trial and the effect of delays on both the accused and the people. The Court also discussed some of the factors to be taken into consideration in determining whether the guarantee to a speedy trial had been violated. In view of the enlightening language of this decision, it is set forth in some detail for review by the reader. The facts of this case reflect that

> On July 20, 1958, in Christian County, Kentucky, an elderly couple was beaten to death by intruders wielding an iron tire tool. Two suspects, Silas Manning and Willie Barker, the petitioner, were arrested shortly thereafter. The grand jury indicted them on September 15. Counsel was appointed on September 17 and Barker's trial was set for October 21. The Commonwealth had a stronger case

against Manning, and it believed that Barker could not be convicted unless Manning testified against him. Manning was naturally unwilling to incriminate himself. Accordingly, on October 23, the day Silas Manning was brought to trial, the Commonwealth sought and obtained the first of what was to be a series of 16 continuances of Barker's trial. Barker made no objection. By first convicting Manning, the Commonwealth would remove possible problems of self-incrimination and would be able to assure his testimony against Barker.

The Commonwealth encountered more than a few difficulties in its prosecution of Manning. The first trial ended in a hung jury. A second trial resulted in a conviction, but the Kentucky Court of Appeals reversed because of the admission of evidence obtained by an illegal search. At his third trial, Manning was again convicted, and the Court of Appeals again reversed because the trial court had not granted a change of venue. A fourth trial resulted in a hung jury. Finally, after five trials, Manning was convicted, in March 1962, of murdering one victim, and after a sixth trial, in December 1962, he was convicted of murdering the other.

The Christian County Circuit Court holds three terms each year—in February, June, and September. Barker's initial trial was to take place in the September term of 1958. The first continuance postponed it until the February 1959 term. The second continuance was granted for one month only. Every term thereafter, for as long as the Manning prosecutions were in process, the Commonwealth routinely moved to continue Barker's case to the next term. When the case was continued from the June 1959 term until the following September, Barker, having spent 10 months in jail, obtained his release by posting a $5,000 bond. He thereafter remained free in the community until his trial. Barker made no objection, through his counsel, to the first 11 continuances.

When on February 12, 1962, the Commonwealth moved for the twelfth time to continue the case until the following term, Barker's counsel filed a motion to dismiss the indictment. The motion to dismiss was denied two weeks later, and the State's motion for a continuance was granted. The State was granted further continuances in June 1962 and September 1962, to which Barker did not object.

In February 1963, the first term of court following Manning's final conviction, the Commonwealth moved to set Barker's trial for March 19. But on the day scheduled for trial, it again moved for a continuance until the June term. It gave as its reason the illness of the ex-sheriff who was the chief investigating officer in the case. To this continuance, Barker objected unsuccessfully.

The witness was still unable to testify in June, and the trial, which had been set for June 19, was continued again until the September term—again over Barker's objection. This time the court announced that the case would be dismissed for lack of prosecution if it were not tried during the next term. The final trial date was set for October 9, 1963. On that date, Barker again moved to dismiss the indictment, and this time specified that his right to a speedy trial had been violated. The motion was denied; the trial commenced with Manning as the chief prosecution witness; Barker was convicted and given a life sentence.

Barker appealed his conviction through the Kentucky Court of Appeals and the United States District Court of Appeals. Both affirmed the conviction. The case was then appealed to the United States Supreme Court on the grounds that the due process of law clause of the Fourteenth Amendment of the United States Constitution had been violated because the defendant had been denied a speedy trial as provided by the Sixth Amendment now made applicable to the states through United States Supreme Court decisions.

In studying the case the United States Supreme Court stated:

The right to a speedy trial is generically different from any of the other rights enshrined in the Constitution for the protection of the accused. In addition to the general concern that all accused persons be treated according to decent and fair procedures, there is a societal interest in providing a speedy trial which exists separate from and at times in opposition to the interests of the accused. The inability of courts to provide a prompt trial has contributed to a large backlog of cases in urban courts which, among other things, enables defendants to negotiate more effectively for pleas of guilty to lesser offenses and otherwise manipulate the system. In addition, persons released on bond for lengthy periods awaiting trial have an opportunity to commit other crimes. It must be of little comfort to the residents of Christian County, Kentucky, to know that Barker was at large on bail for over four years while accused of a vicious and brutal murder of which he was ultimately convicted. Moreover, the longer an accused is free awaiting trial, the more tempting becomes his opportunity to jump bail and escape. Finally, delay between arrest and punishment may have a detrimental effect on rehabilitation.

If an accused cannot make bail, he is generally confined, as was Barker for 10 months, in a local jail. This contributes to the overcrowding and generally deplorable state of those institutions. Lengthy exposure to these conditions has a destructive effect on human character and makes the rehabilitation of the individual offender much more difficult. At times the result may even be violent rioting. Finally, lengthy pretrial detention is costly. The cost of maintaining a prisoner in jail varies from $3 to $9 per day, and this amounts to millions across the Nation. In addition, society loses wages which might have been earned, and it must often support families of incarcerated breadwinners.

A second difference between the right to speedy trial and the accused's other constitutional rights is that deprivation of the right may work to the accused's advantage. Delay is not an uncommon defense tactic. As the time between the commission of the crime and trial lengthens, witnesses may become unavailable or their memories may fade. If the witnesses support the prosecution, its case will be weakened, sometimes seriously so. And it is the prosecution which carries the burden of proof. Thus, unlike the right to counsel or the right to be free from compelled self-incrimination, deprivation of the right to speedy trial does not per se prejudice the accused's ability to defend himself.

Finally, and perhaps most importantly, the right to speedy trial is a more vague concept than other procedural rights. It is, for example, impossible to determine with precision when the right has been denied. We cannot definitely say how long is too long in a system where justice is supposed to be swift but deliberate. As a consequence, there is no fixed point in the criminal process when the State can put the defendant to the choice of either exercising or waiving the right to a speedy trial. If, for example, the State moves for a 60-day continuance, granting that continuance is not a violation of the right to speedy trial unless the circumstances of the case are such that further delay would endanger the values the right protects. It is impossible to do more than generalize about when those circumstances exist.

The nature of the speedy-trial right does make it impossible to pinpoint a precise time in the process when the right must be asserted or waived, but that fact does not argue for placing the burden of protecting the right solely on defendants. A defendant has no duty to bring himself to trial; the State has that duty as well as the duty of insuring that the trial is consistent with due process. Moreover, for the reasons earlier expressed, society has particular interest in bringing swift prosecutions, and society's representatives are the ones who should protect that interest.

The Court stated, however, that the defendant had some responsibility to assert his right to a speedy trial. The approach which the Court accepted was a balancing test in which the conduct of both the prosecution and the defendant was to be weighed. The Court continued by stating:

A balancing test necessarily compels courts to approach speedy-trial cases on an ad hoc basis. We can do little more than identify some of the factors which courts should assess in determining whether a particular defendant has been deprived of his right. Though some might express them in different ways, we identify four such factors: length of delay, the reason for the delay, the defendant's assertion of his right, and prejudice to the defendant.

We have discussed previously the societal disadvantages of lengthy pretrial incarceration, but obviously the disadvantages for the accused who cannot obtain his release are even more serious. The time spent in jail awaiting trial has a detrimental impact on the individual. It often means loss of a job; it disrupts family life; and it enforces idleness. Most jails offer little or no recreational or rehabilitative programs. The time spent in jail is simply dead time. Moreover, if a defendant is locked up, he is hindered in his ability to gather evidence, contact witnesses, and otherwise prepare his defense. Imposing those consequences on anyone who has not yet been convicted is serious. It is especially unfortunate to impose them on those persons who are ultimately found to be innocent. Finally, even if an accused is not incarcerated prior to trial, he is still disadvantaged by restraints on his liberty and by living under a cloud of anxiety, suspicion, and often hostility. . . .

The difficulty of the task of balancing these factors is illustrated by this case, which we consider to be close. It is clear that the length of delay between arrest and trial—well over five years—was extraordinary. Only seven months of that period can be attributed to a strong excuse, the illness of the ex-sheriff who was in charge of the investigation. Perhaps some delay would have been permissible under ordinary circumstances, so that Manning could be utilized as a witness in Barker's trial, but more than four years was too long a period, particularly since a good part of that period was attributable to the Commonwealth's failure or inability to try Manning under circumstances that comported with due process.

Two counter-balancing factors, however, outweigh these deficiencies. The first is that prejudice was minimal. Of course, Barker was prejudiced to some extent by living for over four years under a cloud of suspicion and anxiety. Moreover, although he was released on bond for most of the period, he did spend 10 months in jail before trial. But there is no claim that any of Barker's witnesses died or otherwise became unavailable owing to the delay. The trial transcript indicates only two very minor lapses of memory—one on the part of a prosecution witness—which were in no way significant to the outcome.

More important than the absence of serious prejudice, is the fact that Barker did not want a speedy trial. . . . The probable reason for Barker's attitude was that he was gambling on Manning's acquittal. The evidence was not terribly strong against Manning, as the reversals and hung juries suggest, and Barker undoubtedly thought that if Manning were acquitted, he would never be tried.

. . . We hold, therefore, that Barker was not deprived of his due process right to a speedy trial.

Out-of-State Incarceration

In the past, an acceptable ground for delay in bringing a case to trial was the incarceration of the defendant in another state. Under these circumstances it was assumed that the prosecution had no obligation to bring a defendant to trial if he was unavailable because of imprisonment beyond the jurisdiction of the court in which he was charged with a crime. This viewpoint was changed by the United States Supreme Court in the case of *Smith* v. *Hooey*, 393 US 374 (1969). The Court held that a defendant was entitled to a speedy trial even while serving time in another state, particularly if the defendant demanded to be brought to trial. The facts of the *Smith* case reflect that in 1960 the defendant was indicted in Harris County, Texas, upon a charge of theft. The defendant was then, and still was when the decision was handed down in 1969, a prisoner in the federal penitentiary at Leavenworth, Kansas. Shortly after the Texas charge was filed, the defendant mailed a letter to the Texas trial court requesting a speedy trial. The reply stated that a trial would commence within two weeks of any date the defendant could be present. For the next six years, the defendant made periodic efforts to be brought to trial. Texas authorities made no effort to obtain the defendant's appearance in the Harris County trial court. The defendant appealed the case to the United States Supreme Court on due process of law grounds in that a speedy trial had been denied.

In agreeing with the contention of the defendant the Court stated:

> At first blush it might appear that a man already in prison under a lawful sentence is hardly in a position to suffer from "undue and oppressive incarceration prior to trial." But the fact is that delay in bringing such a person to trial on a pending charge may ultimately result in as much oppression as is suffered by one who is jailed without bail upon an untried charge. First, the possibility that the defendant already in prison might receive a sentence at least partially concurrent with the one he is serving may be forever lost if trial of the pending charge is postponed. Secondly, under procedures now widely practiced, the duration of his present imprisonment may be increased, and the conditions under which he must serve his sentence greatly worsened, by the pendency of another criminal charge outstanding against him.
>
> And while it might be argued that a person already in prison would be less likely than others to be affected by "anxiety and concern accompanying public accusation," there is reason to believe that an outstanding untried charge (of which even a convict

may, of course, be innocent) can have fully as depressive an effect upon a prisoner as upon a person who is at large. In the opinion of the former Director of the Federal Bureau of Prisons,

"It is in their effect upon the prisoner and our attempts to rehabilitate him that detainers are most corrosive. The strain of having to serve a sentence with the uncertain prospect of being taken into the custody of another state at the conclusion interferes with the prisoner's ability to take maximum advantage of his institutional opportunities. His anxiety and depression may leave him with little inclination towards self-improvement."

Finally, it is self-evident that the possibilities that long delay will impair the ability of an accused to defend himself are markedly increased when the accused is incarcerated in another jurisdiction. Confined in a prison, perhaps far from the place where the offense covered by the outstanding charge allegedly took place, his ability to confer with potential defense witnesses, or even to keep track of their whereabouts, is obviously impaired. And, while evidence and witnesses disappear, memories fade, and events lose their perspective, a man isolated in prison is powerless to exert his own investigative efforts to mitigate these erosive effects of the passage of time.

The *Smith* case did not resolve the question as to the action that must be taken, if any, when a defendant does not demand to be brought to trial, and the *Barker* decision was of little assistance. The Court in the *Barker* case stated that the prosecution is responsible for bringing the defendant to trial. However the Court did not absolve the defendant of all responsibility in bringing about the trial. At first glance, it would appear that if the prosecution learns that a defendant is incarcerated in another state that some action should be taken by the prosecution to return the defendant for a speedy trial before the expiration date of the sentence in the other state. Otherwise it could be held that the defendant was denied the right to due process of law. On the other hand, if a defendant knows that he is wanted in another place for a crime committed, the failure to demand to be brought to trial could be interpreted as a waiver of the right to a speedy trial.

Statutory Regulations

In order to assist those involved in the administration of justice, most states have enacted statutes setting forth guidelines as to when a trial should take place, but even these guidelines have much flexibility. For example, many states have passed statutes similar to the following:

The welfare of the people requires that all proceedings in criminal cases shall be set for trial and heard and determined at the earliest

PLACE AND TIME OF THE TRIAL

possible time, and it shall be the duty of all courts and judicial officers and of all prosecuting attorneys to expedite such proceedings to the greatest degree that is consistent with the ends of justice. In accordance with this policy, criminal cases shall be given precedence over, and set for trial and heard prior to any civil matters. Also no continuance of a criminal trial shall be granted except upon sufficient cause shown in open court, and upon reasonable notice to the opposition. It is held also that cases of those accused of a crime who are in custody are to take precedence over those who have been released on bail.

In addition, most states have provisions stating that unless an accused is brought to trial within a set number of days after the filing of the appropriate accusatory pleading, the charge shall be dismissed and, if in custody, the defendant shall be released or bail exonerated. The period of time is usually 30 days if the charge is a misdemeanor, or within a period of 60 to 120 days, depending upon the jurisdiction, if the charge is a felony. This time period may be waived by the defendants. In most instances if a misdemeanor charge is dismissed, further prosecution will be barred on that particular offense, but states vary as to the effect of a dismissal of a felony charge. Some states hold that further prosecution is barred. Other states hold that the defendant must be released after the dismissal, but may be rearrested upon the filing of a new accusatory document, and the time period begins to run again. How many times such procedures could take place before it would be considered a violation of the speedy trial guarantee is uncertain. If it can be proved that the refiling was for harassment purposes, even one refiling would undoubtedly be considered a denial of due process.

It has also been held that unless reasonable efforts are made to execute a warrant of arrest after it has been issued, the accused may have been denied the right to a speedy trial. In one case, for example, a felony warrant of arrest was issued for an accused but no efforts were made to execute the warrant of arrest although the accused had resided at the address listed on the warrant for nearly six months after the warrant was issued. The accused left the area for a few months but returned and again lived at the address listed on the warrant for several months before being arrested on a minor charge. After the conviction on the felony charge, the appellate court held that because of the delay in executing the warrant of arrest, the accused had been denied a speedy trial. However, if a reasonable effort is made to execute a warrant of arrest and the accused cannot be located, the delay in the execution of the warrant will not be interpreted as a denial of a speedy trial. It has been held that if there is a good reason for not serving the warrant of arrest immediately after it is issued, the defendant's right to a speedy trial is not denied. In one case, there was a delay of five months between the time that the warrant of arrest was issued and the time of service. The court held that since the delay was for the purpose of identifying other members of a narcotic ring, and this would have been hampered by an immediate arrest, the delay was justified. Similarly, it has been held that if there is a good cause for a delay in having a warrant of arrest issued after a crime is committed, the defendant has not been denied the right to a speedy trial.

Statute of Limitations

To further assure that one accused of committing a crime is afforded a speedy trial, a statute of limitations is incorporated into the laws of all the states. This has been termed a humanitarian statute since it provides that some prosecutive action must be commenced against an accused within a reasonable time after the crime is committed. The statute prevents the state, or society, from holding the threat of prosecutive action for an indefinite period of time over the head of an offender. The statute has also been described as an act of grace, as there is a surrendering by the sovereignty of its right to prosecute.

The statute forces society to take some action from two aspects. It gives law enforcement the responsibility of taking immediate and continuous action upon a reported crime in order to identify the perpetrator so that he may be afforded a speedy trial. The statute also gives the prosecutive officials the burden of commencing prosecution within a specified time after the identity of an offender is established. There are occasions when a crime is committed and the law enforcement agency involved is unsuccessful in identifying the perpetrators of that crime until after the time stated in the statute of limitations has lapsed. Under those circumstances, the perpetrators may not be brought to trial even if later identified. In most states the statute of limitations is considered to be a jurisdictional matter and may not be waived. If the perpetrators of a crime are identified before the statutory period runs out and their whereabouts are unknown, some prosecutive action, such as filing a complaint or indictment, must still be commenced before the statutory time expires, or future prosecutive action will be barred.

There was no statute of limitations, as we know it today, at common law in England. If a crime was committed at common law, it was a crime against the king, and it was presumed that prosecution might occur at any time. It was particularly true in murder cases. This may be the reason that even today, in the United States, the statute of limitations never lapses on a murder charge. With most other crimes there is a specified time within which prosecutive action must commence. The time varies among states. On a felony charge the statute of limitations varies from three years to six years depending upon the state. On a misdemeanor charge the period is between six months and one year. There are a few states which list other felonies besides murder, such as the embezzlement of public funds or falsification of public records, for which there are not statutory periods. If, during the investigation of a case, it is determined that the perpetrator of the crime has left the state in which the crime was committed, the statute of limitations is suspended, or *tolled,* while the perpetrator is out of the state.

Review Questions

1. Where must a criminal trial take place?
2. What is meant by change of venue?
3. What is meant by a speedy trial?
4. List four factors that the United States Supreme Court set forth in the *Barker* v. *Wingo* decision that should be taken into account in determining whether a defendant has been denied a speedy trial.
5. List three societal disadvantages of lengthy pretrial incarceration.
6. Why should granting continuances be discouraged?
7. What effect, if any, does out-of-state incarceration have on a speedy trial?
8. What is the statute of limitations?

Local Procedure

1. What is the statute of limitations for:
    a. Misdemeanors
    b. Felonies
2. If a felony is dismissed for the failure to bring the defendant to trial within statutory limitations, may the charge be refiled?

seven

TRIAL BY JURY AND PUBLIC TRIAL

Court Trial Versus Jury Trial

By the beginning of the eighteenth century the accused was being confronted by the witnesses against him and hearsay evidence was eliminated. Witnesses were placed under oath to relate facts of their own knowledge. Juries rendered their verdicts upon the testimony of witnesses given in open court and not from what the jurors learned about an accusation outside of court. Rules of evidence were being formulated. The trial by jury as it is known today was rapidly becoming part of the judicial system in Great Britain and was adopted by the colonists. The colonists had deep reverence for trial by jury, and they strongly resented interference by the King of Great Britain in his efforts to subdue them. This resentment was manifested by the colonists in the Declaration of Independence. Among other provisions they included in this declaration the following: "The history of the present King of Great Britain is a history of repeated injuries. . . . To prove this, let facts be submitted to a candid world. . . . For his [the King] depriving us in many cases, of benefits of trial by jury."

Accused's Right to Jury Trial

After the colonists gained their independence from Great Britain, a new government was established. To prevent possible future interference with the right to a trial by jury in this newly formed government, the Sixth Amendment to the United States Constitution contained the provision that all persons accused of a crime had the right to be tried by an impartial jury. The Sixth Amendment right to trial by jury is made binding on the states through the "due process of law" clause of the Fourteenth Amendment, as is the right to a speedy trial. These rights are also contained in all state constitutions or statutes. Although the Sixth Amendment did not mention the number of persons required to constitute a jury, it was generally accepted that the common law rule of twelve persons would prevail. So strongly was it felt that a jury must consist of twelve persons in a criminal case that a trial by jury consisting of less than twelve would be a denial of due process of law. The idea of an accused being permitted to waive a jury and having the case held by a judge alone was practically unthought of. It was not until 1930 in the case of *Patton* v. *United States*, 281 US 276, that the United States Supreme Court held that a verdict rendered by a jury composed of less than twelve members was not a violation of an accused's Constitutional right to a trial by jury. In the *Patton* case the trial started with a jury composed of twelve persons, but during that trial one of the jurors became incapacitated. The defendant agreed to continue the trial with only eleven jurors. He was convicted, and the case was taken to the United States Supreme Court to determine if a defendant had the right to waive a jury trial. The defendant did not waive the entire jury in the *Patton* case, but even the waiver of one juror and continuing with only eleven was so foreign to the common law procedure that the United States Supreme Court felt that the matter was worth their consideration. The Court in the *Patton* case stated that, after an examination of Article III, Section 2, and the Sixth Amendment of the United States Constitution, they had come to the conclusion that a jury trial was a right which the accused might "forego at his election," and that the right to a trial by jury was a privilege and not an "imperative right." As such the defendant could waive a jury composed of less than twelve persons. This decision gave an implied permission to waive the jury entirely and have the case heard by a judge sitting alone.

Even though the Court in the *Patton* case sanctioned the right of an accused to waive his right to a jury, it did emphasize the necessity of preserving the jury trial system. The Court stated:

> Not only must the right of the accused to a trial by a constitutional jury be jealously preserved, but the maintenance of the jury as a fact-finding body in criminal cases is of such importance and has such a place in our traditions, that, before any waiver can become effective, the consent of government counsel and the sanction of the court must be had, in addition to the express and intelligent consent of the defendant.

The United States Supreme Court further emphasized the importance of the right of an accused to a trial by jury in the case of *Duncan* v. *Louisiana* 391 US 145 (1968). The Court in that decision stated:

> Providing an accused with the right to be tried by a jury of his peers gave him an inestimable safeguard against the corrupt or overzealous prosecutor and against the compliant, biased, or eccentric judge. If the defendant preferred the common-sense judgment of a jury to the more tutored but perhaps less sympathetic reaction of the single judge, he was to have it. Beyond this, the jury trial provisions in the Federal and State Constitutions reflect a fundamental decision about the exercise of official power—a reluctance to entrust plenary powers over the life and liberty of the citizens to one judge or to a group of judges. Fear of unchecked power, so typical of our State and Federal Governments in other respects, found expression in the criminal law in this insistence upon community participation in the determination of guilt or innocence. The deep commitment of the Nation to the right of jury trial in serious criminal cases as a defense against arbitrary law enforcement qualifies for protection under the Due Process Clause of the Fourteenth Amendment, and must therefore be respected by the States.

Trial by Judge Alone

Further advantages of a jury trial over a trial by a judge sitting alone, also referred to as a *court trial,* include the belief that a jury of twelve persons, representing a cross section of society, may be better able to evaluate the demeanor of witnesses than a judge sitting alone; that the group judgment of a jury is better than that of a single person—the judge; that there is a value in community participation in the administration of justice; and that the jury injects the common law test into the legal system, instead of the legalistic viewpoint.

With all of these listed advantages to a trial by jury, why would a defendant wish to waive a jury and be tried by a judge sitting alone? Situations arise in which it may be advantageous to the accused to waive his right to a jury trial in favor of a court trial. The crime of which the defendant is accused may be one of a heinous nature. The emotional involvement of the people within the community may make the selection of an impartial jury very difficult. The defendant's general appearance may be such that a jury may become most prejudiced. There may be a serious past criminal record subjecting the defendant to possible impeachment should the witness stand be taken as a defense, and the probability of the jury convicting the defendant on past record rather than on the evidence contended in the present charge is great. Or the defendant may be a part of an organized criminal syndicate, or minority group of which local feeling is against, and the jury may convict the accused by association rather than on the facts of the case. A judge is considered less inclined to be affected by any of these situations than a jury.

Procedure in the Waiver of a Jury.   Prior to the *Patton* decision only a few states had considered allowing a defendant to waive a trial by jury. However after the *Patton* decision a large majority of the states began permitting the defendant to waive his right to a trial by jury. States differ considerably as to the conditions and the procedure to be followed in permitting a waiver of a jury trial. A few states still do not permit the defendant to waive a jury trial. Some states permit the waiver in misdemeanor cases but not on felony charges. Others permit the jury to be waived in all cases except those with a maximum penalty of death. One state permits the defendant to waive the jury in capital cases and be tried by a panel of three judges. A few states permit the jury to be waived in any type of charge, including capital cases.

States differ also as to the procedure to be followed in regard to who must give the consent and how the consent is given. Some provide that the waiver is solely the right of the defendant, while others hold that the waiver must be consented to by the prosecution as well as the defendant. A few states require that the defendant, the prosecution, and the judge all must agree to the waiver of the jury, and a few others provide that the defendant and the judge agree to the waiver, but the consent of the prosecution is not required. This latter position has been criticized as it is believed that the prosecution should be permitted to disagree with the waiver. The reasoning is that a judge may be known to be sympathetic to the defendant, or the judge may be under political pressure making him feel that he is forced to render a verdict in favor of the defendant. In most instances the prosecution will agree with the waiver of the jury since the waiver expedites the trial by eliminating the time-consuming selection of the jury. Time is also saved by not having to stop during a jury trial to explain the law of the case to the jury.

The form in which the waiver of the jury takes place also varies among states. In some states the defendant must waive the jury in open court by an express statement to that effect. Other states require the defendant to consent to the waiver in writing before the date of the trial. Some states hold that unless the defendant demands a jury trial at the time that he enters the plea of not guilty, he automatically waives a jury trial. If the waiver of a jury takes place, it is usually before the jury is selected, but a few states permit the defendant to waive the jury anytime before the verdict is rendered.

A question that sometimes arises is: after consent to a waiver of the jury, may the defendant later demand to be tried by a jury? Generally, unless there is sufficient evidence of a miscarriage of justice, the defendant may not demand a jury trial, particularly if the trial has begun. The reason is that a jury would have to be selected and the trial would have to start over. Once the trial has begun, the waiver of a jury creates no particular difficulty since the judge will have heard all the evidence during the trial's progress and will be in a position to render the verdict. Whether the defendant is permitted to withdraw the waiver of the jury is within the discretion of the trial judge. In making the decision, the judge may consider such matters as the timeliness of the motion to withdraw the waiver, the reason for the requested withdrawal, and the possibility of undue delay of the trial or inconvenience to witnesses that would result from granting the withdrawal of the waiver.

May the Defendant Demand a Court Trial?   As previously pointed out, there are times when a defendant may wish to be tried by a judge sitting alone. Under these circumstances, may the defendant waive the jury and demand a court trial? This question was specifically answered by the United States Supreme Court in the case of *Singer* v. *United States* 380 US 24 (1965). In that decision the Court held that although a defendant could waive the right to a jury trial, there is no correlative right to a court trial. The Court in the *Singer* decision stated:

The ability to waive a constitutional right does not ordinarily carry with it the right to insist upon the opposite of that right. For example, although a defendant can, under some circumstances, waive his constitutional right to a public trial, he has no absolute right to compel a private trial, although he can waive his right to be tried in the State and district where the crime was committed, he cannot in all cases compel transfer of the case to another district, and although he can waive his right to be confronted by the witnesses against him, it has never been seriously suggested that he can thereby compel the Government to try the case by stipulation. . . .

Trial by jury has been established by the Constitution as the "normal and . . . preferable mode of disposing of issues of fact in a criminal case."

In light of the Constitution's emphasis on jury trial, we find it difficult to understand how the petitioner can submit the bald proposition that to compel a defendant in a criminal case to undergo a jury trial against his will is contrary to his right to a fair trial or to due process. A defendant's only constitutional right concerning the method of trial is to an impartial trial by jury. We find no constitutional impediment in conditioning a waiver of this right on the consent of the prosecuting attorney and the trial judge when, if either refuses to consent, the result is simply that the defendant is subject to an impartial trial by jury—the very thing that the Constitution guarantees him.

The Court concluded that it was not a violation of any constitutional right of an accused by forcing a jury trial even though the defendant might feel that it was advantageous to have a court trial. In this regard many states permit the judge to refuse to consent to a court trial in lieu of a trial by jury. Those states adopting this policy feel that protection against community criticism should be provided when the judge might have to render an unpopular verdict.

Denial of a Jury Trial: Petty Offenses

Although the right to a trial by jury is an established guarantee to one accused of a crime, it is not an absolute right in all instances. As early as 1937 the United States Supreme Court in the case of *District of Columbia* v. *Clawans,* 300 US 617, sanctioned a nonjury trial to one accused of a petty offense. This same sanction has been reiterated from time to time by the United States Supreme Court. (See *Duncan* v. *Louisiana; Cheff* v. *Schnackenberg,* 384 US 373 [1966]; and *Frank* v. *United States,* 395 US 147 [1969].)

In the *Duncan* decision, the Court stated:

So-called petty offenses were tried without juries both in England and in the Colonies and have always been held to be exempt from the otherwise comprehensive language of the Sixth Amendment's jury trial provisions. There is no substantial evidence that the Framers intended to depart from this established common-law practice, and the possible consequences to defendants from convictions for petty offenses have been thought insufficient to outweigh the benefits to efficient law enforcement and simplified judicial administration resulting from the availability of speedy and inexpensive non-jury adjudications. These same considerations compel the same result under the Fourteenth Amendment. Of course the boundaries of the petty offense category have always been ill defined, if not ambulatory.

Determining Petty Offenses.   In making a determination as to whether an offense is a "petty" one, the courts have had to turn to some criterion upon which to work. Although the statutes of some states have designated certain offenses as petty ones, this is not conclusive and the courts may render different interpretations as to petty offenses.

As stated by the United States Supreme Court in the *Frank* decision, to determine whether a particular offense could be classified as petty, the Court sought objective indications of the seriousness with which society regarded the offense. The Court stated that the most relevant indication of the seriousness of an offense was the severity of the penalty that could be imposed for the commission of the offense. The severity of the penalty being that authorized by law, and not the penalty actually imposed by the judge, was to be the criterion.

In the *Frank* case, the Supreme Court implied that they were relying upon the criterion set forth in the *Cheff* decision for a definition of petty offense. The *Cheff* decision adopted the definition of the United States Code. A petty offense is defined in 18 United States Code, section 1, as any misdemeanor, the penalty for which does not exceed imprisonment for a period of six months or a fine of $500.

It would appear from these United States Supreme Court decisions that the states could pass statutes denying an accused the right to a trial by a jury for the commission of an offense for which the penalty would not exceed six months imprisonment or a fine of not more than $500, and the accused would not be denied due process of law. A few states grant a defendant the right to a jury trial in all misdemeanor charges irrespective of the penalty but deny him the right to a jury trial on infractions—violations for which no imprisonment may be imposed.

Juries Composed of Less than Twelve

In line with the common-law tradition the laws of the United States, and of most of the states, require that a criminal trial jury consist of twelve persons. There are a few states where the law provides that in misdemeanor violations the jury may be composed of any number less than twelve, agreed upon in open court by the defendant and the prosecution. How many less than twelve is not indicated, but usually a jury will not have less than six members. As in the *Patton* case, in some states it is held that a felony trial must commence with twelve persons on the jury, but if one should become incapacitated and unable to act as a juror the trial may continue with less than twelve if agreed upon by the defendant, his attorney, and the prosecution. If it is not agreed to, the judge must declare a mistrial, and the case will have to be heard again with a new jury.

A few states have broken with the traditional number of twelve in a jury, even in felony cases, and have passed laws providing that a jury may be composed of less than twelve both in misdemeanor and felony cases. The problem which arises is whether trial by a jury composed of less than twelve when not consented to, particularly by the defendant, is a denial of the right to trial by jury. This question was answered in the case of *Williams* v. *Florida,* 399 US 78 (1970), in which the United States Supreme Court held that a jury composed of less than twelve persons, in accordance with the laws of the state involved, did not violate the due process of law clause of the Fourteenth Amendment. The facts in the *Williams* case reflect that Williams was charged with robbery in the state of Florida. Williams, referred to as the petitioner by the Court, filed a pretrial motion to impanel a twelve-man jury instead of the six-man jury provided by Florida law in all but capital cases. The motion was denied, and Williams was convicted and sentenced to life imprisonment. He appealed his case to the United States Supreme Court upon the grounds that his right to a jury trial as provided in the Sixth Amendment to the United States Constitution, made applicable to the states by the Fourteenth Amendment, had been violated by requiring him to submit to a trial by a jury composed only of six persons. The Court stated:

> The question in this case is whether the constitutional guarantee of a trial by "jury" necessarily requires trial by exactly 12 persons, rather than some lesser number—in this case six. We hold that the 12-man panel is not a necessary ingredient of "trial by jury," and that respondent's [state's] refusal to impanel more than the six members provided for by Florida law did not violate petitioner's Sixth Amendment rights as applied to the States through the Fourteenth.

> We had occasion in *Duncan* v. *Louisiana* to review briefly the oft-told history of the development of trial by jury in criminal cases. That history revealed a long tradition attaching great importance to the concept of relying on a body of one's peers to determine guilt or innocence as a safeguard against arbitrary law enforcement. That same history, however, affords little insight into the considerations which gradually led the size of that body to be generally fixed at 12. Some have suggested that the number 12 was fixed upon simply because that was the number of the present-

ment jury from the hundred, from which the petty jury developed. Other, less circular but more fanciful reasons for the number 12 have been given, "but they were all brought forward after the number was fixed," and rest on little more than mystical or superstitious insights into the significance of "12." Lord Coke's explanation that the "number of twelve is much respected in holy writ, as 12 apostles, 12 stones, 12 tribes, etc." is typical. In short, while sometime in the 14th century the size of the jury at common law came to be fixed generally at 12, that particular feature of the jury system appears to have been an historical accident, unrelated to the great purposes which gave rise to the jury in the first place. The question before us is whether this accidental feature of the jury has been immutably codified into our Constitution. . . .

It might be suggested that the 12-man jury gives a defendant a greater advantage since he has more "chances" of finding a juror who will insist on acquittal and thus prevent conviction. But the advantage might just as easily belong to the State, which also needs only one juror out of twelve insisting on guilt to prevent acquittal. What few experiments have occurred—usually in the civil area—indicate that there is no discernible difference between the results reached by the two different-sized juries. In short, neither currently available evidence nor theory suggests that the 12-man jury is necessarily more advantageous to the defendant than a jury composed of fewer members.

Similarly, while in theory the number of viewpoints represented on a randomly selected jury ought to increase as the size of the jury increases, in practice the difference between the 12-man and the 6-man jury in terms of the cross section of the community represented seems likely to be negligible. Even the 12-man jury cannot insure representation of every distinct voice in the community, particularly given the use of the peremptory challenge. As long as arbitrary exclusions of a particular class from the jury rolls are forbidden, the concern that the cross section will be significantly diminished if the jury is decreased in size from 12 to 6 seems an unrealistic one.

We conclude, in short, as we began: the fact that the jury at common law was composed of precisely 12 is an historical accident, unnecessary to effect the purposes of the jury system and wholly without significance "except to mystics."

Since the *Williams* decision has been handed down by the United States Supreme Court, it is highly possible that more and more states will enact laws permitting juries to be composed of less than twelve members in all but capital cases. However, the United States Supreme court, in *Ballew* v. *Georgia*, 55 L Ed 2d 234 (1978), held that a jury may not be composed of less than six persons. Ballew was convicted of a misdemeanor charge by a jury of five persons as provided by a Georgia statute. The conviction was upheld by the Georgia appellate courts. Ballew appealed his case to the United States Supreme Court on the grounds that his constitutional guarantee of a trial by jury had been denied, thereby denying him due process of law. The United States Supreme Court stated that a jury of six persons had been upheld in the Williams case and the "line between five and six member juries is difficult to justify, but a line has to be drawn somewhere if the substance of the jury trial is to be preserved." The Court further stated that assembled research data "raise substantial doubt about the reliability and appropriate representation of panels smaller than six. Because of the fundamental importance of the jury trial to the American system of criminal justice, any further reduction that promotes inaccurate and possibly biased decision making, that causes untoward differences in verdicts, and that prevents juries from truly representing their communities, attains constitutional significance," and such reduction from six-member to five-member juries is not to be permitted.

Public Trial

Not only does the Sixth Amendment to the United States Constitution, as well as the laws of all the states, provide that an accused person is entitled to a trial by jury, but that he also is guaranteed a public trial. The purpose of this guarantee is to ensure that the accused is dealt with fairly and not unjustly convicted. As was stated by the United States Supreme Court in the case of *Estes* v. *Texas*, 381 US 532 (1965):

> History has proven that secret tribunals were effective instruments of oppression. As our Brother Black so well said in *In re Oliver*, 333 US 257 (1948): "The traditional Anglo-American distrust for secret trials has been variously ascribed to the notorious use of this practice by the Spanish Inquisition, to the excesses of the English Court of Star Chamber, and to the French monarchy's abuse of the lettre de cachet. . . . Whatever other benefits the guarantee to an accused that his trial be conducted in public may confer upon our society, the guarantee has always been recognized as a safeguard against any attempt to employ our courts as instruments of persecution."
>
> Clearly the openness of the proceedings (the trial) provides other benefits as well (as a safeguard against oppression): it arguably improves the quality of testimony, it may induce unknown witnesses to come forward with relevant testimony, it may move all the trial participants to perform their duties conscientiously, and it gives the public the opportunity to observe the courts in the performance of their duties and to determine whether they are performing adequately.

What Makes a Trial "Public"

Although an accused's guarantee to a public trial appears on the surface to be a clear and explicit right, it is not without complications. Just what constitutes a "public" trial is not defined either by the Sixth Amendment or by any of the laws of the states. The problems which arise are: What is a public trial? Who constitutes the public? How many persons must be in attendance to make a trial a public one? Also, since the right to a public trial is basically a right of the accused, may the right be waived resulting in a private trial? Over a period of time partial answers to these questions have come from court decisions, but the answers to some questions have not been unanimous. It is unanimously agreed to the overly simple definition that a "public trial" is one that is not secret.

The common-sense interpretation of "public trial" is one which the general public is free to attend. The doors of the courtroom are expected to be kept open. However if no member of the public is in attendance there is no requirement that a trial be stopped in order to satisfy the guarantee of a public trial. Under ordinary circumstances the "public" includes persons of all classes, races, sexes, and ages.

There are times when it may not be necessary to permit every person to attend trial proceedings in order for a trial to be a public trial. It has been held that to satisfy the constitutional guarantee to a public trial it is not necessary to provide a stadium large enough to accommodate all who might want to attend a particular trial. Yet a courtroom should be large enough to permit a reasonable number of the public to observe the trial proceedings. It also has been held that a judge may limit the number of persons attending a trial to the seating capacity of the courtroom facilities without violating the right of a public trial. A judge may eject any spectator, or member of the public, who becomes unruly and disrupts the trial proceedings. The judge may even clear the courtroom of all spectators if they become disruptive. However, that does not permit locking the courtroom doors and prohibiting other members of the public who conduct themselves properly from attending the trial.

Public Right to Attend

The courts were far from unanimous in answering the question of public exclusion from the courtroom. The issue is whether or not the public may be excluded in any situation without violating the guarantee to a public trial. The question usually surfaced when a trial involved salacious testimony. Two cases which addressed the exclusion of the public from trial were *Richmond Newspapers, Inc. v. Virginia,* 448 US 555 (1980) and *Globe Newspapers Co. v. Superior Court for the County of Norfolk,* 457 US 596 (1982).

Closing the Entire Trial. The Court in the Richmond case recognized that the press and public right to access to criminal trials was based on the First Amendment of the United States Constitution and not on the Sixth Amendment right of a defendant to a public trial. The defendant was charged with murder and had been brought to trial on three prior occasions, each time ending in a mistrial. At the time of the fourth trial, the defense attorney requested that the trial be closed to the public because of prior interferences by spectators. The prosecution voiced no objection to a closed trial and the judge granted the defense request to close the courtroom to the press and public. This right was granted to judges by the Virginia statutes. The Richmond Newspapers, Inc. filed an objection to being barred from the courtroom and a hearing was held on the objection. The Virginia Appellate Court upheld the judge's ruling to close the courtroom. The case was appealed to the United States Supreme Court on the grounds that the freedom of the press right of the First Amendment to the Constitution had been violated by barring the press from the trial. Since the defendant had requested the trial be closed, the United States Supreme Court could not consider the case on the Sixth Amendment right to a public trial. Consideration of the case was then based on First Amendment rights. The Court pointed out that the First Amendment does not mention the right of public access to a criminal trial explicitly, but held that the First Amendment is broad enough in scope to encompass certain rights not specifically mentioned, including the right of access to criminal trials. The Court stated:

> Underlying the First Amendment right of access to criminal trials [by the public] is the common understanding that a major purpose of that Amendment was to protect the free discussion of governmental affairs. By offering such protection, the First Amendment serves to ensure that the individual citizen can effectively participate in and contribute to our republican system of self-government. . . . Thus to the extent that the First Amendment embraces a right of access to criminal trials, it is to ensure that this constitutionally protected discussion of governmental affairs is an informed one.

Closing a Portion of a Trial. The *Richmond Newspapers, Inc.* decision pertained to the closing of the entire trial to the press and public, which the Court held was in violation of the First Amendment. That decision still left the question as to whether the press and public could be excluded from a portion of the trial when it may be in the best interest of fairness to make such an exclusion. The United States Supreme Court discussed this issue in the *Globe Newspapers Co.* case. In *Globe* the Court stated:

> Although the right of access to criminal trials is of constitutional stature, it is not absolute. But circumstances under which the press

and public can be barred from a criminal trial are limited; the State's justification in denying access must be a weighty one. Where, as in the present case, the State attempts to deny the right of access in order to inhibit the disclosure of sensitive information, it must be shown that the denial is necessitated by a compelling governmental interest, and is narrowly tailored to serve that interest.

In the *Globe Newspapers Co.* case the defendant was charged with the rape of three teenage girls. The law of Massachusetts required that under all circumstances the press and public must be excluded during the testimony of a minor victim in a sex offense trial. In *Globe,* the Supreme Court focused on the reasons behind the mandatory exclusion. By passing this law, the State of Massachusetts tried to protect minor victims of sex crimes from further trauma and embarrassment and to encourage such victims to come forward and testify in a truthful and credible manner. The Court stated that it agreed with the State of Massachusetts' interest in safeguarding the physical and psychological well-being of a minor, but that this interest did not justify a mandatory exclusion rule for all cases. The Court felt that the trial judge could determine case-by-case whether a closure is necessary to protect the welfare of a minor victim. Among factors to be weighed by the judge are the minor victim's age, psychological maturity and understanding, the nature of the crime, the desires of the victim, and the interests of the parents and relatives.

The Court further stated in the *Globe Newspapers Co.* case that the victims in that case were already a matter of public record and there was no showing that they would not testify in the presence of the public and press. Additionally, there was no showing that a closure of a trial during the testimony of a minor victim would result in others coming forth and reporting such crimes. For these reasons the Court held that the mandatory exclusion of the press and public in all such matters violated the First Amendment to the United States Constitution. The *Globe* decision would appear to allow a trial judge to exclude the press and public during the giving of testimony by a witness when it would be in the best interest of fairness to make that exclusion. The burden of showing that such an exclusion was in the best interest of all would be on the trial judge.

In a state court case the trial judge's exclusion of the press and public during the testimony of the prosecution's principal witness, a 16-year-old pregnant girl, was upheld by the state appellate court. The exclusion order was based partly on concern for the welfare of the young expectant mother and her unborn child and partly on her own subjective fear of reprisal if she testified in public. In another state case the exclusion of the press and public by the trial judge was upheld by the state appellate court during the testimony of an undercover police officer whose safety might have been endangered if his identity had been publicly exposed.

Public Exclusion from Pretrial Hearings.   The *Richmond Newspaper, Inc.* and the *Globe Newspapers Co.* cases are not to be confused with the case of *Gannett Co.* v. *DePasquale,* 443 US 368 (1979). In *Gannett,* the United States Supreme Court held that the press and public may be excluded from pretrial hearings, such as a pretrial hearing on the suppression of evidence or a preliminary hearing. *Gannett* upheld the exclusion of the press and public from pretrial hearings on the grounds that adverse prepublicity given to such hearings could pose a risk to the defendant and prevent a fair trial. The Court pointed out that there is a difference between the trial itself and pretrial hearings. The Court in the *Gannett* case stated that:

> Publicity concerning pretrial suppression hearings such as the one involved in the present case poses special risks of unfairness. The whole purpose of such hearings is to screen out unreliable or illegally obtained evidence and ensure that this evidence does not become known to the jury. Publicity concerning the proceedings at a pretrial hearing, however, could influence the public opinion against a defendant and inform potential jurors of inculpatory information wholly inadmissible at the actual trial. This Court has long recognized that adverse publicity can endanger the ability of a defendant to receive a fair trial.

The *Gannett* decision does not demand that all pretrial hearings be closed to the press and public, but only on request made to the trial judge or on the judge's own discretion.

Fair Trial Versus Freedom of the Press

From our foregoing discussion it may be concluded that the public is entitled to know that justice is taking place during a criminal trial. Therefore the public, with some reservations, is permitted to attend trial proceedings. Since not all the public who may have an interest in a particular trial may be able to attend, the news media have assumed the responsibility of informing the public about what takes place during certain trials. The problem that arises is just how far the news media may go in obtaining information and reporting it to the public. The courts and the news media are often in conflict over the answer to this question. The news media rely upon the First Amendment to the United States Constitution for support in the uninhibited right to exercise their power in getting the news. This amendment provides, among other provisions, that "Congress shall make no law . . . abridging the freedom of speech, or of the press . . ."

When the courts attempt to curtail the media in obtaining news, the media allege violation of their rights under the First Amendment. The courts on the other hand hold that an accused is entitled to a fair trial by an impartial jury, and when the right is interfered with by the news media they have exceeded their prerogative. Because of the right of the public to be informed of what takes place during criminal trials, the courts generally have permitted reporters to be present during criminal trials, and in many instances there are special areas in courtrooms set aside for reporters in order that they may have a vantage point to assist them in obtaining the news. With the advent of the camera, radio, and television, conflicts have arisen as to whether this type of equipment should be permitted in the courtroom. It is conceded by the courts that when the gathering of news during trial proceedings becomes too disruptive, or otherwise denies the defendant a fair trial by an impartial jury, some control must be exercised.

This viewpoint was emphasized by the United States Supreme Court in the *Estes* case. Estes was convicted in the state court in Texas on an extensive swindling charge. His case was taken to the United States Supreme Court on the grounds that, because of massive pretrial and trial publicity, he had been denied the right of due process of law as provided by the Fourteenth Amendment to the United States Constitution. The Supreme Court concluded that the defendant had been denied a fair trial because of the live radio and television coverage, and the conviction was reversed. The Court set forth some pertinent arguments against permitting live news coverage of criminal trials; these arguments are still being presented by those opposing live coverage.

At the time the *Estes* case was heard by the United States Supreme Court, the attorneys representing the state of Texas contended that the television portions of the trial did not constitute a denial of due process since there was no showing of prejudice of Estes resulting from the television coverage. The State also argued that the public has a right to know what goes on in the courts, and that televising criminal trials would be enlightening to the public and promote greater respect for the courts. To this argument the Court stated:

> It is true that the public has a right to be informed as to what occurs in its courts, but reporters of all media, including television, are always present if they wish to be and are plainly free to report whatever occurs in open court through their respective media. . . .
>
> As has been said, the chief function of our judicial machinery is to ascertain the truth. The use of television, however, cannot be said to contribute materially to this objective. Rather its

use amounts to the injection of an irrelevant factor into court proceedings. In addition experience teaches that there are numerous situations in which it might cause actual unfairness—some so subtle as to defy detection by the accused or control by the judge. We enumerate some in summary:

1. The potential impact of television on the jurors is perhaps of the greatest significance. They are the nerve center of the fact-finding process. . . . From the moment the trial judge announces that a case will be televised it becomes a cause celebre. The whole community, including prospective jurors, becomes interested in all the morbid details surrounding it. The approaching trial immediately assumes an important status in the public press and the accused is highly publicized along with the offense with which he is charged. Every juror carries with him into the jury box these solemn facts and thus increases the chance of prejudice that is present in every criminal case. And we must remember that realistically it is only the notorious trial which will be broadcast, because of the necessity for paid sponsorship. The conscious or unconscious effect that this may have on the juror's judgment cannot be evaluated, but experience indicates that it is not only possible but highly probable that it will have a direct bearing on his vote as to guilt or innocence. Where pretrial publicity of all kinds has created intense public feeling which is aggravated by the telecasting or picturing of the trial the televised jurors cannot help but feel the pressures of knowing that friends and neighbors have their eyes upon them. If the community be hostile to an accused a televised juror, realizing that he must return to neighbors who saw the trial themselves, may well be led "not to hold the balance nice, clear and true between the State and the accused. . . ."

2. The quality of the testimony in criminal trials will often be impaired. The impact upon a witness of the knowledge that he is being viewed by a vast audience is simply incalculable. Some may be demoralized and frightened, some cocky and given to overstatement; memories may falter, as with anyone speaking publicly, and accuracy of statement may be severely undermined. Embarrassment may impede the search for the truth, as may a natural tendency toward overdramatization. Furthermore, inquisitive strangers and "cranks" might approach witnesses on the street with jibes, advice or demands for explanation of testimony. There is little wonder that the defendant cannot "prove" the existence of such factors. Yet we all know from experience that they exist.

3. A major aspect of the problem is the additional responsibilities the presence of television places on the trial judge. His job is to make certain that the accused receives a fair trial. This most difficult task requires his undivided attention. Still when television comes into the courtroom he must also supervise it. . . . In addition, laying physical interruptions aside, there is the ever-present distraction that the mere awareness of television's pres-

ence prompts. Judges are human beings also and are subject to the same psychological reactions as laymen. Telecasting is particularly bad where the judge is elected, as is the case in all save a half dozen of our States. The telecasting of a trial becomes a political weapon, which, along with other distractions inherent in broadcasting, diverts his attention from the task at hand—the fair trial of the accused.

But this is not all. There is the initial decision that must be made as to whether the use of television will be permitted. This is perhaps an even more crucial consideration. Our judges are high-minded men and women. But it is difficult to remain oblivious to the pressures that the news media can bring to bear on them both directly and through the shaping of public opinion. Moreover, where one judge in a district or even in a State permits telecasting, the requirement that the others do the same is almost mandatory. Especially is this true where the judge is selected at the ballot box.

Finally, we cannot ignore the impact of courtroom television on the defendant. Its presence is a form of mental—if not physical—harassment. . . . A defendant on trial for a specific crime is entitled to his day in court, not in a stadium, or a city or nationwide arena. The heightened public clamor resulting from radio and television coverage will inevitably result in prejudice.

After the *Estes* decision, courts for a time generally prohibited live coverage of criminal trials. But the news media eventually renewed their pressure to permit live coverage of trials. Many judges and attorneys have resisted this pressure principally on the grounds presented in the *Estes* decision. Regardless of these strong arguments against live coverage, more and more courts are permitting live news coverage of trials. There is still a serious concern of many in the justice system about the effects of this type of coverage, not only from the standpoint of the defendant, but also concerning the safety of witnesses. Great strides have been made to protect the victims of rape cases from embarrassment during trials in order to encourage victims to come forth and report such offenses. It is believed that with live coverage of trials, many victims of all types of crimes will refuse to report offenses rather than face the embarrassment and possible harm from testifying before television cameras.

Gag Orders

Courts throughout the nation are aware that the news media are entitled to report events occurring during a trial as well as crimes taking place, and no effort is made to suppress this type of reporting. However, the courts have periodically issued orders limiting the information that may be given to the press. These are referred to as *gag orders*. They are issued to prevent extensive pretrial or trial publicity which could deny a defendant a fair trial because of the resulting difficulty in selecting and maintaining an impartial jury. But the news media has strongly protested the issuance of gag orders on the grounds that such orders violate the First Amendment. So balancing the right of a defendant to a fair trial with the right of the freedom of the press has continually plagued the courts. In *Sheppard* v. *Maxwell,* 384 US 333 (1966), the United States Supreme Court criticized the trial judge for the failure to restrain pretrial publicity. The facts of that case reveal that Dr. Sheppard was accused of killing his wife. Prior to the trial there were numerous newspaper stories concerning the questioning of the accused as well as articles about his personal life and love affairs. The jury list was published and many of the prospective jurors received telephone calls concerning the case. Inaccurate news releases were given to the press by the police. The judge, who was coming up for election, permitted extensive live news coverage of the trial. Sheppard was convicted and eventually appealed the case to the United States Supreme Court on the grounds that due process of law had been denied during the trial. The United States Supreme Court reversed the conviction because it felt that pretrial publicity and extensive live coverage of the trial had kept the defendant from receiving a fair trial. The Court stated:

> [that the trial judge] should have made some effort to control the release of leads, information, and gossip to the press by police officers, witnesses, and the counsel for both sides. . . . The courts must take steps by rule and regulation that will protect their processes from prejudicial outside interference. Neither prosecutors, counsel for defense, the accused, witnesses, court staff nor enforcement officers coming under the jurisdiction of the court should be permitted to frustrate its function.

Although the Court in the *Sheppard* case stated that trial judges "have the duty of so insulating the trial from publicity as to insure its fairness," the Court did not set down any fixed rules to guide the trial judges and others as to what could and could not be printed. But acting upon the suggestion of the *Sheppard* case, trial judges have occasionally issued gag orders. But in *Nebraska Press Association* v. *Stewart,* 427 US 539 (1976), the United States Supreme Court discouraged, but did not rule out, the use of gag orders. The Court stated: "This Court has frequently denied that the First Amendment rights are absolute and has consistently rejected the proposition that a prior restraint can never be employed." The Court indicated that such prior restraint should be used only when absolutely necessary to assure a fair trial. As stated by one of the justices, before a prior restraint is to be used there must be "a showing that (i) there is a clear threat to the fairness of trial, (ii) such a threat is posed by the actual publicity to be restrained, and (iii) no less restrictive alternatives are available."

The United States Supreme Court in this case felt that the trial judge had overstepped his rights in issuing the gag order. He prohibited the publication of information brought out in an open preliminary hearing that the public was free to attend. The Court did not rule out the possible use of a gag order to prevent pretrial publicity concerning information not otherwise known that would prevent a fair trial from being obtained, when other less restrictive measures were unavailable. But the Court did not indicate what less restrictive measures might be substituted for the gag order.

One less restrictive measure suggested for use instead of issuing a gag order was the granting of a change in venue. But there are many crimes committed that receive such extensive publicity that a change in venue would accomplish little. Under these circumstances, judges may still issue gag orders to prevent undue pretrial publicity, and undoubtedly receive the sanction of the United States Supreme Court.

Even before the *Sheppard* decision, law enforcement officers and prosecuting attorneys were restrictive in the release of certain information to the news media. This restrictive action, taken even without a gag order, was the result of criticism directed at law enforcement officers in *Rideau* v. *Louisiana*, 373 US 723 (1963). The United States Supreme Court in that case was critical of the law enforcement agencies involved in permitting the televising of a confession while it was being given by the defendant. The facts of the case reveal that:

> Some two months before petitioner's (Rideau's) trial began and some two weeks before he was arraigned on charges of robbery, kidnapping and murder, a local TV station broadcast three different times in the space of two days a twenty-minute film of petitioner, flanked by the sheriff and two state troopers, admitting in detail the commission of the various offenses in response to leading questions by the sheriff.

Rideau was convicted of the charges against him and his case was taken to the United States Supreme Court on the grounds that he had been denied due process of law when a change of venue request was denied by the trial judge. The Supreme Court reversed the conviction, stating:

> . . . we hold that it was a denial of due process of law to refuse the request for a change of venue, after the people of the Parish had been exposed repeatedly and in depth to the spectacle of Rideau personally confessing in detail to the crimes with which he was later to be charged. For anyone who has ever watched television the conclusion cannot be avoided that this spectacle, to the tens of thousands of people who saw and heard it, in a very real sense was

Rideau's trial—at which he pleaded guilty to murder. Any subsequent court proceedings in a community so pervasively exposed to such a spectacle could be but a hollow formality.

After the Rideau decision, many law enforcement officers and prosecuting attorneys decided it was generally best not to reveal to the press whether an accused person has confessed, nor to comment on the results of any tests that may have been given. Some officers will not reveal any prior criminal record of an accused. However, not all are in agreement with this viewpoint, as some contend that if an accused has been previously convicted, the court record of the conviction is a public record and the news media should be able to obtain this information. But self-imposed restrictions by officers and prosecutors may help to ensure a fair trial. Judges often impose further restrictions during a trial to prevent jurors from being influenced by news media comments.

Review Questions

1. What amendment of the United States Constitution embodies the right to trial by jury?
2. List three advantages to an accused of a trial by jury over a court trial.
3. Why may an accused wish to waive a trial by jury?
4. What reasons has the United States Supreme Court set forth in prohibiting the accused from demanding and receiving a court trial?
5. Some jurisdictions hold that an accused may be denied a jury trial on petty offenses. What criterion has the United States Supreme Court set forth in determining what qualifies as a "petty offense"?
6. What United States Supreme Court decision upheld that a trial by a jury composed of less than twelve persons was not a denial of the due process clause of the Fourteenth Amendment?
7. What is considered as a public trial?
8. Why is the accused guaranteed a public trial?
9. Must a demand by an accused for a private trial be granted?
10. Why did the *Richmond* case base the public right to access to criminal trials on the First Amendment of the United States Constitution instead of the Sixth Amendment?

11. In what way may a fair trial and the freedom of the press be in conflict?
12. What is meant by a "gag order" and why may one be placed in effect?

Local Procedure

1. May a defendant waive a jury trial? If so, are there any restrictions on the type of offense for which the jury trial may be waived?
2. If a jury trial may be waived, who must give consent to the waiver?
3. Can a jury be composed of less than twelve persons?
4. May a petty offense charge be tried without a jury?

eight

CONFRONTA-TION AND ASSISTANCE OF COUNSEL

The Presence of the Defendant at a Trial

In some countries an accused person may be tried and convicted of a crime without being present and without knowing that a trial has taken place. This procedure is referred to as *conviction in absentia*. To prevent such action from taking place in the United States, the Sixth Amendment of the United States Constitution, as well as the laws of all the states, includes a provision entitling an accused to be confronted with the witnesses for the prosecution. This guarantee has a dual purpose. It guarantees that witnesses against a defendant must appear in person in court to present their facts, and provides a defendant with the right to be present during every phase of trial proceedings.

For many years the interpretation of the right of an accused to be present during a trial was so rigid that, if a defendant was not present, a trial had to be halted until his presence could be obtained. Knowing the court's rigid interpretation of this right, defendants occasionally took advantage by being so disruptive that the trial could not continue with their presence, or by failing to appear in court while out on bail, thus preventing the trial from taking place. Many states included provisions in their statutes stating that in felony cases the defendant had to be present during all phases of the trial. But as time passed, some courts relaxed the rule requiring the defendant's presence when he or she voluntarily was absent.

Disruption of the Trial

A separate issue is raised when the defendant is present and demands to remain present, but becomes so disruptive that the trial cannot take place. This question was answered in the case of *Illinois* v. *Allen*, 397 US 337 (1970), in which the United States Supreme Court held that a defendant had waived his right to be present at his trial by his own disruptive action.

The facts of the *Allen* case state that Allen was convicted of armed robbery by an Illinois jury and was sentenced to serve ten to thirty years in the Illinois State Penitentiary. During the trial Allen insisted upon acting as his own attorney, and when the judge appointed an attorney for him, Allen began to argue with the judge in an abusive and disrespectful manner. The judge ordered Allen to remain silent and to let his attorney speak for him. In spite of this admonition the defendant continued to talk and argue with the judge proclaiming that the appointed attorney was not going to act for him. Allen also informed the judge that "when I go out for lunchtime, you're going to be a corpse here." At the same time Allen tore up his attorney's file and threw the pieces on the floor. The judge informed Allen that he would be removed from the courtroom if another disruption occurred. This warning had no effect upon Allen, and the judge had him removed from the courtroom. The jury was selected in his absence. Later in the day Allen was permitted to return to the courtroom, but became disruptive again, forcing the judge to remove him a second time. Allen remained out of the courtroom during most of the prosecution's presentation of the case, but on promising that he would conduct himself properly, was permitted to return and remain in the courtroom during the presentation by the defendant's attorney.

The *Allen* conviction was upheld by the Illinois appellate courts, but was reversed by the United States District Court of Appeals. This Court held that Allen's removal from the courtroom was a denial of his guarantee of confrontation as provided by the Sixth Amendment to the United States Constitution. The Court stated that Allen could have been bound and gagged to prevent him from being disruptive, and that the judge erred in removing Allen from the courtroom.

The case was then taken to the United States Supreme Court to determine if Allen was denied due process of law because his Sixth Amendment guarantee of confrontation had been violated. The United States Supreme Court upheld the conviction and stated that the Sixth Amendment guarantee of confrontation could be "lost by consent or at times even by misconduct." The Court further stated:

> Although mindful that courts must indulge every reasonable presumption against the loss of constitutional rights, . . . we explicitly hold today that a defendant can lose his right to be present at trial if, after he had been warned by the judge that he will be removed if he continues his disruptive behavior, he nevertheless insists on conducting himself in a manner so disorderly, disruptive, and disrespectful of the court that his trial cannot be carried on with him in the courtroom. Once lost, the right to be present can, of course, be reclaimed as soon as the defendant is willing to conduct himself consistently with the decorum and respect inherent in the concept of courts and judicial proceedings.
>
> It is essential to the proper administration of criminal justice that dignity, order, and decorum be the hallmarks of all court proceedings in our country. The flagrant disregard in the courtroom of elementary standards of proper conduct should not and cannot be tolerated. We believe trial judges confronted with disruptive, contumacious, stubbornly defiant defendants must be given sufficient discretion to meet the circumstances of each case. No one formula for maintaining the appropriate courtroom atmosphere will be best in all situations. We think there are at least three constitutionally permissible ways for a trial judge to handle an obstreperous defendant like Allen: (1) bind and gag him, thereby keeping him present; (2) cite him for contempt; (3) take him out of the courtroom until he promises to conduct himself properly.

Trying a defendant for a crime while he sits bound and gagged before the judge and jury would to an extent comply with that part of the Sixth Amendment's purposes that accords the defendant an opportunity to confront the witnesses at the trial. But even to contemplate such a technique, much less see it, arouses a feeling that no person should be tried while shackled and gagged except as a last resort. Not only is it possible that the sight of shackles and gags might have a significant effect on the jury's feelings about the defendant, but the use of this technique is itself something of an affront to the very dignity and decorum of judicial proceedings that the judge is seeking to uphold. . . . However, in some situations which we need not attempt to foresee, binding and gagging might possibly be the fairest and most reasonable way to handle a defendant who acts as Allen did here.

In citing the unruly defendant for contempt of court, the Court in the *Allen* case stated:

It is true that citing or threatening to cite a contumacious defendant for criminal contempt might in itself be sufficient to make a defendant stop interrupting a trial. If so, the problem would be solved easily, and the defendant could remain in the courtroom. Of course, if the defendant is determined to prevent any trial, then a court in attempting to try the defendant for contempt is still confronted with the identical dilemma that the Illinois court faced in this case. Any criminal contempt has obvious limitations as a sanction when the defendant is charged with a crime so serious that a very severe sentence such as death or life imprisonment is likely to be imposed. In such a case the defendant might not be affected by a mere contempt sentence when he ultimately faces a far more serious sanction. Nevertheless, the contempt remedy should be borne in mind by a judge in the circumstances of this case.

Another aspect of the contempt remedy is the judge's power, when exercised consistently with state and federal law, to imprison an unruly defendant such as Allen for civil contempt and discontinue the trial until such time as the defendant promises to behave himself. This procedure is consistent with the defendant's right to be present at trial, and yet it avoids the serious shortcomings of the use of shackles and gags. It must be recognized, however, that a defendant might conceivably, as a matter of calculated strategy, elect to spend a prolonged period in confinement for contempt in the hope that adverse witnesses might be unavailable after a lapse of time. A court must guard against allowing a defendant to profit from his own wrong in this way.

The trial court in this case decided under the circumstances to remove the defendant from the courtroom and to continue his trial in his absence until and unless he promised to conduct himself in a manner befitting an American courtroom. As we said earlier, we find nothing unconstitutional about this procedure. Allen's behavior was clearly of such an extreme and aggravated nature as to justify either his removal from the courtroom or his total physical restraint. Prior to his removal he was repeatedly warned by the trial judge that he would be removed from the courtroom if he persisted in his unruly conduct, and, as Judge Hastings observed in his dissenting opinion, the record demonstrates that Allen would not have been at all dissuaded by the trial judge's use of his criminal contempt powers. Allen was constantly informed that he could return to the trial when he would agree to conduct himself in an orderly manner. Under these circumstances we hold that Allen lost his right guaranteed by the Sixth and Fourteenth Amendments to be present throughout his trial.

It is not pleasant to hold that the respondent Allen was properly banished from the court for a part of his own trial. But our courts, palladiums of liberty as they are, cannot be treated disrespectfully with impunity. Nor can the accused be permitted by his disruptive conduct indefinitely to avoid being tried on the charges brought against him. It would degrade our country and our judicial system to permit our courts to be bullied, insulted, and humiliated and their orderly progress thwarted and obstructed by defendants brought before them charged with crimes.

Voluntary Absence from Trial

The *Allen* decision definitely established that a trial could take place in the absence of a defendant when he was so disruptive that his removal from the courtroom became necessary. This decision also provided that if a defendant voluntarily absented himself, he waived his right to be present. Even before the *Allen* decision, the courts were beginning to accept that if a defendant was voluntarily absent from his trial, the trial could proceed in his absence. This viewpoint was expressed in the case of *Cureton* v. *United States,* 130 US App DC 22 (1968). The Court concluded that "if a defendant at liberty remains away during his trial the court may proceed provided it is clearly established that his absence is voluntary. He must be aware of the processes taking place, of his right and of his obligation to be present, and he must have no sound reason for remaining away." This is sometimes referred to as the *Cureton* test. In other words, the defendant must have "knowingly and voluntarily absented himself."

As a result of the *Allen* decision and the viewpoint expressed in the *Cureton* case, many states have passed provisions similar to that of the *Federal Rules of Criminal Procedure,* which provides that "in prosecutions for offenses, not punishable by death, the defendant's voluntary absence after the trial has been commenced in his presence shall not prevent continuing the trial to and including the return of the verdict." The federal rule, as well as the provisions of many states, holds that the trial may continue in the absence of the defendant if the trial was commenced in his presence. Under these circumstances, the trial cannot commence unless the defendant is present. After the trial date is set, a defendant out on bail can keep the trial from taking place by merely not showing up for the trial. Of course, the judge could issue a bench warrant for the defendant's arrest, but it could take time to locate the defendant, thus delaying the trial. To overcome this problem, several states have provisions stating that a trial may commence when the defendant, knowing that the case is set for trial, voluntarily fails to appear on that date.

In those states requiring a trial to begin in the defendant's presence, for it to continue if the accused is voluntarily absent, the court must establish that the trial actually began while the defendant was present. Remember that a jury trial begins once the jury is sworn, and a court trial begins when the first witness is sworn. In one case, the defendant was present during the selection of eleven jurors before court was adjourned for the day. The following day the defendant failed to appear for the trial. The judge concluded that the defendant had voluntarily absented himself. Over the objections of the defense attorney, the judge permitted a twelfth juror to be selected, and the trial continued to the verdict stage in the absence of the defendant. The defendant was convicted and he appealed his conviction on the grounds that he had been denied due process. The conviction was reversed since the law of the particular state provided that a trial could continue only if commenced in the presence of the defendant. Since the jury had not been selected and sworn in the presence of the defendant, the trial had not begun.

Even in those states that hold that a trial may continue only if it began in the presence of the defendant, this rule usually refers to felony charges. In a misdemeanor case, most states provide that if a defendant voluntarily fails to appear at the time the case is set for trial or is voluntarily absent during the course of the trial, the judge may proceed when the defendant has full knowledge that the trial was to be held. In most jurisdictions, whether the charge is a felony or misdemeanor, it is not necessary to advise the defendant that this action will take place in the event of voluntary absence.

The problem created by these rules is establishing that the defendant knowingly and voluntarily absented himself from the trial. Establishing this could take time, and the judge would have to delay the progress of the trial until this could be determined. The delay might be only a few hours, but it could take several days. If the court cannot determine satisfactorily whether the defendant was absent knowingly and voluntarily, the judge must declare a mistrial or delay the present trial until the defendant can be located and arrested on a bench warrant. If it cannot be determined that the defendant was absent without cause, and a conviction results, a new trial must be granted unless a satisfactory reason for absence is given. Thus, the courts are cautious in continuing a trial in the absence of a defendant.

The Right to Counsel

Under the common law of England, a person on trial for a felony was not entitled to the assistance of counsel. If the charge was a misdemeanor, however, the defendant had the right of counsel. Various reasons have been given for this paradoxical situation. In felony cases it was thought that the judge would be sympathetic to the defendant because if the defendant was convicted, he would be subjected to severe punishment, and might have his property confiscated by the king. In misdemeanor cases, the judge would have less interest in protecting the accused. Another theory is that because the property of a convicted felon could be confiscated, the king knew that the chances for the defendant's conviction would be greater if assistance of counsel was not allowed. Thus the king did not permit the assistance of counsel in a felony trial.

This denial of the assistance of counsel in felony cases was rejected by the colonists, and in most of the colonies the right of counsel became a part of their due process of law. The right to counsel had become such an accepted practice that when the Bill of Rights was formulated the following provision was included in the Sixth Amendment of the United States Constitution: "In all criminal prosecutions, the accused shall . . . have the assistance of counsel for his defense." This guarantee pertained only to federal prosecutions, but the states included similar provisions in their constitutions or statutes upon admittance to the Union. These provisions are usually worded similar to: "In criminal prosecutions the accused shall have the right to appear and defend, and in person and with counsel."

For many generations this right to the assistance of counsel was interpreted as meaning if an accused appeared in court with an attorney, the accused could not be denied the assistance of the attorney. If, however, the defendant were unable to afford an attorney to assist him in his defense, it was his misfortune. Little thought was given to providing counsel for the accused. Neither was assistance of counsel considered essential for the accused prior to the time of the trial. But as time passed, new interpretations were placed upon the Sixth Amendment guarantee of counsel, particularly by the United States Supreme Court.

Providing the Accused with Counsel

One of the earliest decisions in which the United States Supreme Court held that in certain instances an accused must be provided with an attorney, if he cannot afford one, was the case of *Powell* v. *Alabama*, 287 US 45 (1932). The facts of this case reflect that ignorant and friendless black youths, strangers in the community without means to obtain counsel, were hurried to trial in an Alabama State Court for capital offense without appointment of counsel. The youths were convicted, and their case was taken to the United States Supreme Court on the grounds that the defendants had been denied due process of law. The United States Supreme Court agreed that the defendants had been denied due process of law in that they had not been provided with counsel to assist them in their defense. The Court stated:

> . . . All that is necessary now to decide, as we do decide, is that in a capital case, where the defendant is unable to employ counsel, and is incapable adequately of making his own defense because of ignorance, feeblemindedness, illiteracy, or the like, it is the duty of the court, whether requested or not, to assign counsel for him as a necessary requisite of due process of law. . . .

In the Powell case the charge was a capital offense, and the Court held that in capital offenses the judge must appoint an attorney when the accused is unable to obtain counsel. This decision was in effect until the case of *Gideon* v. *Wainwright*, 372 US 335 (1963), when the United States Supreme Court held that counsel must be provided for any defendant brought to trial irrespective of the charge. The facts of the *Gideon* case reveal that Gideon (the petitioner) was charged in a Florida state court with breaking and entering into a poolroom with intent to commit a misdemeanor. This offense is a felony under Florida law. Appearing in court without funds and without a lawyer, the petitioner asked the court to appoint counsel, but the judge informed the petitioner that under the laws of the state of Florida the only time that the court could appoint counsel to represent a defendant is when that person is charged with a capital offense. Gideon attempted to conduct his own defense by making an opening statement, cross–examining prosecution witnesses, and presenting witnesses in his own behalf. Gideon was convicted and sentenced to five years in the state prison. The case was taken to the United States Supreme Court on the grounds that he had been denied due process of law in that his Sixth Amendment guarantee to the assistance of counsel had been denied. The United States Supreme Court agreed with this contention and reversed the conviction. The Court in its decision stated:

> . . . reason and reflection require us to recognize that in our adversary system of criminal justice, any person haled into court, who is too poor to hire a lawyer, cannot be assured a fair trial unless counsel is provided for him. This seems to us to be an obvious truth. Governments, both state and federal, quite properly spend vast sums of money to establish machinery to try defendants ac-

cused of crime. Lawyers to prosecute are everywhere deemed essential to protect the public's interest in an orderly society. Similarly, there are few defendants charged with crime, few indeed, who fail to hire the best lawyers they can get to prepare and present their defenses. That government hires lawyers to prosecute and defendants who have the money hire lawyers to defend are the strongest indications of the widespread belief that lawyers in criminal courts are necessities, not luxuries. The right of one charged with crime to counsel may not be deemed fundamental and essential to fair trials in some countries, but it is in ours. From the very beginning, our state and national constitutions and laws have laid great emphasis on procedural and substantive safeguards designed to assure fair trials before impartial tribunals in which every defendant stands equal before the law. This noble ideal cannot be realized if the poor man charged with crime has to face his accusers without a lawyer to assist him. A defendant's need for a lawyer is nowhere better stated than in the moving words of Mr. Justice Sutherland in Powell v. Alabama: "The right to be heard would be, in many cases, of little avail if it did not comprehend the right to be heard by counsel. Even the intelligent and educated layman has small and sometimes no skill in the science of law. If charged with crime, he is incapable, generally, of determining for himself whether the indictment is good or bad. He is unfamiliar with the rules of evidence. Left without the aid of counsel he may be put on trial without a proper charge, and convicted upon incompetent evidence, or evidence irrelevant to the issue or otherwise inadmissible. He lacks both the skill and knowledge adequately to prepare his defense, even though he has a perfect one. He requires the guiding hand of counsel at every step in the proceedings against him. Without it, though he be not guilty, he faces the danger of conviction because he does not know how to establish his innocence."

Right to Counsel in Petty Cases

Although the Court in the *Gideon* case held that any person haled into court who is too poor to hire a lawyer cannot be assured a fair trial unless counsel is provided for him, the charge in the *Gideon* case was a felony. Thus there remained some question as to whether counsel must be appointed for one brought to trial on a petty charge. This doubt was resolved in the case of *Argersinger* v. *Hamlin*, 407 US 25 (1972), in which the United States Supreme Court held that no person may be imprisoned for any offense, petty or otherwise, unless he is represented by counsel at his trial. The facts of the case show that Argersinger was charged in Florida with carrying a concealed weapon, an offense punishable by imprisonment up to six months. Argersinger was tried before a judge and was not represented by counsel, as he could not afford such, and the State contended that since the charge was a petty one, counsel did not have to be appointed for the defendant. Argersinger was convicted and sentenced to jail for ninety days. The conviction was upheld by the Florida Supreme Court, and the case was taken to the United States Supreme Court on the grounds that the defendant had been denied the right to counsel. The Court stated:

> . . . The Sixth Amendment, which in enumerated situations has been made applicable to the States by reason of the Fourteenth Amendment . . . provides specified standards for all criminal prosecutions.
>
> One is the requirement of a public trial. . . . the right to a public trial was applicable to a state proceeding even though only a 60–day sentence was involved.
>
> Another guarantee is the right to be informed of the nature and cause of the accusation. Still another, the right of confrontation. And another, compulsory process for obtaining witnesses in one's favor. We have never limited these rights to felonies nor to lesser but serious offenses. . . .
>
> While there is historical support for limiting the deep commitment to trial by jury to serious criminal cases, there is no such support for a similar limitation on the right to assistance of counsel. . . .
>
> The Assistance of counsel is often a requisite to the very existence of a fair trial. . . .
>
> The requirement of counsel may well be necessary for a fair trial even in a petty offense prosecution. We are by no means convinced that legal and constitutional questions involved in a case that actually leads to imprisonment even for a brief period are any less complex than when a person can be sent off for six months or more.
>
> The trial of vagrancy cases is illustrative. While only brief sentences of imprisonment may be imposed, the cases often bristle with thorny constitutional questions.
>
> Beyond the problem of trials and appeals is that of the guilty plea, a problem which looms large in misdemeanor as well as in felony cases. Counsel is needed so that the accused may know precisely what he is doing, so that he is fully aware of the prospect of going to jail or prison, and so that he is treated fairly by the prosecution.
>
> We hold, therefore, that absent a knowing and intelligent waiver, no person may be imprisoned for any offense, whether classified as petty, misdemeanor, or felony, unless he was represented by counsel at his trial.

Waiver of Counsel

Although the Sixth Amendment guarantees the right to counsel, may this constitutional guarantee, like most others, be waived, or is it mandatory that the defendant be represented by counsel? This question was answered in *Adams* v. *United States,* 317 US 269 (1942), in which the United States Supreme Court held that a capable defendant could waive the right to the assistance of counsel. But it must be determined first that the accused is capable of defense without counsel's assistance.

The right of a defendant to represent himself was carried one step further by the United States Supreme Court in *Faretta* v. *California,* 422 US 806 (1975), where the Court held that when a defendant "knowingly and intelligently" waives the right to the assistance of counsel, the defendant has the constitutional right to self–representation. The facts reveal that Faretta was charged with grand theft. At the arraignment the judge appointed a public defender to represent Faretta, but before the trial Faretta requested that he be permitted to represent himself. In an effort to determine if Faretta was capable of representing himself, the judge questioned Faretta and learned that Faretta had represented himself in a prior criminal prosecution, that he had a high school education, and that he did not want to be represented by the public defender. After further questioning by the judge at a later time, the judge concluded that Faretta had not intelligently waived his right to the assistance of counsel. The judge also ruled that Faretta did not have a constitutional right to self-representation. Faretta was represented by a public defender, and was convicted and sentenced to prison. He appealed his case to the United States Supreme Court, which agreed to hear the case to settle the question of whether an accused has a Sixth Amendment right to decline counsel. The Court ruled that there is such a constitutional right. The Court pointed out that in early common law, those accused of serious crimes had to represent themselves, and that only later was an accused given the choice of receiving the assistance of counsel. This was the practice at the time the colonists came to America, and at the time the Sixth Amendment was written. The Court stated that it recognized the advantages of an accused having the assistance of counsel, but was unable to find an instance where a colonial court required an accused to accept an unwanted attorney as his representative. The Court felt that when the framers of the Sixth Amendment included the right of an accused to have the assistance of counsel, they were not denying the accused the right of self-representation. The Court stated:

> . . . in most criminal prosecutions defendants could better defend with counsel's guidance than by their own unskilled efforts. But where the defendant will not voluntarily accept representation by counsel, the potential advantage of a lawyer's training and experience can be realized, if at all, only imperfectly. To force a lawyer on a defendant can only lead him to believe that the law contrives against him. Moreover, it is not inconceivable that in some rare instances, the defendant might in fact present his case more effectively by conducting his own defense. Personal liberties are not rooted in the law of averages. The right to defend is personal. The

defendant, and not his lawyer or the State, will bear the personal consequences of a conviction. It is the defendant, therefore, who must be free personally to decide whether in his particular case counsel is to his advantage. And although he may conduct his own defense ultimately to his own detriment, his choice must be honored out of "that respect for the individual which is the lifeblood of the law." When an accused manages his own defense, he relinquishes, as a purely factual matter, many of the traditional benefits associated with the right to counsel. For this reason, in order to represent himself, the accused must "knowingly and intelligently" forego those relinquished benefits. Although a defendant need not himself have the skill and experience of a lawyer in order competently and intelligently to choose self-representation, he should be made aware of the dangers and disadvantages of self-representation, so that the record will establish that "he knows what he is doing and his choice is made with eyes open." Here, weeks before trial, Faretta clearly and unequivocally declared to the trial judge that he wanted to represent himself and did not want counsel. The record affirmatively shows that Faretta was literate, competent, and understanding, and that he was voluntarily exercising his informed free will.

Knowing and Intelligent Waiver. The Court in the *Faretta* case stated that "in order to represent himself the accused must knowingly and intelligently" waive the right to the assistance of counsel. This statement placed a serious burden on trial judges in determining whether a defendant is capable of knowingly and intelligently waiving the right to the assistance of counsel. The problem created by this decision is that if a trial judge concludes that the defendant is capable of self-representation and the defendant is convicted, the defendant may appeal, and the appellate court may hold that the defendant was not capable of making an intelligent waiver of the right to counsel. On the other hand, as in Faretta's case, if the judge concludes that the defendant was incapable of intelligently waiving the right to the assistance of counsel and is convicted, the appellate court may decide that the defendant had been denied the right of self–representation. The dissenting Justices in the *Faretta* case pointed out that the majority of Justices had created a problem that undoubtedly would cause confusion for trial courts since no guidelines were set forth for the trial courts to follow in their efforts to determine when an accused was capable of self-representation.

Since the United States Supreme Court has held that an accused has the constitutional right of self-representation when the right to the assistance of counsel is knowingly and intelligently waived, a trial court must make a careful evaluation of the accused's ability to make the waiver. When an accused requests permission for self-representation, it is usually necessary for the trial judge to hold a hearing to determine the capability of the accused to make the waiver. This hearing has been referred to as a "Faretta hearing." The time required to conduct this hearing varies with the circumstances of each case. It may become obvious to the judge after a short questioning of the accused that he has a limited educational background and/or knowledge of court procedure. The judge will conclude quickly that such an accused is not capable of making a knowing and intelligent waiver, and will require representation by counsel. Other defendants who have some educational background and some knowledge of court procedures may insist on self-representation, and the hearing can be lengthy. The appellate courts have held that a "perfunctory hearing is improper. The record must show that the defendant made a knowing and intelligent election" to waive assistance of counsel. Further, "the actual conducting of a Faretta hearing may be difficult, time-consuming and trying of the patience of the trial judge, particularly if the defendant is eccentric, or prone to causing exasperation in others, or engages in the playing of games, or harassing the establishment. However the judge should not be misled by a confusion of the issue to be determined, that is, whether the defendant is capable of making the waiver."

Judges are inclined to conclude that a defendant is not capable of intelligently waiving the right to the assistance of counsel because of the many problems encountered by an untrained defendant attempting self-representation. The untrained defendant causes the trial to last longer, tries to introduce inadmissible evidence, makes improper objections to questions, and often argues with the judge over rulings. Deciding if assistance should be provided by the trial judge for the self-represented defendant becomes a further issue. Many judges believe that with all the other duties to be performed during the trial, it is dangerous to try to assist the defendant because of the possibility of mistaken or misunderstood assistance. Yet, some appellate courts have stated that one of the major functions of the trial judge is to make certain that the "innocence or guilt of those accused of a crime is based upon the merits of the trial and not upon their inability to understand legal procedure." Therefore, the trial judge should render that assistance necessary for a fair trial.

The dissenting justices in the *Faretta* case recognized that these problems would be encountered by trial judges, and believed that the majority justices had read into the Sixth Amendment something not intended by its framers.

Standby Counsel.   The majority justices in the *Faretta* case did indicate that a trial judge, even over the objections of the defendant, could appoint a "standby counsel" to aid the defendant if and when the defendant requests help, and to be available to represent the defendant in the event that termination of the defendant's self-representation should become necessary. The appointment of a standby attorney is not a practical solution, however, since trial judges may appoint standby attorneys in most instances, tying up the services of an attorney and increasing court costs.

In *McKaskle* v. *Wiggins,* 79 L.Ed 2d 122 (1984), the United States Supreme Court reaffirmed the *Faretta* ruling that a trial judge may appoint a standby attorney over the objections of the defendant. The Court stated:

> A defendant's Sixth Amendment rights are not violated when a trial judge appoints standby counsel—even over the defendant's objection—to relieve the judge of the need to explain and enforce basic rules of courtroom protocol or to assist the defendant in overcoming routine obstacles that stand in the way of the defendant's achievement of his own clearly indicated goals.

The Court further stated:

> A defendant does not have a constitutional right to receive personal instruction from the trial judge on courtroom procedure. Nor does the Constitution require judges to take over chores for a pro se defendant [one representing himself] that would normally be attended to by trained counsel as a matter of course. The right of self-representation is not a license to abuse the dignity of the courtroom. Neither is it a license not to comply with relevant rules of procedure and substantive law.

Although the *McKaskle* decision reaffirmed a trial judge's right to appoint standby counsel over the defendant's objections, the decision did not solve all the problems connected with the appointment of a standby attorney. The trial judge is still faced with deciding how far a standby attorney may proceed over the defendant's objections without that assistance being a violation of the defendant's right to self-representation. The Court in the *McKaskle* case gave few guidelines in this respect, but stated that a defendant's rights to self-representation:

> are not infringed upon when standby counsel assists the defendant in overcoming routine procedural or evidentiary obstacles to the completion of some specific task, such as the introducing evidence or objecting to testimony, that the defendant has clearly shown he wishes to complete. Nor are they infringed when counsel merely helps to ensure the defendant's compliance with basic rules of courtroom protocol and procedure. In neither case is there any significant interference with the defendant's actual control over the presentation of his defense.

Why an Accused Chooses Self-Representation.   With the advantages to an accused in having the assistance of counsel, and the disadvantages of self-representation, one might ask why a defendant would insist upon self-representation rather than having the assistance of counsel. The saying is that an attorney who chooses self-representation has a fool for a client. Yet many defendants do not trust attorneys or question their capabilities. One defendant, for example, conceded that an attorney had "more on the ball" than he did, but stated that there are certain questions "the attorney might not ask certain witnesses that are very potent, important, in regard to the case itself." Some defendants feel that attorneys do not have their client's best interests at stake, or that attorneys are in collusion with the prosecuting attorney, and the defendants will be railroaded into prison. Other defendants receive a certain gratification from representing themselves. Some are aware that by representing themselves they are entitled to confer with codefendants and witnesses in private, enabling them to conspire against the prosecution.

A defendant who represents himself is referred to as appearing *in propria persona* (in one's own proper person), or in person. This is sometimes referred to by the courts as *pro per*.

When the Right to Counsel Begins

For many years the Sixth Amendment guarantee to the assistance of counsel was interpreted as meaning assistance at the time of trial. The *Gideon* decision did not materially change that interpretation, as that decision referred to the fact that "any person haled into court, who is too poor to hire a lawyer, cannot be assured a fair trial unless counsel is provided for him." It was generally accepted that counsel need not be provided for the indigent defendant until the time of trial. However, later United States Supreme Court decisions established a new interpretation as to when the right to counsel began and when counsel had to be provided for the indigent defendant.

In the case of *Escobedo* v. *Illinois*, 378 US 478 (1964), the United States Supreme Court held that the right to the assistance of counsel begins long before the time of the trial, and may even occur before an arrest is made. The Court stated that when the investigation of a crime "shifts from the investigatory to accusatory," the accused is entitled to the assistance of counsel and such assistance could be very hollow if denied until the time of trial.

The facts of the *Escobedo* case reflect that Escobedo was arrested on a charge of murder. He was taken to the Chicago Police Station for interrogation. In route Escobedo requested the right to consult with his attorney. Shortly after Escobedo arrived at the police station, his attorney arrived and requested permission to talk to Escobedo. Both were advised by the police that they could confer after the interrogation was completed. During the interrogation, Escobedo made certain admissions which implicated him in the murder charge. These admissions were used against him during the trial. Escobedo was convicted of murder and his conviction was upheld by the Illinois Supreme Court. The case was taken to the United States Supreme Court upon the grounds that Escobedo was denied the assistance of counsel in violation of the Sixth Amendment guarantee. The attorneys for the State of Illinois argued that the right to counsel was not operative until the indictment stage of proceedings. To this argument the Court stated:

> . . . In *Gideon* v. *Wainwright* we held that every person accused of a crime, whether state or federal, is entitled to a lawyer at trial. The rule sought by the State here, however, would make the trial no more than an appeal from the interrogation; and the "right to use counsel at the formal trial (would be) a very hollow thing (if), for all practical purposes, the conviction is already assured by pretrial examination." In *re Groban*, 352 US 330 (1957) (Black, J., dissenting): "One can imagine a cynical prosecutor saying: 'Let them have the most illustrious counsel, now. They can't escape the noose. There is nothing that counsel can do for them at trial.'"

> It is argued that if the right to counsel is afforded prior to indictment, the number of confessions obtained by the police will diminish significantly, because most confessions are obtained during the period between arrest and indictment, and "any lawyer worth his salt will tell the suspect in no uncertain terms to make no statement to police under any circumstances." This argument of course, cuts two ways. The fact that many confessions are obtained during this period points up its critical nature as a "stage when legal aid and advice" are surely needed. The right to counsel would indeed be hollow if it began at a period when few confessions were obtained. There is necessarily a direct relationship between the importance of a stage to the police in their quest for a confession and the criticalness of that stage to the accused in his need for legal advice. Our Constitution, unlike some others, strikes the balance in favor of the right of the accused to be advised by his lawyer of his privilege against self-incrimination.

> We hold, therefore, that where, as here, the investigation is no longer a general inquiry into an unsolved crime but has begun to focus on a particular suspect, the suspect has been taken into police custody, the police carry out a process of interrogations that lends itself to eliciting incriminating statements, the suspect has requested and been denied an opportunity to consult with his lawyer, and the police have not effectively warned him of his absolute constitutional right to remain silent, the accused has been denied "the assistance of Counsel" in violation of the Sixth Amendment to the Constitution as "made obligatory upon the States by the Fourteenth Amendment," *Gideon* v. *Wainwright*, and that no statement elicited by the police during the interrogation may be used against him at a criminal trial. . . .

> Nothing we have said today affects the powers of the police to investigate "an unsolved crime" by gathering information

from witnesses and by other "proper investigative efforts." We hold only that when the process shifts from investigatory to accusatory—when its focus is on the accused and its purpose is to elicit a confession—our adversary system begins to operate, and, under the circumstances here, the accused must be permitted to consult with his lawyer.

The *Escobedo* decision provided that once suspicion is focused upon a particular suspect he is entitled to consult with an attorney, but nothing was said about having to furnish the accused with an attorney. In the case of *Miranda* v. *Arizona,* 384 US 438 (1966), the United States Supreme Court held that before an accused could be interrogated the accused must be advised of the right to the assistance of counsel. The accused must be advised, among other things, of the right to remain silent, of the right to the assistance of counsel during the interrogation, and that if the accused cannot afford an attorney, one will be provided free.

Although both the *Escobedo* and *Miranda* decisions are more related to the field of evidence and the admissibility of confessions than to procedure, these decisions emphasized the importance of the assistance of counsel and set forth guidelines as to when that right to assistance begins.

Effective Counsel.

A defendant is entitled not only to the assistance of counsel, but also to effective counsel. An effective counsel is one who has knowledge of the defendant's rights and who is capable of presenting the defenses to which the accused is entitled. Establishing the effectiveness of counsel is not easy. A counsel may be knowledgeable in one field but unfamiliar with crucial problems in another. If counsel does not effectively represent a defendant, whether through lack of knowledge or interest, or because of mere carelessness, a conviction could be overruled upon appeal because of the denial of assistance of counsel.

Farce or Sham Test.   In determining if a conviction should be reversed because of ineffective counsel, many state appellate courts have stated that it must appear that counsel's lack of diligence or competence reduced the trial to a "farce or sham." Today's courts have rejected the traditional "farce or sham" test and have adopted a less stringent criterion for determining competency of counsel. Counsel is considered ineffective if in representing the defendant, the counsel fails to meet the standard of competence expected of criminal case attorneys. Counsel is held as ineffective when not exercising the customary skills and diligence that a reasonably competent attorney would have performed under similar circumstances. Effective counsel has the duty to investigate carefully all defenses of fact and law of a case. If counsel's failure to do so results in the failure to present crucial defense during the trial, the defendant has been denied proper assistance of counsel. Further, mere allegations by the defendant indicating a lack of preparation by or general incompetence of counsel is not enough to show ineffectiveness. The defendant must show acts or omissions resulting in a failure to present a crucial defense. Counsel does not have to interview or call every witness with knowledge of the case since many witnesses may be of little assistance to the defense.

Crucial Error by Counsel.   The effectiveness of counsel issue is usually raised when the court appoints an attorney to represent the defendant who cannot afford to choose an attorney. There are times when a defendant will complain about the effectiveness of chosen counsel. If an attorney selected by the accused is so ineffective that the defendant was denied a fair trial, the conviction will be reversed on appeal. For a time courts were inclined to require a lesser degree of competence from an attorney of the defendant's own choosing. Today it is accepted that whether an attorney is appointed for the defendant or the attorney is one of the defendant's own choosing, competence will be measured by the same degree. As stated by the United States Supreme Court in *Strickland* v. *Washington,* 80 L. Ed 2d 674 (1984), "An accused is entitled to be assisted by an attorney, whether retained or appointed, who plays the role necessary to ensure that the trial is fair." A defendant may not expect an error-free attorney, but if an error is crucial to the defense, effective counsel has been denied. Determining if an error was crucial has been a major problem for appellate courts. Defendants who have been convicted have successfully appealed their convictions on the allegation that effective counsel had been denied. Since no guidelines were set forth to measure effectiveness of counsel, many convictions were reversed. In *Strickland,* the Court endeavored to correct this situation by providing some criteria to measure effectiveness. The Court stated that "when a convicted defendant complains of the ineffectiveness of counsel's assistance, the defendant must show that counsel's representation fell below an objective standard of reasonableness. More specific guidelines are not appropriate."

Burden of Proof.   *Strickland* points out that the burden of proving ineffective assistance of counsel is on the defendant. When a convicted defendant claims that counsel's assistance was so defective as to require a reversal of a conviction or a death sentence, the defendant must prove two things. First, the defendant must show that counsel's performance was deficient. This requires the defendant to show that errors made were so serious that counsel did not function as a reasonably competent attorney. Second, the defendant must show that the deficient performance prejudiced the defense. Council's errors must be so serious as to deprive the defendant of a fair trial.

A defendant may allege ineffectiveness of counsel when there may have been acts or omissions such as the failure of counsel to enter a proper plea when applicable (such as a plea of not guilty by reason of insanity); the failure to raise the defense of diminished capacity; the failure to cross-examine prosecution witnesses; or the failure to object to the introduction of evidence improperly obtained. In one case, an appellate court overruled a conviction when the defense attorney's request for a continuance was denied, and the attorney thereafter refused to assist in the selection of the jury. The appelate court held that the defense counsel had reduced the trial to a sham.

The Public Defender and Appointed Counsel

As has been stated, an accused is entitled to the assistance of counsel when that assistance is requested. If the accused is not in a position to employ private counsel, the court must appoint effective counsel. It is not always easy for a judge to obtain effective counsel to represent one accused of a crime. If effective counsel cannot be readily obtained, all prosecutive action must be suspended. To overcome this problem, many counties have established the public defender, whose function is representing those defendants who cannot afford an attorney of their own. These persons are referred to as *indigent persons* or indigent defendants. The public defender, like the prosecuting attorney, is paid out of public funds. Many do not understand the use of public funds to employ a prosecuting attorney to prosecute offenders and, at the same time, to pay a public defender to defend the accused. But until the indigent defendant is furnished with the assistance of counsel, no prosecutive action can be taken. This delay can be expensive in time and money. If there is no public defender in a particular jurisdiction, the court must draw local attorneys from private practice. This creates a problem since most of these attorneys practice civil law and have little knowledge of the intricacies of a criminal trial; furthermore, in case of a conviction, the question of whether there was assistance of effective counsel could arise.

Before an accused may have the assistance of the public defender or an appointed private attorney, it must be established that the defendant is an indigent person, and this is sometimes a difficult problem. Approximately 85 percent of all those arrested on felony charges are without question unable to afford an attorney. Determining which of the others can afford an attorney is difficult. Some courts have held that if the defendant can post bail, he is not indigent. Others have adopted the test that counsel is to be provided for any defendant who is unable to obtain counsel without serious financial hardship to himself or to his family. The mere fact that friends or relatives have posted bail is not sufficient ground for denying the defendant free counsel. Another test is whether or not a private attorney would be interested in representing the defendant in his present economic circumstances. Undoubtedly, there have been defendants who have taken advantage of these tests to obtain free counsel, but with the large number of defendants who claim indigency a thorough inquiry into each case is impossible. Judges who doubt the indigency status of a defendant have required the defendant to file a financial statement under oath. If it is determined later that the defendant was not indigent, prosecution for perjury as well as civil charges may be filed for the cost of the free counsel.

Review Questions

1. What is the significance of the United States constitutional guarantee that an accused be confronted with the witnesses against him or her?
2. May a trial ever be conducted in the absence of the defendant? If so, under what circumstances?
3. What procedure, suggested by the United States Supreme Court, might be taken against an unruly defendant during trial proceedings, and in what decision was the procedure suggested?
4. In what amendment to the United States Constitution is the right to the assistance of counsel embodied?
5. What was the significance of the *Gideon* v. *Wainwright* decision in reference to the assistance of counsel?
6. In the *Argersinger* v. *Hamlin* decision, what arguments were presented by the Court in granting the accused the assistance of counsel in the trial of a petty charge?
7. Under what circumstances, if any, may an accused waive the assistance of counsel and represent himself during a trial?
8. When does the accused's right to counsel begin?
9. What is the significance of the term "effective counsel"?
10. What is the function of a public defender?

nine

PRETRIAL MOTIONS, HEARINGS, AND PLEA NEGOTIATIONS

Prior to a trial the prosecution and defense each may request that the trial judge take some action on a particular matter. These requests are usually referred to as *motions*. The motion may be made orally to the judge, but in most instances it will be in written form and filed with the appropriate court. Accompanying the motion will be an affidavit setting forth the reasons why the judge should take the action requested. A copy of the motion will be furnished to the opposing side, and generally the judge will hold a hearing on the motion during which each side may present arguments for and against it. However not all motions are opposed, making a hearing unnecessary. It is not mandatory that the defendant be present at these hearings in every instance, but many judges demand that the defendant be present at all proceedings. More motions are filed by the defense than by the prosecution as there are more matters affecting the rights of a defendant than the prosecution. A few more prevalent motions will be discussed, but they are in no way inclusive of all motions that may be filed either before or during a trial. The sequence of the motions discussed here is not necessarily in the same order that will be taken at trial. One of the earliest motions that may be filed is for pretrial discovery.

Pretrial Right of Discovery

The right of discovery, or inspection, is more closely related to the subject of evidence than to the procedures in the justice system. However, one of the responsibilities of the attorneys for both the prosecution and defense is to exercise the right of discovery. The right of pretrial discovery in criminal matters is of comparatively recent origin. It was unknown at common law and still is not recognized in criminal matters in some states. As stated in chapter 5, the right of discovery is the pretrial right of the adversary to inspect, review, and copy certain materials held by the opposition which are anticipated to be introduced as evidence during the trial.

The Defendant's Right of Discovery

The right of pretrial discovery was created primarily for the benefit of the defendant. The theory was that the right would assist the defendant in case preparation and aid in getting a fair trial. The right would also enable the defense attorney to better cross-examine the witnesses for the prosecution and assist in impeaching witnesses who have questionable credibility. The purpose of a trial is to determine the truth of what happened in a particular case. The parties involved in a trial are not to play games or create surprises. As expressed in *People* v. *Riser,* 47 Cal 2d 566 (1956):

Absent some governmental requirement that information be kept confidential for the purposes of effective law enforcement, the state has no interest in denying the accused to all evidence that can throw light on issues in the case, and in particular it has no interest in convicting on the testimony of witnesses who have not been as rigorously cross-examined and as thoroughly impeached as the evidence permits.

The right of pretrial discovery may come into being either by legislative action or by appellate court decisions, and may be exercised in two ways. The defense may make an oral request to the prosecuting attorney, and/or the law enforcement agency involved, for permission to examine the material held in the case. The alternative method consists of a written request by the defendant's attorney in the form of a motion to produce the evidence held by the prosecution. This motion is presented to the appropriate trial judge, who will issue an order to produce the material for examination by the defense.

What the Defendant May Inspect

Even in those states in which the right of discovery is recognized, the material and information that the defendant may examine varies. Some states, and the federal government, are quite liberal in the matters that may be examined. Rule 16 of the Federal Rules of Criminal Procedure is typical of the broader right of discovery by a defendant. This rule provides:

> . . . Upon request of the defendant the government shall permit the defendant to inspect and copy or photograph books, papers, documents, photographs, tangible objects, buildings or places, or copies or portions thereof, which are in within the possession, custody or control of the government, and which are material to the preparation of his defense or are intended for use by the government as evidence in chief at the trial, or were obtained from or belong to the defendant.

The defendant is entitled to the names and addresses of witnesses the government intends to call in the case preparation, as well as any record of prior felony convictions of such witnesses. The defendant is also permitted to inspect and copy any statements made to officers of the government as well as his prior criminal record.

Denial of the Right of Discovery

A few states have not granted the right of pretrial discovery to a defendant in criminal matters. Those states allege that this right is a one-way street created for the defendant. It is also alleged that the defendant already has the balance of advantages in his favor in a criminal trial because the prosecution must prove the defendant guilty beyond a reasonable doubt, and in most jurisdictions the verdict must be unanimous. The right of discovery would be an additional advantage. Further, permitting the defendant the right of pretrial discovery would enable him to secure perjured testimony and to fabricate evidence to meet the prosecution's case. The chance of witnesses for the prosecution being intimidated is increased if the defendant learns prior to the trial the names and addresses of witnesses and the nature of their testimony.

In states where the right of pretrial discovery is not recognized, the defendant must rely on the preliminary hearing, when applicable, for any assistance received in case preparation. In these instances the defendant will probably demand a preliminary hearing even though he knows that he will be held for trial.

Those arguing against permitting a defendant the right of discovery often quote a statement made by Judge Learned Hand, in the case of *United States* v. *Garsson*, 291 F 646 (1923), in which he stated:

> Under our criminal procedure the accused has every advantage. While the prosecution is held rigidly to the charge, he (the defendant) need not disclose the barest outline of his defense. He is immune from question or comment on his silence; he cannot be convicted when there is the least fair doubt in the minds of any one of the twelve. Why in addition he should in advance have the whole evidence against him to pick over at his leisure, and make his defense, fairly or foully, I have never been able to see. . . . Our dangers do not lie in the too little tenderness to the accused. Our procedure has been always haunted by the ghost of the innocent man convicted. It is an unreal dream. What we need to fear is the archaic formalism and the watery sentiment that obstructs, delays, and defeats the prosecution of crime.

Prosecution's Right of Pretrial Discovery

Even those states recognizing the right of pretrial discovery have granted little pretrial right of discovery to the prosecution. This supports the contention that the right of pretrial discovery is a one-way street. The most convincing argument against allowing pretrial discovery by the prosecution is that the right would compel the defendant to be a witness against himself. Many legal scholars are at a loss to understand how furnishing the names and addresses of witnesses, or the defense to be used—such as an alibi or insanity defense—could be self-incrimination, but there are state courts that have prohibited the prosecution from exercising the right of pretrial discovery upon the self-incrimination claim.

In addition to the self-incrimination allegation, the supreme court of California has held that it is the burden of the prosecution to prove the defendant guilty beyond a reasonable doubt, and that any discovery by the prosecution that would lessen that burden is not permissible. It is almost impossible to imagine any discovery that would not in some respect lessen the burden of the prosecution. This holding by that court has been highly criticized in legal circles as being too restrictive and without merit.

However Rule 16 of the Federal Rules of Criminal Procedure grants to the government (the prosecution) almost the identical rights of pretrial discovery that are granted to the defendant. More states in the future may follow the precedent set by the federal government in granting the right of pretrial discovery to the prosecution. Several states and the federal government have adopted the requirement that a defendant advise the prosecution in advance of the trial that an alibi defense is to be used. In an alibi defense, the claim is that the accused was in another location at the time the crime was allegedly committed. This type of defense is most difficult to refute as it usually comes late during the trial, catching the prosecution by surprise. The requirement that this information be furnished to the prosecution upon demand has received the sanction of the United States Supreme Court in the case of *Williams* v. *Florida*, 399 US 78 (1970). The facts of the *Williams* case reflect that prior to his trial for robbery Williams filed a motion with the trial court to be excused from the requirements of the Florida Rule of Criminal Procedure. This rule requires a defendant, on written demand of the prosecuting attorney, to give notice in advance of the trial if the defendant intends to claim an alibi, and to furnish the prosecuting attorney with information as to the place he claims to have been and with the names and addresses of the alibi witnesses. Williams, referred to as the petitioner, claimed that this rule compelled him to witness against himself in violation of the Fifth and Fourteenth Amendment rights. The motion was denied, Williams was convicted, and sentenced to life imprisonment. He took his case to the United States Supreme Court on the grounds that his Constitutional rights had been violated. The Supreme Court upheld the conviction and stated:

> Florida law provides for liberal discovery by the defendant against the State, and the notice-of-alibi rule is itself carefully hedged with reciprocal duties requiring state disclosure to the defendant. Given the ease with which an alibi can be fabricated, the State's interest in protecting itself against an eleventh hour defense is both obvious and legitimate. Reflecting this interest, notice-of-alibi provisions, dating at least from 1927, are now in existence in a substantial number of States. The adversary system of trial is hardly an end to itself; it is not yet a poker game in which players enjoy an absolute right always to conceal their cards until played. We find ample

room in that system, as least as far as "due process" is concerned, for the instant Florida rule, which is designed to enhance the search for truth in the criminal trial by insuring both the defendant and the State ample opportunity to investigate certain facts crucial to the determination of guilt or innocence.

Petitioner's major contention is that he was "compelled to be a witness against himself" contrary to the commands of the Fifth and Fourteenth Amendments because the notice-of-alibi rule required him to give the State the name and address of Mrs. Scotty in advance of trial and thus to furnish the State with information useful in convicting him. No pretrial statement of petitioner was introduced at trial; but armed with Mrs. Scotty's name and address and the knowledge that she was to be petitioner's alibi witness, the State was able to take her deposition in advance of trial and to find rebuttal testimony. Also, requiring him to reveal the elements of his defense is claimed to have interfered with his right to wait until after the State had presented its case to decide how to defend against it. We conclude, however, as has apparently every other court which has considered the issue, that the privilege against self-incrimination is not violated by a requirement that the defendant give notice of an alibi defense and disclose his alibi witnesses.

The defendant in a criminal trial is frequently forced to testify himself and to call other witnesses in an effort to reduce the risk of conviction. When he presents his witnesses, he must reveal their identity and submit them to cross-examination which in itself may prove incriminating or which may furnish the State with leads to incriminating rebuttal evidence. That the defendant faces such a dilemma demanding a choice between complete silence and presenting a defense has never been thought an invasion of the privilege against compelled self-incrimination. The pressures generated by the State's evidence may be severe but they do not vitiate the defendant's choice to present an alibi defense and witnesses to prove it, even though the attempted defense ends in catastrophe for the defendant. However "testimonial" and "incriminating" the alibi defense proves to be, it cannot be considered "compelled" within the meaning of the Fifth and Fourteenth Amendments.

Despite the *Williams* decision, a number of states have not passed legislation requiring a defendant to notify the prosecution that he plans an alibi defense. Some state courts still contend that if furnishing the names and addresses of witnesses will incriminate the defendant, it is not necessary to provide them to the prosecution. Thus the right of pretrial discovery by the prosecution is seriously curtailed.

FIGURE 9-1   Sample motion to suppress evidence

(Title of Court)

In the Matter of Property   Cr. No. _____
Seized from____(Names of persons   NOTICE OF MOTION AND
from whom property was seized)   MOTION TO SUPPRESS EVIDENCE
To (Names of all police officers known to have participated in the seizure of the property)
      PLEASE TAKE NOTICE that on _____, 19____ at _____.m., or as
soon thereafter as the matter can be heard, at the courtroom of (Dept. No. /
presiding Judge/etc.)   .
at (the Courthouse/State or other location of court)   , City of _____.
_____(Names of moving parties)_____
will move the Court for an order directing various levying officers, including the
above-named, to return to the movants forthwith certain personal property,
_____ a schedule of which is attached to this motion, and which on
_____ 19_____, at the premises known as ____(Address)____, was unlawfully seized and taken from the movants by those levying officers, and directing
that the property seized be suppressed as evidence against ____(him/them)____ in
any criminal proceeding.

      This motion is made on the grounds that:
1. ____(Set forth grounds)_____.
2. ____(Additional information)_____.
      This motion is based on this notice, the pleadings, records, and files in this
proceeding, the attached memorandum of points and authorities and the attached
supporting declaration of _____

Dated: _____

                                                          _____
                                                          Attorney for Defendant

The Motion to Suppress Evidence

At common law it was held that any evidence that would assist in determining the truth of what happened in a particular case was admissible
during a trial. The same policy was followed in this country for a number
of years in spite of the constitutional guarantee contained in the Fourth
Amendment of the United States Constitution against unreasonable
searches and seizures. In the early 1920s a few states, either by legislation
or court decisions, began to hold that unlawfully obtained evidence was
not admissible during a trial in attempting to prove a defendant guilty.
The inadmissibility of unlawfully obtained evidence is known as the *exclusionary rule.* In 1961 the landmark case of *Mapp v. Ohio,* 367 US 643,
placed the exclusionary rule in effect for all the states. Since that decision
much use has been made of the *motion to suppress evidence.*

Either as a result of pretrial discovery or through the preliminary hearing, the defense may learn that the prosecution plans to introduce evidence during the trial which in the opinion of the defense was unlawfully acquired. This evidence may be material that the defense alleges was obtained through an unlawful search or seizure, or it may be a confession which the defense states was improperly obtained. When this occurs, the defense counsel will usually file a motion to suppress evidence with the appropriate trial court. A hearing will be held on this motion, and the prosecution will present facts and testimony in an effort to prove that the material or confession was lawfully obtained. The defense may present evidence in an effort to prove that the evidence should be suppressed or not be introduced because of illegality.

Hearing to Suppress

The hearing to suppress evidence must be held prior to the trial time in some jurisdictions, and the hearing is held before a judge alone and not before a jury. If the judge concludes that the evidence was illegally obtained, he will suppress it, or hold that it is not admissible during the trial. If he believes that the material was lawfully obtained, it may be introduced against the defendant during the trial, and the jury will give the evidence the weight to which they feel it is entitled.

The reason that the hearing on the motion must be made prior to the trial in some jurisdictions is that it is felt that the trial judge should not be required to stop in mid-trial to determine whether evidence presented by the prosecution was lawfully obtained. If the evidence is ruled inadmissible, the prosecuting attorney may decide to dismiss the charge if a conviction would not be possible without the suppressed evidence. Thus the time and expense of a trial would be saved.

Some jurisdictions permit the defense to object to the introduction of the evidence again at the trial, and the judge may consider at that time whether the evidence is admissible. A few jurisdictions require the motion to suppress be made prior to trial, holding that unless the motion is made prior to the trial the defendant waives the constitutional right to object to the method of obtaining evidence. In these instances, courts have held that there is no waiver if the defendant could not have reasonably made the motion prior to the trial. A reasonable cause may be that the defendant was unaware of the allegedly illegal search or seizure, or did not have reasonable time to make the motion before the trial.

Other states hold that a pretrial motion to suppress evidence is premature and that the objection should take place during the trial. Pretrial motions and hearings to suppress evidence unnecessarily delay setting the case for trial, and, since an objection to the introduction of the evidence may be made again in most jurisdictions during the trial, it is a duplication of effort.

In jurisdictions where the pretrial motion to suppress is not mandatory, many defense attorneys will not file a pretrial motion. They will wait and object to the introduction of the evidence at the preliminary hearings. It is the prosecution's responsibility to present testimony in an effort to prove that the evidence was lawfully obtained. Through cross-examination by the defense, and the testimony of witnesses, efforts will be made to prove that the offered evidence was unlawfully obtained. If the judge holds that the evidence was illegally obtained, the defendant will be released unless other evidence causes the judge to reasonably believe the defendant should be held for trial. If the evidence is lawfully obtained and the defendant is held for trial, a second objection to the introduction of the evidence may be made during the trial.

Grounds for Evidence Suppression

Obtaining confessions and unreasonable searches and seizures are two areas that include numerous grounds for challenging the introduction of evidence. A confession obtained through the psychological pressure of threats or promises would be suppressed. Search warrants may be improperly issued, or permission for consent searches involuntarily given. An officer exceeding the permissible area on a search incident to arrest provides grounds for a motion to suppress. A sample document for a typical motion to suppress evidence appears in figure 9-1.

The Motion to Dismiss Charges

After a complaint, an information, or an indictment has been filed against a defendant facts are sometimes revealed which, in the interest of justice, demand the charge be dismissed. As pointed out in chapter 5, in some jurisdictions this action may be taken by the prosecuting attorney and is known as entering a *nolle prosequi*. Other jurisdictions do not grant the prosecuting attorney nolle prosequi authority. In these jurisdictions a charge may only be dismissed by a judge, by judicial motion or upon recommendation of the prosecuting attorney.

There are many reasons why a prosecuting attorney may recommend a charge be dismissed after it is filed. The original allegation may be unfounded; the evidence to be introduced may have been unlawfully obtained—making a conviction impossible; or a material witness is no longer available to testify. Dismissals have also been granted to a defendant to allow testimony against codefendants. The defense may file a motion to dismiss on the grounds that the indictment or information was seriously defective, or that a case was not brought to trial within the prescribed time.

A dismissal by a judge on judicial or defense motion is not always a bar to further prosecutive action on the matter, particularly if the charge is a felony. The prosecuting attorney may refile the charge. How many times this action may take place is not firmly established, but the right to a speedy trial prevents too many dismissals and refilings from taking place.

The Motion for Continuance

Criminal cases are to be heard as soon as reasonably possible, and they are to be given precedence over civil matters. Most state codes provide that no continuance of a criminal trial shall be granted except where the ends of justice require a continuance. The codes also provide that the continuance shall not be for a period of time longer than justice requires. In spite of these provisions, perhaps no motion is made with greater frequency than the motion for a continuance, particularly by the defense. What is within the "ends of justice" and how long "justice" requires the continuance to be are primarily within the discretion of the trial judge.

Grounds for a Continuance

There are no specified grounds on which the continuance may be based. Justice requires that a continuance be granted to obtain a material witness. But before a continuance to obtain such a witness will be granted, the side making the request must present further evidence as to why the witness is material, what effort has been made to locate the witness, and how the testimony of this witness is not available through any other witness. Continuances have been granted to defendants that they may obtain effective counsel, and they often take advantage of this opportunity. Defendants have employed counsel, and at trial time discharged counsel and requested a continuance to obtain new counsel. There are cases where this request was made as many as ten to thirteen times. Occasionally the defendant will have employed new counsel just prior to the trial date, and the defense counsel will make a motion for continuance on the grounds that additional time is needed to prepare the defense. Continuances have been granted when a defendant is not physically able to attend trial, or when the defense attorney is ill or engaged in another trial. The length of time a trial may be delayed because of these reasons is undetermined. If the defendant is not feigning illness, the court has no alternative but to grant continuance until the defendant recovers. But how long may defense counsel delay a trial? It has been held that unless a defense counsel is available for trial within a reasonable period of time, the defendant must obtain substitute counsel.

A continuance will not usually be granted for longer than thirty to sixty days. At the end of that period a new request may be made, and frequently is granted. As a result many criminal trials are not heard for more than a year after the crime has been committed.

When a motion for a continuance is to be made, reasonable notice must be given to the trial judge and the opposing side. Reasonable notice is difficult to determine. Unfortunately the notice may be given on the trial date. If a continuance is granted at that time, it works a hardship on everyone involved in the trial proceeding. It may be particularly inconvenient for witnesses who have taken time off from work and have traveled great distances to appear in court. The witnesses will have to reappear on the new date set for the trial. The defense makes these frequent requests for continuances because they usually work to the advantage of the defendant. The possibilities of prosecution witnesses becoming unavailable and memories dulling increase with the passage of time.

The Motion for Severance of Offenses

Criminals often commit a series of crimes in a relatively short period of time. For example, a burglar may commit a number of burglaries within a few days or weeks. If the burglar is caught and charged, it is logical to try the offender on all the charges at one time. Consolidating several charges into one trial saves time and expense by eliminating separate trials for each crime. Most state laws permit a series of crimes committed in one jurisdiction to be combined into one accusatory pleading. Each of the crimes charged in the accusatory pleading is referred to as a *count*. Crimes must be of the same general nature to be consolidated. If the crimes are all similar offenses, such as all burglaries or all robberies, there is no doubt as to consolidating them into one accusatory pleading. It has also been held that if the crimes are of a different nature, but are part of the same transaction, scheme, or plan, they may be consolidated. For example, if an offender should commit a burglary and then commit arson to hide the burglary, these two offenses could be consolidated since they are a part of the same transaction or plan. However, a crime of robbery and a crime of burglary could not be consolidated without being parts of the same transaction.

A defendant having a series of crimes consolidated into one trial has the advantage of avoiding defense in separate trials. Yet there are times when a defendant will make a motion for a severance of offenses.

This motion is based upon the premise that being tried on several counts during the same trial is prejudicial to the defendant. As stated in the case of *Cross* v. *United States,* 335 F 2d 987 (1964):

> Prejudice may develop when an accused wishes to testify on one but not the other of two joined offenses which are clearly distinct in time, place and evidence. His decision whether to testify will reflect a balancing of several factors with respect to each count: the evidence against him, the availability of defense evidence other than his testimony, the plausibility and substantiality of his testimony, the possible effects of demeanor, impeachment, and cross-examination. But if the two charges are joined for trial, it is not possible for him to weigh these factors separately as to each count. If he testifies on one count, he runs the risk that any adverse effects will influence the jury's consideration of the other count. Thus he runs the risk on both counts, although he may benefit on only one. Moreover, a defendant's silence on one count would be damaging in the face of his express denial of the other. Thus he may be coerced into testifying on the count upon which he wished to remain silent.

Also in *Drew* v. *United States,* 331 F 2d 85 (1964), the Court stated:

> The justification for a liberal rule on joinder of offenses appears to be the economy of a single trial. The argument against joinder is that the defendant may be prejudiced for one or more of the following reasons: (1) he may become embarrassed or confounded in presenting separate defenses; (2) the jury may use the evidence of one of the crimes charged to infer a criminal disposition on the part of the defendant from which is found his guilt of the other crime or crimes charged; or (3) the jury may cumulate the evidence of the various crimes charged and find guilt when, if considered separately, it would not so find. A less tangible, but perhaps equally persuasive, element of prejudice may reside in a latent feeling of hostility engendered by the charging of several crimes as distinct from only one. Thus, in any given case the court must weigh prejudice to the defendant caused by the joinder against the obviously important consideration of economy and expedition in judicial administration.

The Motion for Severance of Defendants

The laws of most states hold that when two or more defendants are jointly charged with the same offense, they must be tried jointly unless the judge feels that in the best interest of justice separate trials should be granted. Jointly trying codefendants promotes economy and efficiency and avoids multiplicity of trials. But defendants often file a motion for severance to avoid the possibility of prejudice. The prejudice may stem from the fact that evidence against one defendant is not applicable to others, and a jury may have difficulty in separating the evidence. One defendant may have a particularly bad reputation, and a codefendant could be convicted by association. A defendant may have given a confession implicating other codefendants, and this confession is to be introduced during the trial. Under such circumstances, unless the identifying data concerning codefendants cannot be adequately deleted from the confession, it is not admissible. Otherwise, separate trials must be granted. The jury would then be expected to perform the overwhelming task of considering a confession in determining the guilt or innocence of the confessor, and then ignoring the confession in determining the guilt or innocence of codefendants. (See *Bruton* v. *United States,* 391 US 123 [1968].)

Since the concern with joint trials stems principally from the fact that the jury might be prejudiced against the defendant, should a severance be granted if a jury is waived in favor of a court trial? Jurisdictions are divided on the answer to this question. Some hold that a judge is competent to separate evidence between codefendants, whether it be a confession, testimonial, or physical evidence. Therefore a severance of codefendants may be denied. Other jurisdictions hold that upon an allegation of prejudice a defendant has an absolute right to a severance whether the trial is a court trial or a jury trial.

The Motion to Determine Present Sanity

If the present sanity of the defendant is in question at any time prior to or during a trial, the defense counsel should make a motion for a sanity hearing. A hearing may be ordered on the sanity question if the actions of the defendant would cause doubt in the judge's mind. Present sanity of the defendant must be determined because a person cannot be tried, sentenced, or punished while insane. The procedure of determining present sanity is referred to as both a hearing and a trial. Usually the hearing is conducted before a judge sitting alone, unless the defense demands that a jury trial be held. This hearing should not be confused with a trial on a plea of not guilty by reason of insanity, as discussed in chapter 12. The hearing to determine the present sanity of the defendant has nothing to do with guilt or innocence; it ascertains the defendant's *present* mental capabilities. The test of present sanity determines the defendant's present ability to understand the nature and purpose of the proceedings, and measures the capacity to assist in the defense in a rational manner. If the defendant is unable to understand the charge and possible defenses, and is also unable to properly confer with counsel in regard to the conduct of the trial, the trial should not take place. The test to determine present sanity is not the same as that used in a trial on a plea of not guilty by reason of insanity.

Once the present sanity of the defendant is questioned, all prosecutive proceedings must be halted until the sanity can be determined. The next step is the present-sanity hearing or trial. Prior to the hearing the defendant will have been examined by psychologists or psychiatrists appointed by the court and by those selected by the defense, if desired. During the hearing these specialists and any other witnesses able to shed light on the defendant's present sanity may be called to testify. If the prosecution thinks that the defendant is presently able to defend himself, evidence may be offered in an effort to prove that the defendant is presently sane. If determined presently insane, the defendant must be confined to a mental hospital until recovery. There is no formal procedure to determine that the defendant has recovered his sanity other than certification to that effect by the hospital superintendent. After the defendant has recovered he will be brought back for trial unless the recovery period is extensive and the charge has been dismissed in the interest of justice.

If the present sanity hearing determines that the defendant is presently sane, the prosecutive proceedings will commence again from the point where they stopped. This is true unless the trial on guilt or innocence was in progress and the trial judge dismissed the jury and declared a mistrial. Under those circumstances the trial would be resumed from the beginning with a new jury. Various other motions will be discussed as the trial proceedings unfold.

Pretrial Conference

Pretrial conferences in civil matters have been effectively utilized for years. These conferences are informal meetings, usually in the judge's chambers, between both attorneys and the judge. The strong and weak points of the case are discussed in an effort to arrive at a settlement without going to trial. With court calendars becoming more and more crowded, greater use is being made of the pretrial conference in criminal matters. As the trial date approaches, the trial judge will often call for a pretrial conference. During these conferences the judge will determine whether both sides will be ready for trial on the date set, or if a continuance will be requested. The judge will also try to ascertain the approximate number of days each side anticipates taking to present its case. By gathering this information the judge will be better able to set other cases for trial and decide whether alternate jurors should be selected.

The attorneys may try to arrive at some sequence in calling witnesses, particularly professional persons or expert witnesses. The attorneys will attempt to agree, or to *stipulate,* to certain testimony. There are advantages to each side in stipulating to certain facts that a witness may present if called to testify. The stipulation may concern some uncontroversial matter when the presentation of proof during the trial would be of little consequence—thus saving trial time. The stipulation of some fact that the prosecution can prove convincingly may be to the advantage of the defense because it eliminates a witness from going into great detail to the detriment of the defendant. Those facts having a stipulation are brought to the attention of the jury at the appropriate time, and the jury considers those facts as though they had been presented in testimony during the trial. The presentation of facts by stipulation does not violate the defendant's right of confrontation as the defendant has waived his right of confrontation of that particular witness, or witnesses, by agreeing to the facts.

Plea Negotiation

Plea negotiating, or *plea bargaining* as it is more commonly known, is nothing more than agreement between the prosecuting attorney and the defense to reduce a charge to a lesser crime, to drop certain charges, or to receive a lessened sentence in return for a guilty or nolo contendere plea. Plea negotiating usually takes place shortly after the initial appearance or the arraignment of a defendant. In most jurisdictions the negotiating can continue to the time that the verdict is rendered. Plea negotiating is often discussed during the pretrial conference. Although it has been held that the judge should not be a part of the negotiation, he or she should be made aware of it, and in many instances must, by law, accept the conditions of the plea bargaining before the guilty or nolo contendere plea is acceptable.

Plea bargaining has been both praised and criticized. Some allege that plea bargaining is important in the administration of criminal law, is advantageous to the state by saving time and money, and increases efficiency and flexibility in the criminal process. The advantage to the defendant is reduced punishment. Plea bargaining has been criticized, particularly by some law enforcement officers, because it allows a criminal to take advantage of the justice system by not being convicted and sentenced for the crime actually committed. The result is a much lighter penalty.

Reasons Behind Plea Bargaining

Although the practice of accepting negotiated pleas has been criticized, many prosecuting attorneys state that the acceptance of a negotiated plea often is for more justifiable reasons than lightening case loads and clearing crowded court calendars. Sometimes an offender is initially charged on a more serious crime than is warranted by the evidence. Or an offender may be charged with a more serious crime so that a higher bail will be set. Reducing the number of charges in exchange for a negotiated plea may be justified on the grounds that many judges have a tendency to give concurrent sentences. There would be little advantage in going to trial on a larger number of charges over accepting a plea on a reduced number. As to accepting a negotiated plea on the promise of a lighter sentence, prosecutors point out that they have little or no control over the sentence that may be given one convicted of a crime. Even if the accused was convicted as a result of a trial, the sentence could be the same as that agreed to in the negotiated plea.

In the past plea bargaining was not discussed openly as it was considered to be unethical, if not illegal. Judges seldom were aware of any agreements made by plea bargaining because, to be valid, a guilty or nolo contendere plea had to be freely and voluntarily given. If the plea was induced upon some promise of leniency, there was a question of it being freely and voluntarily given. The secrecy of plea bargaining has been eliminated by legislative action and court decisions, and today plea bargaining is openly engaged in as a part of the justice system.

Supreme Court Sanctions Plea Bargaining

Much of this change in viewpoint was brought about by the case of *Brady v. United States*, 397 US 742 (1970), in which the United States Supreme Court gave sanction to plea bargaining. The facts of the case show that Brady was charged with a kidnapping violation and faced a maximum penalty of death if the verdict of the jury should so recommend. Brady entered a plea of guilty to the charge and was sentenced to thirty years imprisonment. The case was taken to the United States Supreme Court upon the grounds that the plea was not freely and voluntarily given because of representations of a reduction of sentence and clemency. Brady alleged that this inducement was compelling him to be a witness against himself in violation of the Fifth Amendment to the United States Constitution. The United States Supreme Court concluded that the guilty plea "was voluntarily and knowingly made" even though it may have been induced by representations with respect to reduction of sentence and clemency, and, as such, Brady's guarantee against self-incrimination had not been violated.

The Court in this decision stated:

> . . . That a guilty plea is a grave and so solemn act to be accepted only with care and discernment has long been recognized. Central

to the plea and the foundation for entering judgment against the defendant is the defendant's admission in open court that he committed the acts charged in the indictment. He thus stands as a witness against himself and he is shielded by the Fifth Amendment from being compelled to do so—hence the minimum requirement that his plea be the voluntary expression of his own choice.

The voluntariness of Brady's plea can be determined only by considering all of the relevant circumstances surrounding it. One of these circumstances was the possibility of a heavier sentence following a guilty verdict after a trial. It may be that Brady, faced with a strong case against him and recognizing that his chances for acquittal were slight, preferred to plead guilty and thus limit the penalty to life imprisonment rather than to elect a jury trial which could result in a death penalty.

The State to some degree encourages pleas of guilty at every important step in the criminal process. For some people, their breach of a State's law is alone sufficient reason for surrendering themselves and accepting punishment. For others, apprehension and charge, both threatening acts by the Government, jar them into admitting their guilt. In still other cases, the post-indictment accumulation of evidence may convince the defendant and his counsel that a trial is not worth the agony and expense to the defendant and his family. All these pleas of guilty are valid in spite of the State's responsibility for some of the factors motivating the pleas; the pleas are no more improperly compelled than is the decision by a defendant at the close of the State's evidence at trial that he must take the stand or face certain conviction.

Of course, the agents of the State may not produce a plea by actual or threatened physical harm or by mental coercion overbearing the will of the defendant. But nothing of the sort is claimed in this case; nor is there evidence that Brady was so gripped by fear of the death penalty or hope of leniency that he did not or could not, with the help of counsel, rationally weigh the advantages of going to trial against the advantages of pleading guilty.

The issue we deal with is inherent in the criminal law and its administration because guilty pleas are not constitutionally forbidden, because the criminal law characteristically extends to judge or jury a range of choice in setting the sentence in individual cases, and because both the State and the defendant often find it advantageous to preclude the possibility of the maximum penalty authorized by law. For a defendant who sees slight possibility of acquittal, the advantages of pleading guilty and limiting the probable penalty are obvious—his exposure is reduced, the correctional processes can begin immediately, and the practical burdens of a trial are eliminated. For the State there are advantages—the more promptly imposed punishment after an admission of guilt may more effectively attain the objectives of punishment; and with the avoidance of trial, scarce judicial and prosecutorial resources are conserved for those cases in which there is a substantial issue of the defendant's guilt or in which there is substantial doubt that the State can sustain its burden of proof. It is this mutuality of advantage which perhaps explains the fact that at present well over three-fourths of the criminal convictions in this country rest on pleas of guilty, a great many of them no doubt motivated at least in part by the hope or assurance of a lesser penalty than might be imposed if there were a guilty verdict after a trial to judge or jury.

Of course, that the prevalence of guilty pleas is explainable does not necessarily validate those pleas nor the system which produces them. But we cannot hold that it is unconstitutional for the State to extend a benefit to a defendant who in turn extends a substantial benefit to the State and who demonstrates by his plea that he is ready and willing to admit his crime and to enter the correctional system in a frame of mind which affords hope for success in rehabilitation over a shorter period of time than might otherwise be necessary.

The Court further stated that even if a guilty plea were entered through some inducement of leniency, that plea could not be withdrawn at a later date if the plea had been freely and voluntarily given. The standard of voluntariness of a guilty plea was set forth in the *Brady* decision which is as follows:

A plea of guilty entered by one fully aware of the direct consequences, including the actual value of any commitments made to him by the court, prosecutor, or his own counsel, must stand unless induced by threats or promises to discontinue improper harassment, misrepresentation including unfulfilled or unfulfillable promises, or perhaps by promises that are by their nature improper as having no proper relationship to the prosecutor's business (e.g., bribes).

Generally, before a negotiated plea is accepted, the judge and the prosecuting attorney must agree on the terms involved. Some judges have held that they may accept a negotiated plea without the concurrence of the prosecution, and can even accept such a plea over the objections of the prosecutor. This contention is based on the fact that a judge may accept an *unnegotiated* plea without the consent or concurrence of the prosecutor; therefore, it is believed that the judge may accept a *negotiated* plea without the consent of the prosecutor.

Pleas to be Related to the Offense Charged

It has been held that a negotiated plea should be related to the crime charged in the accusatory pleading, but the plea does not have to be confined to the one in the accusatory pleading. The negotiated plea may be to an offense of a lesser degree than the one in the accusatory pleading. For example, a defendant may be charged in the pleading with the crime of murder, but may be permitted to plead guilty to voluntary manslaughter. The plea to the offense of voluntary manslaughter would be a plea to a related crime of murder. It is also held that if the negotiated plea is to a crime committed in the course of conduct that leads to the charge in the accusatory pleading, this plea would be to a related crime. For example, during the course of a robbery, the defendant may take the victim from his home to his place of business to open a safe. The defendant may be charged in the accusatory pleading with kidnapping, but may be permitted to plead guilty to robbery. This would be a related crime since the robbery offense was in the course of conduct that led to the kidnapping charge. It is important that the negotiated plea be to a related crime so that the plea will more nearly reflect the true criminal history of and the crime for which the defendant was arrested.

Withdrawal of the Negotiated Plea

A guilty plea may be withdrawn if the bargain is not complied with by either the judge or the prosecuting attorney. The statutes of those states where negotiated pleas have been enacted usually provide that a negotiated plea of guilty or nolo contendere must be approved by both the judge and the prosecuting attorney. If the approval is not forthcoming, the defendant is permitted to withdraw the plea of guilty or nolo contendere and enter another plea. Once the approval is given, the bargain must be complied with, or the defendant may also withdraw the guilty or nolo contendere plea. This is true even though the defendant may not have been entirely honest in dealing with the court. In *People v. Johnson*, 12 Cal Rptr 556 (1974), for a negotiated plea of guilty the judge promised the defendant that the matter would be handled as a misdemeanor rather than as a felony, and that the defendant would be given probation. After discovering that the defendant had concealed his true identity and past criminal record, the judge sentenced the defendant to the state prison.

Upon appeal the judgment was reversed and the trial court was directed to permit the defendant to withdraw the guilty plea and enter a new plea. The appellate court relied upon the state statute providing that "where such plea [negotiated plea] is accepted by the prosecuting attorney in open court and is approved by the court, the defendant . . . cannot be sentenced on such plea to a punishment more severe than that specified in the plea." The statute further provided that if the court approves the plea the defendant, before accepting it, must be informed that the court might withdraw the approval in light of other consideration of the matter. In such case, the defendant shall have the right to withdraw the plea if so desired.

174

In the *Johnson* case the judge failed to inform the defendant of his right to withdraw the plea. During the argument before the state supreme court in this case, Johnson's attorney requested that, since the trial judge erred, the Supreme Court should give Johnson the alternative of enforcing the original bargain or of withdrawing his plea. The Court held that since there was a serious misrepresentation by Johnson, it was reluctant to create a right, for a defendant, to a specific performance of an original plea bargain rather than permit a withdrawal of the plea of guilty.

Review Questions

1. What is the right of discovery?
2. What is the theory behind the right of discovery as it relates to the defendant?
3. In general what may the defendant inspect by exercising his right of discovery?
4. What reasons have been presented by some states in denying the defendant the right of discovery?
5. What is the chief argument against permitting the prosecution the right of discovery?
6. In relation to the right of discovery by the prosecution, what was the significance of the *Williams* v. *Florida* decision?
7. In general what is the chief argument presented by the defense in support of a motion to suppress evidence?
8. Explain the significance of the exclusionary rule on the admissibility of evidence.
9. List two reasons for granting a trial continuance.
10. List the advantages and disadvantages of granting a motion to separate offenses.
11. What is the primary purpose of a motion to determine the present sanity of an accused?
12. What is the purpose of the pretrial conference?
13. What is a negotiated plea?
14. What are some of the advantages and disadvantages in plea bargaining?

Local Procedure

1. Is the defendant granted the right of discovery?
2. Is the prosecution afforded any right of discovery? If so, to what extent?
3. At what point must the motion to suppress evidence be made during a criminal proceeding?

THE TRIAL: ROLES OF MAJOR PARTICIPANTS

The Adversary System

Before discussing the actual trial proceedings, the roles of the other major participants in a criminal trial, in addition to the defendant, should be examined. These include the judge, prosecuting attorney, defense counsel, clerk of the court, bailiff, and court reporter. All are considered officers of the court. An examination of the function of the jury and the witnesses will be made later. By the trial time the law enforcement officer will have completed his or her major role in the administration of justice. The investigation will be finished, and the final duty will be serving as a witness and testifying in a truthful, convincing manner.

The criminal trial procedure varies little—whether the charge is a felony or misdemeanor, or the trial is a court trial or jury trial. The defendant is entitled to a fair trial before an impartial judge, an honest jury, and in an atmosphere of judicial calm.

Our justice system is an adversary system, meaning that it has two sides. In a criminal trial these are the prosecution and the defense. Each is permitted to present evidence in its own behalf. Theoretically, both sides come into the trial on an equal basis. But Justice White of the United States Supreme Court, in *United States* v. *Wade,* 388 US 218, (1967), pointed out that our system is not a true adversary system with both sides entering the trial on an equal footing. He stated:

> Law enforcement officers (and prosecuting attorneys) have the obligation to convict the guilty and to make sure they do not convict the innocent. They must be dedicated to making the criminal trial a procedure for the ascertainment of the true facts surrounding the commission of the crime. To this extent, our so-called adversary system is not adversary at all: nor should it be. But defense counsel has no comparable obligation to ascertain or present the truth. Our system assigns him a different mission. He must be and is interested in not convicting the innocent, but absent a voluntary plea of guilty, we also insist that he defend his client whether he is innocent or guilty. The State has the obligation to present the evidence. Defense counsel need present nothing, even if he knows what the truth is. He need furnish no witnesses to the police, reveal any confidences of his client, nor furnish any other information to help the prosecution's case. If he can confuse a witness, even a truthful one, or make him appear at a disadvantage, unsure or indecisive, that will be his normal course. Our interest in not convicting the innocent permits counsel to put the State to its proof, to put the State's case in the worst possible light, regardless of what he thinks or knows to be the truth. Undoubtedly there are some limits which defense counsel must observe but more often than not, defense counsel will cross-examine a prosecution witness, and impeach him if he can, even if he thinks the witness is telling the truth, just as he will attempt to destroy a witness who he thinks is lying. In this

respect, as part of our modified adversary system and as part of the duty imposed on the most honorable defense counsel, we countenance or require conduct which in many instances has little, if any, relation to the search for truth.

The Judge

Although the terms *judge* and *the court* are used interchangeably, they should be distinguished. The judge presides over the trial proceedings and exercises those duties and power imposed by law. The court is a judicial proceeding presided over by a judge. The judge plays a very important role both before and during the trial. There is a great deal of power and authority, and many decisions are solely at the judge's discretion. Since unscrupulous acts could seriously affect the administration of justice, the judge's actions are subject to review by appellate courts. This avoids any abuse of power or authority by the judge. Fortunately most are honest individuals who endeavor to do a conscientious job.

Superior Court Judges

In most states the judges of the superior court, or its equivalent, are elected by the people of the judicial district where they serve. This district is often the county. These judges are attorneys with past experience in the practice of law. One might wonder why an attorney with a number of years in law practice would wish to become a judge. Probably the most prevalent reason is the prestige that the office holds. Judges are generally held in high esteem within a community. One might be fearful that a judge, being an elected official, would have political obligations interfering with the ability to carry out functions impartially. As practicing attorneys, most candidates for a judgeship are fairly well known to the people of the community. The campaigning is primarily through personal contacts and the assistance of friends, and does not place the victorious judge in a position where he is bound to grant political favors. This does not mean that members of organized crime have not tried to influence elections, as well as judges, in some areas. But the great majority of judges have proven to be above this corrupt influence.

Inferior Court Judges

As in the case of the superior court judges, inferior court judges are elected in most states. They are elected by the people of the judicial district where they serve, but this district is only a portion of a county. The qualifications for this position vary greatly among states. In many outlying rural areas there is not enough court business to justify a full-time judge, so the judge may be a local practicing attorney elected to act as the judge when court business is required. The judge may also be the operator of a local market, service station, or a retired person who needs a part-time job, as usually there is no requirement that the judge of these courts be trained in law. These judges are often poorly paid, encouraging bribery. Some work on a commission receiving a percentage of fines levied, often creating the temptation to fine excessively, particularly in traffic violation cases. The brand of justice meted out in such courts sometimes leaves a great deal to be desired. But again, like superior court judges, most of the judges are honest individuals elected because of the community's faith in their honesty and integrity. However some inferior courts, like municipal courts in some districts, require the judge be an attorney before acting in the capacity of judge, and the judges of these courts are capable of handling the responsibilities imposed on them.

The Function of the Trial Judge

As pointed out in previous chapters, many duties have already been performed by the judge prior to the trial. With the judge sitting as magistrate, arraignments and preliminary hearings will have been held. As a judge decisions will have been made on motions presented, appointments of counsel for indigent defendants will be completed, and the right to a speedy and fair trial will have been preserved. Though a fair trial is essential, a perfect trial is not expected.

During the trial, the judge has the primary responsibility for seeing that justice is carried out. The judge has a duty not only to protect the interests of the defendant, but to protect the interests of the public, ensuring that the guilty are convicted. The judge controls all proceedings during the trial, and limits the introduction of evidence and arguments of counsel to relevant and material matters, with a view to the expeditious and effective ascertainment of the truth. The judge must control the conduct of the defendant and the spectators; determine the competency of witnesses and the admissibility of evidence; rule on objections made to questions asked by the attorneys; protect witnesses from harassment during cross-examination; interpret for the jury the laws involved in the particular case; and in some jurisdictions, comment on the weight of the evidence presented and the credibility of witnesses. In many jurisdictions, the judge sentences the defendant after conviction. If the trial is a court trial, the judge renders a verdict of guilt or innocence. Additional duties during the trial will be enumerated as the discussion of the trial progresses.

Contempt of Court.   A trial is to be conducted in a calm, dignified atmosphere. It is the responsibility of the judge to maintain such an atmosphere. Assisting in this regard, is the authority to punish one who interrupts this atmosphere by declaring the offender in contempt of court. Contempt is an act that is disrespectful to the court or adversely affects the administration of justice. Any act that embarrasses, hinders, or obstructs the court in the administration of justice may be declared by the judge as contempt of court. Typical acts falling within this category include contemptuous or insulting remarks made to the judge and counsel's persistent arguments with the judge after an admonition to desist has been given. A judge may not go so far as to hold a defense counsel in contempt when counsel is merely defending his client vigorously. Disorderly conduct by a defendant or by the spectators may cause the judge to exercise the right of contempt. A witness who refuses to be sworn in and testify could be held in contempt of court. These acts generally take place within the presence of the judge and are known as *direct* contempt. The judge may punish the offender summarily—that is, there and then—without any hearing or other procedure taking place. The punishment may be imprisonment and/or a fine.

Not only are insulting remarks made toward a judge possible contemptuous acts, but such remarks between the prosecuting attorney and the defense counsel may also be contempt. In one case where the two attorneys had exchanged a series of acrimonious remarks, the judge held both in contempt of court. The defense counsel accused the prosecuting attorney of "indulging in crap," to which the prosecuting attorney, according to the judge, "sank to the occasion by voicing an epithet denoting fecal matter of a male bovine." See *People* v. *Fusaro,* 18 Cal App 3rd 877, (1971). On another occasion a prosecuting attorney was held in contempt upon using an old southern colloquialism implying that the defendant was the incestuous son of a canine mother.

An interesting development arose out of the *Fusaro* case. The defense counsel was held in contempt and was imprisoned in the middle of the trial. The facts of the case reflect that: "The record reveals an acrimonious five day trial in which the attorneys mistook bickering and side remarks for vigorous advocacy. The prosecutor . . . was guilty of at least one act of misconduct," and the defense attorney:

> . . . in his turn cluttered and interrupted the trial with frivolous objections. He aroused the trial judge's ire by permitting a witness to remain in the courtroom despite an exclusion order. He was twice late in returning to the trial after a recess. On the afternoon of the third day he was 15 minutes late, apologized and explained that the judge of another court had detained him. Outside the jury's presence the trial court held him in contempt for tardiness and imposed a one-day suspended jail sentence.

This exchange of remarks between the prosecuting attorney and defense counsel concerning "indulging in crap" took place thereafter:

182

> At that point the judge recessed the trial, rebuked the attorneys, indicated that he wanted to consider their behavior and put the matter over to the next morning.
>
> The next morning, outside the jury's presence, the court found both attorneys in contempt.

The prosecuting attorney apologized, and the judge fined him $50. The defense counsel endeavored to justify the language. The judge:

> . . . imposed a 24-hour jail sentence on defense counsel, refused to stay the execution and committed him to jail immediately. In view of the jailing, defendant's trial was recessed until the following morning.

The defendant was convicted on four narcotics charges. The conviction was appealed on the grounds that the judge had abused discretion in holding the defense counsel in contempt and immediately imposing a jail sentence. The defendant alleged that the jailing of the counsel prejudiced the defendant in the eyes of the jury, and that a speedy trial was denied because of the interruption. Although the Appellate Court upheld the conviction, the Court took a dim view of jailing a defense counsel in the middle of a trial. The Court stated:

> A trial court has inherent statutory power to exercise reasonable control over the trial in order to insure the orderly administration of justice and to maintain the dignity and authority of the court; it has power to punish summarily for contempts committed in its immediate view and presence. [In accordance with the code of the State] as punishment for contempt a court may impose a fine not exceeding $500 or up to five days imprisonment or both.

Attorneys as well as others may be held in contempt more than once during a trial, and may be punished for each time they are so held. Offenders have been known to receive sentences running into years if the sentences are made to run consecutively. The United States Supreme Court has held that under these circumstances the offender is entitled to a trial on the contempt charge. The Court stated that criminal contempt is a crime and that the offender is entitled to the same trial procedure as in any other crime. If total sentences exceed six months, the offender is entitled to a trial by jury. If the sentence is not more than six months, the offender may be tried by a judge sitting without a jury, but the Court stated that the trial should be conducted by a judge other than the one holding the offender in contempt because of the possible emotional involvement in the matter. (See *Taylor* v. *Hayes,* 418 US 488 [1974], and *Codispoti* v. *Pennsylvania,* 418 US 506 [1974].) Some states grant a person accused of a crime a jury trial for all violations. The offender would then be entitled to a jury trial even though the sentence would not exceed six months.

As stated by the dissenting Justices in the *Hayes* and *Codispoti* decisions, the United States Supreme Court has considerably restricted the right of a trial judge to take summary contempt action and confused the action that may be taken. But the Court apparently did not eliminate the right entirely. The wording of the Court indicated that it is necessary to preserve the calm atmosphere and dignity of the court, a judge may exercise the contempt action right at the time of the misconduct, and may even sentence the person involved. But if the judge waits until the conclusion of the trial to take the contempt action, the offender is entitled to a trial on the contempt charge.

Defense counsels are held in contempt more frequently than prosecuting attorneys. If a prosecuting attorney indulges in misconduct, the misconduct may be considered prejudicial error, and a conviction may be reversed on appeal.

Other acts not performed in the presence of the judge may also be declared as contempt. These acts are known as *indirect,* or constructive, contempt, and they are usually the results of failures to abide by court orders. For example, jurors may discuss the facts of the case during a recess—in violation of the judge's order not to discuss the case, a juror may refuse to appear in court without sufficient good reason after receiving a summons to appear, or a witness may not appear as directed. Since indirect contempt does not occur in the presence of the judge, a hearing is held to determine if the alleged offender should be held in contempt. Prior to the hearing the judge will issue an order requesting the offender to show cause why he should not be held in contempt of court. Witnesses both for and against will be questioned at the hearing to assist in determining if the accused should be held in contempt. If the judge determines that the person should be held in contempt, it would appear from the *Taylor* and *Codispoti* decisions that the offender is entitled to a trial on the contempt charge since the act was not committed in the presence of the judge.

The right of contempt is a powerful weapon and it is meant to be. It permits a judge to prohibit court proceedings from getting out of hand because of misconduct. It also protects those involved in the court proceedings. If a judge should abuse his power of contempt, appeals may be made to a higher court for review and possible remedy.

The Prosecuting Attorney

The prosecuting attorney is known by a variety of names. In some places he or she is known as the *district attorney,* or the D.A., and in other areas as the *county attorney*. In the federal system, the title is the *United States Attorney*. The "public official" role of the prosecuting attorney is comparatively recent. For many years it was the responsibility of the victim or relatives to prosecute when a crime was committed. Attorneys were employed by these persons to assist in the prosecution. As time passed it was deemed advisable to have a full-time public prosecutor since the offense was actually committed against society, and the office of the prosecuting attorney was established.

In most states the prosecuting attorney is an elected official of the county. In large urban areas it is a sought-after position, as it holds prestige, pays well, and the prosecuting attorney has a number of deputies for assistance. In many places there may be no staff, and in sparsely settled counties, the position may be only a part-time job. When not engaged in handling official duties, the prosecuting attorney in such counties may have a private law practice. A few states have permitted several counties to form a *judicial district* and employ a single prosecuting attorney to handle the duties. Many attorneys have no interest in running for the position of prosecuting attorney since their private practices are more lucrative. Others shun the idea of running as a candidate in an election. As a result, in many counties the office of the prosecuting attorney is a training ground for younger attorneys willing to run for the office to gain experience and tide them over financially while building a private practice. In most counties the prosecuting attorney is a capable and reputable local attorney, and has a sincere interest in making certain that justice is done.

Responsibilities of the Prosecuting Attorney

The prosecuting attorney has a great deal of power, irrespective of personal capabilities or jurisdiction of service. The prosecuting attorney is charged with grave responsibilities to the public demanding integrity, zeal, and conscientious effort in the administration of justice. As stated by the Court in the *Gideon* decision, prosecuting attorneys "are everywhere deemed essential to protect the public's interest in an orderly society." The public prosecutor institutes proceedings before magistrates for the arrest of persons charged with or reasonably suspected of committing a public offense. In addition to acting as prosecutor, in most instances he represents the county on all civil matters.

The prosecuting attorney enters the justice procedural picture early in the prosecutive process. A great number of arrests are made by law enforcement officers on their own determination that there is reasonable cause to believe a crime has been committed. Unless the alleged offender is released by the arresting agency without further action being taken, the prosecuting attorney must be consulted to determine whether prosecutive action will be taken against the arrested person. The prosecuting attorney evaluates the weight of evidence against the accused and the nature of the charge in making the decision whether to prosecute. If the prosecuting attorney decides against prosecution, the accused will be released. If it is decided that prosecutive action should be taken, a complaint will be prepared by the prosecuting attorney and filed with the appropriate court. The accused is then taken before a committing magistrate for the initial appearance, or arraignment as it is referred to in some jurisdictions. Often law enforcement agencies conduct an investigation of alleged violations before making an arrest. In these instances the prosecuting attorney is usually consulted to determine whether there is sufficient evidence against the accused to justify prosecutive action, if a complaint should be filed, and a warrant of arrest obtained. As pointed out in chapter 5, the prosecuting attorney may prefer to present the charge to the grand jury to determine whether prosecutive action should be taken, or a secret indictment should be sought. This procedure is followed in felony charges. If the crime for which the arrest was made is a less serious misdemeanor, the prosecutive decision may be left to the discretion of the law enforcement agency involved. Even the preparation of the complaint and the prosecution during the trial may be handled by the officer, and the prosecuting attorney may not even appear on the scene unless some special problem should arise. In the more serious misdemeanor cases and on felony charges the prosecuting attorney will be involved from the time of arrest through the appeal.

If the charge is a serious one and the prosecuting attorney decides to prosecute, there are many decisions and duties to perform. The first decision is to determine what charge, or charges, the evidence will support so that the appropriate accusatory pleading may be filed. The prosecuting attorney must decide whether the charges, when more than one, are to be separated into different trials or consolidated into one. In some jurisdictions, if the charge is a felony, it must be decided whether the facts are to be presented in a preliminary hearing or to a grand jury. The information or the indictment must be prepared depending on the type of hearing conducted. Where appropriate the granting of motions requested by the defense must be disputed. At the time of the trial another responsibility is to present enough evidence to prove the defendant guilty beyond a reasonable doubt. The prosecuting attorney must also assist in the selection of the jury, decide what witnesses to call, and determine what physical evidence should be introduced. It is not necessary that every person who has some knowledge of the facts in the case be called, nor is it necessary that all physical evidence collected by the law enforcement officers during an investigation be presented during a trial. The prosecuting attorney must present enough witnesses and physical evidence to ensure the defendant a fair trial, and may not withhold any evidence that would be advantageous to the defendant. If the defense presents witnesses in its behalf, the prosecuting attorney must corss-examine them. The responsibilities of making recommendations to the judge on the severity of the sentence and assisting the state attorney general with appeals also fall to the prosecuting attorney.

The State Attorney General

In most states the attorney general has broad authority to coordinate local prosecutions. This authority includes the right to prosecute on his own and to supervise, assist, and consult local prosecuting attorneys. If a local prosecuting attorney needs assistance or fails to perform his duties, the attorney general is free to act. Unless called on by the local prosecutor, or unless the local prosecutor fails to prosecute when the facts warrant it, the state attorney general does not ordinarily intervene. There are a few states where the attorney general has no authority over local prosecutions. If there should be a malfeasance in office by the local prosecuting attorney in those states, the governor could be called to appoint a special prosecutor to perform the duties of the local prosecutor. When a case is appealed, in most jurisdictions it is the responsibility of the state attorney general to present the case to the appellate court. The attorney general will be assisted by the prosecuting attorney of the county in which the trial took place.

The Defense Counsel

Obtaining Counsel

Considerable discussion has already taken place concerning the right of an accused to the assistance of counsel. When an accused is unable to afford counsel, one will be provided free of charge. If able to afford one, the accused may choose the attorney. One problem faced by the accused is the method of finding effective counsel to assist in the defense. Looking through the yellow pages of a phone book for an attorney causes the risk of selecting an attorney not knowledgeable in criminal law. The accused may have confidence in an attorney known through a prior business matter, but be refused assistance due to a feeling of incompetence in criminal law. This attorney, however, can usually assist the accused in obtaining a criminal law specialist.

Criminal Law Specialist

The specialist is generally referred to as a *criminal lawyer.* Being few in number, criminal lawyers are usually well known in a community and locating one is a relatively easy task. The court often appoints this criminal law specialist to defend the indigent defendant because there is no doubt as to the effectiveness of counsel. Under the circumstances the indigent defendant may have the advantage over the accused who can afford counsel, as the accused may be a person of medium income who cannot afford the services of a criminal lawyer of great repute.

Many people look upon the criminal defense attorney as a threat to society. There are also criminal lawyers who seemingly become overzealous in their attempts to have an accused acquitted. It is their feeling that any attorney can have an innocent person acquitted, but that it takes a real specialist to obtain an acquittal for one who is guilty. These attorneys assume the attitude that society has established the presumption of all persons being innocent until proven guilty beyond a reasonable doubt. If the prosecution fails to meet the challenge of that responsibility because of clever defense, the accused is entitled to an acquittal. Likewise, if the defense is able to get an accused freed on some legal technicality, it is the privilege, duty, and right of an attorney properly and effectively defending a client. Some of these attorneys are not beyond vigorously cross-examining prosecution witnesses merely for the purpose of devaluating the testimony in the minds of the jury, and not to assist in arriving at the truth of what happened. Nor do they hesitate to present defense witnesses who are willing to perjure themselves in behalf of the defendant. Fortunately there are few defense attorneys who feel that they must go this far in defending an accused. However most defense attorneys, whether they are privately employed by the defendant, appointed by the court, or acting as public defender, do a sincere job in assisting and defending an accused in an ethical manner.

Except for those few criminal lawyers who receive some diabolical satisfaction out of having guilty defendants acquitted, the role of defense counsel is not an easy or highly satisfying job. In most instances the attorney and his client are thrust on each other without a choice by either party. The client often loses respect in the community because of the run-in with the law, and the defense counsel is often condemned by association. Frequently the client will not be honest with counsel, much to counsel's surprise and possible embarrassment during the trial. On the other hand, the client may be entirely honest with the defense counsel by admitting guilt, but refuse to enter a plea of guilty—even though there is no chance of an acquittal. Yet the defense counsel must see that the client receives a fair trial.

Privileged Communication

Defense counsels are often placed in a most awkward position because of the age-old relationship of *privileged communication* between attorney and client. This relationship provides that information furnished to an attorney in confidence by his client may not be revealed without the permission of the client. Law enforcement agencies may be unaware of crimes discussed by a client. In one instance a client told his attorney about two murders he had committed and where the bodies were buried. The problem created by receiving this information is whether the attorney should furnish it to the appropriate law enforcement agency or keep it in strictest confidence. The answer to this question has been debated by many legal scholars with no concrete answer forthcoming. It would appear that the better view would be to furnish the information to the appropriate law enforcement agency in order that the bodies be recovered and relatives notified. Society, as well as the criminal, is entitled to some consideration and justice. In most instances prosecutive action could not be taken since the exclusionary rule would prohibit the use of the information as evidence.

If the facts of a case are such that an attorney absolutely cannot accept the responsibility of effectively defending a client, the case should be refused. Once the case is accepted, it is the attorney's duty to remain until it has been brought to a logical conclusion. The defense attorney has many functions to perform, both before and during the trial. A conference with the accused should be held as soon as practically possible. This conference should be private and unobserved even though the accused is in jail at the time. If there are codefendants, the defense counsel must decide whether all can be effectively represented without a conflict of interest. If either counsel or one of the defendants feels that being represented by just one counsel would result in prejudice, each defendant is entitled to and must be provided with individual counsel.

The defense counsel will advise the defendant on the plea that should be entered at the arraignment, and counsel will be present for the purpose of cross-examining witnesses at the preliminary hearing. Counsel also has a right to be present during an identification "line-up" procedure if the defendant has been formally charged; however, the attorney has no right to interfere with the line-up or to prohibit the defendant from participating. The counsel will file those motions that are in the best interest of the defendant. At the time of the trial counsel has the duty and authority to conduct the defense. The counsel will determine the tactics and strategy to be used—even if they are opposed by the defendant. Unless the defendant can show that appointed counsel is ineffective, counsel may not be replaced merely because of a conflict in ideas. The defendant is entitled to sit with counsel at the counsel table during the trial so they may confer on the defense. This assistance is another reason why a defendant is entitled to be present during a trial. Defense counsel will cross-examine prosecution witnesses when appropriate, and will present such evidence on behalf of the defendant deemed necessary under the circumstances. Further duties of the defense counsel will be pointed out in the discussion of trial procedures.

The Clerk of Court

With the judge, the prosecuting attorney, and the defense counsel all playing dramatic roles during a criminal trial, one could easily overlook the clerk of the court, or county clerk, as the position is also known. This official also has a most important function in the justice system not only during the trial but before and after as well. The main function of the court clerk is to maintain all records of a particular case. These records include items such as copies of all the accusatory pleadings and motions that have been filed. The clerk also issues subpoenas and, in many jurisdictions, prepares the jury panel. He or she attends trials to swear in witnesses, mark exhibits, and maintain the evidence that is introduced. The clerk also keeps copies of the court transcripts, judgments rendered, and motions for appeals.

The Bailiff

The court bailiff may be a permanent member of the justice system or an individual appointed to assist in a particular trial. In some jurisdictions the bailiff is a member of the county government and carries the title of marshal. The bailiff assists the judge in maintaining order in the court and calls the witnesses to testify. If the defendant has not been released from custody, it is the duty of the bailiff to guard the defendant in the courtroom. When the jury is sequestered, it is the responsibility of the bailiff to make certain that the jurors are free from all contact with the public; the bailiff will return the jury to the courtroom after they have reached a verdict. In many jurisdictions the bailiff serves court orders and other court papers.

The Court Reporter

The responsibility of recording everything said during the trial proceedings belongs to the court reporter. This includes the testimony of all the witnesses, objections made to the attorneys' questions, rulings made by the judge, and conferences between the attorneys and the judge. If the case is taken up on appeal, the recorded notes must be transcribed.

The court reporter must be highly skilled to record transactions as they take place, often at a rapid pace. The reporter may record the proceedings in shorthand or with a stenotype machine. Tape recorders have been used, but these machines have not proved satisfactory. Often it has been discovered that the machine was not recording or that testimony was accidentally erased because the machine was not used properly.

The Court Commissioner

In many judicial districts, court commissioners are appointed to assist trial judges. In most instances they must possess the same qualifications as the judge, and a commissioner may substitute for a judge in an emergency situation. Otherwise the commissioners hold hearings on motions filed, set and accept bail, and perform other duties as may be imposed on them by law.

Review Questions

1. What is the primary function of the judge?
2. List four duties of the judge during trial proceedings.
3. What is contempt of court?
4. Name three types of misconduct that might cause one to be held in contempt of court.
5. List five duties and/or responsibilities of the prosecuting attorney.
6. What are some of the problems that a defense attorney encounters with a client?
7. List four duties of a defense counsel.
8. Describe the functions of the following:
     a. the clerk of court
     b. the bailiff
     c. the court reporter

Local Procedure

1. Does the state attorney general have the authority to assist local prosecuting attorneys in handling prosecutions?

THE JURY

eleven

Once the trial date has arrived and the prosecution and defense indicate their readiness, the selection of the jury begins the jury trial procedure. Before entering this phase of the trial proceedings, a few questions need to be answered. First, who are these persons who serve on a jury and where do they come from? Also, what qualities must they possess to qualify as jurors? A defendant is entitled to be tried in the judicial district in which the crime was committed, and an impartial jury is to be selected from that district. A criminal would not pick a particular judicial district in which to commit a crime because of greater faith in a jury from that district. This right to be tried within the judicial district in which the crime was committed is included in the Sixth Amendment of the United States Constitution. It was included because of experiences that the colonists suffered from being "hauled away" to Great Britain for trials of crimes allegedly committed in the colonies. The jurors were thus picked in Great Britain. Therefore, unless a change of venue is granted because an impartial jury cannot be selected within that district, one committing a crime rests his fate with those in the judicial district where the crime was committed.

A Jury of One's Peers

The only jury qualification set forth in the Sixth Amendment is that it be an "impartial jury" chosen from the judicial district in which the crime was committed. Similar provisions are included in the constitutions or statutes of the states. Any additional qualifications believed necessary for service as a juror come from suppositions of legislative action. Though not specifically provided for in most state statutes, it is generally conceded that the jury is to be composed of the accused's peers. This concept stems from a provision in the Magna Charta that provides that no freeman shall be seized and imprisoned except by judgment of "his peers." This provision did not pertain to a trial jury but to an accusatory jury. The Magna Charta was prepared by noblemen for their own benefit. It was to prohibit the king from seizing and imprisoning a nobleman merely on a whim. Seizure and imprisonment were to be made only after an accusation was determined to be well founded by the judgment of fellow noblemen. Although the Magna Charta was designed primarily for the benefit of noblemen, other lower classes of persons in Great Britain at the time also received benefit from this provision, and it became a part of the due process of law of Great Britain.

Trial by One's Peers

As the trial jury was created, it was assumed that it would be composed of one's peers. This concept was brought to America by the colonists. Yet

192

the provisions of all but a few states directly state that a trial jury must consist of one's peers. This concept today, more than ever before, seems to be directing the selection of trial juries. In the past, if the jury were composed of twelve men "good and true" picked from the community where the trial was to be held, the nebulous "peers" qualification had been satisfied. In recent years a closer look has been taken at the term "one's peers," and whether the requirement, though not specifically and formally set forth in the statutes, is met. The dictionary defines "peers" as one's equals, or of equal status; one's friends; or associates. To take this definition too literally in composing a jury would imply that a medical doctor could be tried only by a jury composed of other doctors; a farmer by farmers; a former convict by other convicts; or a sixteen-year-old defendant by a jury of only other sixteen-year-old persons. Such juries would undoubtedly fulfill the "peers" qualification, but would be most difficult to find in some jurisdictions. If such a jury were possible, the chances for jury impartiality would be low. Fortunately courts have not gone this far in selecting juries. As long as the jury is composed of persons representing a cross section of the community in which the trial takes place, it is considered as being composed of one's peers.

At one time only white males were qualified to serve as jurors. In fact, most states did not permit women to serve on juries until they were granted the right to vote with the passage of the Nineteenth Amendment to the United States Constitution in 1920. Persons of certain races, religions, and national origin were excluded, if not by statutory provision, by those making the jury panel selection. These exclusions were justified by those responsible for the jury panel, as they were to select only persons who were males, over twenty-one years of age, honest, intelligent, and of good character and sound judgment. It was alleged that members of minority groups did not meet these qualifications. To overcome this practice, the federal government passed legislation stating that no citizen shall be excluded from service on the federal grand jury or a federal petit jury because of race, color, religion, sex, national origin, or economic status, and that persons are to be selected at random from a fair cross section of the community. (See 18 United States Code, section 1861.)

Cross Section of the Community Standard

Many states have adopted the *cross section of the community* standard to meet the peer group regulation, particularly in view of United States Supreme Court decisions. In *Glasser v. United States,* 328 US 128 (1942), the Court stated: "The American tradition of trial by jury, considered in connection with either criminal or civil proceedings, necessarily contemplates an impartial jury drawn from a cross section of the community."

The Court has also stated that it is part of the established tradition in the use of juries as instruments of public justice that the jury be a body truly representative of the community. However, what is a truly representative body? Does it pertain only to races, education, age, sex, religion, economic status, or philosophical thinking, or must *all* of these matters be taken into consideration when composing a jury panel? These questions were partially answered by the United States Supreme Court in *Fay* v. *New York,* 332 US 261 (1947), when the Court stated:

> There is no constitutional right to a jury drawn from a group of uneducated and unintelligent persons. Nor is there any right to a jury chosen solely from those at the lower end of the economic and social scale. But there is a constitutional right to a jury drawn from a group which represents a cross section of the community. And a cross section of the community includes persons with varying degrees of training and intelligence and with varying economic and social positions. Under our Constitution, the jury is not to be made the representative of the most intelligent, the most wealthy or the most successful, nor of the least intelligent, the least wealthy or the least successful. It is a democratic institution, representative of all qualified classes of people.

Only by being able to select a jury from persons who truly represent a cross section of a community can the accused be assured of an impartial jury.

In order to have a truly representative cross section of a community on a jury panel, more and more jurisdictions are conducting surveys to determine the percentage of persons of minority races and different national origins within the community. In this way a like percentage can be included on jury panels. Younger people make up a larger percentage of those selected to serve on jury panels. In the past juries were frequently composed of older persons, as they were less likely to suffer financially by serving on juries. As idealistic as it may be to have a truly representative cross section of the community, juries often are not truly representative because many classes of persons suffer financial hardships by serving and are thus excused. However, as long as there is no systematic exclusion of any class of persons, the cross section requirement is fulfilled. As pointed out by the courts, it is not necessary that a jury include one of each class of persons to be truly representative of a cross section of a community.

When the courts use the term *community,* they generally mean the judicial district in which the crime was committed. In most instances the judicial district is the county, but in the case of inferior courts, the judicial district may be only a portion of a county.

When a jury is challenged as not being a true representation of a cross section of a community, the challenge usually is made by a defendant who fails to find one of his particular sex, race, or group among those from whom the jury may be chosen. But in *Taylor* v. *Louisiana*, 419 US 522 (1975), the United States Supreme Court held that a defendant may object to the exclusion of a class of persons from the jury panel even though the defendant was not one of the excluded class. In that case, a male defendant objected to the exclusion of women from the jury unless they volunteered for jury duty. The Court pointed out that although 53 percent of persons eligible for jury duty in the judicial district were female, only 10 percent of these had volunteered, and thus there was not a true representation of the cross section of the community. The defendant had a right to object to the exclusion of women from his jury even though he was not a member of the excluded class.

The Jury Panel or Jury List

The procedure of jury selection varies somewhat among states and even among districts within a state. In some larger metropolitan districts a *jury commissioner* is often appointed, whose duty it is to select persons within his district to be available for jury duty. This group of persons is referred to as a *jury panel* or *jury list*. In other districts the selection of the panel may fall to the court clerk.

In most jurisdictions the selection of a jury panel is made annually, usually at the beginning of the calendar year. There are generally no guidelines set forth for selection. As noted, the federal government provided that no person was to be excluded from serving on a jury because of race, religion, and so forth, and that the persons were to be a community cross section picked "at random." No procedure was set forth as to *how* those persons were to be randomly selected. This regulation did provide that each federal judicial district devise and place into operation a written plan as to how the jurors were to be selected— whether from voter registration lists or some other source. In this way the courts would have some record to verify that no class of persons had been systematically excluded.

The official making the selection has almost complete power over the selection of names to be placed on the jury panel, and, in most districts, the sources from which he obtains the names are solely at his discretion. Whatever list is used, the names will be individually placed in a box from which the official will randomly pull those to be placed on the jury panel. As a matter of convenience officials often used the voter registration list, but it is generally not required that a juror be a registered voter. However this list is often utilized with greater frequency than any other list for two reasons. First, the list is more likely to be representative of a cross section of the community than other lists. Second, the qualifications for voting more nearly coincide with those that a juror must possess. However, the supreme courts of some states have held that the use of only voter registration lists is too restrictive since many members of minority groups do not register to vote. These courts have suggested that other sources in addition to voter registration lists be utilized to get a better cross section of a community. Tax assessors' lists have been utilized but this source has been criticized as it has been held that property owners are more likely to be "convicting" juries than nonproperty owners. Church membership lists have also been used, but with such lists religious conflicts ensue. Some officials have selected names randomly from telephone books in the area, or they select every tenth name or some similar numerical sequence. In sparsely settled districts, the officials have made selections through personal contact or by selecting names furnished by acquaintances. On one occasion an official used the membership list of the area League of Women Voters to get a representative number of women on the panel. The use of this list was criticized as it was too restrictive in the class of women selected and was not a cross section of the women of the community. (See *Glasser* v. *United States.*)

Qualifications to be a Juror

Although individual juror qualifications may vary somewhat among states, the general qualifications are the same. The person must be a citizen of the United States, eighteen years of age or over, and a resident of the judicial district for a specified time, usually one year. This latter qualification has been criticized by some as being too restrictive and not representative of a community because many residents of a community move more frequently than once a year. In view of this contention, the legislatures of some states have changed the residence requirement from one year to one month. Those upholding the one year requirement contend that it takes at least a year for a person to learn the thinking and moral standards of a community. For this reason, many states still use the one year residence requirement.

The person must be in possession of his natural faculties, meaning that the person must be able to see, hear, talk, feel, smell, and be comparatively mobile. Some states have passed legislation that a person is not disqualified as a juror because of loss of sight, hearing, or other disabilities that substantially interfere with mobility. This legislation is criticized as unrealistic by many within the justice system. The belief is that the amount of physical evidence presented during a trial prevents a blind person from adequately functioning as a juror. Similarly, since most evidence presented during a trial is through testimony of witnesses, a person unable to hear the testimony would be unable to perform duties as a juror. A person with limited or impaired mobility may be in a better position to act as a juror, unless that impairment prevents the person from sitting where the sights and sounds of the trial are adequate. The proponents of this legislation argue that such persons should not be deprived of performing their civic duty merely because of an impairment. They allege if there is a reason that the impaired person could not perform in a particular case, a challenge for cause could be made. This challenge, however, is not without its complications as we will see later.

Some states hold that a decrepit person may not qualify as a juror. While the law does not specify the characteristics that make a person decrepit, it appears to be aimed at someone who is of advanced age, cannot move about freely, and may be senile. Determining when one has reached this condition is difficult.

A person must also be of "ordinary" intelligence to qualify as a juror in most states. This is another nebulous term. What might be considered ordinary intelligence by some might not be considered ordinary by others. And by what standards is intelligence to be measured? This qualification has led to the exclusion of competent persons from the jury panel. To establish whether a prospective juror is of ordinary intelligence, many conscientious efforts have been made to devise tests to assist in making the determination. These tests have been challenged by many defendants. They maintain that words unfamiliar to many ethnic groups are included in the tests, thus preventing a jury from being truly representative of the community. Because of these challenges, most such tests have been eliminated.

The prospective juror must have sufficient knowledge of the English language to communicate properly and to understand the trial proceedings. Not all persons on voters lists understand English, nor do all have the full use of their natural faculties. Thus, registered voters are not necessarily qualified as jurors.

Aliens, those convicted of malfeasance in office, any felony, or other high crime are excluded by most jurisdictions from jury duty. However, even this exclusion has been challenged as excluding a cross section of society.

Some jurisdictions exclude persons who have served as a juror during the preceding year. This is to discourage the "professional jurors" who continually hang around courthouses attempting to serve on juries because they have nothing else to do. Whether there is anything wrong with the professional juror is subject to debate.

Obtaining Jurors

Because of the number of persons in a community who do not qualify as jurors, are exempt, or are excused, obtaining a sufficient number of persons who are available for jury duty is not an easy task. In one large metropolitan area the jury commissioner selected 300,000 names in order to maintain a panel of 15,000 persons—the estimated need for the coming

FIGURE 11-1 Sample of potential jury member questionnaire

Name _____ Address_____

1. Occupation _____ Employed by _____
   If retired, state former occupation _____
2. Do you own your own business? _____ (Yes or No) Firm name _____
   How many employees? _____
3. Age _____ Condition of hearing _____ Eyesight _____
4. Do you have any physical or mental disability that would interfere with or
   prevent you from serving as a juror? _____ (Yes or No) If so, describe if fully
   _____
   _____
   Doctor's name _____
5. Can you read and understand English? _____ (Yes or No)
6. Have you ever been convicted of any felony in a State or Federal Court?
   _____ (Yes or No) If your answer is yes, have your civil rights been restored
   by pardon or amnesty? _____ (Yes or No)
7. Have you been a resident of this County and State for one year immediately
   before this date? _____ (Yes or No)
8. Have you served as a juror in this State within the last two years? _____ (Yes
   or No) If yes, when? _____
9. Do you have minor children? _____ Ages: _____
10. Do you have dependents who require your personal constant care? _____ If
    yes, please explain: _____
11. If you are entitled to legal exemption or have legal grounds for excuse
    from jury duty, do you claim it? _____ (Yes or No) If so, explain fully the
    ground of your claim. _____
    _____

I certify (or declare) under penalty of perjury that the answers to the foregoing
questions are true and correct.
Executed in _____ County, State of _____, on the ____ day of _____ 19____.

Signature _____

year in that district. Generally it is the responsibility of the official in charge of the jury panel to determine whether the persons selected are qualified to serve or are exempt. To facilitate this determination many officials will mail a questionnaire to the selected person, requesting certain information. A sample questionnaire may be seen in figure 11-1.

The procedure of mailing questionnaires to prospective jurors also has been challenged by defendants. They contend that many members of minority groups do not respond to the questionnaires and thus do not become eligible to be placed on the jury panel. Regardless of these challenges, many jurisdictions still send out questionnaires to assist in obtaining competent persons to act as jurors. The courts recognize that while there is no ideal way to select prospective jurors, the system used is acceptable if no groups of people are eliminated.

When the selection of prospective jurors is completed, those persons found to be competent are placed on the jury panel. As each trial date is set, a number of these persons will be notified to appear in court on that date. The notice is usually by legal document, referred to as a *summons,* served on the prospective juror by the sheriff, marshall, or other official of the district involved. If the person does not appear as directed after being personally served with the summons, a contempt charge may result unless good cause is shown for not appearing. For example, a prospective juror with a serious illness could not be expected to appear. From this group appearing in court, the trial jury is selected.

The number of persons called to appear in court varies with the type of crime charged and the amount of pretrial publicity that may have been given the case. Usually not less than twenty-five persons will be summoned to appear in court, and if the charge is murder and the case has received wide publicity, as many as one hundred persons may be summoned. There have been times when even with this number a trial jury could not be picked and additional persons from the panel had to be called to appear in court. The first twelve names called by the clerk at the time of the trial may not be those of the ones who will serve on the jury.

In some districts the official will not establish a jury panel very far in advance of a trial. As juries are needed the official will have a number of persons summoned to appear in court on a particular day. At this time it will be determined if those summoned are qualified to serve on a jury. The difficulty with this procedure is that many of those summoned may not qualify for jury duty and more will have to be notified to appear in order that a trial jury may be selected.

When it is established that those persons appearing in court qualify for jury duty, their names will individually be written on slips of paper and placed in a box. When the trial jury is to be selected, the clerk will pick, at random, twelve individuals (or a lesser number depending upon the jurisdiction) who are to act as the trial jurors. They will take seats in an area provided for them, commonly known as the *jury box.* The prosecuting attorney and the defense counsel very closely scrutinize the jurors to determine if this is the group with which they wish to rest their case. If not, the attorneys may decide to replace all or a few of the jurors.

Exemption from Jury Duty

There are many persons who have the qualifications to be a juror but are exempt from jury duty because of their occupations. It is believed that the functions they perform within a community outweigh their responsibility to serve on a jury. Included among those most often exempted from jury duty are: members of legislative bodies; members of the armed services on active duty; attorneys and their staffs; ministers and priests; teachers; physicians; correctional officers; law enforcement officers; firemen; mail carriers; and most public officers of the county, state, or federal government. However, those persons exempt from jury duty do not have to claim the exemption, and are free to serve as jurors if they so choose.

Some state statutes do not designate any class of persons who are exempt from jury duty, but include a provision that the court has the authority to excuse a person upon finding that jury service would entail undue hardship on the person or on the public. However, since it is a citizen's civic duty to serve on juries when called, a person may not be excused for a trivial cause or because of mere inconvenience. The courts are considerate of those for whom jury duty would create a real hardship. This includes persons operating one-person businesses requiring individual attention, students in the midst of a school year, mothers with small children, and persons caring for sick dependents. Since jury duty is an inconvenience if not an actual hardship for most persons, many districts will excuse a person from further jury duty during the year if he has served as many as twenty days, or some other predetermined number, as a juror. This does not mean that a juror may be excused in the middle of a trial after serving his twenty days. The juror must continue serving until that particular trial is completed, even if it takes several more weeks.

Challenging the Jurors for Cause

In most instances, by the time the jurors reach the jury box it will have been determined that each possesses the qualifications necessary to act as a juror. If this has not been determined, the judge or prosecuting attorney will read to the jurors the qualifications necessary, and if any seated in the jury box does not possess those qualifications, that juror will be excused and another name will be pulled from the box to replace the excused juror. There have been instances where a person selected to act as a juror did not qualify, yet refused to acknowledge the lack of qualification. If either the prosecuting attorney or defense attorney knows that the juror is not qualified, that attorney may challenge the juror's right to serve. For example, it may be known that one of the jurors has been convicted of a felony. That person could be challenged. These challenges are referred to as *challenges for cause*. In other words, there may be some cause why a person should not serve on the jury. There are a number of other reasons why a juror may be challenged for cause besides not being qualified. After viewing the jury, the defense counsel may conclude that it does not represent a cross section of the community because there is no member of the same race, national origin, or age level as the defendant. The defense counsel may then challenge the entire jury panel. If this challenge is made and the judge knows that there was no systematic exclusion of any class of persons, the judge will deny the challenge, and the trial activities will proceed. If any other challenges are forthcoming, they will have to be made on other grounds. If the judge should question the possibility of certain classes of persons being excluded, a recess may be declared until doubt is resolved by determining the method used to select the panel.

Preconceived Ideas of Guilt or Innocence

One of the grounds for challenging a juror for cause is preconceived ideas about the guilt or innocence of the defendant. A juror is often asked the question of how much has been heard or read about the case through newspapers, radio, and television. In many instances the juror, or all of them, may admit hearing or reading about the case. The juror will then be asked if an opinion has been formed as to the guilt or innocence of the defendant. If it has, the juror will be challenged for cause, and the judge will undoubtedly excuse that juror unless there is an indication that the opinion could be changed as a result of evidence presented during the trial. The problem is whether a juror can in reality throw off an opinion of guilt or innocence already formed irrespective of how strong the evidence may be on either side. The questioning of a prospective juror on a challenge for cause is often referred to as a *voir dire examination.*

In almost all instances the prospective juror who has formed an opinion about guilt or innocence prior to a trial has formed that opinion as a result of pretrial publicity given to the case. This creates a continuing battle between the freedom of the press and the defendant's right to a fair trial by an impartial jury. Publicity is given to many cases, particularly murder charges, and it is next to impossible for prospective jurors not to have learned something about the case. As stated by United States Supreme Court Justice Clark in the case of *Irvin* v. *Dowd,* 366 US 717 (1961):

> It is not required . . . that the jurors be totally ignorant of the facts and issues involved (in a case). In these days of swift, widespread and diverse methods of communication, an important case can be expected to arouse the interest of the public in the vicinity, and scarcely any of those best qualified to serve as jurors will not have formed some impression or opinion as to the merits of the case. This is particularly true in criminal cases. To hold that the mere existence of any preconceived notion as to the guilt or innocence of an accused, without more, is sufficient to rebut the presumption of a prospective juror's impartiality would be to establish an impos-

sible standard. It is sufficient if the juror can lay aside his impression or opinion and render a verdict based upon the evidence presented in court.

In the *Irvin* case pretrial newspaper stories described the defendant as a confessed slayer of six and a parole violator. Because of deep-seated preconceived opinions of the guilt of the defendant by members of the jury, the Court felt that the defendant had been denied a fair trial by an impartial jury.

Returning again to the *Sheppard* v. *Maxwell* case discussed in Chapter 7, the United States Supreme Court held that the defendant had been denied a fair trial, as in the *Irvin* case. In the *Sheppard* decision, extensive pretrial publicity accusing the defendant of the crime was given to the case, even though he had not been arrested or charged with the crime. Headlines such as "Why Don't Police Quiz Top Suspect" appeared, with a demand that Sheppard be taken to the police headquarters for questioning. One newspaper described Sheppard in the following language: "Now proved under oath to be a liar, still free to go about his business, shielded by his family, protected by a smart lawyer who has made monkeys of the police and authorities, carrying a gun part of the time, left free to do whatever he pleases." After the arrest of the defendant, the publicity intensified and continued throughout the trial. The Court felt that if the prospective jurors did not have a preconceived opinion of the guilt of the defendant, they reached that opinion during the trial primarily from the publicity given the case and not from the evidence presented.

Although the trial judge in the *Sheppard* case endeavored to keep the jurors from being exposed to publicity, the effort was apparently not successful. At the beginning of the trial, the judge stated: "I would suggest to you and caution you that you do not read any newspapers during the progress of this trial, that you do not listen to radio comments nor watch or listen to television comments, insofar as this case is concerned. . . . After it is all over, you can read it all to your heart's content." At intervals during the trial, the judge repeated his suggestions. But the "jurors were thrust into the role of celebrities by the judge's failure to insulate them from reporters and photographers. The numerous pictures of the jurors, with their addresses, which appeared in the newspaper before and during the trial itself exposed them to expressions of opinion from both cranks and friends."

As a result of these United States Supreme Court decisions, local courts have been encouraged to control information released to the news media. This control does not interfere with the freedom of the press, but assists in picking jurors without preconceived opinions on the guilt or innocence of the defendant because of pretrial publicity. The control is designed to prevent the jury from being influenced during the trial by extensive publicity, some of which may be inaccurate. Because of the freedom of the press in this country, much pretrial and during-the-trial publicity is given many cases, despite "gag order" controls. Because of pretrial publicity, extensive questioning of prospective jurors takes place to determine whether the prospective juror has a deep-seated opinion of guilt or innocence that cannot be overcome by the evidence presented during the trial. In some of the more notorious cases it has taken several weeks just to select a jury.

Challenging the Jurors for Bias

A preconceived idea on guilt or innocence is not the only grounds for challenging a juror for cause. Another is *bias,* either *implied* or *actual.*

Implied bias is set by law and disqualifies a juror from serving. Implied bias may include consanguinity or affinity (that is, kinship or relationship) to within the fourth degree to the victim of the crime or to the defendant. Other examples of implied bias are having a relationship of employer and employee, or landlord and tenant, to either the victim of the crime or to the defendant, or having served on a jury that tried another person for the offense charged.

Actual bias is prejudice that a juror may admit to having because of a dislike for a particular race, religion, national origin, or class of persons. For example, the juror may admit to a bias against law enforcement officers that would create prejudice against the prosecution.

Since some states do not disqualify prospective jurors because of blindness, an attorney might challenge a blind person for cause if there will be evidence presented during the trial requiring visual examination. However, because of the general sympathy for blind people, an attorney should be cautious in excusing a blind person for cause under these circumstances. That same sympathy might be given a prospective deaf juror, causing other jurors to become prejudiced against the attorney. Even though a challenge is made, complications in executing the challenge can occur as in the following instance. A hearing impaired person was challenged in a criminal case because of the inability to hear the testimony. The excluded person countered the challenge for cause, alleging an inherent right to be a juror. He stated that it was the court's responsibility to supply an interpreter capable of using sign language to translate the testimony to the hearing impaired juror. The judge concluded that persons could be challenged for cause on other grounds permitted by law, and that there was no inherent right to be a juror in all circumstances. The judge further pointed out that even if an interpreter was a practical solution to the challenge, there was always the danger of misinterpretation of the testimony by the interpreter or misconception in the translation by the juror. To further complicate the matter, at the final deliberation only jurors could be present. The judge's position was further supported by the fact that a person without a sense of smell or feeling could be excused for cause if these faculties were important to the evidence examination.

Prospective Jurors Opposed to the Death Penalty

Prior to the United States Supreme Court decision in *Witherspoon* v. *Illinois,* 391 US 510 (1968), if a juror was against the death penalty, a challenge for cause could be made in cases carrying a maximum penalty of death. The facts of the *Witherspoon* case show that Witherspoon, the petitioner, was brought to trial in Cook County, Illinois, on a charge of murder. The jury found him guilty and fixed the penalty at death. At the time of trial an Illinois statute provided: "In trials for murder it shall be a cause for challenge of any juror who shall, being examined, state that he has conscientious scruples against capital punishment or that he is opposed to the same."

During the trial the prosecution eliminated approximately one half of the jury panel on a challenge for cause when prospective jurors expressed any qualms about capital punishment. Those persons chosen for the trial jury were ones with no conscientious scruples against the death penalty. Witherspoon took the case to the United States Supreme Court on the grounds that a fair trial by an impartial jury representative of the cross section of the community had been denied. Witherspoon maintained that persons who were not against the death penalty were more likely to be convicting jurors. Since many persons were against the death penalty, eliminating those persons from a jury resulted in a jury that was not representative of the community. The Supreme Court agreed with Witherspoon and held that merely having conscientious scruples against capital punishment was not a sufficient cause to disqualify a person from serving on a jury. The Court did state that if a prospective juror advised that under no circumstances could he vote to convict a defendant if the death penalty was the sentence, that person could be excused on a challenge for cause.

In those states in which the death penalty may be imposed upon conviction of certain crimes, the prosecuting attorney may ask if a prospective juror is opposed to the death penalty. If the juror indicates opposition, the prosecuting attorney may then ask if the juror could vote for conviction knowing that the death penalty could be imposed. If the prospective juror states that he could, then he may not be challenged for cause. The problem created by the *Witherspoon* decision is just what action may be taken against the prospective juror who merely indicates some reservations about being able to vote for conviction. Some appellate courts have held that the prospective juror must state positively that he could not consider a guilty verdict, if the penalty is death, in order to have the person challenged for cause. There were three dissenting justices in the *Witherspoon* decision who felt that permissible questioning of prospective jurors on the death penalty would not result in a different kind of jury and that prosecutors would be put to a great deal of trouble for nothing.

The *Witherspoon* decision has caused great complication in the voir dire examination of prospective jurors in capital punishment cases. Some appellate courts have adopted the view that the *Witherspoon* decision holds that to constitutionally excuse a prospective juror for cause due to opposition to the death penalty, the juror must make it unmistakably clear that first, the juror would automatically vote against the death penalty without regard to evidence presented, or second, that this attitude toward the death penalty would prevent the prospective juror from making an impartial decision on the defendant's guilt.

Prosecuting attorneys and judges have attempted to abide by the *Witherspoon* decision, but just how positive must the feeling be against the death penalty before a prospective juror is excused? In one case a prospective juror stated on voir dire examination that she was against the death penalty. The judge asked: "Are you so against the death penalty that you would just automatically vote against the death penalty?" To this the prospective juror stated: "I think there might be a hypothetical case in which so heinous a crime was committed that I would consider the death penalty. But I have not been able to think of a hypothetical case that heinous." With this statement the judge excused the prospective juror for cause. The defendant in that case was convicted and the case was automatically appealed to the state supreme court, which reversed the death penalty on the grounds that the prospective juror had been improperly excused as not stating that she would automatically vote against the death penalty. There was a dissenting justice in that case who felt that the juror had been properly excused. The case indicates the difficulty facing the courts in determining when a prospective juror was properly excused for cause in being against the death penalty. (See *People* v. *Velasquez*, 26 Cal. 3d 425 [1980].)

In another state case, a prospective juror was asked if any personal feelings might prevent participation in the deliberation of a case carrying a possible death sentence. The prospective juror replied that he was a born-again Christian and did not think that he could have any part of sitting in on a case that would send anyone to the electric chair. With this reply the judge excused the man. After the defendant was convicted and given the death penalty, the state supreme court in that case reversed the death penalty on the grounds that the prospective juror was improperly excused since it was not made unmistakably clear that the juror's participation in the deliberation of the case was not possible because of the penalty. The dissenting justice in that case felt that the court was only seeking a way to reverse death penalties. Justices who have personal feelings against the death penalty have been able to effectively overrule death penalty sentences by holding that a prospective juror was improperly excused in violation of the *Witherspoon* decision. This has brought about criticism of those justices for not upholding the will of the people.

In the case of *Wainright* v. *Witt,* 83 L. Ed 2d 841 (1985), the United States Supreme Court somewhat relaxed the strict rule of the Witherspoon decision. In this case the Court set forth a new standard for determining when a prospective juror may be excused for cause because of his or her views on capital punishment. "That standard is whether the juror's views would prevent or substantially impair the performance of his duties as a juror in accordance with his instructions and his oath. We [the Supreme Court] note that, in addition to dispensing with Witherspoon's reference to 'automatic' decision making, this standard likewise does not require that a juror's bias be proved with 'unmistakable clarity.' "

It is important to remember that state appellate courts have the power to make rules for their own trial courts. These may be more restrictive than the ones set forth by the United States Supreme Court, and as such may still adhere to the strict rule set forth in the *Witherspoon* decision.

The voir dire examination of prospective jurors can be extensive in any type of case. To limit this examination some states have passed legislation permitting the trial judge to conduct the voir dire examination. In other states the trial judge will often call into the courtroom all of the jury panel selected to appear for the particular trial, and the judge will conduct a portion of the voir dire examination. The panel will be asked if they have any preconceived opinions on guilt or innocence as a result of pretrial publicity given to the case. The judge may also go into other phases of possible bias. Even though this procedure is followed, the prosecuting attorney and particularly the defense counsel are permitted a reasonable voir dire examination opportunity. Some judges conduct no voir dire examinations, as they believe that selecting the jury is the prerogative of the attorneys involved and that any interference with it is a denial of their rights. Most attorneys enjoy the privilege of conducting voir dire examinations in challenging for cause since it gives them an opportunity to become better acquainted with the jurors who are finally selected. Some courts frown on this reason for voir dire examinations as having no place in the justice system. These courts hold that voir dire examinations by the attorneys are for determining whether a juror should be disqualified by a challenge for cause. In these courts the attorneys are limited to questions pertinent to the cause for which they may be attempting to disqualify the juror. Other courts permit a certain freedom when questioning a prospective juror. This aids the attorneys in determining whether a peremptory challenge should be exercised when an undesired juror cannot be disqualified for cause. As long as the attorneys' questions relate to a challenge for cause, the questioning can be almost limitless, particularly when the cause is for bias. For this reason some judges try to limit the questioning to matters directly relating to the particular case involved. If a judge should be too restrictive in permitting the questioning by the defense counsel, a conviction could be reversed on appeal through the allegation that the jury was not impartial.

Peremptory Challenge

After the prosecution and defense have exhausted their challenges for cause, there is one more opportunity to remove an undesired juror or jurors. Each attorney is given the right to excuse a juror whom he may not want on the jury. The right to excuse a juror under these circumstances is known as a *peremptory challenge*. Both the prosecution and defense have a certain number of peremptory challenges that permit either attorney to excuse a juror without stating a reason. The challenges are granted upon the theory that they assist the attorneys in more nearly selecting an impartial jury. A prosecuting attorney, for example, may exercise the right of peremptory challenge to excuse a juror who, during challenge for cause, indicated reservations against the death penalty but could vote for a conviction if the evidence against the defendant was strong enough. Even though this is the real reason the juror was excused, the attorney does not have to give the reason. A defense attorney may excuse a juror who stated during challenge for cause that there was a feeling that the defendant was guilty but that it could be controlled with the juror guided by the evidence of the case.

Prohibiting the Peremptory Challenge

Generally, the judge has no authority to prohibit the juror from being excused on a peremptory challenge. However, the supreme court of one state held that when a prosecuting attorney used his peremptory challenges to exclude all black persons from the jury, the prosecutor was denying the defendant a fair trial. The court reversed the conviction, stating that it should have been obvious to the judge what the prosecutor was doing, and that the judge should have taken action to prevent the use of peremptory challenges in this manner. The holding of this state court was contrary to the ruling of the United States Supreme Court in *Swain* v. *Alabama*, 380 US 202 (1965), where it was held that the attorneys for each side were entitled to exercise their right of peremptory challenges without being supervised by the judge. The Court stated that if a contrary rule were adopted the challenge "would no longer be peremptory, each and every challenge being open to examination, either at the time of the challenge or at a hearing afterwards. The prosecutor's judgment underlying each challenge would be subject to scrutiny for reasonableness and sincerity." As these cases indicate, a state supreme court may make a ruling that is *more* restrictive than that of the United States Supreme Court of the prosecution's right to prove the defendant guilty beyond a reasonable doubt, but it may not make one that is *less* restrictive.

As in the case of the challenge for cause, when a juror is excused by the peremptory challenge, the court clerk will pick another name from the jury panel box, and that prospective juror will take the seat of the excused juror in the jury box. That juror and any others who may replace excused jurors may be questioned to determine if they should be challenged for cause. Thus another time-consuming procedure occurs in the selection of the jury. The number of peremptory challenges for the prosecution and the defense varies among states. Some states grant the prosecution and defense an equal number of peremptory challenges, usually ten each. Other states grant the defense ten challenges and the prosecution only five. Some jurisdictions grant more peremptory challenges for felony trials than for misdemeanor trials. Where the maximum penalty is death, most jurisdictions permit twice as many peremptory challenges as in noncapital cases.

Holding Challenges in Reserve

Both the prosecuting attorney and the defense attorney will hold one or two of their peremptory challenges in reserve. The reason is that a person who is most unsatisfactory to one side or the other may have his name drawn from the panel, leaving no way to disqualify this person for cause. If all the peremptory challenges have been exhausted there is no way of preventing that person from being a juror. The person may have a history of never having voted for conviction, or a known dislike for a particular race or religion, yet this dislike cannot be established in questioning for cause. Defense attorneys generally do not like to have law enforcement officers, either active or retired, on a jury, as such a person has a tendency to assume guilt from the mere arrest and formal charging of the defendant. This type of tendency may be impossible to establish in order to excuse the officer on cause, but no cause is needed in the peremptory challenge. Both prosecuting attorneys and defense attorneys will question prospective jurors for cause as extensively as the court will permit. This questioning enables them to get a better idea as to how a particular prospective juror may think or react in reaching a verdict. The attorneys may then utilize their peremptory challenges more effectively.

Who Make the Best Jurors?

All attorneys engaged in the trial of cases, whether civil or criminal, constantly try to analyze persons in an effort to determine who make the best jurors. There is no way to predict how a person will react in each instance, but attorneys feel that certain groups or classes of persons tend to react in more definite patterns than others. For example, defense attorneys feel that minority groups who have encountered hardships and discrimination tend to be more tolerant of defendants than members of the white Anglo groups of medium or higher income. Younger persons are alleged to be more permissive and forgiving in their attitudes toward a defendant, particularly if the defendant is also a younger person. This is why defense attorneys try to have more persons between the ages of eighteen and twenty-one on jury panels as well as more members of minority groups. But obtaining these classes of people for jury duty is not easy. Many younger persons attending school are excused so that their school year will not be interrupted. If not in school many are married and are in a lower income bracket, as are many in minority groups who are excused from jury duty because of the extreme financial hardship that might be suffered. In most jurisdictions the compensation for jury duty is meager, as it is considered to be a civic duty to serve on a criminal trial jury. Jurors in some areas receive only $5 a day plus a small mileage fee. It has been recommended that the compensation be increased in order that younger persons and those of minority groups in lower income brackets may afford to serve on the jury. But court costs are already extremely high and each increase in jury fees makes the court costs that much greater, another burden on the taxpayer. A few jurisdictions have increased the jurors' compensation to ease the financial hardship suffered by those who serve as well as to obtain a wider selection of persons.

Many attorneys feel that the middle-aged housewife is the most satisfactory juror because she takes pride in serving on a jury; takes the duty seriously; endeavors to conscientiously evaluate the evidence presented during the trial; and attempts to arrive at a just verdict. The financial burden upon her is not as great as on others, and she is not worried about small children who may need her attention at home.

After the prosecution and defense have exhausted their challenges for cause, have no desire to further exercise their right of peremptory challenges, and indicate to the judge that they are satisfied with the jury selected, the jury will then be sworn to perform their duty. The oath administered to the jurors will in substance be that each of them will endeavor to reach a true and just verdict based on the evidence of the case. After the jurors have been sworn in, the trial begins. Some jurisdictions still swear jurors individually, but most jurisdictions will administer the oath to the jury as a group once they have been selected and accepted by both sides and the judge.

Alternate Jurors

Records reveal that often during a lengthy trial one or more jurors become incapacitated and cannot continue as a juror. If this happens and the defendant does not agree to continue the trial with those jurors remaining, the judge must declare a mistrial, and the trial must be restarted. If several weeks have elapsed before the juror becomes incapacitated, having to start the trial over is most frustrating, as well as expensive. To avoid the possibility of having to start a new trial, most states have statutes providing that alternate jurors may be selected at the discretion of the trial judge. Determining the approximate time that the prosecution and defense plan to take in presenting their sides of the case enables the judge to decide if and how many alternate jurors should be selected.

Alternate jurors are selected in the same manner as regular jurors. The alternates may be challenged for cause, and usually one additional peremptory challenge is granted for each alternate selected. The judge may decide that only one alternate will be necessary, or he may decide on more if the trial is to be extremely lengthy. Usually not more than four alternates are selected. If there is more than one alternate and one of the regular jurors becomes incapacitated, the clerk will draw the name of the alternate who will be substituted for the incapacitated juror. Some states permit an alternate to be substituted for an incapacitated juror up to the time that the case is given to the jury for deliberation. Other states permit an alternate to be substituted any time before the verdict is reached. The alternate jurors must be situated in the courtroom where they can observe all of the proceedings and can hear all that takes place. Usually an area next to the jury box is reserved for alternate jurors to facilitate their being able to see and hear. After selection, the alternate jurors are given the same oath as the regular jury.

The use of the alternate juror system has been criticized by some legal scholars. They allege that the alternate juror creates a jury of thirteen instead of twelve, particularly if the alternate is substituted during the deliberation. It has been alleged that permitting a substitution during the deliberation handicaps the alternate juror as he has not had the benefit of the group dynamics during the preceding deliberation. Because of these criticisms some states do not permit substitution after the deliberation begins, and once the case is given to the jury for a verdict, the alternate juror or jurors are discharged. The problem created by discharging alternate jurors at the time of deliberation is that, after a lengthy trial, the deliberation could take several days and a juror could possibly become incapacitated during that time. If this happens, the jury would have to be dismissed and the trial started over, thus defeating the purpose of the alternate juror system. Those jurisdictions permitting a substitution of an alternate during deliberation believe that there is no reason why the alternate could not be thoroughly briefed on the deliberation up to the time of the substitution, thus enabling the alternate to cast an intelligent vote for the verdict.

The alternate jury system has also been criticized as unfair to the defendant because the alternate juror, knowing that chances of substitution are slight, may not take much interest in the case and be unable to properly evaluate the evidence during deliberation if substituted. To overcome this possibility it has been proposed that, if alternate jurors are to be selected, the entire jury—including alternates—be selected at one time. At the time the case is given to the jury for deliberation, the court clerk would draw twelve names from the jury selection box. In this way none of the jurors would know who were regulars and alternates until all the evidence of the case had been presented, and all would have an equal interest in the presentation.

Although the alternate juror system has been criticized by some as being unfair to the defendant, these criticisms seem shallow compared to the benefits gained by having a juror who can replace one who may become incapacitated. It must be remembered that the alternate juror system was established because, in most instances, a defendant will not agree to continue a trial with less than a full jury should one of the jurors become incapacitated. The refusal to continue with the trial is usually based on the belief that delays in a trial work to the defendant's advantage. In addition, it is impossible to make every situation arising in the justice system idealistic for the defendant. In fact, many in the justice system feel that the system is already balanced heavily in favor of the defendant.

Sequestering the Jury

Once the jury has been selected and sworn in, the judge must decide whether it is to be *sequestered,* or "locked up." When a jury is sequestered, it is segregated from all outside contact. The primary reason for the sequestering of the jury is to protect its members from possible outside influence in arriving at their verdict. When not in the courtroom, the jurors are kept together as a body at all times under the guard of a bailiff or some other court officer. They eat together and are housed in a hotel, motel, or some other convenient place until the trial is concluded. Even the newspapers that they may be permitted to read or the news broadcasts that they may listen to must be monitored to ensure that nothing which might affect their verdict is brought to their attention. As was pointed out in the *Sheppard* case, the jury was aware of the extensive news media publicity throughout the entire trial. According to the United States Supreme Court, it influenced the jury in their opinion on guilt, and the United States Supreme Court reversed the conviction. The Court suggested that the judge should have had greater control over the news releases or sequestered the jury during the trial to prevent undue influence. Generally it is held that when a jury is not sequestered, the judge has the authority to forbid the jurors from reading any newspapers or listening to any broadcasts about the case, and if they should inadvertently read about or listen to something about the case, they are to disregard it.

In a few states the jury must be sequestered during a trial on certain charges, but otherwise sequestering is at the discretion of the judge. The jury may be sequestered at any time during the trial proceedings. The jury may be sequestered on the judge's own decision or at the request of either the prosecution or defense. If the jury is not sequestered during the presentation of the evidence, it will usually be sequestered during the deliberation when the trial pertains to a serious charge. In a few jurisdictions the jury must be sequestered during the deliberation. If the jury is sequestered, the alternate jurors are sequestered also, but are generally sequestered separately from the regular jury.

In those jurisdictions where it is at the judge's discretion to sequester the jury prior to the time of deliberation, most judges hesitate to sequester the jury because of the hardship imposed. The jurors lose all contact with their families and friends during the period of sequestration. Most of the jurors are unacquainted with one another before the trial begins, yet must be housed together. Often personality clashes occur, affecting their judgment during the deliberation. From the standpoint of the taxpayer, sequestering a jury is an expensive proposition because taxes pay for housing and feeding the jury during this period.

Most jurors dislike being sequestered, and when that possibility is apparent, prospective jurors will do everything possible to be excused from that particular trial. Thus in addition to the hardships experienced by the jurors themselves, selecting a jury becomes even more difficult than usual. When a jury is sequestered during a trial at the request of the prosecution or defense, it is the policy of the judge not to inform the jury which side made the request in order to avoid any prejudice by the jurors toward that side. Whether the jury is sequestered or not, each time the court is adjourned, the judge must advise the jurors against discussing the facts of the case among themselves or with others, and against forming any opinions about the case until the time of deliberation.

The Future of the Jury System

Interviews with persons who have accepted their duty to serve on criminal juries reveal that many become disenchanted with the jury system.

The most common complaint is the time spent by prospective jurors waiting to be called for duty on a particular case. Many wait hours in the uncomfortable surroundings of the courthouse halls. Some even wait all day without being called, only to be ordered to return the next day to suffer a similar experience. This waiting usually stems from last-minute requests for continuances, hearings on other motions presented, or plea bargainings.

Many persons believe that average jurors are neither able to cope with the facts of the more complex trials, nor able to understand and abide by the instructions given them by the judge. There are those who feel that too many jurors permit emotions and personality conflicts to interfere with judgment in arriving at a verdict. In those states where the unanimous verdict must be returned, one juror may prevent such a verdict from being rendered just because of an emotional or personality conflict thereby hampering the justice system. Many persons believe that our justice system would not come to a sudden halt if the jury system were abolished and verdicts were decided by a body of three or more judges. Irrespective of what persons may think or believe, as long as the Sixth Amendment guarantee to a trial by jury is in effect, the jury system will not be eliminated.

Review Questions

1. Who are one's peers as the term relates to a jury?
2. In what amendment is the right to trial by an impartial jury found?
3. What is a jury panel or jury list?
4. List four qualifications for being a juror.
5. What persons may be exempt from jury duty and why is the exemption granted?
6. What is meant by challenging a juror for cause?
7. List three possible challenges for cause.
8. What is the purpose of permitting a challenge for cause?
9. What is a peremptory challenge?
10. Who are alternate jurors and why are they selected?
11. What is meant by sequestering the jury?
12. Explain the purpose of sequestering a jury.

Local Procedure

1. What are the qualifications for a juror?
2. If a juror becomes incapacitated may he or she be replaced by an alternate during the deliberation?
3. Must the jury be sequestered? If so, at what point during the trial?
4. How many peremptory challenges are permitted to the prosecution and the defense?

TRIAL PROCEDURE

twelve

Opening Statements

In order that the jury may be informed of both the charge against the defendant and the plea entered, it is the policy of most courts to have the accusatory pleading read to the jury. If the charge is a felony the accusatory pleading will be an information or an indictment, depending on the circumstances. If the charge is a misdemeanor the accusatory pleading is usually a complaint that may or may not be read depending upon the custom of the jurisdiction.

Prosecuting Attorney Opening Statement

After the jury has been sworn in and the charge read to them, the prosecution is the first to present its evidence. Prior to calling the first witness the judge will ask the prosecuting attorney if he or she wishes to make an opening statement. An opening statement will be made in most instances, as it provides an opportunity to further explain the charge against the defendant. By making an opening statement the prosecuting attorney is able to outline the evidence planned for the trial, thereby allowing the jury to more intelligently follow the presentation of the prosecution's side of the case. The opening statement is probably more important in jury trials than in court trials because it orients the jury as to what is to follow and prepares them for the evidence.

The prosecuting attorney has considerable latitude in referring to the evidence that he plans to introduce during the trial, but the statements are not considered facts of the case. If for some reason the evidence is not admitted, the jury may not consider the attorney's statements as evidence of the case. It has been held to be *prejudicial error* for a prosecuting attorney to mention evidence known to be inadmissible. Prejudicial error may result from a statement or an act of misconduct by a prosecuting attorney or a witness that will prevent the defendant from getting a fair trial, or that is so prejudicial that either a mistrial will be declared, or a conviction reversed on appeal. It is also prejudicial error for a prosecuting attorney to refer to the defendant as an ex-convict, or to imply that he has committed prior crimes. A defendant is entitled to be tried on the facts stated in the accusatory pleading; any reference to other crimes or prior convictions is considered to be so prejudicial against the defendant that the judge may declare a mistrial at that time. If the judge does not declare a mistrial and the defendant is convicted, the conviction may be reversed on appeal.

Defense Counsel Opening Statement

After the prosecuting attorney has completed the opening statement, the judge will often ask if the defense attorney wishes to make an opening statement. In some jurisdictions, the judge may delay the defense attorney's opening statement until after the prosecution has presented its side of the case. Many defense attorneys believe that it is a mistake to make an opening statement before the prosecution has completed its side of the presentation of the evidence, as the defense strategy may change. If an opening statement is made before the prosecution presents its side of the evidence, statements may be made that will not conform with the defense strategy, and the jury may be confused as to what happened or question the innocence of the defendant. In making an opening statement immediately after the prosecuting attorney has made his opening statement, the defense attorney alerts the prosecution to the anticipated defense—which most defense attorneys try to avoid. Many defense attorneys waive the right of making an opening statement at any time, as they feel that the disadvantages of making one outweigh the advantages. Often defense witnesses do not measure up to expectation or do not appear at all. If their testimony has been previously outlined, the jury may question the validity of the defense.

On the other hand some defense attorneys believe that it is a mistake not to make an opening statement immediately following the opening statement of the prosecuting attorney. They theorize that the prosecuting attorney will have made a favorable impression on the jury and it is dangerous not to challenge those statements immediately. These defense attorneys state that it is not necessary to go into any detail of the defense at that time. They can merely inform the jury that the defense plans to present evidence to prove that the facts of the case are not as alleged by the prosecuting attorney. These defense attorneys will request the jury to keep an open mind until the defense has the opportunity to present contrary evidence.

Reasonable Doubt

In our system of justice the defendant in a criminal case is presumed to be innocent until proved otherwise. It is the burden of the prosecution to prove the defendant guilty beyond a reasonable doubt. The United States Supreme Court has held in a number of cases that proof of a criminal charge *beyond a reasonable doubt* is constitutionally required though not included in the Bill of Rights. This Court stated in the case of *In re Winship*, 397 US 358 (1970):

> . . . it is the duty of the Government to estabish guilt beyond a reasonable doubt. This notion—basic in our law and rightly one of the boasts of a free society—is a requirement and safeguard of due process of law in the historic, procedural content of due process . . . that guilt in a criminal case must be proved beyond a reasonable doubt and by evidence confined to that which long

experience in the common-law tradition, to some extent embodied in the Constitution, has crystallized into rules of evidence consistent with that standard. These rules are historically grounded rights of our system, developed to safeguard men from dubious and unjust convictions, with resulting forfeitures of life, liberty and property. . . .

The requirement of proof beyond a reasonable doubt has this vital role in our criminal procedure for cogent reasons. The accused during a criminal prosecution has at stake interests of immense importance, both because of the possibility that he may lose his liberty upon conviction and because of the certainty that he would be stigmatized by the conviction. Accordingly, a society that values the good name and freedom of every individual should not condemn a man for commission of a crime when there is reasonable doubt about his guilt. . . .

Moreover, use of the reasonable doubt standard is indispensable to command the respect and confidence of the community in application of the criminal law. It is critical that the moral force of the criminal law not be diluted by a standard of proof which leaves people in doubt whether innocent men are being condemned. It is also important in our free society that every individual going about his ordinary affairs have confidence that his government cannot adjudge him guilty of a criminal offense without convincing a proper factfinder of his guilt with utmost certainty.

The term *reasonable doubt* is familiar to all. Yet many jurors are confused concerning the real meaning of the term and when it has been reached. They desire some explanation, but the more one tries to interpret the meaning of reasonable doubt, the more confusing it becomes. To further confuse the issue some courts and statutes have provided that the defendant must be proved guilty beyond a reasonable doubt and to a moral certainty. A statute of one state defines reasonable doubt as follows:

It is not a mere possible doubt; because everything relating to human affairs, and depending upon moral evidence, is open to some possible or imaginary doubt. It is that state of the case, which, after the entire comparison and consideration of all the evidence, leaves the minds of jurors in that condition that they cannot say they feel an abiding conviction, to a moral certainty, of the truth of the charge.

After reading this definition there is some question as to whether the jury would have any better understanding as to the meaning of reasonable doubt than before. To state it in a simpler form, it is that doubt which a juror may have after weighing all the evidence of the case and is still not satisfied that the defendant is guilty of the crime charged.

Witnesses

The defendant is entitled to be confronted by the witnesses against him or her. As stated by the United States Supreme Court in *California* v. *Green,* 399 US 149 (1970), this confrontation:

> . . . (1) insures that the witness will give his statements under oath—thus impressing him with the seriousness of the matter and guarding against the lie by the possibility of a penalty for perjury; (2) forces the witness to submit to cross-examination, the "greatest legal engine ever invented for the discovery of the truth"; (3) permits the jury that is to decide the defendant's fate to observe the demeanor of the witness in making his statement, thus aiding the jury in assessing his credibility.

Since the defendant has the right to be confronted by opposing witnesses, most of the prosecution's evidence attempting to prove guilt beyond a reasonable doubt will be presented through the testimony of witnesses.

There are two kinds of witnesses, the *lay* or ordinary witness and the *expert* witness. The lay witness is an individual who has some personal knowledge of the facts of the case derived from personal perceptions, that is, from what was seen, heard, or felt. An expert witness is an individual who has knowledge and skill in a particular field that is beyond the knowledge of the average man on the street. The expert witness gives the judge and the jury the benefit of acquired knowledge, often in the form of an opinion, to assist them in arriving at the truth of a matter. The jury may accept the opinion of the expert or reject it as they see fit. Before an expert witness may testify, the side calling this witness must qualify him or her as an expert. By training, experience, or education, the expert witness must prove knowledge or skill in a particular field above that of the average person on the street. This ability is established by questioning the witness concerning ability in a particular field. The judge must then declare the witness to be qualified as an expert before testimony or an opinion on the facts of the case may be given. Establishing the qualifications of the expert witness is referred to as a voir dire examination.

It is not necessary for the prosecution to call every person who has some knowledge about the facts of the case to be a witness. The prosecuting attorney must call enough witnesses to prove the defendant guilty beyond a reasonable doubt. It is difficult to determine how many witnesses this will take in any given case. At first glance, it may appear that the prosecuting attorney should not gamble on how many witnesses should be called, but should call all that may know something about the case. However to accept testimony from every person who may have some personal knowledge about the case could be most time consuming and cause the jury to become weary and lose interest in the prosecution's presentation. But the prosecution will call all the witnesses necessary to completely relate the story of what happened in the case. In addition, a few witnesses will probably be called to corroborate the testimony of other witnesses. The prosecution will have to present those witnesses necessary to establish that a crime was committed—that is, it will have to prove the elements of the crime. This process of proving that a crime was committed is known as establishing the *corpus delicti.*

The sequence in which the witnesses are called to testify may not result in the events being related in the same sequence in which they occurred. The prosecuting attorney will decide the sequence in accordance with how the facts can best be presented in a logical, understandable manner.

The Subpoena

Persons are officially notified to appear in court as witnesses by a legal document known as a subpoena. Subpoenas will be issued for the attendance of both prosecution and defense witnesses. Depending upon the jurisdiction, a subpoena may be issued by a judge, prosecuting attorney, clerk of the court, or public defender. A copy of a typical subpoena appears in figure 12-1.

Occasionally a witness will be commanded to bring books, papers, documents, or other physical evidence with him. If so, a *subpoena duces tecum* will be issued to the witness. The subpoena duces tecum follows the same general form as the subpoena, but includes a description of the material that the witness is to produce in court.

Generally a subpoena or subpoena duces tecum may be served by anyone, but most frequently it will be served by an officer of the court. Service is made by personally delivering a copy of the subpoena to the witness. After the service is made, the person serving the subpoena will make a written return on a copy of the subpoena stating the date, time, and place that the service was made.

It has been held that a person owes a duty to society to appear and testify as a witness in criminal cases when subpoenaed to do so. Because of this duty, witnesses generally are not compensated when appearing to testify. Yet it is recognized that a witness should not suffer undue financial hardship in performing duty as a witness. Since a subpoena is valid anyplace within the state in which it is issued, most jurisdictions provide for the payment of reasonable travel expenses to a witness who must travel a great distance to testify. Before a witness can be com-

FIGURE 12-1 Sample of a subpoena

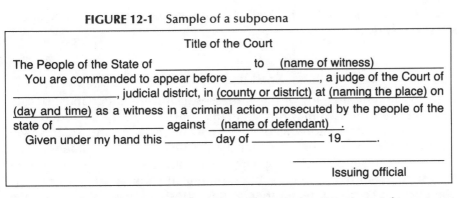

pensated in some jurisdictions, the judge involved in the trial must endorse the subpoena with a statement that the witness is a material witness and that this attendance is absolutely necessary.

Witnesses Failing to Appear

The failure of a witness to appear as commanded in a subpoena can bring about contempt of court charges unless good cause for not appearing can be shown. In addition to being held in contempt the witness, if subpoenaed by the defense, can in some states be civilly sued by the defendant for failure to appear. It is not necessary for a person to be served with a subpoena to be a witness. The witness may orally agree to appear, but cannot be held in contempt for failing to be present at the trial.

In the past, since a subpoena was good only within the state in which it was issued, there was no way to command the appearance of a witness who was out of the state. Today most states have adopted the "Uniform Act to Secure the Attendance of Witnesses from without the State in Criminal Cases." This Act enables a court to command the appearance of a material witness beyond the jurisdiction of the court because the witness resides in another state. The court in which the witness is needed to appear will issue a certificate naming this person as a material witness, the date and place that he is to appear, and the approximate number of days that the person will be needed as a witness. This certificate is transmitted to the appropriate court in the state where the needed witness resides. The court in that state will order the witness to come before it for a hearing to determine if the person is a necessary and material witness, and whether any undue hardship will be caused by the person appearing in the other state as a witness. If the judge concludes that the person is a necessary and material witness and that no hardship will be suffered, the person will be tendered expense money and ordered to appear in the demanding court as a witness. Should the person fail to appear as commanded, contempt of court charges may be filed in the state where the material witness resides. This witness is immune from arrest on any prior crimes committed in the demanding state while in the state to testify.

Excluding Witnesses

Prior to the time that any of the witnesses testify, the judge must decide whether the witnesses may remain in the courtroom or be excluded until after they have testified. This decision may be made on the judge's own motion or on the request of either the prosecution or the defense. The primary purpose for excluding witnesses from the courtroom is to prevent them from trying to corroborate the testimony of other witnesses. The effort to corroborate another witness's testimony is not always done with an intent to falsify. It may be done because one witness may be uncertain of some of the facts. Although witnesses are excluded from the courtroom, it is almost impossible to keep them from conversing about their testimony even though the judge admonishes them against such action.

Examination of Witnesses

The Oath

Before being permitted to testify, an oath must be administered in which the witness promises to tell the truth. Throughout the history of trial by jury, witnesses have given an oath that their allegations are true. In the past, these oaths have involved a call to the deity to assist the oathgiver in substantiating the truthfulness of the statements made, as well as a call for assistance in telling the truth. It was the general belief that, after giving such an oath, should one falsely testify, divine punishment would result. So strong was the belief in divine punishment at common law that if one did not believe in God, the person was considered incompetent to testify.

Although most jurisdictions presently do not prescribe wording for the oath administered to a witness, generally a call to the deity to assist the witness in telling the truth is still included. Oaths which are administered to witnesses today are substantially as follows: "Do you hereby solemnly swear to tell the truth, and nothing but the truth, in the matter now pending before this court, so help you God?" At one time while this oath was being administered, the witness was required to raise the right hand and lay the left hand on a Bible. Most jurisdictions have dispensed with the use of the Bible in administering the oath, but the witness is still required to raise his right hand during administration of the oath.

Affirmation.   Although there is no requirement that the word God be mentioned in the oath, it usually is included. Some persons find that "swearing to God" to tell the truth is objectionable. They feel this way either because they believe that the use of the word God under the circumstances is sacrilegious, or because they do not believe in a God and object to swearing to something in which they have no belief. To accommodate these individuals, courts permit them to *affirm* to tell the truth. When the court clerk, or other court officer, administers the oath, or *swears in* the witness as the procedure is known, the witness is asked to stand and be sworn. If the oath is found objectable, the witness will advise the officer that the truth will be affirmed. The officer will then require the witness to raise the right hand and the officer will state words to this effect: "Do you hereby solemnly affirm to tell the truth and nothing but the truth in the matter now pending before this court?" This procedure has been referred to as an *affirmation*. Whether a witness swears to tell the truth or affirms to tell the truth, both procedures are technically known as the "oath."

There are a few legal scholars who argue that administering the oath is a useless procedure and a waste of time as it does not guarantee that the witness will testify truthfully. But the great majority of persons engaged in the trial of cases believe that administering the oath to the witness gives a certain legal solemnity to the occasion, and may cause the witness to reflect upon the necessity to tell the truth. As is stated in the federal procedure, the wording of the oath may be of any nature that will awaken the witness to the necessity of telling the truth.

Even though the oath may not guarantee that the truth will be told, the witness may be prosecuted for perjury if testimony is intentionally falsified after the oath is administered. This threat may be enough to encourage some to testify truthfully, where they might not otherwise.

Refusal to be Sworn.   If a witness refuses to be sworn, a contempt of court charge can be filed against the witness. The only exception to the administration of the oath to a witness is in the case of a small child or a mentally retarded person who may not understand the meaning of the oath. Under these circumstances before the child or mentally retarded person is allowed to testify, the judge will conduct a voir dire examination to determine if the prospective witness knows that it is wrong to tell a falsehood and of the necessity to tell the truth. If this can be established by the judge through the questioning of the prospective witness, the oath will be eliminated.

Direct Examination

After the oath has been administered to the witness, he will begin his testimony, that is, facts will be related within the witness's knowledge of the case. Prior to making any statements about the case, the witness will be required to state name, address, and in some instances occupation for identification purposes. Because of threats that have been made to law enforcement officers and their families, some jurisdictions permit the officers to give the address of their headquarters instead of their home address. After the identification data is furnished by the prosecution witness, the prosecuting attorney will start the examination. The questioning of the witness by the side that calls him is known as *direct examination.* The prosecuting attorney may approach the direct examination in one of two ways or in a combination of both. The prosecuting attorney may request the witness to relate in his own words the facts about the case. This procedure is sometimes referred to as the *narrative* approach. The prosecuting attorney may also use the *short question and answer* approach. Both procedures have their advantages and disadvantages. The narrative approach permits the witness to tell the story in a more logical form so that the jury may be better able to follow the testimony. But unless the witness is familiar with the rules of evidence, irrelevant material and hearsay evidence may be included, or facts may be related that the prosecuting attorney wishes to avoid. By asking the witness short direct questions, the prosecuting attorney has greater control over the facts to be related and can limit the testimony to relevant facts. The short question and answer form of examination is frequently time consuming, and sometimes this type of testimony becomes boring to the jury. If a witness is shy or perhaps somewhat reluctant to testify, it may be necessary to revert to the short question and answer procedure.

During the direct examination the attorney may not ask the witness leading questions. A leading question is one that indicates the desired answer to the witness. For example, the attorney may ask the witness: "You did see the defendant threaten the victim with a knife, didn't you?" Clearly the attorney wants a "yes" answer. But by rephrasing the question, the witness may be asked: "Did you see the defendant threaten the victim with a knife?" Although the attorney may still desire a "yes" answer, it has not been indicated to the witness, and the witness is free to give either a "yes" or "no" answer. The mere fact that a question calls for a "yes" or "no" answer does not make it a leading one, but if phrased to indicate the answer desired, it is a leading question. The reason why these questions are not generally permitted during direct examination is that the side that calls the witness is usually favored, and there may be a tendency to assist that side irrespective of the truth, if a desired answer is indicated.

Occasionally a witness called by the prosecution will display hostility toward the prosecution, making the expected testimony most difficult to obtain. Under these circumstances the prosecuting attorney may request the judge to declare for the record that the witness is a *hostile witness*. If the witness is declared to be hostile, the prosecuting attorney may then ask leading questions. This is permitted because it is assumed that the witness will answer truthfully, because of the displayed hostility, even though a desired answer is indicated. Even though a hostile witness may be asked leading questions during direct examination, that does not mean that obtaining the desired testimony from the witness will become any less difficult. To be declared a hostile witness, a person must display hostility and uncooperativeness. The mere fact that a witness does not meet expectations or is reluctant to furnish information will not be sufficient grounds for the judge to declare the witness hostile.

A limited use of leading questions is permitted in the examination of children, senior citizens, and mentally retarded persons, in order to assist them in telling their stories. Leading questions may also be asked concerning identifying matters, such as name, address, and place of employment, pertaining to the witness, since these matters are usually not in controversy. Occasionally a leading question may be permitted to assist in refreshing the memory of a witness.

Objections to Questions

During the direct examination by the prosecuting attorney, the defense attorney may object to some of the questions asked. If so, the objection will be indicated to the judge who must rule upon the objection. After an objection is made the witness should not answer the question until the judge has ruled on it. If the judge believes that the objection is well founded, he or she will *sustain* the objection, meaning that the witness may not answer the question. If the judge does not agree with the objection, he will *overrule* the objection, whereupon the witness must answer. There are any number of reasons why the defense attorney may object to a question. The question may call for an answer that would be hearsay information; it may be leading; or it may require the witness to state an opinion about some matter. If the prosecution asks an improper question or one that calls for information that is not admissible, unless the defense attorney objects, the answer is permitted to go into the record of the case and generally is not grounds for appeal should the defendant be convicted. For this reason defense attorneys make frequent objections during the trial. From a psychological standpoint, defense attorneys may also inject objections from time to time in an effort to lessen the impact of the testimony of the prosecution's witness.

Occasionally a witness will become overzealous in answering the prosecuting attorney's questions and will answer a question to which an objection is made before the judge is able to rule on it. If the objection is overruled no serious consequences result, other than the judge becoming irritated because the witness did not wait for the ruling. However if the objection is sustained the answer has been improperly given, and it must be stricken from the record with the jury being advised to disregard the answer. But the problem is, can a jury completely forget such a statement? Knowing the difficulty of disregarding some statements, especially if the answer is highly prejudicial against the defendant, the judge may declare a mistrial, and the case will have to be restarted with a different jury. In addition the witness could be held in contempt of court particularly if previously admonished against answering before the judge could rule on an objection.

Cross-examination

After the prosecuting attorney has concluded questioning the witness on direct examination, the defense attorney is permitted to cross-examine the witness. The primary purpose of cross-examination is to assist in arriving at the truth. Cross-examination enables the opposition or adversary to challenge the witness's veracity, accuracy, and prejudices. One of the basic reasons that the accused is entitled to confront adverse witnesses is to enable cross-examination. This right was made mandatory on the States by the case of *Pointer* v. *Texas,* 380 US 400 (1965). The United States Supreme Court stated in the *Pointer* decision:

> . . . We hold today that the Sixth Amendment's right of an accused to confront the witnesses against him is likewise a fundamental right and is made obligatory on the States by the Fourteenth Amendment.

> It cannot seriously be doubted at this late date that the right of cross-examination is included in the right of an accused in a criminal case to confront the witnesses against him. And probably no one, certainly no one experienced in the trial of lawsuits, would deny the value of cross-examination in exposing falsehood and bringing out the truth in a trial of a criminal case . . . the right of cross-examination is one of the safeguards essential to a fair trial.

If the defense attorney believes that the witness told the truth during the direct examination and nothing is to be gained by cross-examining the witness, the right to cross-examine that particular witness may be waived. Cross-examination is at best a dangerous procedure for a defense attorney. Before deciding whether to cross-examine a witness, the defense counsel must carefully weigh whether there is more to be lost than gained by the cross-examination. If a witness was telling the truth during direct examination, the cross-examination may merely result in the witness being able to re-emphasize the story to the jury. There is also the possibility that the witness may become emotionally upset by vigorous cross-examination, thus often receiving the sympathy of the jury.

Impeachment. On the other hand, if a witness testified falsely during direct examination, has made prior inconsistent statements, or has colored the testimony because of some prejudice, these facts may only be disclosed to the jury through cross-examination. Cross-examination under these circumstances is necessary in order that the jury may disregard the testimony or give it the proper weight. This devaluation of the testimony by cross-examination is referred to as *impeachment* in the field of evidence.

Generally cross-examination is an unpleasant experience for both the witness and the attorney. As was pointed out, if the witness told the truth during direct examination and cannot be upset by cross-examination, the defense attorney may suffer the unpleasantness of the witness retelling the story to the jury. Many times a defense attorney does not receive the answer anticipated during cross-examination, but is usually bound by the answer and often is powerless to overcome the damage it may cause. If a witness testifies truthfully during direct examination, there is usually little to fear from cross-examination. However, there are a few attorneys who feel that the only way to properly represent the defendant in a criminal case is to vigorously cross-examine all witnesses. If the witness has given testimony particularly damaging to the defense, the defense attorney may endeavor to devaluate the testimony by belittling or embarrassing the witness during cross-examination. Although having the responsibility of protecting a witness from overzealous cross-examination, the judge may not unduly restrict the defense attorney from vigorous cross-examination. Occasionally a witness may have been indiscreet in some action or statement made that may be brought out during cross-examination, and the judge would be powerless to prevent this embarrassment. If the witness, and particularly the law enforcement officer, has testified discreetly in conduct and content, any attempt at embarrassment by the defense attorney may result in the officer's favor. Juries often react unfavorably to this cross-examination tactic.

Although leading questions may not generally be asked during direct examination, they are permitted on cross-examination if the attorney feels that utilizing them is an advantage. Leading questions are frequently asked during vigorous cross-examination. The reason that these questions are permitted during cross-examination is that usually the witness who is being cross-examined is not favorable to the side doing the cross-examining, and the witness will not give a desired answer even though it is indicated unless it is the truth.

Limited Cross-Examination. States differ as to the extent of the cross-examination. A majority of the states limit the cross-examination to the facts brought out during direct examination. This procedure is referred to as *limited* or *restricted cross-examination.* Other states permit the witness to be cross-examined about any pertinent facts in the case that may be within the knowledge of the witness. This procedure is known as *unlimited* or *unrestricted cross-examination*. Those favoring the restricted cross-examination allege that attorneys are able to control the material that is presented by a witness, and may prepare the presentation in a more logical manner. This enables the jury to more closely follow the facts as they unfold. Those who advocate the unrestricted cross-examination allege that the unrestricted procedure saves time. A witness may be examined extensively while on the stand rather than being recalled at a later time. Also the procedure eliminates objections by the opposing side that the questions asked during cross-examination did not pertain to matters brought out during direct examination. In those states following the restricted cross-examination procedure witnesses are usually cautioned to confine their answers to questions asked during direct examination and not to volunteer additional information, as they may subject themselves to unnecessary and extensive cross-examination. This is one of the dangers of permitting the story to be told in the witness's own words, as facts may be included that could be used to devaluate the testimony during cross-examination. Whether the restricted or unrestricted procedure is followed, witnesses are seldom permitted to give the facts in their own way during cross-examination. The cross-examiner desires to control the testimony and can better do so by confining the questions to ones that require short answers, often only a "yes" or "no."

Redirect Examination and Recross-Examination.   After the defense attorney has completed his cross-examination, the judge will permit the prosecuting attorney to further question his own witness. This questioning is known as *redirect examination*. The questioning must be confined to clarifying facts brought out during cross-examination. Sometimes the defense attorney will require that the witness answer a question with only a "yes" or "no," but the answer does not reflect the true situation without further explanation. When the prosecuting attorney further questions the witness after cross-examination, the answers can be explained more fully by the witness. Seldom will a judge permit any new material to be brought forth during the redirect examination. To do so would start the whole questioning process again and could encourage sloppy practice by attorneys by not properly preparing the direct examination. Unless the prosecuting attorney believes that redirect examination will be beneficial, it may be waived.

If the prosecuting attorney further questions the witness on redirect examination, at the conclusion of this questioning the defense attorney is entitled to recross-examine the witness on facts stated on redirect examination. After this series takes place the witness is excused, and the next witness is called. The same sequence of examinations may take place with each prosecution and defense witness that is called, or the sequence could stop after the direct examination. When the whole series is repeated with each witness, criminal trials can become most lengthy.

Refusal to Answer Questions

The witness must answer all questions asked throughout the entire examination. The only exception is that if the answer to a question will incriminate the witness, the witness may refuse to answer the question. An incriminating answer is one that would subject the witness to prosecution. The Fifth Amendment to the United States Constitution provides that one may not be compelled to witness against oneself. But all other questions must be answered even though the answer may be embarrassing or life-endangering to the witness or his family. The degrading or endangering questions must be pertinent to the case, however, and not asked merely to embarrass the witness. Otherwise the judge may not permit the question to be answered. Refusal to answer questions occurs more frequently during cross-examination than during direct examination. It is during the cross-examination that the witness is questioned by the adversary, and it is then that questions may be asked that the witness would be hesitant to answer. If a witness persists in refusing to answer a question that is not incriminating, the entire testimony may be stricken from the record and the jury advised to disregard it. It is held that a witness may not testify to those facts that may be favorable and refuse to testify concerning matters that may be unfavorable. In addition to having the testimony stricken from the record, the witness could be held in contempt of court until the questions were answered.

There are times during a trial when arriving at the truth of what happened is more important than the prosecution of some witness incriminated by answering a question. Under these circumstances the witness may be granted immunity from prosecution by the judge. If immunity is granted, the witness must answer all questions.

Examination by the Judge and Jury

Although it is the primary responsibility of the prosecution and defense to call and examine the witnesses that they believe necessary, witnesses may also be called by the trial judge if deemed necessary in the interest of justice. Most jurisdictions permit the judge to question prosecution and defense witnesses if it may furnish further information not brought forth by the prosecutor or defense counsel. Occasionally a juror may wish to question a witness in order that some point may be clarified. Most judges will permit a limited amount of questioning by a juror if it is felt that the questioning is in good faith, but such questioning could very easily get out of hand as some jurors may desire to get into the "act" and become counsels. The questioning of witnesses by jurors is generally not encouraged. When a juror wishes to ask a witness a question, the judge usually will require the juror to write the question on a slip of paper and have it handed to the judge, who will ask the question for the juror. This keeps a juror from trying to become one of the questioning attorneys.

Introduction of Physical Evidence

During the investigation of a crime, officers will usually discover physical evidence, or material objects, that are pertinent to the crime. These objects, such as a latent fingerprint developed at a crime scene and identified as that of the defendant, often assist in connecting the defendant with the crime. Physical evidence may include objects taken during a robbery or burglary that were found in the possession of the defendant. These objects may be described by the officer who found them, and it is not necessary that they be presented in court. But in almost all instances the prosecuting attorney will introduce these objects as evidence in order to substantiate the officer's testimony and to emphasize the facts of the case. These physical objects must be introduced by some witness who can connect the objects with the crime charged. The witness will have to describe where the object was found, when, and under what circumstances. Once the object is introduced into evidence the jury may examine it and consider it as part of the facts of the case.

Viewing the Crime Scene

There are times when a judge may feel that a jury can better follow the testimony of the witnesses if it views the area in which the crime was committed. Under these circumstances the judge will order the jury, as a body, to be taken to the crime scene by an officer of the court. Since viewing the crime scene is in a sense receiving facts of the case, the viewing in some jurisdictions is considered as evidence of the case. For that reason the prosecuting attorney, defense attorney, defendant, and judge must accompany the jury. It has been established as improper for a jury, either as individuals or as a group, to view the crime scene without authorization from the judge.

In making the decision, the judge must take into consideration several factors. Can photographs of the crime scene be displayed to the jury and accomplish as much as the actual viewing? Have material changes taken place in the crime scene that may cause more confusion than clarification?

Prosecution Rests

After presentation of all the prosecution witnesses and physical evidence that the prosecuting attorney believes is necessary, the prosecuting attorney will usually state "the prosecution rests, your honor." This statement is an indication to all those involved in the trial that the prosecution has presented the evidence that it believes is sufficient to convince the jury that the defendant is guilty beyond a reasonable doubt. In other words, the prosecution rests its side of the case in the hands of the jury with the hope of getting a favorable verdict.

Judgment of Acquittal

After the prosecution rests, the defense may present evidence in its own behalf. Before doing so, however, the usual procedure is for the defense counsel to request permission from the judge to *approach the bench*—that is, permission to speak to the judge. Permission is usually granted, and the defense attorney then will request that the jury be excused so that a motion can be made for a judgment of acquittal.

If the judge permits the motion to be argued, the defense attorney will endeavor to convince the judge that the prosecution failed to establish that a crime was committed, or that the defendant committed it. Or the defense attorney may contend that the prosecution failed to present enough evidence to substantiate, or uphold, a conviction on appeal. If the judge agrees with the defense attorney, the judge has the authority to take the case out of the hands of the jury and enter a judgment of acquittal, which is a bar to any further action against the defendant on the crime charged. This procedure also is commonly referred to as a motion for a *directed verdict*. However, the directed verdict has another meaning in some states. In such states if a motion for a directed verdict is granted, the judge instructs the jury to return a verdict of not guilty. The jury is not bound by this direction in some states. The jury may disregard the motion and return a verdict of guilty. A few states contend that a judge does not have the right to either enter a motion of acquittal or a directed verdict, as the procedure takes the case out of the hands of the jury who are the exclusive judges of the facts of the case.

The reason that a defense attorney will request the jury to be excused during the time the motion is made for a judgment of acquittal is that if the motion is not granted, the jury may be convinced that the judge believes the defendant guilty. This belief could affect their verdict. The motion for a judgment of acquittal or a directed verdict does not always have to be argued. The judge may be convinced that the evidence presented by the prosecution does not support a conviction. The judge may then make a motion to enter a judgment of a acquittal or direct a verdict of acquittal.

However, even though convinced at the time the prosecution rests that the defendant is guilty beyond a reasonable doubt, the judge may not enter a judgment of conviction nor direct a verdict of conviction. Such action would be denying the defendant the right to a trial by jury.

Defense Presentation

If the judge does not agree to enter a judgment of acquittal or direct a verdict of acquittal, the defense attorney must make a decision. It must be decided whether to allow the case to go to the jury at that time with the hope that they have some doubt as to the guilt of the defendant, or whether evidence should be presented in behalf of the defendant in an effort to create such a doubt. Generally, if there is any defense that can be presented, the defendant's attorney will present evidence rather than take a chance on the jury returning a guilty verdict. If the defendant has admitted guilt to counsel but refuses to enter a plea of guilty, presenting a defense may be a difficult task for the defense attorney.

Defense Approaches

If the charge is homicide or aggravated assault, the defense may attempt to prove that the defendant committed the act in self-defense. In the case of a forceful rape, the defense may allege that the victim consented to the act of intercourse with the defendant. One of the more prevalent defenses is the alibi defense. Also a defense attorney will occasionally endeavor to prove that the defendant is of such good character that a crime as charged in the accusatory pleading could not have been committed. This is not always an easy defense to present, particularly if the defendant has a past criminal record. The moment that the defendant endeavors to prove reputable character through witnesses, the prosecution can discredit the testimony by showing the defendant's past criminal record. This is one of the few times that the past record of a defendant may be introduced in evidence.

Should the Defendant Testify?

While planning the defense, an attorney must decide whether the defendant should be permitted to testify. Often it is not an easy decision to make, as many factors must be considered. The attorney must consider the impression that the defendant may make on the jury while testifying. If the defendant has a past criminal record, and particularly a conviction on a felony, this may be brought out during cross-examination. On the stand the defendant is treated the same as any other witness in most jurisdictions, and witnesses may be impeached by revealing certain past convictions. Being aware of the defendant's past record of convictions could affect the jury's verdict. If the defendant does not take the stand, what will be the jury's reaction to this failure to testify and explain personal knowledge of the facts?

In the past if the defendant did not take the stand in his own defense, the failure to do so could be commented on by the prosecuting attorney and the judge as the case was being summarized to the jury. But in the case of *Griffin* v. *California*, 380 US 609 (1965), the United States Supreme Court held that such comments were improper since they tend to force the defendant to be a witness against oneself in violation of the Fifth Amendment of the United States Constitution. The facts of the *Griffin* case reflect that the defendant was convicted of murder in a jury trial. The defendant did not testify at the trial on the issue of guilt, and

> . . . the trial court instructed the jury that a defendant has a constitutional right not to testify. But it told the jury: "As to any evidence or facts within his knowledge, if he does not testify or if, though he does testify, he fails to deny or explain such evidence, the jury may take that failure into consideration as tending to indicate the truth of such evidence and as indicating that among the inferences that may be reasonably drawn therefrom those unfavorable to the defendant are the more probable." . . .
>
> The petitioner (the defendant) had been seen with the deceased the evening of her death, the evidence placing him with her in the alley where her body was found. The prosecutor made much of the failure of petitioner to testify, (and made the following statements to the jury).
>
> "The defendant certainly knows whether Essie Mae (the deceased) had this beat up appearance at the time he left her apartment and went down the alley with her.
>
> What kind of a man is it that would want to have sex with a woman that beat up if she was beat up at the time he left?
>
> He would know that. He would know how she got down the alley. He would know how the blood got on the bottom concrete steps. . . .
>
> These things he has not seen fit to take the stand and deny or explain. And in the whole world, if anybody would know, this defendant would know. Essie Mae is dead, she can't tell you her side of the story. The defendant won't."

The case was taken to the United States Supreme Court on a writ of certiorari to consider whether comment on the failure to testify violated the self-incrimination clause of the Fifth Amendment made applicable to the States by the Fourteenth Amendment. The Supreme Court pointed out that a defendant has a constitutional right to remain silent and not testify, and permitting the prosecuting attorney and judge to comment on the defendant's failure to testify was

> . . . a penalty imposed by the courts for exercising a constitutional privilege. It cuts down on the privilege by making its assertion costly. It is said, however, that the inference of guilt for failure to testify as to facts peculiarly within the accused's knowledge is in any event natural and irresistible, and that comment on the failure does not magnify that inference into a penalty for asserting a constitutional privilege. What the jury may infer, given no help from the court, is one thing. What it may infer when the court solemnizes the silence of the accused into evidence against him is quite another.

The defendant's Fifth Amendment right against self-incrimination and the fact that the exercise of that right may not be called to the attention of the jury were both clearly illustrated by the *Griffin* case. However in most jurisdictions if the defendant does take the stand and fails to explain certain facts that logically should have been explained, it may be commented on by the judge and prosecuting attorney. The theory behind this permitted comment is that it is held that a defendant should not be able to testify concerning only those matters that are beneficial and fail to explain other facts that may be unfavorable.

Another problem created for a defense attorney arises when the client insists on taking the stand, and the attorney does not believe such action to be wise. Does a defendant have a right to testify in his own behalf over the objections of counsel? This question has not been answered in all jurisdictions, but a few have held that a defendant does have a right to present evidence in one's own behalf, even to testifying over the objections of counsel. The court of one state made this comment concerning the right of a defendant to testify:

> We are satisfied that the right to testify in one's own behalf is of such fundamental importance that a defendant who timely demands to take the stand contrary to the advice given by his counsel has the right to give an exposition of his defense before a jury. The defendant's insistence upon testifying may in the final analysis be harmful to his case, but the right is of such importance that every defendant should have it in a criminal case. Although normally the decision whether a defendant should testify is within the competence of the trial attorney where, as here, a defendant insists that he wants to testify, he cannot be deprived of that opportunity. (See *People* v. *Robles*, 85 Cal Rptr 166 [1970])

Rebuttal by the Prosecution

After the defense has presented its side of the case and rests, the prosecution may present additional evidence to meet or rebut that presented by the defense. The presentation of rebuttal evidence is permitted because in most instances the prosecution will have no advance knowledge of the approach that the defense may take in an effort to prove the defendant not guilty. Although after resting the prosecuting attorney may have felt that the defendant was proved guilty beyond a reasonable doubt, the defense may have created some new doubt by presenting its evidence. The evidence presented by the defense may not have been based upon true facts. For example, the defense may have tried to prove that the defendant was at some place other than where the crime was committed, creating a doubt in the minds of the jury as to the guilt of the defendant. This alibi evidence may have been attempted through perjured testimony. To allow this testimony to stand unchallenged by the prosecution would be an injustice to society. The only way that this testimony can be effectively challenged, except through cross-examination, is for the prosecution to present further testimony to prove that the defendant was at the scene of the crime.

Generally no new evidence pertaining to the guilt of the defendant may be presented during the rebuttal. This is because permitting new evidence would cause the whole sequence of the trial examination procedure to take place again. The only time that additional evidence may be introduced is when new material evidence has been discovered. The prosecution must be in a position to convince the judge that the newly discovered evidence was not available when the prosecution first presented its side of the case, and that its discovery was not due to carelessness, inadequate investigation, or preparation. In the interest of justice the judge may permit the newly discovered evidence to be introduced, but the defense may again present evidence in an effort to overcome that presented by the prosecution. This presentation is sometimes referred to as the *rejoinder* in some jurisdictions, and in others it is known as the *defense rebuttal*.

After the prosecution has finished the rebuttal, the defense may again make a motion for a judgment of acquittal to be entered. If this motion is denied by the judge, the next procedure, depending upon the procedure of the jurisdiction, is either presentation of closing arguments by the prosecution and defense, or instructing the jury on the law of the case.

Depositions

Sometimes during a trial a witness for one side or the other is unable to attend court to testify, yet the testimony of that witness is material to the case. Rather than continuing the trial until the witness is able to appear in court, an out-of-court written statement, or *deposition,* given under oath, will be taken from the witness. Before a deposition may be taken, the opposing side must be notified that a deposition is to be taken at a particular time, date, and place. This notice is necessary so that the opposing side may be present to cross-examine the witness. The deposition is usually in a question and answer form much as the testimony would be given in court. The deposition will be read to the jury at the appropriate time during the trial, and the information will become part of the facts of the case. Because of the right of the defendant to be presented with the witnesses against him, some states do not permit the prosecution to introduce depositions in evidence.

Not Guilty by Reason of Insanity

Because the procedure on the defense of not guilty by reason of insanity differs among states, it is believed that a discussion of that defense is in order at this time. Not all states permit a separate plea of not guilty by reason of insanity. In those states where this plea is not permitted, the insanity defense is alleged by the defense after the prosecution rests, in the same manner as other defenses that the defendant may utilize, such as the alibi or self-defense. Under these circumstances the prosecution will present its evidence to prove the defendant guilty beyond a reasonable doubt.

After the presentation of this evidence, the defendant alleges he cannot be held criminally liable for the crime, as he was insane at the time he committed the act. He then presents evidence in his behalf in an endeavor to prove that he was insane at the time. This type of defense can catch the prosecution by surprise and the obtaining of rebuttal evidence may be difficult. Also, with this type of defense being alleged, the prosecution has a double burden. Not knowing of the insanity defense in advance, the prosecution usually must present much evidence to prove that the defendant committed the crime, but by claiming the insanity defense, the defendant is in a sense admitting the act but alleging that there is no criminal liability. To rebut this allegation the prosecution must prove that the defendant was sane at the time the crime was committed. Because of the element of surprise to the prosecution by the insanity defense and the double burden imposed upon the prosecutor, efforts have been made to have this defense included in the right of discovery by the prosecution. In those jurisdictions permitting a separate plea of not guilty by reason of insanity, the prosecuting attorney is not surprised and usually has ample opportunity to prepare the case to meet the allegation.

In those states where a separate plea of not guilty by reason of insanity is permitted, unless the defendant enters that plea, sanity is presumed at the time that the crime was committed, and no defense of insanity may be entered. As pointed out in chapter 5, a few states permit the defendant to enter dual pleas. The defendant may enter a plea of "not guilty" and at the same time enter a plea of "not guilty by reason of insanity." When the dual pleas are entered, the trial on the not guilty plea will be tried first. If the defendant is found not guilty, no further action may take place. But if the defendant is found guilty, a second trial takes place to determine the sanity of the defendant at the time the crime was committed. These trials may be heard by the same jury or different juries depending on the wishes of the defendant or the procedure of the jurisdiction involved. In some states the two trials are consolidated into one trial.

The Burden of Proof

States differ in their approach as to the burden of proof on the insanity issue. Some states contend that, by entering the plea of not guilty by reason of insanity, the defendant has admitted guilt. Having admitted guilt the defendant is not entitled to the presumption of innocence, and the prosecution has no burden of proof on the guilt issue. Since it is presumed that all persons are sane unless, and until, proved otherwise, in some states the defendant has the burden of proving insanity at the time the crime was committed. Having this burden, the defense will open the trial proceedings by presenting the defendant's evidence first, followed by the prosecution. In the effort to prove insanity, the defendant may produce expert witnesses in the field of psychology who after examining the defendant, may express their opinions as to the defendant's mental state at the time the crime occurred. The defense counsel may produce lay witnesses acquainted with the defendant at or about the time the crime was committed, to express their opinions on the defendant's sanity in corroboration with the opinions of the experts. The amount of proof that the defendant must present differs among states. Some states require the defendant to prove insanity by a preponderance of evidence; other states require that insanity be proved to the satisfaction of the jury. The line of demarcation between these proofs is very fine, but it is conceded that the defendant does not have to prove beyond a reasonable doubt that the crime was committed while insane.

After the defendant has presented evidence to prove insanity, the prosecution has the responsibility of going forward with the evidence and proving that the defendant was sane at the time of the act. How much evidence must the prosecution present to prove sanity? Merely going forward with the evidence generally implies meeting the evidence of the opposition. The general consensus of opinion is that the prosecution must do more than meet the evidence. There must be more than a doubt as to the sanity of the defendant before the jury may conclude that the defendant was sane at the time the crime occurred. Most jurisdictions contend that the prosecution still has the burden of proving the defendant sane beyond a reasonable doubt. In fact, in some jurisdictions if the defendant enters the plea of not guilty by reason of insanity, the prosecution opens the trial and presents evidence to prove the defendant sane beyond a reasonable doubt, and the defense may meet that evidence by merely creating a doubt as to sanity at the time the act was committed.

The Test for Sanity

Determining sanity is not easy. Whatever procedure is followed, the ultimate determination to be made is whether the defendant was in such a state of mind at the time the crime was committed that he cannot be held legally responsible. Some acceptable test must be applied. The problem becomes more complicated by the fact that it is not the present state of mind of the defendant that is in issue. As has been previously pointed out, unless a defendant is mentally capable of defending himself, the trial cannot take place. Since the case is going to trial it has been adjudged that the defendant is presently sane. It is necessary then to go back in time in attempting to establish the sanity of the defendant. Even the most knowledgeable experts in the field of psychology can only give an opinion of the mental condition at the time of the crime, unless the defendant was under a doctor's treatment.

Devising a test that will accurately establish a defendant's mental condition months before has been most difficult. For many years in England the "wild beast test" was used. This test has also been referred to as the "good and evil" test. It was held that if an accused did not know any more than a wild beast would when the crime was committed, then no criminal responsibility could result from the act. In other words, if the accused had no more conception of good and evil than a wild beast while committing the crime, he could not be held responsible.

The good and evil test was used until it was replaced by the *right and wrong test* in 1843, resulting from the case of Daniel M'Naghten, 8 Eng Reprint 718. In that case Daniel M'Naghten was indicted for the murder of Edward Drummond, private secretary to Sir Robert Peel, Prime Minister of England. M'Naghten mistook Drummond for Peel, whom M'Naghten felt was persecuting him. M'Naghten was found not guilty by reason of insanity. The acquittal generated so much public indignation in London, including that of the Queen, that the judges were called before the House of Lords and requested to explain the test that was used to determine the sanity of M'Naghten. The judges answered the House of Lords inquiry with the following test, which the jury was to consider in making a determination as to the sanity of one accused of a crime. The judges stated:

> . . . the jurors ought to be told in all cases that every man is to be presumed to be sane, and possess a sufficient degree of reason to be responsible for his crimes, until the contrary be proved to their satisfaction; and that to establish a defense on the ground of insanity, it must be clearly proved that, at the time of the committing of the act, the party accused was labouring under such a defect of reason, from disease of mind, as not to know the nature of the act he was doing; or, if he did know it, that he did not know he was doing what was wrong. The mode of putting the latter part of the question to the jury on these occasions has generally been, whether the accused at the time of doing the act knew the difference between right and wrong.

The test has been referred to as the *M'Naghten test.* It has been followed since in England, and has been adopted by a majority of the states in this country. Although the test has been criticized by some legal scholars and psychologists, it has been replaced in only a few states. The M'Naghten test continues to have acceptance because it is generally felt that no better test has been devised, and the jury is better able to understand it than other tests that have been suggested.

In the case of *Durham* v. *United States,* 94 US App DC 228 (1954), the following test, known as the *Durham test,* was set forth to be followed by the courts in the District of Columbia. The Court stated that the "rule" to be followed in determining criminal responsibility is as follows:

> . . . It is simply that an accused is not criminally responsible if his unlawful act was the product of mental disease or mental defect. . . .
>
> Whenever there is some evidence that the accused suffered from a diseased or defective mental condition at the time the unlawful act was committed, the trial court must provide the jury with guides for determining whether the accused can be held criminally responsible. We do not, and indeed could not, formulate an instruction which would be either appropriate or binding in all cases. But under the rule now announced, any instruction should in some way convey to the jury the sense and substance of the following: If you the jury believe beyond a reasonable doubt that the accused was not suffering from a diseased or defective mental condition at the time he committed the criminal act charged, you may find him guilty.

The Durham test has been severely criticized in that it is too vague and indefinite to be workable in the determination of criminal responsibility, as was stated in the case of *United States* v. *Currens,* 290 F 2d 751 (1961). The Durham test does not give the jury any real guidelines to determine if an unlawful act was the product of a mental disease or mental defect. In the *Currens* case the Court endeavored to develop a more workable tool for the jury in determining criminal responsibility. The Court in that case stated:

> We are of the opinion that the following formula most nearly fulfills the objectives just discussed: The jury must be satisfied that at the time of committing the prohibited act the defendant, as a result of mental disease or defect, lacked substantial capacity to conform his conduct to the requirements of the law which he is alleged to have violated.

There is some question whether the test set forth in the *Currens* decision is any more workable for a jury than the Durham test. For that reason some judges have included the *irresistable impulse test*. These judges inform the jury that if they are of the opinion that the defendant's state of mind was such that an impulse to commit the unlawful act could not be controlled, then no criminal responsibility should result.

Although efforts have been made to formulate a modern workable test which juries may apply in making the determination of criminal responsibility, generally it is felt that little has been accomplished in creating a more understandable test than the M'Naghten "right and wrong" test. This probably is the reason the M'Naghten test is still utilized by the courts in a majority of the states. But the test for insanity now utilized by most of the United States Courts of Appeal, and by about one-third of the states, is that a person is not responsible for criminal conduct if at the time of such conduct, as a result of mental disease or defect, one lacks substantial capacity to appreciate the wrongfulness of one's conduct or to conform that conduct to the requirement of the law.

Some efforts have been made by defense attorneys to utilize the alleged effects of the *XYY Syndrome* as an insanity defense. This defense is based upon the theory that individuals with an abnormal complement of chromosomes are legally insane, and as such cannot be held criminally responsible for their acts. Generally courts have been rejecting this defense, primarily because the geneticists, in studying the extra Y chromosomes, differ in their opinions as to the effects. It is generally conceded that not all individuals with an abnormal complement of chromosomes are, by nature, involuntarily aggressive. Also these experts hold that it cannot be stated for a certainty that a criminal act is the result of an abnormal complement of chromosomes.

Irrespective of the test that is applied, if the jury finds the defendant to have been sane at the time the crime occurred, the only procedure left is sentencing. On the other hand, if the jury finds that the defendant was insane when the crime was committed the accused is theoretically entitled to be released. As pointed out in chapter 5, if the defendant was found to have been insane when committing the crime, in most jurisdictions confinement will be in a mental hospital under a civil commitment to make certain that there is no threat to society. One court went so far as to hold that "an accused person who is acquitted by reason of insanity is presumed to be insane and may be committed for an indefinite period to a hospital for the insane." (See *Orencia* v. *Overholser,* 82 US App DC 285 [1947].) In another decision it was stated that "even where there has been a specific finding that the accused was competent to stand trial and assist in his own defense, the court would be well advised to invoke the code provision so that the accused may be confined as long as the public safety and his welfare require." (See *Barry* v. *White,* 62 US App DC 69 [1933].)

Closing Arguments

After both sides have presented their evidence, the next procedure in most jurisdictions is the closing arguments by the prosecuting attorney and the defense attorney. Closing arguments are merely a summarization of the evidence presented during the trial. Attorneys have mixed emotions on the value of closing arguments. Some attorneys allege that the closing arguments have no effect on the jury and that the arguments are a waste of time. Other attorneys feel that a closing argument may be the difference between losing a case and winning it. Irrespective of viewpoints, in most criminal trials both the prosecution and defense will give closing arguments. There is no limit as to the length of time of a closing argument. The attorneys may only take a few minutes or several days, depending on the length of the trial. The judge does have the right to limit the time involved, but may not be too restrictive. With the possible exception of an insanity trial, the usual procedure is for the prosecuting attorney to give the closing argument first, followed by the defense. After the defense has completed its closing argument, the prosecuting attorney may give a rebuttal argument. Some jurisdictions reverse this procedure and permit the defense attorney to present the closing argument first, followed by the prosecution.

It is considered improper for the attorneys to appeal to the sympathy or emotions of the jurors, but frequently the closing arguments are a most dramatic performance that results in an appeal to the emotions. In fact, during the questioning of the jurors for cause, attorneys may inject questions designed to later enable them to weave the personal life of some of the jurors into the closing arguments. At this point in the trial, each side is endeavoring to sell the jury on the fact that it is entitled to the verdict.

Closing Argument by the Prosecution

During the closing argument the prosecuting attorney will summarize the evidence presented, emphasizing the strong points that indicate guilt. To substantiate the closing statements, the physical evidence already introduced may be displayed again. The prosecuting attorney may state that the evidence clearly proves that the defendant is guilty of the crime charged. It is held to be prejudicial error, however, for the prosecuting attorney to state that from personal knowledge the defendant is known to be guilty, implying that information not brought forth during the trial is in his possession. The courts have stated that the right to discuss the merits of a case, both as to the law and facts, is very wide, and the prosecuting attorney has the right to state what the evidence shows, and the conclusions to be drawn. The adverse party cannot complain if the reasoning is faulty and the deductions illogical, as such matters are ultimately for the consideration of the jury. It has been held that the prosecuting attorney should be most circumspect in remarks concerning the defendant and counsel, but the use of derogatory epithets does not necessarily represent misconduct.

In the case of *People* v. *Jones,* 86 Cal Rptr 516 (1970), the prosecuting attorney referred to the defendant's behavior as consistent with animalistic and felonious tendencies, and that there was a strange, twisted reason for the actions of the accused. The Court in that case stated:

> We recognize that prosecutors, like all others who have responsible roles in the trial of a criminal case, are human; as humans they may be affected by the tensions of a trial to the point of error and, on occasion, even to misconduct. We recognize, too, that the great increase in crime and the corresponding increase in the number of prosecutions in recent years has placed a heavy burden on district attorneys, who frequently must rely on inexperienced deputies to try cases. Be that as it may, prosecutors should be ever aware that in all they do and say they are representatives of the government of whom the public, including those who are prosecuted, are entitled to expect a high degree of ethical conduct.
>
> . . . while some of the references to the appellant (defendant), more particularly, "animalistic tendencies" and "felonious tendencies" were quite strong, we hold that, under the facts of this case, they were within the bounds of legitimate argument and did not constitute misconduct.

Following such arguments by the prosecuting attorney, the judge will often instruct the jury that the closing arguments are not to be considered as evidence in the case and that the jury is to disregard any statements not based on the evidence. If a prosecuting attorney does indulge in misconduct during the closing argument, a mistrial could be declared at the time, or could lead to a reversal of a conviction on appeal.

Closing Argument by the Defense

Technically the same rules of conduct which apply to the prosecuting attorney are applicable to the defense attorney. Since defense counsel misconduct is not appealable if the defendant should be acquitted, the defense attorney often engages in considerable freedom in arguing the case to the jury. An appeal will often be made to the sympathy of the jury. It may be pointed out that in rendering a guilty verdict, the jury will deprive the defendant of freedom and companionship with family. In one case the defendant appeared in court wearing long hair and a shaggy beard. In the defense attorney's argument to the jury, counsel stated that in looking over the jury no member representative of the defendant's peer group could be seen. The defense attorney recalled a trial some two thousand years before where the defendant also was wearing a beard, had long hair, and was tried without peer group representation. Keeping that fact in mind, the defense attorney felt the appearance of the defendant would not deter the jury from rendering a verdict in favor of acquittal. Although the defense attorney may be most dramatic in appealing to a jury, there are times when the jury may resent what they feel to be an insult to their intelligence in defense counsel arguments.

Even though represented by an attorney, occasionally a defendant will insist upon making a closing argument in addition to the one given by the attorney. It is at the judge's discretion whether the defendant may make a closing argument. If the defendant is self-represented, a closing argument is always permitted.

Rebuttal Closing Argument

After the defense attorney has concluded the closing argument for the accused, the prosecuting attorney is entitled to make a rebuttal closing argument. Statements and challenges presented during the defense attorney's closing argument can be met. At this time the prosecuting attorney's final remarks must be circumspect to avoid making statements amounting to misconduct in response to challenges presented by the defense.

Review Questions

1. What is the purpose of the opening statement?
2. Define reasonable doubt.
3. What amendment guarantees a defendant the right to be confronted with the witnesses against him?
4. What is the purpose of a subpoena?
5. In what way does the oath differ from the affirmation?
6. Why was the affirmation adopted?
7. What is direct examination?
8. Define a leading question.
9. What is the primary purpose of cross-examination?
10. Must the defendant present evidence in his own behalf?
11. What is the purpose of rebuttal by the prosecution?
12. State the purpose of the M'Naghten test.
13. What purpose do closing arguments serve?

Local Procedure

1. May a defendant enter a plea of not guilty by reason of insanity or is insanity raised only as a defense?
2. Is the M'Naghten or some other test followed?

THE JURY: INSTRUCTIONS AND DELIBERATION

thirteen

Instructions to the Jury

On completion of the closing arguments, in most jurisdictions, the judge instructs the jury on the law applicable to the case. Instructing the jury is also known as *charging the jury* or as the *charge to the jury*. In a few states the judge may instruct the jury prior to the closing arguments in order that the attorneys involved may include comments on the instructions during their closing arguments. Although the procedure of instructing the jury follows the presentation of the evidence, the judge has the responsibility of explaining the law to the jury as the trial progresses for their guidance in following the evidence. During the charge to the jury the judge will summarize the points of law explained to them during the trial and instruct them on their function as jurors. The judge will instruct the jury on any additional laws applicable that were not explained as the trial progressed.

Defense and Prosecution Recommendations

As a general rule the prosecuting attorney and defense attorney prepare written instructions that they desire to be given to the jury. These instructions will be furnished to the judge prior to the closing arguments. After reviewing these instructions, the judge selects those that appear to be applicable. Other instructions not suggested by the attorneys may also be given. The judge has the responsibility of instructing the jury on the laws applicable whether requested to do so or not.

The defendant is entitled to instructions being given on all pertinent evidence regardless of its importance. The failure to give an instruction concerning pertinent evidence, whether requested or not by the defense, could be grounds for the reversal of a conviction on appeal. However, a judge does not have to give instructions that are repetitive or that include some statement of fact in the form of evidence in the case.

The judge also has the responsibility of instructing the jury in clear and understandable language. Too often the instructions are lengthy, complicated, and difficult for the jury to understand. For example, an instruction on the meaning of reasonable doubt may be most confusing to the jury, but the defendant is entitled to this instruction and on the presumption of innocence. The judge will read to the jury the definition of reasonable doubt as set forth in chapter 12. The jury will be informed that a defendant in a criminal action is presumed innocent until the contrary is proved, and if there is a reasonable doubt as to guilt, the defendant is entitled to an acquittal. The effect of this presumption places on the state the burden of proving guilt beyond a reasonable doubt.

The following are samples of additional instructions generally given to a jury. The jury will be informed that it is the function of the judge to interpret the law but that the jury is the exclusive judge of the facts. The jury must determine those facts only from the evidence presented in court, and it must conscientiously consider and weigh the evidence during the trial. It must also carefully determine the credibility of each witness. In measuring the credibility of the witness, the jury may consider the demeanor of the witness as each testifies, the opportunity of the witness to have gained the facts about which each testifies, and the ability to observe, retain, and communicate the matters. The jury will be informed that it must not consider as evidence any statement made by the attorneys involved nor is the jury to speculate on what an answer to a question may have been when an objection to the question was sustained. Neither may the jury consider in its deliberation on the verdict any statement that was stricken from the record. The jurors will be advised that they must not be governed by mere sentiment, sympathy, passion, or prejudice in arriving at a verdict and that they must reach a just verdict regardless of the consequences of that verdict. The jurors will also be informed that it is their duty to consult one another and deliberate on a just verdict but that the verdict is to express the individual opinion of each juror. The jury will then be advised of the previously mentioned presumption of innocence and reasonable doubt instructions.

The foregoing instructions are applicable in all criminal trials. In addition to these general instructions, more specific instructions applicable to the particular case will be included. Instructions may be given on the meaning of direct and circumstantial evidence. The jury will be informed that direct evidence directly proves the fact in issue whereas circumstantial evidence proves a fact by an inference drawn from another set of facts having been proven. At this point in the instructions the jury is often again hopelessly lost in the explanation. The right of an expert witness to give an opinion on controversial questions is explained. It will be explained that the jury may consider the qualifications of the expert and give the testimony the proper weight. The meaning of intent and motive may be explained. If an alibi defense was alleged, the judge will inform the jury that if they have reasonable doubt about the defendant being present at the scene of the crime, an acquittal should result. The meaning of *consciousness of guilt* will be explained, as well as those acts that may fall within that category, such as a suspect running from a crime scene. The jury will be informed that the defendant has a right not to testify and that no inference of guilt is to be drawn from the failure to testify. Since most jurisdictions permit a jury to return a verdict to a lesser degree of crime than that charged in the accusatory pleading, the jury will be given an instruction to this effect. Most jurisdictions permit the jury to take the written instructions given by the judge with them during deliberations. The foregoing instructions are in no way all inclusive of those that may be given in any trial proceeding.

Comments by the Judge

States differ materially in permitting a judge to comment on the evidence of a case and the credibility of witnesses. About one half of the states prohibit comments by the judge on the evidence and credibility of the witnesses as it is believed that such comments are an invasion of the function of the jury. A few states grant considerable freedom to a judge to comment on the evidence and credibility of the witnesses. It has been stated that the judge should be a real factor in the administration of justice and not a mere referee of the adversary system. The judge must summarize the evidence in an impartial and instructive manner, but may point out weaknesses in the evidence of the prosecution and defense, or question the credibility of witnesses. However, the judge's right to comment on the evidence and witnesses is not unlimited. Courts have stated that the judge must be "fair, objective and impartial and must not ignore evidence favorable to the defendant." It has been held improper for the judge to directly state the belief that the defendant is guilty. Comments in one case were considered improper when the judge indicated to the jury that in viewing the evidence in its most favorable light to the defendant, one was still left with the conclusion that the defendant was guilty. The judge further stated that if he were deciding the case, the accused would be found guilty.

Comments to the jury may be made before or after the instructions, at the judge's discretion. Except in states where the judge gives the instructions to the jury prior to the closing arguments, the jury begins its deliberations once the instructions are given.

Deliberation

If the jury has not been sequestered prior to the case being given to the jury, the judge must decide whether or not to do so during deliberation. As was pointed out, in some states the jury must be sequestered during the deliberation. In other states it is at the discretion of the judge. The jury may decide on the verdict in the courtroom, but in most instances will retire to some private and convenient place for deliberation. This is generally referred to as the *jury room.*

Inside the Jury Room

While deliberating, the jurors will be under the guard of some officer of the court. The court officer will have been sworn to keep the jurors together, not permit any person to speak to them, and possibly not personally speak to them except on orders of the court. During the deliberation no one may be present in the jury room except the jurors—not even the officer in charge of the jury. On one occasion an alternate juror was inadvertantly given permission by the officer in charge of the jury to sit in the jury room merely to observe during the deliberation. On learning of the presence of the alternate juror during the deliberation, the judge declared a mistrial, although the alternate juror did not in any way engage in the deliberation. The courts of a few states, however, have permitted an alternate juror to be sequestered with the other jurors during the deliberation, but only after the judge has instructed the alternate juror not to participate in the deliberation.

In one case, the officer in charge of the jury was also a material witness for the prosecution. He and other officers transported the jury back and forth to their hotel while the jury was being sequestered, and these officers also ate at the same table with the jurors and conversed with them. Although it was alleged that there was no conversation about the facts of the case during these associations, the United States Supreme Court held that the presence of the officer interfered with the defendant's right to be tried by an impartial jury. The presence of the officer, according to the Court, may have established a favorable rapport with the jury that may have affected their verdict of guilty. (See *Turner* v. *Louisiana,* 379 US 466 [1965].)

In reference to only jurors being present during the deliberation, we return to the problem encountered by the hearing impaired person who becomes a juror. By necessity, this juror's interpreter must be present during the deliberation to interpret the communication that takes place among the jurors as they attempt to arrive at a verdict. How may it be determined that the deliberation was accurately interpreted, or was that juror somehow influenced by the interpretation? Would it be held that the interpreter was an extra juror present during the deliberation? If the defendant was convicted, could the defense challenge on appeal the presence of the interpreter during deliberation, or would this challenge have been waived by the lack of challenge for cause during jury selection? Only future cases will decide the answers to these questions.

Prior to beginning the deliberation, the jury will select one of their members to act as the foreman—their leader and spokesman. If, during the deliberation, the jury desires further instructions on the law or information concerning the case, the foreman will advise the officer in charge, who in turn will notify the judge of the request. The judge in most instances will require that the jury be returned to the courtroom for the requested information. It is considered improper for the officer in charge to act as a messenger carrying information from the judge to the jury.

Materials Inside the Jury Room

On entering deliberation the jury may take with them any and all documents introduced during the trial. However, in many jurisdictions the jury may not take any depositions with them. The reason for this prohibition is that to permit the jury to take the depositions would possibly allow them to give greater weight to the testimony of a witness not present over one who was present. The rules of evidence in most states provide that the jury may take any document introduced, and also permits the jury to take any exhibits or physical evidence, such as a gun, plaster of paris cast, or fingerprint, that may have been introduced. Courts in some jurisdictions have held that the jury should be permitted to take with them all evidence introduced, including depositions, any prepared transcript or recorded testimony, and personal notes as long as the defendant is not unduly prejudiced and the jury is not likely to improperly use the evidence.

A great majority of the states permit jurors to take notes at the discretion of the judge. Judges differ in their attitudes toward note taking. Some judges argue that most jurors are not trained in the art of taking notes. Not being trained, they may take down trivial matters and overlook important facts, or may try to take down everything and get hopelessly lost in the process, missing material testimony as it is presented. It is argued also that the better note takers will have a tendency to dominate the deliberation, or that jurors will argue as to whose notes are a correct record of the testimony. Those arguing in favor of note taking by jurors allege that it is asking too much of a juror to remember all the testimony during a lengthy trial and that permitting notes to be taken enables the juror to refresh the memory during the deliberation. Usually the reporter's transcript is not available at the time of the deliberation, and unless the jurors have their notes, the only way testimony may be recalled in some instances is to have the jury returned to the courtroom and the reporter's notes read to the jury. This is time consuming, and judges often frown on this activity when engaged in too frequently by a jury. It is argued that the benefits derived from a juror taking notes during a trial far exceed any detriment that may be suffered.

Length of Deliberation

How long the jury may deliberate on a case before reaching a verdict will depend largely upon the length of the trial, and how convincing the evidence may have been. The jury may decide on a verdict after conferring for a few minutes, or they may take days to decide upon a verdict. In many instances they cannot agree at all. When the jury cannot agree upon a verdict, it is referred to as a *hung jury.* When a jury cannot agree upon a verdict, it is discharged, and a mistrial may be declared by the judge. The trial will have to be restarted with a new jury. It is not unusual for a trial to end with a hung jury. As was previously pointed out, most juries in a criminal case must consist of twelve persons. In a great majority of the states the verdict must be unanimous, that is, all of the jurors must agree on either guilt or innocence. To get twelve people to agree on the guilt or innocence of an accused is often most difficult.

Judges would rather permit a reasonable amount of time for deliberation than have to start the case over with a new jury, as this is both time consuming and expensive. Most judges will do their utmost to encourage a jury to reach a verdict. A judge may call the jury back into the courtroom from time to time to determine if the foreman believes that a verdict can be reached. The judge may even inquire as to how the jury is numerically split in reaching a verdict, but it is considered improper for the judge to ask how they are split as to guilt or innocence. If the foreman should inadvertently state how the jury is split on guilt or innocence it is not generally considered to be a reversible error. The judge must be most circumspect in urging the jury to reach a verdict. He must not do or say anything that may be interpreted as a threat to the jury or as forcing a verdict on the jury. Any statement or instruction to the jury at this point that could be interpreted as coercive is considered improper and could result in the reversal of a conviction on appeal. An instruction has been held to be coercive when a judge emphasizes that a verdict must be reached because of the simplicity of the evidence, or when a judge threatens to lock up the jury until the verdict is agreed on. In one case, a jury had been deliberating from Monday until Wednesday afternoon before Thanksgiving. Late Wednesday afternoon the judge called the jurors in and indicated that it would be wise for them to agree on a verdict soon so that it would not be necessary to sequester them over the Thanksgiving holidays. After deliberating for a few more hours, the jury returned a guilty verdict. The conviction was reversed on appeal because of the threat by the judge to the jury.

After a judge has made an inquiry about the possibility of the jurors reaching a verdict, the judge will undoubtedly discharge the jury if the foreman feels that the jury is hopelessly deadlocked and cannot possibly agree on a verdict. If possible, the judge will avoid this action. The jury may be asked to further consider the matter, particularly if a majority are for a verdict with only one or two disagreeing. In some states, the judge may read to the jury what is referred to as the *Allen charge,* or *Allen instruction.* This instruction has been called the "dynamite charge," since its purpose is to blast the jury into action so that it will arrive at a verdict. This charge was originally approved by the United

252

States Supreme Court in the case of *Allen* v. *United States,* 164 US 492 (1896). The Allen instruction is substantially as follows:

> Ladies and gentlemen of the jury, in a large proportion of cases and perhaps strictly speaking, in all cases, absolute certainty cannot be attained or expected. Although the verdict to which a juror agrees must, of course, be his own verdict, the result of his own convictions and not a mere acquiescence in the conclusion of his or her fellows, yet in order to bring twelve minds to a unanimous result, you must examine the questions submitted to you with candor and with a proper regard and deference to the opinions of each other. You should consider that the case must at some time be decided, that you are selected in the same manner and from the same source from which any future jury must be selected, and there is no reason to suppose the case will ever be submitted to twelve men or women more intelligent, more impartial or more competent to decide it, or that more or clearer evidence will be produced on the one side or the other. And with this view, it is your duty to decide the case, if you can conscientiously do so.

> In order to make a decision more practicable, the law imposes the burden of proof on one party or the other in all cases. In the present case, the burden of proof is on the prosecution to establish every part of it beyond a reasonable doubt. And if in any part of it you are left in doubt, the defendant is entitled to the benefit of the doubt and must be acquitted. But in conferring together, you ought to pay proper respect to each other's opinions and listen with a disposition to be convinced to each other's arguments.

> And on the other hand, if much the larger of your panel are for a conviction, a dissenting juror should consider whether a doubt in his or her own mind is a reasonable one, which makes no impression upon the minds of so many men or women equally honest, equally intelligent with himself or herself and to have heard the same evidence with the same attention and with an equal desire to arrive at the truth and under the sanction of the same oath.

> And on the other hand, if a majority are for acquittal, the minority ought seriously to ask themselves whether they may not reasonably and ought not to doubt the correctness of a judgment, which is not concurred in by most of those with whom they are associated, and distrust the weight or sufficiency of that evidence which fails to carry conviction to the minds of their fellows.

> That is given to you as a suggestion of the theory and rationale behind jurors coming to a decision one way or the other. So the Court is going to ask you to retire and continue in your deliberations.

The courts in some states are opposed to the reading of the Allen instruction to a jury. These courts are of the opinion that the jury may interpret the instructions as commanding them to reach a verdict. Yet many courts consider the Allen instruction to be a proper reminder to the jurors of their obligation to attempt to arrive at a just verdict and not allow personal pride, prejudice, or personalities to interfere with their judgment. As was stated by Justice Burger in the case of *Fulwood* v. *United States,* 125 US App DC 183 (1967):

> The Allen charge is a carefully balanced method of reminding jurors of their elementary obligations, which they lose sight of during protracted deliberations. It is perfectly valid to remind them that they should give some thought to the views of others and should reconsider their position in light of those views. The charge as given here did not require the jury to reach a verdict but only reminded them of their duty to attempt an accommodation. While it suggests to the minority that they reconsider their position in light of a majority having a different view, it reminds them that they should not acquiesce in a verdict which does not represent their own convictions.

Instead of using the Allen instruction to encourage jurors to arrive at a verdict, the courts of some states have adopted the instruction recommended by the American Bar Association, which is in substance:

> It is your duty, as jurors, to consult with one another and to deliberate with a view to reaching an agreement, if you can do so without violence to individual judgment. Each of you must decide the case for yourself, but do so only after an impartial consideration of the evidence with your fellow jurors. In the course of your deliberations, do not hesitate to reexamine your own views and change your opinion if convinced it is erroneous. But do not surrender your honest conviction as to the weight or effect of evidence solely because of the opinion of your fellow jurors, or for the mere purpose of returning a verdict.

Even if the jury is read the Allen instruction or a similar instruction, it still may be unable to reach a verdict. Some persons may have sincere doubts about the guilt or innocence of a defendant and will not retract that doubt regardless of the urging of the majority of the jurors. Unfortunately, there are also persons who, for reasons of their own, take a delight in opposing the majority on any issue. When these individuals are on juries, reaching a verdict is next to impossible. As the old story goes, when the judge inquired of a jury foreman regarding the possibility of reaching a verdict, the foreman replied that the jury was still attempting to arrive at an agreement, but that it would take time. The foreman then suggested that the judge order eleven dinners and one bale of hay in order that they might eat before further deliberations.

Less-than-unanimous Verdicts

To avoid hung juries caused by one or two jury members, some states have broken with the traditional unanimous verdict rule in criminal trials. Legislation has been passed in these states permitting less than the unanimous verdict to be reached in certain criminal cases. All states require that the verdict be unanimous in cases where the maximum penalty may be death, but vary somewhat in the number required to arrive at a verdict. Some require an eleven-to-one verdict, some as few as nine-to-three. The less-than-unanimous verdict has received the sanction of the United States Supreme Court in two companion cases decided in 1972. (See *Johnson* v. *Louisiana* 406 US 356 [1972], and *Apodaca* v. *Oregon,* 406 US 404 [1972].) In the *Johnson* case the defendant was convicted of robbery by a nine-to-three verdict in the Criminal District Court of the Parish of Orleans. In the *Apodaca* case, the facts reveal that "Robert Apodaca, Henry Morgan Coopers, Jr., and James Arnold Madden were convicted respectively of assault with a deadly weapon, burglary in a dwelling, and grand larceny before separate Oregon juries, all of which returned less than unanimous verdicts. The vote in the case of Cooper was ten to two, the minimum requisite vote under Oregon law for sustaining a conviction." Johnson as well as the defendants in the *Apodaca* case took their convictions to the United States Supreme Court on the ground that they had been denied their guarantee of a trial by jury as provided by the Sixth Amendment and made applicable to the States by the Fourteenth Amendment. These defendants contended that permitting the conviction of a less-than-unanimous verdict did not constitute a trial by jury.

Johnson alleged that when a jury rendered such a verdict, the prosecution had failed to prove the defendant guilty beyond a reasonable doubt, thus violating the right to due process of law. The Court did not agree with this contention and stated:

> We conclude that as to the nine jurors who voted to convict, the State satisfied its burden of proving guilt beyond a reasonable doubt. The remaining question under the Due Process Clause is whether the vote of three jurors for acquittal can be said to impeach the verdict of the other nine and to demonstrate that guilt was not in fact proved beyond such doubt. We hold that it cannot.
>
> Of course, the State's proof could be regarded as more certain if it had convinced all 12 jurors instead of only nine; it would have been even more compelling if it had been required to convince and had, in fact, convinced 24 or 36 jurors. But the fact remains that nine jurors—a substantial majority of the jury—were

convinced by the evidence. In our view disagreement of three jurors does not alone establish reasonable doubt, particularly when such a heavy majority of the jury, after having considered the dissenters' views, remains convinced of guilt. That rational men disagree is not in itself equivalent to a failure of proof by the State, nor does it indicate infidelity to the reasonable doubt standard. Jury verdicts finding guilt beyond a reasonable doubt are regularly sustained even though the evidence was such that the jury would have been justified in having a reasonable doubt; even though the trial judge might not have reached the same conclusion as the jury; and even though appellate judges are closely divided on the issue whether there was sufficient evidence to support a conviction.

In the *Apodaca* decision the Supreme Court further discusses the reasonable doubt argument as well as upholding the rights of the States to permit less than a unanimous verdict and still be within the due process of law clause. In the *Apodaca* decision the Court stated:

In *Williams* v. *Florida*, we had occasion to consider a related issue: whether the Sixth Amendment's right to trial by jury requires that all juries consist of 12 men. After considering the history of the 12-man requirement and the functions it performs in contemporary society, we concluded that it was not of constitutional stature. We reach the same conclusion today with regard to the requirement of unanimity.

Like the requirement that juries consist of 12 men, the requirement of unanimity rose during the Middle Ages and had become an accepted feature of the common-law jury by the 18th century.

Our inquiry must focus upon the function served by the jury in contemporary society. As we said in *Duncan*, the purpose of trial by jury is to prevent oppression by the Government by providing a safeguard against the corrupt or overzealous prosecutor and against the compliant, biased, or eccentric judge. Given this purpose, the essential feature of a jury obviously lies in the interposition between the accused and his accuser of the common-sense judgment of a group of laymen. A requirement of unanimity, however, does not materially contribute to the exercise of this commonsense judgment. As we said in *Williams,* a jury will come to such a judgment as long as it consists of a group of laymen representative of a cross section of the community who have the duty and the opportunity to deliberate, free from outside attempts at intimidation, on the question of a defendant's guilt. In terms of this function we perceive no difference between juries required to act unanimously and those permitted to convict or acquit by votes of 10 to two or 11 to one. Requiring unanimity would obviously produce hung juries in some situations where nonunanimous juries will convict or acquit. But in either case, the interest of the defendant in having the judgment of his peers interposed between himself and the officers of the State who prosecute and judge him is equally well served.

The defendants in the *Apodaca* case, as did Johnson, contended that a unanimous verdict was necessary in order to comply with the beyond a reasonable doubt requirement for guilt, but the Court stated:

> We are quite sure that the Sixth Amendment itself has never been held to require proof beyond a reasonable doubt in criminal cases. The reasonable doubt standard developed separately from both the jury trial and the unanimous verdict. As the Court noted in the *Winship* case, the rule requiring proof of crime beyond a reasonable doubt did not crystalize in this country until after the Constitution was adopted. And in that case, which held such a burden of proof to be constitutionally required, the Court purported to draw no support from the Sixth Amendment.
>
> Defendant's argument that the Sixth Amendment requires jury unanimity in order to give effect to the reasonable doubt standard thus founders on the fact that the Sixth Amendment does not require proof beyond a reasonable doubt at all. The reasonable doubt argument is rooted, in effect, in due process and has been rejected in *Johnson* v. *Louisiana*.

Mr. Justice Powell in his concurring opinion made some comments worthy of noting in upholding the less than unanimous verdict. Among other comments he stated:

> . . . There is no reason to believe, on the basis of experience in Oregon or elsewhere, that a unanimous decision of 12 jurors is more likely to serve the high purpose of jury trial, or is entitled to greater respect in the community, than the same decision joined in the 10 members of a jury of 12. The standard of due process assured by the Oregon Constitution provides a sufficient guarantee that the government will not be permitted to impose its judgment on an accused without first meeting the full burden of its prosecutorial duty. . . .
>
> Removal of the unanimity requirement could well minimize the potential for hung juries occasioned either by bribery or juror irrationality. Furthermore, the rule that juries must speak with a single voice often leads, not to full agreement among the 12 but to agreement by none and compromise by all, despite the frequent absence of a rational basis for such compromise. . . .

The petitioners (defendants) contended that their right to a jury composed of a cross section of a community was interfered with by

the less-than-unanimous verdict. Their petitions alleged that unless unanimity is required, the viewpoint of a minority of the jurors representing
minority groups is excluded from discussion during the deliberation.
They also alleged that whether the verdict is conviction or acquittal, it
may be the unjust product of racism, bigotry, or an emotionally inflamed
trial. To this contention Mr. Justice Powell stated:

> Such fears materialize only when the jury's majority, responding to
> these extraneous pressures, ignores the evidence and the instruc-
> tions of the court as well as the rational arguments of the minority.
> The risk, however, that a jury in a particular case will fail to meet its
> high responsibility is inherent in any system which commits deci-
> sions of guilt or innocence to untrained laymen drawn at random
> from the community. In part, at least, the majority-verdict rule must
> rely on the same principle which underlies our historic dedication
> to jury trial; both systems are premised on the conviction that each
> juror will faithfully perform his assigned duty. . . . Even before the
> jury is sworn substantial protection against the selection of a repre-
> sentative but wilfully irresponsible jury is assured by the wide avail-
> ability of peremptory challenges and challenges for cause. The
> likelihood of miscarriage of justice is further diminished by the
> judges' use of full jury instructions, detailing the applicable bur-
> dens of proof, informing the jurors of their duty to weigh the views
> of fellow jurors, and reminding them of the solemn responsibility
> imposed by their oaths. Trial judges also retain the power to direct
> acquittals in cases in which the evidence of guilt is lacking, or to set
> aside verdicts once rendered when the evidence is insufficient to
> support a conviction. Furthermore, in cases in which public emo-
> tion runs high or pretrial publicity threatens a fair trial, judges
> possess broad power to grant changes of venue, and to impose
> restrictions on the extent of press coverage.
>
> In light of such protections it is unlikely that the
> Oregon "ten-of-twelve" rule will account for an increase in the
> number of cases in which injustice will be occasioned by a biased
> or prejudiced jury. It may be wise to recall Mr. Justice White's
> admonition in *Murphy* v. *Waterfront Comm'n.*, 378 US 52 (1963),
> that the Constitution "protects against real dangers, not remote
> and speculative possibilities."

Since the United States Supreme Court has given sanction to less than a
unanimous verdict, it is highly possible that other states in the future will
adopt this verdict requirement.

It has been argued that there is no sound reason, other than
tradition, for the requirement of the unanimous verdict. The origin of the
unanimous verdict is unclear. By the latter part of the fourteenth century
the unanimous verdict was required, but it was not the jury verdict as we
know it today. As pointed out in the history of the jury trial, in the four-

teenth century convicted persons were often subject to cruel and unusual punishment. It has been alleged that one of the reasons for the unanimous verdict at that time was to avoid such punishment as often as possible. Those who are for the less-than-unanimous verdict allege that the convicted person is not subjected to cruel and unusual punishment today, thus there is no need for the unanimous verdict. This verdict would also eliminate many hung juries, resulting in fewer retrials and saving court costs.

The arguments of those who oppose the less-than-unanimous verdict are just as strong. It is stated that abolishing the unanimous verdict in order to prevent hung juries is a shallow argument and not sufficient reason for such an action. Some argue, as did Mr. Justice Douglas in his dissent in the *Johnson* case, that the less-than-unanimous verdict prohibits the minority members of the jury from presenting their arguments, that might prevent a conviction when the minority have a real doubt as to guilt. It is also argued that if this verdict is permitted, the next step may be eliminating the presumption of innocence or proving the defendant guilty beyond a reasonable doubt. It should be pointed out that the Bill of Rights says nothing about a specific number of twelve persons being required to compose a jury, a verdict being unanimous, proving the defendant guilty beyond a reasonable doubt, or presuming innocence. These rights of the accused have been established by tradition, but allegedly have a constitutional standard, and any break with this standard will weaken our justice system.

The United States Supreme Court, however, in *Burch* v. *Louisiana*, 60 L Ed 2d 96 (1979), held that the verdict of a jury composed of only six persons must be unanimous for "nonpetty offenses." The court stated that "to hold anything less than a unanimous verdict by a jury of only six persons would be a threat to the constitutional guarantee of a trial by an impartial jury.

Review Questions

1. What is the purpose of the charge to the jury?
2. List five points of law that a judge may explain to the jury before it goes into deliberation.
3. What is the purpose of the deliberation?
4. What may the jury take with it during the deliberation?
5. Define a hung jury.
6. What is the purpose of the Allen instruction?

Local Procedure

1. May the judge comment on the weight of the evidence and the credibility of the witnesses?
2. May the Allen instruction be read to the jury?
3. Must the jury reach a unanimous verdict?
4. May an alternate juror be sequestered with the jury during deliberation?

THE VERDICT, APPEALS, AND APPELLATE CITATIONS

fourteen

The Verdict

Derived from the Latin word *verdictum,* the word *verdict* means a true declaration. In a criminal trial the verdict is the decision of the jury. In a court trial the verdict is the decision of the judge, as to the guilt or innocence of the defendant. Once the verdict has been agreed upon, the foreman will so advise the bailiff, the officer who is in charge of the jury. The bailiff will then inform the judge who will reconvene court in order that the verdict may be received. Since the deliberation often takes considerable time, the judge usually will adjourn court on the case while the jury is deliberating. This permits the judge to perform other duties, while being available at all times to furnish further instructions or information that the jury may request while deliberating. After the court is reconvened the judge will instruct the bailiff to return the jury to the courtroom. On their arrival the judge may request that their names be called to make certain that all the jurors are present. If a juror should be missing, the judge may have to declare a mistrial unless the juror's whereabouts can be determined, and his or her presence can be immediately obtained.

After all the jurors are accounted for, the judge will ask the foreman if the jury has agreed upon a verdict. If answering in the affirmative, the judge may ask the foreman to announce the verdict, or if the verdict is in writing the judge may request that it be given to the clerk of the court to read. Not all jurisdictions require that the verdict be in writing and signed by the foreman. Whether required to be in writing or not, most jurisdictions furnish forms to the jury on which they may record their verdict. The defendant must be present at the time the verdict is announced in open court, unless his whereabouts cannot be determined. In that case the verdict may be announced in the absence of the accused.

After the verdict is announced the prosecution or the defense may request that the jurors be polled individually to determine how each voted on the verdict. When the verdict must be unanimous, if one or more jurors allege that the verdict does not express all of the jurors' opinions, the judge may instruct the jury to return to the jury room for further deliberation. If the facts should warrant such action, the judge may discharge that jury and declare a mistrial.

If the jury finds the verdict to be not guilty, the defendant is entitled to immediate release if in custody. If the defendant is out on bail, the security will be returned to the person who posted it, as it will have served its purpose. In either event the defendant is free from further prosecution on the crime charged.

If the defendant is found guilty, the next procedural step is sentencing. A few other matters should be considered before the discussion of the sentencing. The jury may have found the defendant guilty as charged in the accusatory pleading, or the jury may have found the defendant guilty of a lesser degree. It is possible that the jury found the defendant guilty on some of the charges stated in the accusatory pleading and not guilty on others. In addition to finding the defendant guilty, the jury may be called upon to determine whether the defendant was armed at the time that a crime was committed. All of these matters may affect the sentence imposed. Once the verdict is announced in open court it will be recorded in the record of the case. At this point the jury is entitled to be discharged, as they will have fulfilled their function, unless they are involved in the sentencing procedure. If it is a court trial, the judge has the responsibility of rendering the verdict.

Even though the jury returns a verdict of guilty, most jurisdictions permit the judge to modify the verdict. If the judge believes that the evidence shows the defendant not guilty to the degree that the jury found him or her guilty, the judge may modify the verdict by finding the defendant guilty of a lesser degree or lesser crime included in the criminal act. A few states permit the judge to go one step further. The guilty verdict of a jury may be set aside and a judgment of acquittal entered or the judge may set aside the verdict and dismiss the charge. In either event the judge's action in this regard is usually a bar to any further prosecutive action against the defendant. The right of a judge to set aside the entire verdict is very powerful. But such action is permitted on the grounds that if the evidence is insufficient to establish the defendant guilty beyond a reasonable doubt, the judge must set aside the verdict in the interest of justice. However, a judge may not set aside a verdict of not guilty, as this would deny the defendant the right of a trial by jury.

New Trial and Mistrial

As stated, if a judge believes that the prosecution has failed to prove the defendant guilty beyond a reasonable doubt, the judge may enter a judgment of acquittal in some jurisdictions. This action occurs before the case is turned over to the jury for deliberation, and takes the case out of their hands. But by permitting the judge to set aside the jury's guilty verdict, the case is taken from the jury after it has fulfilled its function. This action often draws criticism from jurors since it voids their function. To avoid this criticism, judges will grant a motion for a new trial rather than enter the judgment of acquittal or set aside the verdict.

After a jury has returned a verdict of guilty, the defense may request that a new trial be granted. Generally, a new trial may be granted only on the motion, or request, of the defendant, and not on the judge's own motion. If a new trial is granted, it means that the case will be heard again from the beginning, usually before the same judge but with a new jury. The grounds for granting a new trial are specifically set forth in the codes of most states. These grounds usually include such matters as the jury receiving evidence of the case out of court; the jurors separating without permission of the court after being sequestered; the verdict being decided on by lot, or by means other than a fair expression of opinion; misconduct of the jurors, preventing the defendant from receiving a fair trial; or a guilty verdict being returned that was not supported by the evidence. Although it has been stated that a new trial may be granted only on statutory grounds, courts have held that new trials should be granted on nonstatutory grounds when a failure to do so would result in a denial of a fair trial to the defendant. In one case, the judge stated in comments to the jury that, in all his experience as a lawyer and judge, he had never seen so many defense witnesses, including the defendant himself, whose truthfulness was in doubt. Even though the judge informed the jurors that it was their duty to weigh the credibility of the witnesses, he felt that, after a guilty verdict was returned by the jury, a new trial should be granted in the interest of justice. In this way, the judge was correcting his own remarks that bordered on directing the jury to return a verdict of guilty.

One of the more frequent grounds utilized for granting a new trial is newly discovered evidence by the defense. In order for a defendant to avail oneself of this ground, the defense must be in a position to prove to the satisfaction of the judge that the newly discovered evidence was material and that the evidence could not with due diligent search have been discovered by the time of the first trial. It has been held by some courts that the newly discovered evidence must be of sufficient importance to indicate a probable acquittal in a new trial. This evidence must be more than just a repetition of the evidence presented by the defense during the first trial, unless the repetitive evidence would materially strengthen previously presented evidence.

The prosecution has the right to argue against the granting of a new trial. It may endeavor to prove that there was not due diligent search before the first trial to justify a new trial, or may argue against other grounds presented by the defense. It is not always necessary for the prosecution to argue against the motion for a new trial. The judge may deny the motion without any argument being presented.

Granting a new trial is not to be confused with declaring a mistrial. The motion for a new trial may not be made until a verdict of guilty has been rendered. A mistrial may be declared any time during the trial proceedings, on the judge's own motion or at the request of the defense. The right of the prosecution to request a mistrial is somewhat restricted and not permitted in all jurisdictions. A mistrial may be declared at any time there is misconduct that is so prejudicial that the defense would be denied a fair trial. The misconduct may occur early in the trial proceedings. For example, if during the opening statement by the prosecuting attorney, he should refer to the defendant as an "ex-con" or otherwise imply a past criminal record, the judge may decide that the remarks were so prejudicial that the defendant could not get a fair trial. The judge may at that time declare a mistrial. If the mistrial is declared at that point in the proceedings not too much trial time is lost, but if the misconduct comes late in the trial, such as just before deliberation, much time, energy, and money will have been wasted. Sometimes, rather than declare a mistrial, the judge will instruct the jury to disregard the misconduct and inform them that it is not to affect them in rendering a verdict. This admonition is not always effective as jurors cannot always erase something that they have heard. If the defendant is convicted, the failure to declare a mistrial may be grounds for reversal on appeal. As stated, a judge may declare a mistrial when the jury cannot agree on a verdict. Defendants have argued that the inability of a jury to agree on a verdict indicates both that the prosecution has not proved the defendant guilty beyond a reasonable doubt, and that the defendant is entitled to a judgment of acquittal. This argument has been rejected by the United States Supreme Court. The Court has held that the defendant may be retried under these circumstances. The Court stated that it recognizes "society's interest in giving the prosecution one complete opportunity to convict those who have violated its laws." (See *Arizona* v. *Washington*, 54 L Ed 2d 717 [1978].) However, before a mistrial may be declared when a jury cannot agree on a verdict, the judge must weigh the situation carefully. Courts have held that if a judge declares a mistrial too quickly when further deliberation would have resulted in a verdict, the defendant has been deprived of his "valued right to have his trial completed by a particular tribunal." But if the judge fails to declare a mistrial when the jury cannot agree on a verdict after lengthy deliberation, there is a risk that a verdict may result from pressure by some jurors on others that would deny the jurors an opportunity for individual expression.

If a mistrial is declared at the request of the defense, generally the case can be tried again at the discretion of the prosecuting attorney. The retrial is not considered a violation of the double jeopardy guarantee since the defendant, in requesting a mistrial, waives the guarantee against double jeopardy. However, some jurisdictions hold that unless there is sufficient cause to declare a mistrial or unless the defendant agrees to the mistrial, jeopardy may have set in, and the defendant cannot be retried. If the misconduct prejudicial to the prosecution was committed by defense counsel or the accused, the prosecution may have little or no remedy.

However, in the *Arizona* v. *Washington* case, the United States Supreme Court did uphold the action of the trial judge in declaring a mistrial at the request of the prosecution when a defense attorney made improper statements to the jury during the opening argument. The trial judge concluded that the remarks were so prejudicial that the prosecution would be denied the right to have the case tried before an impartial jury. The Supreme Court stated that before a trial judge could declare a mistrial over the objections of the defense, it must be established that there was a "manifest necessity" for such action. In other words, there must be sufficient evidence to prove that such action should be taken. The Court stated:

> Because of the variety of circumstances that may make it necessary to discharge a jury before a trial is concluded, and because those circumstances do not invariably create unfairness to the accused, his valued right to have the trial concluded by a particular tribunal is sometimes subordinate to the public interest in affording the prosecutor one full and fair opportunity to present his evidence to an impartial jury. Yet in view of the importance of the right, and the fact that it is frustrated by any mistrial, the prosecutor must shoulder the burden of justifying the mistrial if he is to avoid the double jeopardy bar. His burden is a heavy one. The prosecutor must demonstrate "manifest necessity" for any mistrial over the objections of the defendant.

Yet in *Carsey v. United States,* 392 F 2d 810 (1967), the Court of Appeals held that the improper remarks made by the defense attorney to the jury during the closing argument could have been corrected if the judge had instructed the jury to disregard the improper remarks of the defense attorney. The Court held that declaring a mistrial was improper and that the defendant had been placed in jeopardy and could not be retried.

In a dissenting opinion in the *Carsey* case, Justice Tamm took the opposite view from that of the majority, stating:

> When appellant's (defendant's) trial counsel, in his closing plea to the jury, advised the jury of two prior mistrials he did it deliberately for the purpose of creating doubt of the defendant's guilt in the minds of the jurors who, understandably, would ask themselves whether a reasonable doubt of guilt had not been established when two prior juries, upon the same evidence, had been unable to reach a verdict. If the prosecutor had made the same statement to the jury for the purpose of injecting into their thinking a fact completely outside of the evidence before them, we would label it as both a "foul blow" and an "improper method calculated to produce a wrongful conviction." I am unwilling and unable to agree that the questioned statement herein was proper when made by defense counsel when it so obviously would have been improper if made by Government counsel. The statement would have been adequate and proper basis for the granting of a mistrial if the prosecutor had made it, and I must conclude that it was proper and adequate for the trial judge's action when it was made by defense counsel. Defense counsel's initial statement created and triggered

the factual situation resulting in the mistrial, despite the majority's feeble attempt to transfer the responsibility to the prosecuting attorney.

The majority opinion places a premium on chicanery and invites defense counsel to engage in it by its "you cannot lose" result. If this opinion is to prevail, defense counsel may resort to trickery in the court room secure in the knowledge that if he gets by with it he will have the benefit of his misconduct, and if he does not a mistrial will be declared and thereby he reaps an even greater reward for his unethical behavior.

The facts of another case reflect that during the trial recess the defendant, who was out on bail, approached a drinking fountain in the courthouse hall and drew a cup of water and handed it to one of the women jurors, at the same time carrying on a conversation with her. Thereafter the defendant proceeded to give other members of the jury drinks of water. This conduct was observed by an officer who informed the judge. After court reconvened, the judge questioned the officer on the stand about the incident, and the judge declared a mistrial. The defense attorney endeavored to place the defendant on the stand to prove that no conversation pertaining to the facts of the case took place. The defense attorney also tried to accept the blame for the misconduct of the defendant by stating that he had failed to admonish the defendant against having any contact with the jury. The judge's opinion was that the defendant was endeavoring to make a favorable impression on the jury, and a mistrial was declared. In addition the defendant was held in contempt of court. On retrial the defendant entered a plea of once in jeopardy that the judge refused to accept, and the defendant was found guilty on the original charge of attempted robbery. The defendant appealed the conviction on the grounds that the guarantee against double jeopardy had been violated by the retrial. The Appellate Court agreed with the defendant. The Court stated:

> Once a jury has been impaneled and sworn to try a defendant, jeopardy attaches, and its subsequent discharge when not authorized by law or by defendant's consent, is equivalent to an acquittal and constitutes former jeopardy barring retrial.
>
> As to what constitutes sufficient cause to authorize the discharge of a jury, the courts have required a showing that there exists some legal necessity resulting from physical causes beyond the control of the court.
>
> The determination as to whether the required legal necessity exists is a matter left to the discretion of the trial court. However, "the power of the Court to discharge a jury without the consent of the prisoner is not an absolute, uncontrolled discretionary power. It must be exercised in accordance with established

268

legal rules and a sound legal discretion in the application of such rules to the facts and circumstances of each particular case, and in this State is subject to review by an appellate Court."

The trial court's action in summarily declaring a mistrial solely on the basis of the officer's testimony that he had observed defendant talking with two of the jurors during the recess on their way back to the court room from the water cooler was unjustified and constituted an abuse of discretion. Before the matter was ruled on defendant should have been given a reasonable opportunity to present his version of the incident and with proper participation by his counsel. (See *People* v. *Huff,* 63 Cal Rptr 317 [1967].)

This decision has been criticized by many legal scholars on the basis that the judge did have sufficient cause to declare a mistrial. It is alleged that the misconduct by the defendant in contacts with the jury could not help but create some favorable impression to the detriment of the prosecution. It is further alleged that if a material witness for the prosecution had made this contact with the jury, the judge undoubtedly would have declared a mistrial, as the defendant could not have received a fair trial from an impartial jury (See *Turner* v. *Louisiana*).

Arrest of Judgment and Pronouncement of Judgment

If a new trial is not granted after the verdict is rendered, the next procedure is the *pronouncement of judgment* by the judge. Pronouncement of judgment is usually thought of as the oral sentencing of the defendant by the judge. But technically, pronouncement of judgment entails more than the oral statement of what the sentence will be. The pronouncement of judgment will be reduced to a written document generally known as the *judgment.* This judgment will set forth the plea entered; the verdict; and, if guilty, will reflect the sentence or other disposition of the case—all of which are entered in the case record. Technically the pronouncement of judgment is made whether there is an acquittal or a conviction, but in many jurisdictions it is synonymous with the pronouncement of the sentence. In misdemeanor cases, most jurisdictions permit the pronouncement of judgment in the absence of the defendant. In a felony conviction, the presence of the defendant is required unless the accused cannot be located after due diligent search. In this case pronouncement of judgment may be made in his absence.

Jurisdictions vary some in the time within which the pronouncement of judgment must take place after a guilty plea is entered or a guilty verdict is returned. In misdemeanor convictions in some jurisdictions the pronouncement may be made immediately; if not, it must be pronounced within a few days. Other jurisdictions provide that the pronouncement of judgment may not occur in less than six hours and not more than five days. The six-hour limit allows time for the convicted defendant to arrange personal affairs before serving time. In felony convictions there is usually a considerable delay permitted in the pronouncement of judgment. The delay permits time for a presentence investigation, conducted in order that a more equitable sentence may be imposed. The delay is usually not longer than one month. It is to the advantage of both society and the convicted defendant to have sentence pronounced without unnecessary delay. The defendant is entitled to know the sentence as soon as possible in order that the term may begin. As for society's interest, there is little comfort in having a convicted felon free on bail who may be in a position to commit other crimes while awaiting the pronouncement of sentence.

Prior to the pronouncement of judgment, the defendant may file a motion in the *arrest of judgment,* or in most jurisdictions the judge may enter the motion. In many jurisdictions the law provides that at the time the convicted defendant is brought before the judge for pronouncement of judgment, the judge must inquire of the defendant "if there is any legal reason why judgment should not be pronounced." It is at this time that the defendant will show legal cause for the arrest of judgment. Some jurisdictions hold that making the inquiry of the defendant is a useless procedure, and the defendant is entitled to make a motion any time after the verdict is rendered.

The motion for the arrest of judgment is made on statutory grounds. These grounds include such matters as present insanity of the defendant. If it is determined that the defendant is insane at the time of the pronouncement of judgment, it must be postponed until sanity has been restored since a defendant may not be sentenced while insane. The motion may be made on the grounds that there was some defect in the accusatory pleading that had not been successfully challenged previously, such as the failure to state that a crime had been committed. If the motion for arrest of judgment is denied or none is entered, the next procedure is the pronouncement of the sentence. In most jurisdictions, before the sentence is pronounced the defendant is entitled to make a statement in his or her own behalf if wished. This statement is generally a plea for leniency or consideration in the sentencing. If a judge fails to grant the defendant an opportunity to make a statement, the sentence may be set aside on appeal. The case does not have to be retried under the circumstances but the sentence will be set aside and the case will be sent back to the trial court for resentencing after the defendant has been given an opportunity to speak.

After the defendant has made a plea, if any, to the judge or jury, he or she will be sentenced. Before entering into the sentencing procedure, the appeals that may be taken by the defendant or the prosecution should be discussed. The outcome of the appeal could determine whether a defendant serves a sentence.

Appeals

Appeal by the Defendant

If convicted, a defendant will usually appeal the conviction to the appropriate appellate court if there is any basis at all for the appeal. The defendant's appeal may be well-founded as there may have been some error committed during the trial that was prejudicial. Or the defendant may attempt to appeal the case merely to delay serving the imposed sentence.

Freedom Pending Appeal. Generally the defendant must file a notice of appeal within a few days after the pronouncement of judgment. Whether the defendant remains free on bail pending the outcome of appeal is largely within the discretion of the judge. There is no inherent right to remain free from custody once convicted, as the presumption of innocence is lost. In determining whether a defendant should be free pending the appeal, the judge may consider whether the efforts to appeal were based upon frivolous grounds; whether the appeal was merely a delaying tactic to avoid serving the sentence; whether there may be a temptation to flee the jurisdiction of the court pending the appeal; or whether the defendant may be a threat to the community if free on bail.

Whether the defendant remains free on bail or is incarcerated, the judge in most instances will have sentenced the defendant. If remaining free on bail, no time will be served until the outcome of the appeal is determined. If the conviction is reversed, the defendant will not have served any time. But if the defendant is incarcerated pending the appeal, the sentence will have begun to be served. If the conviction is reversed and the defendant is not retried or cannot be retried, there is little that can be done to compensate for the time spent other than to clear the name of the accused. But if the conviction is affirmed or if the defendant is retried after a reversal, credit will be given for the time spent in incarceration pending the appeal. It should be pointed out that not all appeals are made immediately after a conviction. An appeal may not be taken until several years of a sentence have been served. These appeals are usually based on the result of some United States Supreme Court decision that changes the justice procedure in some manner and is made retroactive, that is, the decision is applicable to all convictions irrespective of when the case was tried. If the decision is not made retroactive, it is only applicable to those defendants whose cases have not been finally decided previous to the United States Supreme Court's decision.

Not all efforts by a defendant to appeal a conviction to an appellate court are successful. Sufficient grounds must be alleged in order for the appellate court to hear the appeal. The grounds on which a defendant may appeal a case are numerous. Whatever grounds are alleged, it must be shown that the error committed during the trial was sufficiently prejudicial that the defendant was denied a fair trial or that there was a miscarriage of justice. Some of the grounds most frequently alleged on appeal are: there was insufficient probable cause to make a lawful arrest; a confession that was improperly obtained was admitted as evidence; physical evidence was introduced that was unlawfully seized; a failure to grant a change of venue; insufficient representation of competent counsel; failure to give pertinent instructions to the jury; a denial of a new trial; or the failure to declare a mistrial when there was prejudicial misconduct.

Method of Appeal.   Upon appealing the case the defendant, through counsel or on one's own, will submit to the appropriate appellate court a brief setting forth the alleged error committed during the trial with citations of appellate court decisions upholding the contended error. A transcript of the trial proceedings will accompany the brief. The prosecution will submit a brief in an effort to show why the conviction should be affirmed and not reversed. The appellate court will review the briefs and the transcript. After doing so, it may conclude that there is no ground for appeal and the court will deny a hearing on the matter. A hearing date will be set if the appellate court feels that the appeal is worthy of a hearing. At the hearing the defense attorney and prosecution's representative, usually the state attorney general, assisted by the prosecuting attorney who was responsible for the conviction, will be present to argue their sides of the case. The defendant is usually not present, as it is not an inherent right to be present at an appeal hearing. After the hearing the appellate court justices will consider the matter and come to some conclusion as to whether the conviction should be affirmed or reversed. In making its determination, the appellate court will consider whether there was error or conduct that was so prejudicial that the defendant was denied a fair trial. Sometimes the appellate court will hold that there was error or misconduct during the trial, but that this was not serious enough to deny the defendant a fair trial. Under these circumstances the error is referred to as "harmless error."

If the appellate court denies the defendant a hearing on the appeal, there is little the defendant can do about the decision. The appellate court may be called the court of "last resort"; its decision is usually final unless the defendant can prove that one of the United States constitutional guarantees was violated, and then the defendant may eventually appeal to the United States Supreme Court. The Supreme Court may or may not grant a hearing, depending upon the validity of the alleged violation. It may grant a hearing in an effort to determine if there was a violation; if there was, the Supreme Court will reverse the conviction. If the Supreme Court denies the hearing or affirms the conviction, there is no further appeal that can be taken by the defendant.

Retrial After Reversal.   If a conviction is reversed by either the state appellate court or the United States Supreme Court, the states differ concerning whether the defendant may be retried. If the reversal is based on the fact that a law is unconstitutional, that jeopardy had attached, or that a law is too vague in wording to indicate the violation, there cannot be a retrial. But if the reversal is based upon the introduction of illegally seized evidence or an improperly obtained confession, in many states the defendant may be retried, and the improperly introduced evidence will not be admissible during the retrial. The prosecuting attorney has to determine whether the other evidence was sufficient in obtaining a conviction. If not, the charge will undoubtedly be dismissed. A few states do not permit a retrial on reversal of a conviction, as it would be a violation of the guarantee against double jeopardy. Other states hold that on appealing a conviction the defendant waives the double jeopardy guarantee.

   If a defendant is successful in getting a conviction reversed on appeal and is retried and convicted, may the judge impose an increased sentence after the new trial? This question was answered by the United States Supreme Court in the case of *North Carolina* v. *Pearce,* 397 US 711 (1969). The Court in that decision held that if identifiable misconduct by the defendant took place after the first trial the judge might impose an increased sentence, but the increase should not be based on the fact that the defendant had appealed his case. The Court stated:

> Due process of law requires that vindictiveness against a defendant for having successfully attacked his first conviction must play no part in the sentence he receives after a new trial. And since the fear of such vindictiveness may unconstitutionally deter a defendant's exercise of the right to appeal or collaterally attack his first conviction, due process also requires that a defendant be freed of apprehension of such a retaliatory motivation on the part of the sentencing judge.
>
>   In order to assure the absence of such a motivation, we have concluded that whenever a judge imposes a more severe sentence upon a defendant after a new trial, the reasons for his doing so must affirmatively appear. Those reasons must be based

upon objective information concerning identifiable conduct on the part of the defendant occurring after the time of the original sentencing proceedings. And the factual data upon which the increased sentence is based must be made part of the record, so that the constitutional legitimacy of the increased sentence may be fully reviewed on appeal.

Justice White, who concurred in part with the majority opinion, stated that in his opinion he would "authorize an increased sentence on retrial based on any objective, identifiable factual data not known to the trial judge at the time of the original sentencing proceeding." Only future decisions will tell whether the Court would sanction this reason for an increased sentence, rather than the majority's limited reason of "identifiable conduct" by the defendant after the original sentence. The Court did conclude that on an increased sentence after a new trial, the defendant must be given credit for the time served on the original sentence.

Appeal by Prosecution

States vary considerably concerning the prosecution's right of appeal. A few states deny the prosecution any right to appeal as it would result in a violation of the guarantee against double jeopardy. Some permit a limited right of appeal by the prosecution when the appeal does not involve the double jeopardy guarantee. Generally, an appeal may be taken by the prosecution on a judge's order setting aside or dismissing an accusatory pleading. But the appeal may be taken only when the setting aside or dismissal was before the trial began; otherwise, jeopardy will have set in. An appeal may also be taken on a grant of a new trial, an arrest of judgment, or a modification of a verdict or punishment imposed. In most states, there is no right by the prosecution to appeal a case when an acquittal verdict has been rendered. As stated in *Washington* v. *Arizona*, a judgment of acquittal is final regardless of how erroneously it may have been arrived at. However, a few states do allow an appeal by the prosecution after a verdict of acquittal has been returned. The appeal is allowed when the prosecution alleges that a serious error was made by the judge on a ruling of law or procedure. The appeal is permitted so that guidelines may be established for future cases, but the appellate court has no authority to reverse the acquittal.

An increasing number of states allow the prosecution to appeal a judge's order suppressing evidence. It is generally held that where such an appeal is permissible, the appeal may be taken only on an order suppressing evidence that was made before the trial began and not during the trial. Some states do not permit an appeal of an order suppressing evidence that was made even before the trial. The courts of these states hold that the prosecution is no more disadvantaged by an erroneous ruling before the trial than one during the trial, when such ruling leads to an acquittal.

Appeal of a Guilty Plea

As previously discussed, a plea of guilty is equal to a conviction, and this must be explained to the defendant before the plea may be accepted. Therefore, it is paradoxical to permit a defendant to appeal a conviction resulting from a voluntary plea of guilty, but some states do permit a defendant to appeal a guilty plea. The grounds for the appeal are based upon some alleged constitutional, jurisdictional, or other grounds concerning the legality of the proceedings. For example, the defendant may allege that the judge failed to explain the significance of the guilty plea as required by *Boykin* v. *Alabama;* that the judge denied the defendant the right to withdraw the guilty plea; or that there was a violation of the agreement pertaining to the plea bargain. There have been times when a defendant was denied a request for suppression of evidence, and thereafter entered a plea of guilty knowing that the trial would result in conviction. Under these circumstances, the defendant may appeal the guilty plea in an effort to determine if the evidence should have been suppressed.

Appellate Court Citations

Judges of the appellate courts are generally referred to as *justices*. The number of justices comprising an appellate court varies from one state to another as well as from one appellate court to another. As pointed out in chapter 2, many states have only a single appellate court that is generally referred to as the supreme court. Other states have a bilateral appellate court system in which there is an appellate court and a supreme court. Usually only three justices will comprise an appellate court, whereas the supreme court varies usually from five to nine justices. Not all justices must agree on the decision—only a majority. Once the decision is made, one of the justices agreeing with the majority will put the decision in writing, stating whether the conviction was upheld or reversed, and the reasoning behind the decision. A dissenting justice, if any, may or may not decide to write a dissenting opinion, setting forth the reasons for disagreement with the majority.

Recording Court Decisions

The decisions handed down by the appellate courts are recorded in official publications so they may act as guidelines for future cases. Each decision is given a *citation* number in order that the decision may be filed, indexed, and located by attorneys, judges, and others having occasion to refer to a particular decision. The citation will include the name, or title, of the case; the name of the official record book; the volume and page number; and the year in which the decision was handed down by the appellate court.

The following is a typical example of an appellate court citation: *Bridges* v. *State,* 247 Wis 350 (1945). *Bridges* v. *State* is the title of the decision; 247 refers to the volume number of the official record; the "Wis" is an abbreviation for the state of Wisconsin, indicating that the decision is that of the Wisconsin Supreme Court; 350 is the page number where the decision begins; 1945 is the date, or year, in which the decision was handed down by the Wisconsin Supreme Court. Sometimes the date will precede the volume and page number. The way that the titles of the decisions refer to the persons involved varies among the states. Instead of the title being *Bridges* v. *State,* the title may be *State* v. *Bridges,* depending on the manner in which the appeal was taken. In some states the word "People" or "Commonwealth" is substituted for "State."

In addition to the appellate decisions being published in official publications, the decisions, particularly those of the Supreme Court, are included in the publications of private companies. A different citation is reflected for these publications. In order that a particular decision may be more readily located by a judge or attorney, both the official citation and citation of private companies are included when a case decision is referred to. For example, the West Publishing Company, St. Paul, Minnesota, publishes the decisions of the supreme courts of the various states. These decisions are reported by geographical areas. This reporting system is known as the *National Reporter System.* The supreme court decisions of the states of Iowa, Michigan, Minnesota, Nebraska, North Dakota, South Dakota, and Wisconsin are published in the *North Western Reporter,* and the citation carries the abbreviation of "NW." Returning to the case of *Bridges* v. *State,* 247 Wis 350, there may be the additional citation of 19 NW 2d 529 (1945). The figure "2d" following the initials "NW" indicates a second series of *North Western Reporter* volumes.

The supreme court decisions of the states of Connecticut, Delaware, Maine, Maryland, New Hampshire, New Jersey, Pennsylvania, Rhode Island, and Vermont are published in the *Atlantic Reporter,* abbreviated as "A." The supreme court decisions of the states of Illinois, Indiana, Massachusetts, New York, and Ohio are published in the *North Eastern Reporter.* The decisions of the supreme courts of the states of Alaska, Arizona, California, Colorado, Hawaii, Idaho, Kansas, Montana, Nevada, New Mexico, Oklahoma, Oregon, Utah, Washington, and Wyoming are published in the *Pacific Reporter.* The *South Eastern Reporter* includes the supreme court decisions of the states of Georgia, South Carolina, Virginia, and West Virginia. The *Southern Reporter* publishes the decisions of the supreme courts of the states of Alabama, Florida, Louisiana, and Mississippi. The *South Western Reporter* publishes the decisions of the supreme courts of the states of Arkansas, Missouri, Kentucky, Tennessee, and Texas.

If a decision is handed down by the United States Supreme Court on an alleged violation of a constitutional guarantee, the following is an example of the official citation that would be used: *Pointer* v. *Texas,* 380 US 400 (1965). The United States Supreme Court decisions are published also by the West Publishing Company in a publication known as the *Supreme Court Reporter,* abbreviated as "S Ct." The *Pointer* decision would be cited as 85 S Ct 1065. The Lawyers Co-operative Publishing Company, Rochester, New York, also publishes the United States Supreme Court decisions in a publication known as the *Supreme Court Reports Lawyer's Edition,* abbreviated as "L Ed." Thus the *Pointer* decision may be cited as follows: *Pointer* v. *Texas,* 380 US 400, 85 S Ct 1065, 13 L Ed 2d 923 (1965).

In those states in which there is an appellate court below the supreme court, the decisions of these appellate courts are also published in an official publication. These decisions can usually be distinguished from the decisions of the supreme courts by the abbreviation "App" appearing after the abbreviation of the state.

Review Questions

1. What is a verdict?
2. Where is the verdict announced?
3. Must the defendant be present when the verdict is announced?
4. In what way are a mistrial and a new trial alike? In what way do they differ?
5. What is meant by an "arrest of judgment"?
6. What does the term "pronouncement of judgment" mean?
7. List three grounds on which the defendant may appeal a conviction.
8. Why is the prosecution limited in its right to appeal a verdict of acquittal in most jurisdictions?
9. What is the purpose of an appellate citation?
10. Explain the meaning of the following citation: *Pointer* v. *Texas,* 380 US 400 (1965).

Local Procedure

1. May the prosecution appeal a verdict of acquittal?
2. If an appellate court reverses a conviction, may the defendant be retried?

THE SENTENCE AND CORRECTIONAL PROCEDURES

fifteen

History of Punishment

In order to more fully understand the history of punishment and its severity, we begin by discussing early societies. The social world of early mankind was composed of separate isolated groups, referred to as clans. These clans were an aggregate of families. Each family was a unit within the clan. The eldest male was the ruler in these ancient societies. If harm was done to some member of the clan by another member of the clan, it was the ruler's responsibility to right the wrong. If he were unable to right the wrong, other clan members were pressed into service for assistance. If the wrong was committed by a neighboring clan member, it was a religious duty of each wronged clan member to avenge the wrong. The belief was that an injury to any clan member was an injury to the entire clan. This philosophy of revenge usually ended with the clan waging war on the offender. If the offender could not be located, the revenge could be inflicted on any member of the neighboring clan.

The Blood Feud

As time passed, avenging the wrong became more of a family responsibility. The offended family member had the first and foremost responsibility to avenge the wrong. If the victim should be killed by the offender or die before the crime had been avenged, other family members had the responsibility to avenge the wrong. Again, if the offender could not be located, then the revenge would be inflicted on other family members. As pointed out in Chapter 2, this procedure resulted in what was known as the *blood feud*. Retaliation during a blood feud was often brutal and usually ended in the death of the offender.

In ancient days when the vengeance took the form of the blood feud there was little that the offender could do to escape. Even the members of the offender's own family would provide little protection since they would become the victims of the blood feud if the offender were not found. When time passed without a crime being avenged, family members often became disenchanted with carrying on the blood feud, particularly when they were not personally offended. Consequently members of the offended family became willing to accept money or property in return for inflicting physical retaliation on the offender or relations. This procedure became known as *atonement*. By the twelfth century atonement had grown in popularity, and the blood feud had been all but abolished. In the beginning atonement was primarily a family affair. But as families and clans were taken over by kingdoms, atonement was a source of revenue for kings or the church, depending on the crime. By this time the church had begun to take a dominant part in the affairs of mankind and sought sources of revenue. Not all crimes could be atoned, so the offender was required to stand trial. Trial could be by ordeal, battle, or compurgation. If found guilty by trial, the offender was subjected to the punishment prescribed for that particular crime. In many instances the punishment was death. If the death penalty were not imposed, the convicted offender would often be subjected to another form of severe physical punishment such as having a hand or ear amputated, or an eye gouged out. On display in the Marksburg Castle in Germany is a hinged metal, helmet-type face mask that was heated red hot and applied to the head of anyone convicted of treason. If a person bearing the scars of such punishment were later seen in public, anyone could kill that person without recourse being taken against the slayer.

As late as the middle of the twentieth century, certain primitive societies inflicted forms of unusual punishment on offenders. In New Guinea for example, an unusual form of punishment was meted out to men caught in the act of adultery. The offended husband was permitted to shoot an arrow at the groin of the offender, who stood fifty paces away. If the wife got pregnant, the husband was permitted to chop off the offender's head. This method of avenging the wrong was probably a carry over from ancient societies. Adultery was considered to be the worst offense that could be committed among clan members. It was thought that adultery disrupted the family unit more than murder, and threatened the foundation of the tribal religion.

Protection within a Church

A study of early judicial procedure reveals that offenders in Great Britain were also subjected to many forms of severe punishment. Often to escape punishment, an offender entered a church for sanctuary from pursuers attempting to inflict punishment. The offender was safe as long as he or she remained inside the church. Sometimes the pursuers surrounded the church and remained there for days to prevent escape. Often the pursuers would try to have the priests or clergy starve the offender into submission. Usually, the priests would not have anything to do with matters that interfered with the holiness of the sanctuary. This was the beginning of what became known as the *benefit of clergy*. Generally, whatever punishment was imposed for conviction of a particular crime was a mandatory sentence carried out regardless of severity.

Imprisonment as Punishment

Imprisonment as a form of punishment was not used at that time. In fact, under Roman law, imprisonment as punishment was illegal. In early English history, imprisonment was a means of holding the offender for trial and sentencing, but not for punishment. The imprisonment of convicted offenders was, and still is, a troublesome and expensive form of punishment.

Thus we find that in earlier times, swifter and less expensive forms of punishment were inflicted. Some use of imprisonment as a form of punishment was used at common law in England for a few minor offenses, such as vagrancy. The ecclesiastical courts also imposed imprisonment on convicted clergymen in some instances. But the death penalty, mutilation, and banishment were still the most frequently imposed forms of punishment. When a convicted person was banished from England, not only was the offender required to leave home, family, and friends, but his property was also confiscated by the king or the church. Banishment became another source of revenue for both king and church. It is alleged that as many as 100,000 persons were banished to the American colonies from England before the colonies received independence. As late as the early 1800s England had over 200 violations carrying a possible death penalty. But shortly thereafter imprisonment and banishment to Australia were substituted for the death penalty as a form of punishment.

Punishment in Early America

As the colonies were being settled, the colonists brought with them much of the criminal procedure that they had known in England. At that time retribution, or vengeance, was still the philosophy behind punishment. This philosophy was also brought to the colonies; consequently the royal colonial governors continued to inflict cruel and unusual punishment on offenders in the colonies. The death penalty was frequently inflicted, and the manner in which it was carried out was many times as inhumane as it had been in England. Other forms of cruel and unusual punishments, such as mutilation, were also practiced. Much corporal punishment was inflicted—particularly whipping—and the pillory, stocks, and public cage were also used. It is little wonder that, with such practices existing, the framers of the United States Constitution included the Eighth Amendment guarantee against "cruel and unusual punishment." However after a time, the colonists began substituting imprisonment for the death penalty allegedly as a more humane form of punishment. But early imprisonment in most instances was far from humane, and most imprisoned offenders would probably have preferred other forms of punishment, even death, at that period in history. Since retribution was still the primary force behind punishment, little consideration was given to the imprisoned offender. Food furnished, if any, was meager; no thought was given to providing any comforts of warmth, lighting, ventilation, or sanitation. Prisoners often died of neglect. Each small community was responsible for providing places of confinement, which in many instances were abandoned stockades or fortresses.

William Penn, himself a prisoner for nine months in the Tower of London, is given credit for the first improvement in prison conditions, as well as for reforms in the types of punishment imposed. In 1681 Penn received the charter to a large tract of land, known as Pennsylvania, in payment of a debt owed to his father. Shortly thereafter Penn moved to a new city that he named Philadelphia, and established a government along the lines of republicanism and religious freedom. The death penalty was abolished for all offenses except murder. Around 1683 a jail was erected to replace the fort that had been used to confine offenders. This jail was nothing more than a box-like room, and soon became inadequate, so other houses were erected to confine convicted offenders. Penn had further reforms in mind, but he died in 1718 before they could be completed. Almost immediately thereafter Queen Anne reinstituted some of the harsh penalties. The death penalty was imposed as the punishment for thirteen different crimes. Whipping and mutilation were again inflicted for a number of offenses.

Penalty reforms for convicted offenders were begun after the colonies achieved independence from England. Improvements were also made in the conditions of confinement. In 1786 an act was passed that provided for imprisonment at hard labor for many crimes that previously carried the death penalty or corporal punishment. Although the act was an improvement, much reform was still needed. Places of confinement soon became overcrowded. There was little in the way of supervision. There was no segregation as to sex, age, or offense committed. Liquor was freely sold to inmates, and prostitution was practiced. In 1790 a block of cells was added to the Walnut Street Jail in Philadelphia. It was to house the more hardened criminals, and was referred to as the "penitentiary house." Inmates began to be separated according to sex, age, and offense committed, and were sent to this jail from other parts of the state. It became a focal point of study by persons interested in prison reform.

Present Sentencing Procedure

Each rule of conduct written throughout history has required that a punishment be established for convicted violators. Usually the more serious the crime, the more severe the punishment. But which punishments should be inflicted for each particular crime has plagued society for centuries. Even today the sentencing of a convicted offender may be the most complex part of the judicial process. Convicting the offender may be easier than deciding what should be done after the conviction. In primitive times *retaliation* was the philosophy behind punishment, and the victim inflicted any punishment he desired. As more organized

Imprisonment is based on a philosophy of punishing by isolation to protect society from the offender. (Photo by Strix Pix)

societies were developed, those in the judicial process began to make an effort to fit the penalty to the crime committed. Yet vengeance or retaliation against the offender was still prevalent in the thoughts of those trying to establish appropriate punishments. The problem became what penalty the offender should be subjected to in order to satisfy society's desire for vengeance and still have the penalty fit the crime. Thus in the early sentencing process, a thief might have a hand cut off, a perjurer might have the tongue cut out, the male adulterer might be castrated. The punishment continued to be cruel and severe.

As time passed imprisonment became the generally accepted way of punishing an offender, and society turned from the retaliatory approach to the *isolation philosophy of punishment*. Instead of trying to get even with the offender, society attempted to protect itself by imprisonment. As long as the offender was confined, society would be free of recurrent harm. As a result, when penitentiaries were first built in the United States, they were built with the idea of confining the offenders in maximum security to isolate them from society for the prescribed length of the sentence. The offenders became known as *inmates*. These penitentiaries were fortress-like structures. There were high walls with gun towers surrounding the buildings and cell blocks. Inmates spent much time locked in their cells. They were required to wear a distinctive uniform; for a long time the uniform was made of black and white striped material. Many of the penitentiaries built in the late 1800s and early 1900s are still currently in use.

Length of Isolation

With punishment based on the isolation theory, the problem was how long an offender should be isolated for society's protection. Early in our history the sentencing of an offender to imprisonment was solely the responsibility of the trial judge. In most instances, there were no guidelines to assist in making the determination on how long an offender should be confined. As a result, there was a great discrepancy between judges as to the sentence imposed for the same offense. Much depended on the judge's attitude and personal philosophy. When legislators began to establish appropriate penalties for each crime, they concentrated on the felony. There is considerable difference between states on the sentences that may be imposed. In some states legislation has been passed providing a minimum and maximum number of years that an offender must serve for the conviction of a particular crime. For example, an offender convicted of burglary may receive a sentence of not less than one year in prison and not more than ten years. In other states the law sets forth the maximum length of imprisonment that may be imposed. The law may provide that an offender may not be sentenced for a term longer than ten years. Under this system an offender could be sentenced to a single hour in confinement, and this has happened in a few instances. As will be seen, under both systems the trial judge has great leeway in the sentence to be imposed. As legislators considered the penalties for felonies, misdemeanors were also considered. As with felonies, the length of time to be imposed was usually left to the trial judge, with the maximum set forth in the state statutes.

Other Possible Penalties

While imprisonment became one form of punishment, it is not the only penalty that may be imposed on a convicted offender. The types of sentences possible for criminal offenders are set forth in the codes of the various states. Penalty is still referred to as punishment in most codes. A penalty may be one or a combination of the following: imprisonment, fine, probation, suspended sentence, and in some states, the death penalty. Removal from public office and the disqualification to hold public office are also listed as forms of punishment in some states.

In a few jurisdictions the terms "punishment" and "sentence" imply imprisonment. Therefore probation is not considered to be a sentence, but rather a disposition of the case. However in most jurisdictions the term "sentence" is the judgment of the court after conviction. The sentence is the final disposition of the trial, whether by imprisonment, suspended sentence, probation, or fine. But punishment is sometimes more closely associated with imprisonment than are other forms of

THE SENTENCE AND CORRECTIONAL PROCEDURES

sentence. Technically, punishment means any unpleasantness that the convicted offender may suffer. Any restrictions placed upon the offender, whether by imprisonment, suspended sentence, or probation, are forms of unpleasantness, as is the financial hardship imposed by a fine.

Deterrence

As reformists in the justice system continued to study punishment, its purpose shifted from isolation theory to *deterrence*. The movement to rehabilitate the offender followed. As our study will emphasize, the isolation approach has not been entirely abandoned, as there are inmates from whom society is safe only during their confinement. Neither deterrence nor rehabilitation is applicable to some hardened criminals.

Whatever sentence is imposed, its primary purpose is for the *protection of society*. The protection may be a result of isolating the offender from society, or by deterring the offender from committing future crimes, thus serving as an example to others inclined to commit crimes. The protection may also be through rehabilitation, so the offender will refrain from committing future crimes.

Types of Sentencing

To better understand the deterrence and rehabilitation theories of sentencing, we should discuss the type of sentence to be imposed. Perhaps in no other area of the justice system is there a greater variance between states than in the sentencing phase of the justice proceedings.

Misdemeanor Sentencing

Upon conviction of a misdemeanor charge, the statutes of most states provide that the penalty imposed shall not exceed one year imprisonment and/or a $1,000 fine. As stated, in most jurisdictions the sentence is imposed by the trial judge, and if imprisonment is imposed, the time is generally served in a county or city jail. Most jurisdictions permit the judge to either suspend the sentence and place the offender on probation; grant probation with the provision that a certain amount of time must be spent in imprisonment; or merely impose a fine.

Although the laws of most states provide that an offender convicted on a misdemeanor charge may not be sentenced for a period of more than one year, it is possible for him or her to serve more than a single year. This results when the offender is convicted on more than one misdemeanor charge. The judge may impose a sentence for one year on each charge and have the sentence run *consecutively*. A consecutive sentence is one that must be served before the next begins. A consecutive sentence for minor convictions is the exception; in most instances, if the offender is convicted on more than one charge, the judge will provide that the sentences are to be served *concurrently*, that is, at the same time.

Felony Sentencing

In a majority of the states it is still the prerogative of the trial judge to impose the sentence. But in some states the jury will impose the sentence, and in a few states a jury must be impaneled to impose the sentence even though a jury trial has been waived. If the convicted offender is imprisoned, in some states the length of time that must be served is determined by a board or committee appointed for that purpose. Generally, depending upon the jurisdiction, the types of imprisonment or sentence that may be imposed are the definite sentence, the indefinite sentence, or the indeterminate sentence. Although the sentences are classified as such, confusion has arisen because a "definite sentence" in one state is known as an "indefinite sentence" in another state. Irrespective of their names, each classification will be discussed in order that the reader will have some insight regarding the sentencing procedures followed in the various states.

The Definite Sentence

As imprisonment began to be substituted for other forms of punishment there were few guidelines to assist judges in deciding the number of years to be imposed. Since retribution, or social retaliation, was still the primary purpose behind punishment, lengthy sentences were often imposed. Some judges became arbitrary and discriminatory in imposing sentences. To overcome this practice, legislation was passed in most states setting forth a prescribed sentence, or a definite mandatory sentence, to be required of one convicted of a particular offense. The theory behind the definite sentence was that it would be applied equally to all, irrespective of race, religion, social or economic status. The judges no longer had any control over the length of time to be served. On conviction the mandatory sentence was imposed, and the offender was required to serve that period of time. After serving the prescribed period of time the offender was released back into society, but in no way was the offender released prior to that time.

The first major change in the definite sentencing procedure came with the introduction of the *conditional release*. A few states passed legislation permitting the governing board of the penal system to grant time off from the definite sentence for good behavior. If as an inmate the convicted offender's behavior was proper, the sentence was reduced by a few days each month. Good behavior principally consisted of complying with prison rules.

The definite sentence was severely criticized by reformists as being inflexible and rigid. The definite sentence did not permit any aggravating or mitigating factors, such as age of the offender, prior criminal record, or other circumstances surrounding the commission of the crime to be taken into consideration. Since the definite, or mandatory, sentencing procedure was inflexible, judges often would dismiss a charge against an offender rather than impose a severe definite sentence when there were mitigating circumstances. An offender would then be permitted to go unpunished. Because of the inflexibility of the definite sentence, it has all but disappeared from the justice system.

The Indefinite Sentence

As the definite sentence lost favor, it was replaced by the indefinite sentence. In some states the indefinite sentence is referred to as the *indeterminate sentence,* or as the *determinate sentence.* Technically, there is a difference in the application of the indefinite, or determinate, sentence and the indeterminate sentence. With the appearance of the indefinite sentence, legislative bodies passed statutes prescribing the maximum penalty that could be imposed on the convicted offender. For example, if an offender were convicted of armed robbery, the statute might read that the offender "shall not be imprisoned for a period of more than thirty-five years." Under the indefinite sentencing procedure the imposition of the sentence was returned to the judge in most states. A few states provided for the jury to impose the sentence.

The theory behind the indefinite sentence was that it enabled the sentence to fit the offender and not the crime. The sentencing body would weigh the situation and impose the number of years deemed just under the circumstances. Since sentencing is far from an exact science, the determination of the number of years to be served was, and still is, a most difficult problem. The problem is magnified by the fact that an individual's future conduct is most difficult to predict. Society's reaction to imposed sentences is also unpredictable. There are persons who would lead us to believe that vengeance plays no part in the sentencing procedure of our civilized society. However, realistically, society's vengeance may still be felt in a community when an atrocious crime is committed. Thus in imposing a sentence it must be of sufficient length to satisfy the desire for social retaliation, but not so long as to discourage the offender from wanting to reform. In most instances when legislation was passed prescribing the maximum sentence to be imposed, that time was long enough that the most vengeful individual could not take exception. It was the duty of the sentencing body to impose the exact length of a sentence. Since there were no guidelines as to the length of an equitable sentence, it often reflected the judge's or the jury's feelings and philosophy. There were wide discrepancies between judges and juries in the sentences imposed for the same offenses. Some judges became very lenient in the sentences they imposed.

To overcome this leniency and to assist in establishing some sentencing guidelines, the legislatures of several states passed statutes that prescribed both a minimum and a maximum sentence. For example, on a conviction of armed robbery, the penalty prescribed may state that the offender "shall not serve less than five years and not more than thirty-five years imprisonment." It became the responsibility of the judge or jury to decide on an appropriate number of years between the minimum and maximum.

Presentence Investigations.   To assist judges in attempting to arrive at an equitable sentence and to more nearly make the sentence fit the offender, many judges require a *presentence investigation.* The presentence investigation is usually conducted by a staff member of the probation department. The investigation generally includes such matters as the offender's family status, educational background, work experience, and prior criminal record. It also includes circumstances surrounding the commission of the crime. Whether it was a crime of passion, thrill, or emotional involvement may have an impact on the sentence to be prescribed. The offender's attitude towards the crime will be reported. The investigation will also show whether the offender is remorseful over having committed the crime, or is only unhappy about being caught. Even with the assistance of the information contained in a presentence report, the sentence to be imposed still involves a difficult decision for the judge. Not all judges have staffs available to them to make presentence investigations, so in most instances they must rely solely upon their contact with the offender during the trial and their own insight as to what sentence should be imposed. The judge may consider the mental state of the offender at the time the crime was committed. Was the offender in a state of *diminished capacity?* Was the mental condition so diminished by intoxication or drugs that the offender could not have formulated an intent, created a motive, or entertained malice toward the victim? If so, the judge may impose a lesser penalty. Some states have permitted diminished capacity to be pleaded as a defense to a criminal charge, but currently this use has been abolished in most states, and may be considered only by the judge at the time of sentencing.

Juries Imposing Sentences.   Juries generally do not have access to any presentence investigative material. When the jury imposes the sentence, it is too often nothing more than a calculated guess as to what is appropriate. Often juries will be either extremely harsh or very lenient in sentencing because of deep emotional involvement with a crime committed in their community. The sentence of the jury is many times the result of a compromise brought about by bargaining over the verdict. Attempting to get a jury to arrive at what may be an equitable sentence is often more difficult than reaching a unanimous verdict. One may wonder why juries are permitted to impose the sentence in some states in view of the problems involved. This practice is a carryover from colonial days. The colonists frequently had unpleasant experiences with the royal judges, as well as some post-independence judges, as being too arbitrary and discriminatory in the imposition of sentences. To overcome this practice a few state legislatures provided that the imposition of the sentence was to be the prerogative of the jury.

Whether a sentence is imposed by a judge or a jury, it will stipulate the exact number of years to be served. At first glance it would appear that this sentencing procedure is of the definite type. The definite and indefinite sentences differ in that with the definite sentence the law prescribes a definite mandatory number of years that must be served by all offenders on conviction of a particular crime. With the indefinite sentence the law prescribes either a maximum amount of time that may be imposed, or a minimum and maximum, and from this indefinite period of time the judge or jury will decide upon a definite amount of time for the sentence.

With the passing of time and the growing interest in rehabilitation, the indefinite sentence has become even more indefinite because, after serving a portion of the sentence, the inmate may become eligible for parole, thereby shortening the time to be served. Parole will be discussed more fully later in the chapter. Because the exact number of years that must be served is indefinite, or indeterminate, and because of the possibility of parole, this sentencing procedure is referred to as the *indeterminate sentence* in some states.

The Indeterminate Sentence

The true indeterminate sentence removes the sentencing of a prescribed number of years from the hands of a judge or a jury. The length of sentence is determined by a board or committee appointed for that purpose sometime after the imprisonment has commenced. The primary purpose of the indeterminate sentence is to permit the sentence to more nearly fit the offender and to assist in the rehabilitation process. But this was not the original purpose of the indeterminate sentence when it first appeared on the justice scene. On the continent of Europe during the seventeenth and eighteenth centuries the indeterminate sentence was used to lengthen the sentences of dangerous criminals for protective detention after they had served their original sentences. This procedure eventually died out in Europe. The indeterminate sentence was adopted in this country but for a different reason. This sentence permitted a mitigation of the sentence that might otherwise have been imposed with the view that the indeterminate sentence would assist the offender in reforming. When first adopted in this country, the offender was imprisoned for an indeterminate time in order to accomplish physical, emotional, and mental rehabilitation so that his renewed freedom would no longer endanger the welfare of society. Once the offender arrived at this status as decided by a board of managers of the penal system, the inmate was entitled to be released. Thus the inmate could be held for an indeterminate period of time—even for an entire life—until reaching that point of physical, emotional, and mental rehabilitation where there was no threat to society on release.

Very few states have adopted the true indeterminate sentencing procedure. Under the indeterminate sentencing procedure the legislature prescribes both the minimum and maximum terms for each offense punishable by imprisonment in the state prison. Upon conviction of such offense, and if neither a new trial nor probation is granted, the trial judge does not specify the length of imprisonment but merely sentences the defendant as "prescribed by law." A board appointed by the governor on a permanent basis then determines, within statutory limits, the length of time that the offender will actually be required to serve. This board is frequently referred to as the *parole board*.

The indeterminate sentence has been interpreted to mean that on being sentenced as prescribed by law, the offender has been sentenced to the maximum time prescribed by the statutes for the particular offense. But the indeterminate sentence process permits the shortening of the offender's sentence on a showing of rehabilitation. The theory behind the indeterminate sentence is to place before the inmate a great incentive to reform in order that the sentence be reduced in length from the maximum prescribed.

When is an Offender Rehabilitated?

Determining when an offender has been rehabilitated to a point where there is no longer a threat to society on release is an almost impossible task. Some never reach that point and have to serve the maximum time. However, each inmate is entitled to eventually have the length of his or her sentence determined by the board. In making the determination the board will take many things into consideration. Each penal institution maintains a file or cumulative folder on each inmate. The board will study these files and hold a hearing at which the inmate may appear to plead the case. Generally the hearing will not be held until the inmate has served six months to one year of the maximum time prescribed. By holding the hearing after the inmate has started serving a portion of the sentence, the board has an opportunity to study the inmate's reaction to incarceration since this data, as well as much other information, will be included in the cumulative file. The file will contain the name and age of the inmate, place and time of conviction, the charge for which the inmate was convicted, and the minimum and maximum sentence prescribed by the statutes. The presentence investigative report will be included in order that the board may have background knowledge on the inmate. Also included may be the results of tests given to the inmate upon incarceration, as well as a record of the inmate's efforts to improve academically by attempting to learn some salable work skill. The board will take into consideration the general attitude of the inmate toward society, law, and authority as expressed by the inmate in the appearance before the board.

After a review of the entire matter, the board will endeavor to arrive at some equitable length of time to be served. The board may conclude that the inmate should serve six years on a sentence prescribed by law to be not less than one year and not more than ten years. The board may conclude further that the inmate should serve four of those years in actual confinement and the other two years on parole. After the time has been set, if the inmate should demonstrate an inability to conform to prison regulations or that no attempt to reform has been made, the board has the authority to reset the length of the sentence—even as much as requiring the inmate to serve the maximum time. For this reason it has been interpreted that an offender sentenced under the indeterminate sentence procedure is sentenced to the maximum prescribed, and any time less than the maximum is determinate on the rehabilitation of the inmate. It has been held that the indeterminate sentence grants the inmate no vested right to a permanently fixed length of sentence at any time.

Advantages and Disadvantages of the Indeterminate Sentence

The indeterminate sentence has been attacked by inmates on the allegation that it violates the due process of law because of its uncertainness, and as such is cruel and unusual punishment. However, to date, these attacks have been unsuccessful as the courts have interpreted the sentence as fixed at the maximum and it is the inmate's reformation that permits the maximum to be reduced. The courts have held that as long as a minimum and maximum sentence prescribed by the legislature is not disproportionate to the offense committed, the sentence is not cruel and unusual. It has been stated that whether a particular punishment is disproportionate to the offense is a question of degree. Courts have described a disproportionate punishment as one in which the length of the sentence is so disproportionate as to shock the moral sense of all reasonable men as to what is right and proper, or so disproportionate as to shock the moral sense of the community.

The proponents of the true indeterminate sentencing procedure allege that a board is in a better position than a judge to determine the sentence that should be imposed. The board comes in contact with all convicted offenders who are imprisoned, whereas judges are in contact with only those convicted in their particular court. The board therefore is able to view the inmates' progress in an overview as one large unit and can follow this progress during confinement as well as parole. As such the board can weigh what sentence is more likely to be equitable. The board also has personal contact with the inmate during confinement and, before determining the sentence, can study responses to treatment over a period of months. The judge must make a sentence determination at the end of a trial—without any guidelines as to a defendant's reaction to the rehabilitation processes. As previously stated, judges under both the indeterminate and the indefinite sentencing procedures are able to retain jurisdiction over a defendant by granting probation in lieu of imposing a sentence of imprisonment.

The Suspended Sentence and Probation

The right of *benefit of clergy* was carried a step further in Great Britain during the thirteenth and fourteenth centuries. The right of benefit of clergy may be called the forerunner of the suspended sentence. Under certain circumstances, an accused was permitted to have a trial transferred from the king's court to the ecclesiastical court. By so doing the offender was able to avoid the death penalty, but still might be imprisoned for life. However, in most instances, the offender was only mutilated in some minor way and released back into society. The philosophy of the right of benefit of clergy was brought to America by the colonists. Instead of a transfer of courts being possible, there was either a substitution of some other punishment for the death penalty, or the judge might suspend carrying out the death penalty for the lifetime of the offender dependent on good behavior.

The suspended sentence is recognized in our system of justice today, but in most instances it is coupled with a period of probation. In many jurisdictions there cannot be a suspended sentence without probation being imposed for a prescribed period of time. In those jurisdictions that the suspended sentence is permitted without probation the judge merely suspends imposing a sentence. The offender is free to return into society. Generally there are no restrictions placed on the offender other than good behavior during the period of the suspended sentence. If the offender breaks the law again, the judge may impose a sentence on the original charge as well as the new charge, if convicted.

Probation, like the suspended sentence, permits the convicted offender to remain free from custody, but by being placed on probation the offender is under the supervision of some person who assists him or her in leading a law-abiding life. The person is usually a public officer known as a *probation officer*. The primary purpose of the suspended sentence and probation is for the rehabilitation of the offender. By granting the convicted offender a suspended sentence or probation, it is assumed that there is no threat to society by the offender remaining free from custody.

Origins of Probation. Probation, primarily of American origin, is an outgrowth of the suspended sentence and is the newest form of correctional treatment for the offender. Probation is believed to have begun in America when a cobbler, John Augustus, attended a police court in Boston, Massachusetts in August 1841. He decided to post bail for a man charged with being a common drunkard. The judge permitted Augustus to post the bail and ordered the defendant to return in three weeks for sentencing. When the man returned, the judge noted an improvement in the defendant's attitude. Instead of sentencing the defendant to imprisonment, the judge fined the defendant one cent and court costs. Encouraged by his first experience, Augustus posted bail for other first offenders who seemed worthy of consideration. In each case, Augustus agreed to supervise the activities of the offenders and to report back to the judge on their progress. Augustus continued this work until his death in 1859. His work was continued by Rufus R. Cook, a chaplain of a county jail. In 1878, Massachusetts passed a law providing for the appointment of a paid probation officer for the courts in Boston. At the same time, experiments were being made in the use of probation in England. Although probation made its appearance in America in the mid–1800s, it was not until well into the twentieth century that probation as a form of sentencing came into extensive use.

Probation is a form of clemency and an offender has no inherent right to demand to be placed on probation. In most states there are certain violations for which probation may not be granted. Otherwise in most jurisdictions the judge has wide discretionary power to grant probation. In most instances the judge's decision is final. Prior to granting probation, the judge may, or in some cases must, have a probation or presentence investigation conducted to determine if the offender could benefit from probation. This investigation is generally conducted by a probation officer who may or may not give a recommendation as to whether probation should be granted. In most states the recommendation is not binding upon the judge, and probation may be granted even though not recommended by the probation officers, or vice versa. Probation is often granted as a result of plea bargaining. But the mere fact that an offender enters a guilty plea is no assurance that there will be benefits from probation or that society is better protected by the granting of probation.

One of two procedures is usually followed in granting probation. On conviction the judge merely suspends pronouncing any sentence and places the offender on probation for a prescribed period of time. Or the judge may impose a sentence such as a prescribed period of imprisonment, but the execution of the sentence will be suspended and the offender will be placed on probation for a prescribed period of time. The time that the offender may be placed on probation is generally at the discretion of the judge, but in most instances it is not for a period longer than the maximum time of imprisonment for the particular crime.

Conditions of Probation. The general condition imposed on the offender, when placed on probation, is that he be a law-abiding individual during the period of probation. Many other restrictions may also be imposed at this time. For example, the judge may restrict the offender's area of travel and associates, or the offender may be prohibited from patronizing bars. Restitution for damages or injuries caused while violating the law may be required. In some instances, as a condition of probation, the offender must agree to having his or her person or home searched without a warrant at any time by either a probation officer or a law enforcement officer. When these conditions are imposed, however, it is generally held that the search may not be a harassment procedure, but is to be made only when there is probable cause to believe that the offender has violated probation. Whenever restrictions are placed on an offender, it has been stated that the restrictions should have some connection with the crime committed. For example, in one case the defendant was convicted of grand theft. Prior to the conviction, the defendant had given birth to three illegitimate children fathered by different men. As a condition of probation, the judge advised the defendant that she was not to become pregnant out of wedlock again during the probation period. She did become pregnant out of wedlock, and the judge revoked her probation and sentenced her to prison. She appealed the sentence as constituting cruel and unusual punishment. The appellate court agreed with her and reversed the case, sending it back to the judge for further consideration. The appellate court stated that the trial judge might be commended for the attempt to prevent illegitimacy, but that it should have been attempted in a different manner since the restriction on pregnancy had no connection with the crime committed. However, judges frequently require a person placed on probation to do work for charity organizations, a requirement that appears to have no connection with the crime committed. There are times when a judge may grant probation with the stipulation that a short period of time be spent in imprisonment. Some reformists have criticized the use of imprisonment for one placed on probation as being a handicap to the rehabilitation process. Others justify the imprisonment as being a means of awakening the offender to the realization of what could happen if probation is violated.

There is a difference among states on the question of whether a convicted offender may refuse probation. In some states it is held that the offender does not have to give consent to being placed on probation; therefore, there is no right to refuse to accept probation. In other states it is held that the convicted offender must give consent to be placed on probation. Although probation is generally preferable to imprisonment, a judge, in granting probation, may impose certain restrictions that the offender may feel are intolerable. In this case the offender may prefer a limited time of imprisonment. Since probation is not considered to be a form of punishment, but a rehabilitation process, it is believed that the convicted offender should be willing to be placed on probation. Otherwise the rehabilitative effect of probation is lost. There are a few states in which an offender may be placed on probation prior to conviction. On a complaint being filed, an offender can be placed on probation, thereby avoiding a conviction. It is felt that the consent of the offender is necessary under these circumstances. In some states permitting this procedure, it is known as *diversion.*

Revocation of Probation. If during the period of probation the offender, known as a *probationer,* violates the law or fails to abide by other restrictions that may have been imposed, the probation may be revoked and the probationer sentenced to imprisonment. Whether or not probation is revoked is at the discretion of the trial judge. Before the probation may be revoked the probationer is entitled to a hearing, as was stated in the case of *Gagnon* v. *Scarpelli,* 411 US 778 (1973). In that case the United States Supreme Court held that

> Probation revocation, like parole revocation, is not a stage of a criminal prosecution, but does result in a loss of liberty. Accordingly, we hold that a probationer, like a parolee, is entitled to a preliminary and final revocation hearing, under the conditions specified in *Morrissey* v. *Brewer.* . . .

The *Morrissey* v. *Brewer* decision will be discussed in the next section.

Criticism of Probation. Generally, one would not quarrel with the primary purpose of probation, which is rehabilitating the offender. But many persons both in and out of the justice system believe that judges grant probation too often. Probation has been granted to prevent overcrowding of prisons. It has also been granted to offenders who have no incentive to mend their ways. In one case, for example, an offender was convicted of burglary and placed on three years probation. While on probation, the offender was convicted on another burglary charge and the same judge again placed the offender on probation, to run concurrently with the probationary period of the prior conviction. It is for this reason that some states have passed legislation that prohibits an offender from being placed on probation after conviction for certain crimes or for using a gun while committing crimes. In spite of the efforts to curb the use of probation, it is still extensively utilized. At any given time there are over one million persons on probation in the United States.

Parole

Purpose of Parole

The release of an offender from a correctional institution prior to the expiration of an imposed sentence is known as *parole*. Parole is granted after the offender has served a portion of his or her sentence and the parole board feels that the offender can be released without being a threat to society. Parole has two purposes. It is to assist in rehabilitating the offender through release from imprisonment and promote a useful life in society. It is also to protect society by placing some restrictions on the offender after release from custody. The paroled offender, referred to as a *parolee,* is placed under the supervision of a *parole officer,* who assists the parolee in adjusting to society's regulations and in resisting the temptation to commit other crimes.

In the case of *Morrissey* v. *Brewer,* 408 US 471 (1972), the United States Supreme Court reviewed the purpose of parole as well as some of the restrictions that may be imposed on a parolee. The Court stated:

> During the past 60 years, the practice of releasing prisoners on parole before the end of their sentences has become an integral part of the penological system. Rather than being an *ad hoc* exercise of clemency, parole is an established variation on imprisonment of convicted criminals. Its purpose is to help individuals reintegrate into society as constructive individuals as soon as they are able, without being confined for the full term of the sentence imposed. It also serves to alleviate the costs to society of keeping an individual in prison. The essence of parole is release from

prison, before the completion of sentence, on the condition that the prisoner abide by certain rules during the balance of the sentence. Under some systems parole is granted automatically after the service of a certain portion of a prison term. Under others, parole is granted by the discretionary action of a board which evaluates an array of information about a prisoner and makes a prediction whether he is ready to reintegrate into society.

To accomplish the purpose of parole, those who are allowed to leave prison early are subjected to specified conditions for the duration of their terms. These conditions restrict their activities substantially beyond the ordinary restrictions imposed by law on an individual citizen. Typically parolees are forbidden to use liquor or to have associations or correspondence with certain categories of undesirable persons. Typically also they must seek permission from their parole officers before engaging in specified activities, such as changing employment or living quarters, marrying, acquiring or operating a motor vehicle, traveling outside the community and incurring substantial indebtedness. Additionally, parolees must regularly report to the parole officer to whom they are assigned and sometimes they must make periodic written reports of their activities.

The parole officers are part of the administrative system designed to assist parolees and to offer them guidance. The conditions of parole serve a dual purpose; they prohibit, either absolutely or conditionally, behavior which is deemed dangerous to the restoration of the individual into normal society. And through the requirement of reporting to the parole officer and seeking guidance and permission before doing many things, the officer is provided with information about the parolee and an opportunity to advise him. The combination puts the parole officer into the position in which he can try to guide the parolee into constructive development.

The enforcement leverage which supports the parole conditions derives from the authority to return the parolee to prison to serve out the balance of his sentence if he fails to abide by the rules. In practice not every violation of parole conditions automatically leads to revocation. Typically a parolee will be counseled to abide by the conditions of parole, and the parole officer ordinarily does not take steps to have parole revoked unless he thinks that the violations are serious and continuing so as to indicate that the parolee is not adjusting properly and cannot be counted on to avoid antisocial activity. The broad discretion accorded the parole officer is also inherent in some of the quite vague conditions, such as the typical requirement that the parolee avoid "undesirable" associations or correspondence. Yet revocation of parole is not an unusual phenomenon, affecting only a few parolees. It has been estimated that 35–45% of all parolees are subjected to revocation and return to prison. Sometimes revocation occurs when the parolee is accused of another crime; it is often preferred to a new prosecution because of the procedural ease of recommitting the individual on the basis of a lesser showing by the State.

Implicit in the system's concern with parole violations is the notion that the parolee is entitled to retain his liberty as long as he substantially abides by the conditions of his parole. The first step in a revocation decision thus involves a wholly retrospective factual question: whether the parolee has in fact acted in violation of one or more conditions of his parole. Only if it is determined that the parolee did violate the conditions does the second question arise: should the parolee be recommitted to prison or should other steps be taken to protect society and improve chances of rehabilitation? The first step is relatively simple; the second is more complex. The second question involves the application of expertise by the parole authority in making a prediction as to the ability of the individual to live in society without committing antisocial acts. This part of the decision, too, depends on facts, and therefore it is important for the Board to know not only that some violation was committed but also to know accurately how many and how serious the violations were. Yet this second step, deciding what to do about the violation once it is identified, is not purely factual but also predictive and discretionary.

If a parolee is returned to prison, he often receives no credit for the time served on parole. Thus the returnee may face a potential of substantial imprisonment.

The Parole Board

The decision as to whether an inmate is to be released on parole is generally at the discretion of a *parole board*. This board is usually appointed on a permanent basis to make these decisions. Whether an inmate should be released on parole is no small decision. The future conduct of an individual is impossible to predict. Will an offender who has been isolated from society for a number of years and whose daily activities have been controlled and regulated by signals, bells, and the custody staff adjust to the freedom of society? Not all inmates released on parole are able to make the adjustment. When they do not, in most instances their paroles are revoked, and they are returned to prison to serve the remainder of their sentences. With the help of the parole officer many parolees are able to adjust to society. But becuse of the number who do not adjust and who commit other crimes while on parole, the parole system has been severely criticized. Those who criticize the system overlook the fact that the great majority of offenders imprisoned will eventually be released from custody. In the long run releasing an offender under supervision and assistance is preferable to releasing an inmate, after completing an entire sentence, with no supervision or assistance. It is easy to understand why there are those who are critical of paroling inmates. Many parolees commit other crimes while on parole. When this happens, people wonder why such offenders were released from custody to prey upon society again. The increase of crimes committed by parolees in recent years may stem from the fact that greater use is being made of parole to relieve the overcrowded condition of prisons. Consequently, the parolees are not always screened as well as they might be, and greater chances are taken that the parolees will conform to the regulations of society. Not all inmates are released on parole. The parole boards know that there are many inmates who will not be able to adjust to society. The hostility and hatred toward society is so ingrained within many of them that they have no desire to conform. These inmates are not paroled and serve their entire sentences in prison. On completion of their sentences these inmates are discharged without any restrictions—other than the loss of certain civil rights by having been convicted of a felony.

Criteria for Release on Parole

Since very few offenders are sentenced to imprisonment without the possibility of parole, most inmates become eligible for parole consideration after a certain period of time. In order to make an intelligent evaluation whether an inmate should be granted parole, many factors will be taken into consideration. One of the first things to be considered is whether there is a reasonable and adequate parole plan. This plan must include some provision for employment and a place to reside. Also taken into consideration is the intelligence of the inmate; prior employment record, if any; the family status; the prior criminal record; the type of crime committed; the attitude of the inmate toward society, law, and authority; and the efforts made by the inmate to improve while incarcerated. After weighing these matters as they relate to each inmate, a decision will be made as to granting the inmate a parole. Yet with all this information, it is still impossible to know in each instance whether the inmate will be able to conform to the regulations of society. When the released offender returns to a pattern of criminal activity, he is referred to as a *recidivist*.

Revocation of Parole

The chief restriction placed on a parolee is that of being a law-abiding person. A failure in this respect is almost certain to result in revocation of the parole. Repeated violations of less rigid restrictions may also result in revocation. Whether or not an inmate's parole becomes revoked is largely at the discretion of the parole board. Before parole may be revoked the parolee is entitled to a hearing, as provided by the case of *Morrissey* v. *Brewer*. The facts of *Morrissey* reflect that two Iowa convicts, Morrissey and Booher, had their paroles revoked without hearings. The Court held that the due process of law clause of the Fourteenth Amendment ensures that before a person's liberty can be taken a hearing must be granted. The Court stated:

> There must also be an opportunity for a hearing, if it is desired by the parolee, prior to the final decision on revocation by the parole authority. This hearing must be the basis for more than determining probable cause; it must lead to a final evaluation of any contested relevant facts and consideration of whether the facts as determined warrant revocation. The parolee must have an opportunity to be heard and to show, if he can, that he did not violate the conditions, or, if he did, that circumstances in mitigation suggest the violation does not warrant revocation. The revocation hearing must be tendered within a reasonable time after the parolee is taken into custody. A lapse of two months, as the State suggests occurs in some cases, would not appear to be unreasonable.
>
> We cannot write a code of procedure; that is the responsibility of each State. Most States have done so by legislation, others by judicial decision usually on due process grounds. Our task is limited to deciding the minimum requirements of due process. They include (a) written notice of the claimed violations of parole; (b) disclosure to the parolee of evidence against him; (c) opportunity to be heard in person and to present witnesses and documentary evidence; (d) the right to confront and cross-examine adverse witnesses (unless the hearing officer specifically finds good cause for not allowing confrontation); (e) a "neutral and detached" hearing body such as a traditional parole board, members of which need not be judicial officers or lawyers; and (f) a written statement by the factfinders as to the evidence relied on and reasons for revoking parole. We emphasize there is no thought to equate this second stage of parole revocation to a criminal prosecution in any sense; it is a narrow inquiry; the process should be flexible enough to consider evidence including letters, affidavits, and other material that would not be admissible in an adversary criminal trial.
>
> We do not reach or decide the question whether the parolee is entitled to the assistance of retained counsel or to appointed counsel if he is indigent.
>
> We have no thought to create an inflexible structure for parole revocation procedures. The few basic requirements set out above, which are applicable to future revocations of parole,

should not impose a great burden on any State's parole system. Control over the required proceedings by the hearing officers can assure that delaying tactics and other abuses sometimes present in the traditional adversary trial situation do not occur. Obviously a parolee cannot relitigate issues determined against him in other forums, as in the situation presented when the revocation is based on conviction of another crime.

Parole versus Probation

Many persons are confused concerning the difference between parole and probation. In both instances an offender is freed from custody, when he or she is not a threat to society, to participate in a supervised rehabilitation process. In the case of probation, it is often granted *in lieu* of any imprisonment. The probationer is under the supervision of a probation officer, who is considered to be an officer of the court. The probation officer may be a part of the trial court system, or may be provided to the court by a state or county probation department. Because the probationer is under the supervision of a probation officer, any violations of the probation conditions will be reported by the probation officer to the trial court having jurisdiction over the case for possible revocation of probation.

In a few states the trial court has the authority to grant *summary probation*. After being placed under summary probation, the probationer is directly responsible to the trial judge and not to a probation officer. Summary probation is usually granted only in misdemeanor convictions and when a trial judge may have a particular interest in the matter.

Parole is granted to an offender to permit a release from custody *before serving the complete sentence*. It is usually granted to one who is serving time in a state prison, generally on a felony charge. However a few states have provisions for the parole of an offender serving time on a misdemeanor charge in a county jail. In most instances the parole officer is a state officer responsible to the parole board.

Parole, like probation, may be refused. Although freedom from confinement is generally preferable to imprisonment, many imprisoned persons are apprehensive as to being able to conform to the restrictions imposed during parole. These persons would rather serve the entire sentence and receive a final discharge than to risk having the parole revoked and being returned to prison to serve an even longer term. Both the parolee and probationer are entitled to be discharged on completion of parole or probation. The discharge means that the conditions of parole or probation have been fulfilled and the sentence completed.

The Fine

The origin of the fine as a form of punishment is lost in history. Its early use as a form of punishment served a dual purpose. Money or property was taken from the wrongdoer and paid to the victim of the crime or to relatives. The fine was also a source of revenue to the king or church, depending on the law that was broken. As other means of reimbursing the victim of a crime became available, such as civil suits, the fine was no longer used for that purpose, but fines were levied as a source of revenue for government. The fine is still employed as a form of punishment for minor crimes.

The use of the fine as punishment in serious cases has dwindled considerably since the decision of *Williams* v. *Illinois*, 399 US 235 (1970), was handed down by the United States Supreme Court.

The statutes of most states provide for a penalty of imprisonment plus a specific amount of money that can be imposed in the form of a fine. This provision is applicable to most felonies as well as misdemeanors. As a result judges, in the past, were able to impose a maximum time of imprisonment plus a fine. If unable to pay the fine, the convicted offender was imprisoned and "worked out" the fine by being given credit in a prescribed daily amount. In the *Williams* case, the United States Supreme Court held that imprisoning one who was indigent and unable to pay the fine beyond the maximum amount of imprisonment prescribed by law was in violation of the equal protection clause of the Fourteenth Amendment. The facts of the *Williams* case show that Williams was convicted of petty theft and received the maximum sentence provided by law, which was one year imprisonment and a $500 fine. Williams was also taxed $5 court costs. "The judgment directed, as permitted by statute, that if Williams was in default of payment of the fine and court costs at the expiration of the one-year sentence, he should remain in jail pursuant to the Illinois Criminal Code to 'work off' the monetary obligations at the rate of $5 per day." The Court in that case stated:

> . . . Thus, whereas the maximum term of imprisonment for petty theft was one year, the effect of the sentence imposed here required appellant (Williams) to be confined for 101 days beyond the maximum period of confinement fixed by the statute since he could not pay the fine and costs of $505. . . .
>
> We conclude that when the aggregate imprisonment exceeds the maximum period fixed by the statute and results directly from an involuntary nonpayment of a fine or court costs we are confronted with an impermissible discrimination which rests on ability to pay, and accordingly, we reverse.

Nothing in today's decision curtails the sentencing prerogative of a judge because, as noted previously, the sovereign's purpose in confining an indigent beyond the statutory maximum is to provide a coercive means of collecting or "working out" a fine. After having taken into consideration the wide range of factors underlying the exercise of his sentencing function, nothing we now hold precludes a judge from imposing on an indigent, as on any defendant, the maximum penalty prescribed by law.

It bears emphasis that our holding does not deal with a judgment of confinement for nonpayment of a fine in the familiar pattern of alternative sentence of "$30 or 30 days." We hold only that a state may not constitutionally imprison beyond the maximum duration fixed by statute a defendant who is financially unable to pay a fine. A statute permitting a sentence of both imprisonment and fine cannot be parlayed into a longer term of imprisonment than is fixed by the statute since to do so would be to accomplish indirectly as to an indigent that which cannot be done directly. We have no occasion to reach the question whether a State is precluded in any other circumstances from holding an indigent accountable for a fine by use of penal sanction. We hold only that the Equal Protection Clause of the Fourteenth Amendment requires that the statutory ceiling placed on imprisonment for any substantive offense be the same for all defendants irrespective of their economic status.

Although the United States Supreme Court did not rule out the alternate penalties, such as thirty days in jail or $30 fine, some appellate courts contend that application of such alternate penalties necessarily results in different treatment for the rich offender and the poor one. The nature of the penalty actually inflicted by the thirty days in jail or $30 fine depends on the offender's financial ability and personal choice. If the offender chooses and is able to pay the fine, imprisonment may be avoided. If he chooses imprisonment, the fine may be avoided. If unable to pay the fine, imprisonment cannot be avoided. Thus the indigent offender has no choice, and the alternate penalties work as a violation of the equal protection clause. However, to date, the alternate penalty procedure has not disappeared from the justice system, and fines will continue to be imposed as a form of penalty for some time to come, particularly in less serious charges.

Review Questions

1. What amendment includes the guarantee against cruel and unusual punishment?
2. Why was imprisonment not used as a form of punishment in early criminal procedures?
3. What contribution did William Penn make to the sentencing procedure?
4. What is the primary purpose behind sentencing an offender?
5. List the different forms of punishment that may presently be imposed upon a convicted offender.
6. Explain the significance of each of the following types of sentences:
   a. the definite sentence
   b. the indefinite sentence
   c. the indeterminate sentence
7. What is the primary purpose of granting probation?
8. What is parole?
9. List five factors that may be taken into consideration in granting parole.
10. What procedure must be followed before parole may be revoked?
11. In what way do probation and parole differ? In what way are they alike?
12. Why has the alternate sentence of a fine of $30 or thirty days in jail been criticized?
13. What is a recidivist?

Local Procedure

1. Which sentence is imposed, the indefinite or indeterminate?
2. Who sentences the defendant—the judge, the jury, or some other body?

SENTENCING PHILOSOPHY AND CLEMENCY

Punishment as a Deterrence

As previously discussed, punishment was originally based upon retaliation against the offender, for punishment is an ancient institution. As time passed society endeavored to justify punishment for other reasons than retribution. Punishment was deemed necessary to protect society. It became necessary to isolate the offender from society by imprisonment. Following the isolation theory, punishment was justified on the grounds of deterrence. It was to be imposed to discourage the offender from committing future crimes because of the unpleasantness of imprisonment, and the imprisonment was to serve as an example to others in deterring them from committing crimes. Many contend that punishment does not deter persons from committing crimes, and that this is particularly true regarding the death penalty. They relate the adage about the pickpocket working his trade at a public hanging in England while a convicted pickpocket was being hanged. In answer to those who allege that deterrence has no effect on curbing crime, this simple illustration of deterrence is often related. The example reflects a driver of a vehicle driving down the highway exceeding the speed limit who sees a highway patrol car parked beside the road. It is almost automatic that the speeder will decease in speed to the legal limit before reaching the patrol car. If not, it is alleged that the driver is eligible for a not guilty by reason of insanity defense. The driver slows down to avoid suffering the consequences of a speeding ticket.

There are an equal number who believe that punishment does deter crime. There is no doubt that deterrence plays little or no part in curbing certain crimes that may be committed in passion. Deterrence is difficult to measure, and it might be compared with the immunization against disease. Medical science has seen poliomyelitis all but wiped out during the pasty fifty years. Credit is given to the vaccine that was developed against the disease. Yet one may question if that were the reason for its elimination or would nature have caused the disease to eventually decline? That question cannot be dogmatically answered. It is known that crime continually increases beyond the proportionate growth in population, so deterrence has not stopped crime. But the question that remains unanswered is: how much more crime would there be if there were not some deterrence resulting from the punishment of offenders? That question cannot be answered.

In discussing the effectiveness of deterrence many factors must be taken into consideration. For any punishment to act as a deterrence it must be sufficiently severe to discourage criminal activity, but not so disproportionate to the crime that the courts will declare it cruel and unusual. Also, to be a deterrence, the punishment must be swift and sure in being imposed and executed. Today with the frequent granting of continuances and delays in bringing cases to trial, there is nothing swift about the imposition of punishment. With the number of trials ending in hung juries and the number of reversals of convictions on appeal, there is no certainty that a sentence will be carried out. Under these circumstances deterrence has not had an opportunity to manifest full effectiveness.

For deterrence to be effective, it must pose a threat to one's social status. If the businessman or banker entrusted with large sums of money should embezzle that money, the lasting humiliation and degradation to social status in a community caused by imprisonment could be even more devastating than the unpleasantness of the imprisonment itself. Yet not all individuals, including some in higher levels of the social strata, are deterred from committing crimes. It is also known that many criminals are in such low strata that imprisonment holds no threat to them except the loss of freedom. Even the loss of freedom may hold little threat as imprisonment may not be any more unpleasant than the conditions under which they are accustomed to living. In addition, the more that a criminal indulges in recidivism, the less there is to lose and the less deterrent that punishment will be.

Rehabilitation

Shortly after the close of World War II, reformists interested in correctional systems contended that since neither isolation nor deterrence had effectively curbed crime, greater thought should be given to the rehabilitation of the offender as a purpose of imprisonment. As stated, the primary purpose of punishing the offender is to protect society. Since most offenders must eventually be released into society, if these offenders could be released without being a threat to society, society would receive the protection that it is entitled. Reformists believed that the offender not only should be rehabilitated, but also that offenders could be. Concentrated efforts were begun to rehabilitate offenders. In many places, offenders were placed on probation instead of being sentenced to prison if there was any possibility that probation would assist in their rehabilitation. Those offenders sent to prisons were tested and classified in an effort to determine the best possible correctional treatment that could be given under the circumstances. Yet as idealistic as the rehabilitation philosophy for punishment may be, many handicaps must be overcome before rehabilitation of all offenders becomes a reality. Recent studies of rehabilitation programs have revealed that many experts in correctional systems who were enthusiastic about rehabilitation now question its merits. These experts point out that the success of rehabilitation programs has not been worth the effort and expense involved. The rehabilitation philosophy, however, will undoubtedly continue to be advocated, and it is well to discuss some of the problems and handicaps encountered in the effort to rehabilitate the criminal.

How is an Offender Rehabilitated?

Perhaps the first and most difficult handicap to be overcome is our present lack of knowledge on how to rehabilitate the offender. Such rehabilitation is still in its infancy and there is much yet to be learned. Studies are being made in an effort to determine why an individual commits a crime. The offender may be striking out against a society felt to be cruel because of repeated rejection and abandonment. Hostility is so ingrained in the offender that innocent victims are hurt merely because they are a part of that society. How do we reach that mind and remold it into one that entertains respect, rather than hostility, for society? There is no simple solution to this problem. We can work with the offender, converse, try to convince him or her that society is not completely wrong, and that not all of society is to blame for the rejection and abandonment. These talks take time, effort, and skill in dealing with the human mind. They may even be completely ineffectual, with the offender becoming even more hostile toward society because of prison confinement. It may be that another individual has committed crimes to satisfy an ego or to get luxuries not obtainable by legitimate means. With this type of offender a different rehabilitation approach must be taken. Thus what may be effective with one offender may be completely inapplicable to another. Further study in this area is vitally necessary if our system is to remold these people into wholesome persons.

Another major handicap to any rehabilitation program is the offender's attitude. It is well known that many hardened criminals have no desire to conform to the regulations of society. Unless the offender cooperates with a rehabilitation program, there is very little change that will occur. It becomes necessary to make further studies to determine how to overcome the resistance to rehabilitation. This is particularly true in relation to the hardened criminal from whom society is protected only while the individual is incarcerated, but who will eventually be returned to society. Society must first learn how to reach the mind of this type of offender in order to encourage rehabilitation, and then it must be in a position to follow through with a process that will accomplish that purpose.

Public attitude is also a major handicap to rehabilitation programs. The mere mention of the term "rehabilitation" causes many persons to create a mental block to any intelligent discussion of the subject. Many persons still feel that the offender should suffer some particularly harsh punishment, so retribution still holds sway in the minds of much of the public. With such a viewpoint these persons do not condone what they term as "molly-coddling" the offenders by furnishing them with educational and training facilities and an environment necessary for a successful rehabilitation program. Other citizens have closed minds to rehabilitation programs as a result of what they refer to as its failures. True rehabilitation is still in the formative stage. Those alleged failures are the results of experiments that have been made with resources now available and with most of the questions of rehabilitation still to be answered. The fact that rehabilitation has not been successful in every instance does not justify the abandonment of the effort, any more than medical science should abandon its search for a cancer cure simply because of previous failures. Many administrators and staff members of correctional institutions have not accepted the rehabilitation of inmates. It is difficult to have a successful rehabilitation program when those responsible for its operation have not wholeheartedly accepted it.

Prison Rules and Structures

In chapter 15 it was pointed out that the indeterminate sentence was adopted in order that an offender could be released when physically, emotionally, and mentally rehabilitated. For a rehabilitation program to be successful there must be an atmosphere that enables those involved to physically, emotionally, and mentally rehabilitate the offender. If a conscious effort were made to structure an atmosphere disastrous to a program, it would be difficult to create a worse atmosphere than the one most rehabilitation programs are presently forced to put up with. The physical structure of the buildings containing most rehabilitation programs are prisons that were built in the late 1800s, when isolation was the prime purpose of confinement. Even the most enthusiastic advocate of rehabilitation concedes that it is next to impossible to successfully remold an offender to reenter society as a wholesome individual while housed in a fortress-type structure where much of the time is spent in a cell.

The prison rules reduce the inmate to a robot. These rules, however, are necessary to maintain security in most large maximum custody prisons where violent offenders are confined. On entering prison the inmate is furnished with a set of prison rules. At the same time it is pointed out that, for the inmate's protection and for the protection of others, discipline is necessary. Strict rules must be established and followed by all inmates. It is further explained that to get along well while incarcerated, the inmate should assume a cooperative attitude and comply with the regulations set forth. The inmate is also advised that violating any of the rules will result in disciplinary action being taken that could mean a loss of privileges, such as right to the exercise yard, to receive

The rules necessary to maintain security in maximum custody prisons reduce the inmates to robots. (Photo © Billy E. Barnes)

visitors, or to receive mail. Violations of the rules could also cause the inmate to lose the "good time off" of the sentence and a possible delay in being paroled. If the violation is a serious one the inmate may be placed in solitary confinement.

The following are samples of some of the rules furnished to the newly arrived inmate:

1. Keep your cell neat and clean—including your toilet and wash basin.

2. You are to arise at the sound of the first bell in the morning—not before. You are to wash, dress, make your bed, sweep out your cell and be ready to march out.

3. On the sound of the second bell in the morning your cell door will be unlocked—you are to open the door step out—close the cell door without slamming it—form a line as directed and wait until the order to march— keep your place in line—there will be no talking while in line or while marching—while marching keep one arm's length between you and the person in front of you.

4. On entering the dining hall, take your seat promptly, position erect with eyes to the front until the signal is given to commence eating—strict silence must be observed while eating—eating or drinking before or after the bell sounds, using vinegar in your drinking water or putting articles of food on the table is strictly pro-

hibited—after finishing eating remain seated until signal to march is given.

5. On returning to your cell block—go at once to your cell—never enter any cell but your own—you are not to pass any articles from one cell to another.

6. At the 10 P.M. signal go to bed—sleep with your head uncovered and your feet toward the door.

7. Talking from one cell to another is prohibited.

8. At the count time stand by cell door with one hand on the bars.

9. You will not be permitted to have any contraband items on your person or in your cell—contraband is defined as weapons, alcoholic liquors, drugs, tools, explosives, and money.

In addition to the breaking of any of the foregoing rules, the following are violations for which disciplinary action can be taken:

1. altering clothing
2. defacing anything
3. wasting food
4. dirty cell
5. spitting on the floor
6. hands in pockets
7. communicating by signs
8. hands or face dirty
9. failure to bathe at least once a week
10. using vile language
11. disobeying orders

Not only are the prison structures and strict disciplinary rules a handicap to rehabilitation, but the society within those structures is foreign to that found in a free society. In describing the situation one inmate stated that the worst thing about being in prison was living with prisoners. In a free society one is able to select friends and associates. In prison there is no choice of associates. Those associates consist of robbers, burglars, murderers, rapists, narcotic peddlers, and many other offenders. Each tries to justify his or her own crime. The only thing they have in common is that they are all serving time. The prison society is foreign to that of a free society in other ways. A free society is composed of persons of all ages, of men and women, and of persons of generally equal status. In prison it has been deemed necessary to segregate younger offenders from older ones, and in most institutions it is necessary to separate the men and women. The inmate is a subservient member of the prison society controlled and dominated by the custody staff.

Caste Systems within Institutions

The inmates create their own caste system. The robber looks down on the embezzler, confidence man, or sneak-thief, boasting that when a person was held up, they knew they were being robbed. The robber will also state that money obtained in a robbery is "honest money," and that no trust was violated. The burglar alleges that no one was ever threatened or placed in danger. Instead he or she entered a building and took what was wanted when no one was present. The narcotic peddler claims people asked him to sell them drugs in order that they might feel better, claiming that the person was actually receiving a favor. Any racial or religious prejudices which inmates may have entertained before being imprisoned seem to be magnified by the tensions of confinement. These are only a few of the justifications and segregations.

Although most prisons in use today are not conducive to rehabilitation programs, they are still being used out of necessity. The expense of replacing them with more modern institutions is more than the taxpayer is willing to assume. In addition, not all inmates can be rehabilitated with our present knowledge of the procedure. These inmates can be housed in the older prisons with less psychological harm than the ones that may be selected for rehabilitation experimentation. Many states, as well as the federal government, are building new correctional institutions that are more conducive to rehabilitation. These new institutions resemble dormitory complexes rather than fortresses. The inmates are housed in individual rooms often with wall-to-wall carpeting. There are lounges with television and recreational facilities. The grounds are surrounded by high chain link fences instead of rock walls. In some institutions the men and women occupy the same buildings. The inmates are referred to as guests, patients, or residents instead of inmates, convicts, or prisoners. The institutions are known as *correctional facilities* rather than prisons or penitentiaries. The grounds are often called campuses. Efforts are being made to overcome the stigma of being a prisoner. Even the prison uniform has been discarded and casual clothing may be worn. Most of these institutions house selected offenders nearing the end of the confinement period and who may be able to benefit from this type of atmosphere. The transition from total confinement in a small cell to complete freedom can be more easily made by spending the last few months in dormitory surroundings. In a few states, when the possibility of rehabilitation seems great for an offender, he or she may spend the major portion of a sentence in such an institution.

One of the major obstacles to total rehabilitation appears when the inmate returns to society. Too often the inmate returns to the same environment that caused the initial downfall. Often the same frustrations and temptations are re-experienced. Even those who are most anxious to return to society as wholesome individuals need an environment that encourages continued rehabilitation. It is obvious that there should be someone and somewhere for these people to turn. Gainful employment should be available in order for the releasee to be self-sustaining. These things are not yet possible for all releasees. A new world cannot be created for each.

Statistics reflect that there are over 400,000 adults serving sentences on felony convictions in our prisons at any given period. Of this number between 12,000 and 15,000 are women. Finding homes and employment for such a number of inmates who are constantly being released is a monumental, if not impossible, task. Most prospective employers have reservations about employing a person who has been convicted of robbery or burglary, as well as most other crimes. So when the releasee cannot find a job because of being an ex-con, too often the temptation to continue committing crimes is overwhelming. The result is another recidivist, and one more effort toward rehabilitation is wasted. These are the ones to whom the rehabilitation critics point as proof of the program's lack of success. Those who are released and adjust to society's regulations are soon forgotten, and their successful adjustments are relatively unpublicized.

Rehabilitation on the Local Level

Penologists have described the county or local jail as the weakest link in our penal system. Most jails in use today were built in the early 1900s at a time when the number of persons arrested and held in jail was only a small portion of the number arrested and held today. In most instances there has been little, or no, enlargement of the jail facilities and serious overcrowding occurs. In one county a jail was built in 1927 to hold 400 prisoners. Approximately 800 are housed in that jail at present.

Early in our history the local jail was only used to hold an offender until trial. The county jail is still used for that purpose. All persons arrested and unable to post bail are housed in the county or local jail to await trial. This includes persons arrested on felony charges as well as on misdemeanors. Usually there is no segregation of offenders in accordance with the crime charged. A first offender arrested on a minor charge may find that a cellmate with a long criminal record is accused of a violent murder. In many jails there are tanks, or large cells, where a number of offenders are housed together. Included in the group may be vagrants, drunks, murderers, rapists, and sex deviates. In addition to housing those awaiting trial are those persons who have been convicted of some minor charge and are serving their time in the county or local jail. These individuals are usually not segregated from those awaiting trial.

Very little interest has been shown in attempting any rehabilitation program at the county or local jail level. Thousands of those housed in these jails are awaiting trials on misdemeanor charges. Usually the period of time between the arrest and the trial is short and there is little opportunity to even consider a rehabilitation process. Those who are serving their sentences are only incarcerated a comparatively short time and very little can be done in the way of rehabilitation for these offenders. A large majority of the sentences being served do not exceed more than ninety days. Much of that time is spent in a cell, but many counties maintain road camps where the convicted offender may be sent. However, other than getting out of the cell and getting some exercise, little is accomplished in the way of rehabilitation. Some counties have programs where the alcoholic and drug addict does get some treatment. But to thousands the confinement is nothing but a marking of time until the release date.

Some reforms in the local jail situation have been recommended. It has been suggested that the offenders awaiting trial be segregated from those who are serving their sentences. It is also suggested that those awaiting trial on misdemeanor charges be segregated from those arrested on felony charges. Some reformists advocate area jails, or state-maintained facilities, where offenders convicted on minor charges could serve their sentences, and where some rehabilitation could be attempted. But with the thousands presently housed in local jails, the funds necessary for such facilities will be difficult to obtain. Most persons display little interest in the minor offender because, except to the victim, the crime is comparatively inoffensive.

Correctional Facilities

As idealistic as rehabilitation of offenders may be, the task of rehabilitation is almost an impossible one at any level. First, we do not know how to deal with inmates who have an ingrained hostility toward society. Second, the mass of offenders that must be dealt with make the job of rehabilitation unwieldy. As a result, the rehabilitation of offenders has taken a back seat in the thinking of most justice system personnel. Current thought is returning to the view that if society is to be protected from the criminal, isolation may be the only practical approach. Still, not all efforts toward rehabilitation have been abandoned.

Inmates of medium custody institutions have some freedom of the grounds surrounding the cell blocks. (Photo courtesy Ohio Department of Rehabilitation and Correction.)

Types of Correctional Facilities

Three types of institutions are often considered when new correctional facilities are being built. The most hardened criminal is confined in a *maximum custody institution*. This type of institution has a two-fold purpose. It enables serious offenders to be segregated from the less violent offenders and minimizes the escape risk. Many older prisons built at a time when isolation was the chief approach to confinement are being used as maximum custody institutions. This saves funds for other types of facilities.

A facility currently being built in many places is the *medium custody institution*. Inmates within this type of facility are most often housed in cell blocks, but are usually surrounded by a high chain link fence instead of the traditional block walls. Inmates confined in these facilities have greater freedom of the grounds, and may work under supervision in fields outside the facilities. Many first offenders are housed in these facilities, even though their conviction may have been a more violent crime such as robbery or aggravated assault. Second offenders may also be confined in medium custody institutions. They may have committed burglaries, sex offenses, or forgeries.

The final type of facility is known as the *minimum custody institution*. Inmates may be housed in barracks or in a dormitory setting. Chain link fences will generally surround the housing facilities as in the medium custody institutions. Offenders housed in this type of facility may vary considerably among states. First offenders of non-violent crimes may be confined in this institution. The minimum custody institution may house those offenders who have already served a major portion of their sentence in other institutions. Prior to their release into free society, these inmates have the opportunity to begin to adjust to a freer atmosphere. Work camps are often associated with this type of institution. Inmates may be sent to work on projects such as road maintenance, forest restoration, or forest fire fighting.

The Guidance or Screening Center

Where these types of correctional facilities are available, there is usually a guidance or screening center where all offenders sentenced to confinement on serious charges will be sent for a complete screening and testing process. The inmate is first given a thorough physical examination to determine his or her physical condition. Particular care is taken to determine whether the inmate is suffering from any communicable disease that would require the inmate to be segregated from other inmates. This physical examination will be followed by a battery of tests to determine the inmate's intelligence, educational potentials, and occupational aptitudes. An interview will be conducted to establish the inmate's general attitude toward society, and to find out whether he or she is remorseful for the criminal act, or is just sorry about getting caught. An effort will be made to find out if there is an escape risk. Determining the inmate's propensity toward escape is not easy since there is a natural tendency to attempt to gain freedom from confinement. An assessment of the past record of the inmate will be made. This assessment will include the educational background, past work record, past criminal record, and social environment. The total information obtained from the entire screening process will be used for placement in a facility that best fits the inmate's needs and best protects society.

The Correctional Officer

Once the offender is sentenced to confinement in a penitentiary, the law enforcement agencies and the courts have completed their assignments. The correctional officer is now responsible for the offender. Our discussion encompasses all of the numerous roles of the correctional officer in the correctional system. No one officer will be responsible for the various functions that are performed within the system.

Function of the Correctional Officer

Whether involved with a maximum, medium, or minimum custody institution, the correctional officer is engaged in a business common to all three types of institutions. That business is custody and treatment. Except for a few minimum custody institutions, custody responsibilities overshadow those of treatment. Custody of the inmates is the primary function of all types of institutions, and may be defined as the maintenance of the inmates in confinement for their period of sentence and the prevention of escape. Compared to the large number of inmates in custody at any given time, few escape and most are apprehended in a short time.

Orientation of the prisoner.   Even though custody is the chief responsibility of the correctional institutions, some treatment programs must be performed in all facilities. In maximum custody institutions treatment is often minimal. The treatment begins with the arrival of the new inmate at the reception center of the correctional facility. Here the inmate receives an orientation period. Institution rules and the reasons behind them will be explained to the inmate. The explanations are primarily for the benefit and safety of the inmate and to assist in the peaceful maintenance of the institution. Also during the orientation process the general function of the institution and the part to be played by the inmate will be discussed. Many inmates enter a prison with no idea what to expect or what is expected of them. Any available work programs will be explained, and the inmate will be advised of certain productive duties that will be required. Through the orientation session the conscientious correctional officer can greatly assist the inmate in adjusting to confinement. The officer can help the inmate understand the situation and accept what must be done to make the best of confinement.

Efforts are made to alleviate the trauma that will be experienced by the inmate in being confined. This is especially true for the first time offender. Confinement is a demoralizing experience, and the entire environment is contrary to normal everyday life. The inmate has little control over his or her life until the sentence has been served. The inmate is told where to live, what time to go to bed and when to get up. There is no choice of food or associates. Why there is no choice over these matters will be explained to the inmate as will the reason why most personal belongings were taken at the time of confinement. The taking of a wedding ring from a female inmate can be the cause of severe depression. But jewelry or clothing of value may be used as barter to obtain favors, or can be stolen by other inmates.

Following the orientation session, there will be a classification period. Efforts are made to determine which resources of

320

the particular institution can best be applied to the particular inmate. These resources include work programs, educational opportunities, training programs, and medical facilities.

Keeping the Peace.   One of the major functions of the correctional officer in a maximum custody institution is keeping the facility peaceful. This is not an easy task, as inmates in these institutions are prone toward rioting, uprisings, and assaults. Much of the inmate's time is spent in idleness, as there are not enough work assignments available within the prison walls to occupy their time. In addition, many of these inmates have limited productive skills or are reluctant to perform duties. Boredom results, and any small incident may spark trouble among the inmates. One of the major causes for rioting within such institutions is dissatisfaction with the food served. The correctional officer in charge of planning and preparation of the food within any correctional institution is thus of prime importance. The food must be nourishing and as palatable as possible.

Use of Prison Labor.   Regardless of the type of correctional institution involved, work projects are of a limited nature, and most are of little value in a treatment process designed to return the inmate to a free society as a better person. The reason for the limitation on work projects is that various state and federal laws prohibit the sale of prison-made goods on the public market. The laws were enacted during the early 1930's when businesses and labor unions became fearful that they could not compete with manufactured goods made by free prison labor. Prior to that time, many states were using prison labor as a source of revenue to help make correctional facilities self-supporting. Inmates were leased out to contractors in private industry for work assignments, and the correctional institutions received minimum fees for the use of this labor. Today, goods manufactured in correctional institutions are limited to those items that can be utilized by state and local governmental agencies and institutions. Included are items such as brooms, clothing, and furniture. Most vehicle license plates are made in correctional institutions. Those officers responsible for work projects within the correctional institutions have a major function in providing some treatment for the inmate. But their efforts are limited because of the lack of work projects and the large number of inmates to be assigned. This leads to a great amount of idle time being spent by the inmates in their cells, particularly in maximum custody institutions. In medium and minimum custody institutions, many farms projects are available. These farms projects not only give the inmate an opportunity for work assignments outside the prison confines, but produce food stuffs for the various state institutions.

Correctional officers in minimum custody institutions have added responsibilities since the major portion of inmate treatment takes place in these institutions. Much time is spent counseling the inmates on an individual basis in an effort to return them to society as law-abiding citizens. The difficult and varied tasks of the competent correctional officer illustrate the importance of this position within the justice system.

The Death Penalty

Heated arguments have taken place over the years concerning the merits of the death penalty. Those who oppose the death penalty do so principally on the grounds that it has no place in a civilized society. They hold that the death penalty is a form of cruel and unusual punishment, and further allege that the death penalty does not act as a deterrent. An equal number contend that the death penalty is a deterrent and as such should be retained. But they concede that the deterrent effect does not function effectively because, as previously pointed out, for any deterrent to be effective the punishment must be swift and sure. Certainly the delays between the imposition of the death penalty and the execution make the death penalty anything but swift in coming and sure in being carried out.

Cruel and Unusual Punishment

The question of whether or not the death penalty is cruel and unusual punishment in violation of the Eighth Amendment was placed before the United States Supreme Court in the case of *Furman* v. *Georgia,* 408 US 238 (1972). The Court held in that case that the death penalty as such was not cruel and unusual punishment, but the indiscriminatory manner in which it was applied made the death penalty cruel and unusual punishment in violation of the Eighth Amendment.

The Court in the *Furman* decision indicated that perhaps if the death sentence was to be made mandatory on all of equal guilt, the sentence would not be indiscriminatory, and thus would not violate the cruel and unusual punishment provision of the Eighth Amendment. As a result, many state legislatures passed statutes making the death penalty mandatory on conviction for certain crimes. This mandatory sentence took from the jury or judge the right to determine the sentence to be imposed on conviction for crimes previously carrying the *alternate sentence* of life imprisonment or death.

However, the United States Supreme Court, in *Woodson* v. *North Carolina,* 428 US 280 (1976), overruled a North Carolina statute making the death penalty mandatory as cruel and unusual punishment. The Court held that such a statute did not allow any consideration to be given to the character and record of the offender. The Court stated:

"Consideration of both the offender and the offense in order to arrive at a just and appropriate sentence has been viewed as a progressive and humanizing development."

Consequently, those state statutes making the death penalty mandatory had to be revised to conform with the *Woodson* decision. Statutes were then passed allowing the jury or judge to take into consideration aggravating or mitigating circumstances in imposing the alternate sentence of life imprisonment or death. A Georgia statute of this nature was upheld by the United States Supreme Court in *Gregg* v. *Georgia*, 428 US 153 (1976). In reaffirming that the death penalty was not in violation of the Eighth Amendment guarantee against cruel and unusual punishment, the Court stated:

> The imposition of the death penalty for the crime of murder has a long history of acceptance both in the United States and in England. The common-law rule imposed a mandatory death sentence on all convicted murderers. And the penalty continued to be used into the 20th century by most American States, although the breadth of the common-law rule was diminished, initially by narrowing the class of murders to be punished by death and subsequently by widespread adoption of laws expressly granting juries the discretion to recommend mercy.

> It is apparent from the text of the Constitution itself that the existence of capital punishment was accepted by the Framers. At the time the Eighth Amendment was ratified, capital punishment was a common sanction in every State. Indeed, the First Congress of the United States enacted legislation providing death as the penalty for specified crimes. The Fifth Amendment, adopted at the same time as the Eighth, contemplated the continued existence of the capital sanction by imposing certain limits on the prosecution of capital cases: "No person shall be held to answer for a capital, or otherwise infamous crime, unless on a presentment or indictment of a Grand Jury . . .; nor shall any person be subject for the same offense to be twice put in jeopardy of life or limb; . . . nor be deprived of life, liberty, or property, without due process of law . . ." And the Fourteenth Amendment, adopted over three-quarters of a century later, similarly contemplates the existence of the capital sanction in providing that no State shall deprive any person of "life, liberty, or property" without due process of law.

> For nearly two centuries, this Court, repeatedly and often expressly, has recognized that capital punishment is not invalid per se.

In holding the death penalty is not a violation of the guarantee against cruel and unusual punishment, the dissenting justices in the Furman case stated:

Punishments are cruel when they involve torture or a lingering death; but the punishment of death is not cruel, within the meaning of that word as used in the Constitution. It implies there something inhuman and barbarous, something more than the mere extinguishment of life. . . .

The traditional humanity of modern Anglo-American law forbids the infliction of unnecessary pain in the execution of the death sentence. . . . The cruelty against which the Constitution protects a convicted man is cruelty in the method of punishment, not the necessary suffering involved in any method employed to extinguish life humanely.

The gas chamber, electric chair, hanging, lethal injection and firing squad have all been sanctioned by the court as humane means of carrying out the death penalty.

In the *Gregg* decision, the Court made some interesting comments on the death penalty as a deterrent as well as a necessary form of punishment to satisfy society's demand for justice. The Court stated:

The death penalty is said to serve two principal social purposes: retribution and deterrence of capital crimes by prospective offenders.

In part, capital punishment is an expression of society's moral outrage at particularly offensive conduct. This function may be unappealing to many, but it is essential in an ordered society that asks its citizens to rely on legal processes rather than self-help to vindicate their wrongs. "The instinct for retribution is part of the nature of man and channeling that instinct in the administration of criminal justice serves an important purpose in promoting the stability of a society governed by law. When people begin to believe that organized society is unwilling or unable to impose upon criminal offenders the punishment they deserve, then there are sown the seeds of anarchy—of self-help, vigilante justice, and lynch law." Retribution is no longer the dominant objective of the criminal law, but neither is it a forbidden objective nor one inconsistent with our respect for the dignity of men. Indeed, the decision that capital punishment may be the appropriate sanction in extreme cases is an expression of the community's belief that certain crimes are themselves so grievous an affront to humanity that the only adequate response may be the penalty of death.

Statistical attempts to evaluate the worth of the death penalty as a deterrent to crimes by potential offenders have occasioned a great deal of debate. The results simply have been inconclusive. Although some of the studies suggest that the death penalty may not function as a significantly greater deterrent than lesser penalties, there is no convincing empirical evidence either supporting or refuting this view. We may nevertheless assume safely that there are murderers, such as those who act in passion, for whom the threat of death has little or no deterrent effect. But for many others the death penalty undoubtedly is a significant deterrent.

The Alternate Sentencing Procedure

Since the *Woodson* decision held that the alternate sentencing procedure must be followed, it is important to discuss the procedure's development. For many years the death penalty was made mandatory upon the conviction of certain specified crimes in most states. Jurors aware of this situation knew that on voting for a guilty verdict they were voting for the execution of a human being. Many jurors had reservations about the death penalty. When it came time to vote on the verdict they could not bring themselves to vote guilty irrespective of the strength of the evidence as to guilt. This inability to vote for a guilty verdict caused many trials to end with hung juries. In an effort to overcome this problem the legislatures of many states enacted statutes setting forth alternate sentences of life imprisonment or death on conviction of certain crimes. The statutes further provided that the jury in the jury trial, or the judge in a court trial, was to make the decision as to which penalty was to be imposed. Under these circumstances the juror with reservations about the death penalty could still vote for a guilty verdict but be in a position to vote for life imprisonment after the conviction.

When the alternate sentence was made possible, one of two procedures was generally followed. In some states a trial was first held to determine the guilt or innocence of the accused. If the accused was found guilty, a second trial was held to determine if the death penalty was to be imposed or if the sentence was to be life imprisonment. In other states only one trial was held. The jury would deliberate first on the guilt or innocence of the accused, and, if the jury voted a guilty verdict, they would then deliberate on the penalty to be imposed. Both procedures have received the sanction of the United States Supreme Court. Under both procedures the juror with reservations about imposition of the death penalty could still vote for a guilty verdict without voting for the death of the defendant.

During the trial or sentence determination hearing, the jury or judge must consider both aggravating and mitigating circumstances, and weigh them against each other. The *Gregg* decision listed such aggravating circumstances as a murder committed by a convict under a sentence of imprisonment; a murder committed by one previously convicted of murder or a felony involving violence; a murder committed at the time the defendant committed another murder; a murder committed while committing or attempting to commit robbery, rape, arson, burglary, or kidnapping; a murder committed for the purpose of avoiding arrest; and a murder committed in an especially cruel or atrocious manner.

As to mitigating circumstances, the Court suggested that it be taken into consideration whether the defendant had no significant prior criminal record; whether the murder was committed while the defendant was under some emotional stress; whether the defendant was an accomplice of another who actually did the murder, and the defendant's participation in the homicidal act was relatively minor; whether at the time of the murder the defendant was acting under a diminished capacity; and whether the defendant was of youthful age.

In most jurisdictions, when the death penalty is imposed the case is automatically appealed to the highest appellate court within the jurisdiction. The court will review the facts of the case to determine if the conviction should be affirmed and if the death penalty is justified from the evidence presented. The appellate court may affirm both the conviction and the death penalty, or it may affirm the conviction but hold that the death penalty is not justified under the circumstances. In this instance, the case will either be returned to the trial court for revision of the sentence, or depending on the court, the life sentence may be imposed automatically. If the appellate court reverses the conviction the penalty phase will not be considered.

The death penalty may be imposed in approximately two-thirds of the states and within the federal system, yet opponents undoubtedly will continue to attempt to have the death penalty abolished as being cruel and unusual punishment. In fact, in their dissenting opinions in the *Gregg* decision, Justices Marshall and Brennan were adamant in their contention that the death penalty is cruel and unusual punishment and thus a violation of the Eighth Amendment guarantee.

Death Penalty as Excessive Punishment for Crime of Rape

Appellate courts have from time to time held that a particular sentence was excessive and disproportionate to the crime committed, and thus was cruel and unusual punishment. When this happens, the sentence will be set aside and the case referred back to the trial court for resentencing. What is considered excessive punishment is not easily determined, and often rests largely upon the personal viewpoints of the justices involved. In *Coker v. Georgia*, 53 L Ed 2d 982 (1977), the United States Supreme Court held that the death penalty for the rape of an adult woman was excessive and disproportionate to the crime. The Court stated:

> We do not discount the seriousness of rape as a crime. It is highly reprehensible, both in a moral sense and in its almost total contempt for the personal integrity and autonomy of the female victim and for the latter's privilege of choosing those with whom intimate relationships are to be established. Short of homicide, it is the

"ultimate violation of self." It is also a violent crime because it normally involves force, or the threat of force or intimidation, to overcome the will and the capacity of the victim to resist. Rape is very often accompanied by physical injury to the female and can also inflict mental and psychological damage. Because it undermines the community's sense of security, there is public injury as well.

Rape is without doubt deserving of serious punishment; but in terms of moral depravity and of the injury to the person and to the public, it does not compare with murder, which does involve the unjustified taking of human life. Although it may be accompanied by another crime, rape by definition does not include the death or even the serious injury to another person. The murderer kills; the rapist, if no more than that, does not. Life is over for the victim of the murderers; for the rape victim, life may not be nearly so happy as it was, but it is not over and normally is not beyond repair. We have the abiding conviction that the death penalty, which "is unique in its severity and irrevocability," is an excessive penalty for the rapist who, as such, does not take human life.

One of the justices who voted with the majority in the Coker decision dissented in one respect. He felt that the majority went beyond what was necessary in that decision when it held:

. . . that capital punishment always—regardless of the circumstances—is a disproportionate penalty for the crime of rape. . . .

The plurality (the majority) draws a bright line between murder and all rapes—regardless of the degree of brutality of the rape or the effect upon the victim. I dissent because I am not persuaded that such a bright line is appropriate. There is extreme variation in the degree of culpability of rapists. The deliberate viciousness of the rapist may be greater than that of the murderer. Rape is never an act committed accidentally. Rarely can it be said to be unpremeditated. There is also wide variation in the effect on the victim. The plurality opinion says that "life is over for the victim of the murderer; for the rape victim, life may not be nearly so happy as it was, but it is not over and normally is not beyond repair." But there is indeed 'extreme variation' in the crime of rape. Some victims are so grievously injured physically or psychologically that life is beyond repair.

Thus it may be that the death penalty is not disproportionate punishment for the crime of aggravated rape. Final resolution of the questions must await careful inquiry into objective indicators of society's "evolving standards of decency," particularly legislative enactments and the responses of juries in capital cases. The plurality properly examines these indicia, which do support the conclusion that society finds the death penalty unacceptable for the crime of rape in the absence of excessive brutality or severe injury. But it has not been shown that society finds the penalty disproportionate for all rapists. In a proper case a more discriminating inquiry than the plurality undertakes well might discover that both juries and legislatures have reserved the ultimate penalty for the case of an outrageous rape resulting in serious, lasting harm to the victim. I would not prejudge the issue.

This statement indicates that if legislation was passed making it possible to impose the death penalty in aggravated rape cases, such a penalty might not be declared excessive. However, the *Coker* decision, in which four justices declared the death penalty excessive in all instances except where murder was involved, may make the passage of such legislation difficult. And even if such legislation was passed, there is no assurance that the United States Supreme Court would not hold the death penalty excessive.

Chief Justice Burger and Justice Rehnquist expressed concern in the *Coker* case over the majority's decision in holding the death penalty as excessive. These justices pointed out the following facts:

On December 5, 1971, Coker raped and then stabbed to death a young woman. Less than eight months later Coker kidnapped and raped a second young woman. After twice raping this 16 year-old victim, he stripped her, severely beat her with a club, and dragged her into a wooded area where he left her for dead. He was apprehended and pleaded guilty to offenses stemming from these incidents. He was sentenced by three separate courts to three life terms, two 20-year terms, and one eight-year term of imprisonment. Each judgment specified that the sentences it imposed were to run consecutively rather than concurrently. Approximately one and one-half years later, on September 2, 1974, petitioner escaped from the state prison where he was serving these sentences. He promptly raped another 16-year-old woman in the presence of her husband, abducted her from her home, and threatened her with death and serious bodily harm. It is this crime for which the sentence now under review was imposed.

The Court today holds that the State of Georgia may not impose the death penalty on Coker. In so doing, it prevents the State from imposing any effective punishment upon Coker for his latest rape. The Court's holding, moreover, bars Georgia from guaranteeing its citizens that they will suffer no further attacks by this habitual rapist. In fact, given the lengthy sentences Coker must serve for the crimes he has already committed, the Court's holding assures that petitioner (Coker) and others in his position will henceforth feel no compunction whatsoever about committing further rapes as frequently as he may be able to escape from confinement and indeed even within the walls of the prison itself.

328

> To what extent we have left States "elbow room" to protect innocent persons from depraved human beings like Coker remains in doubt.

These two dissenting justices were also concerned over the *Coker* decision because there was an indication that the majority would declare the death penalty excessive for any crime in which there was not a murder involved. These justices stated:

> Since the Court (the majority) now invalidates the death penalty as a sanction for all rapes of adults at all times for all circumstances, I reluctantly turn to what I see as the broader issues raised by this holding.
>
> The plurality acknowledges the gross nature of the crime of rape. A rapist not only violates a victim's privacy and personal integrity, but inevitably causes serous psychological as well as physical harm in the process. The long-range effect upon the victim's life and health is likely to be irreparable; it is impossible to measure the harm which results. Volumes have been written by victims, physicians and psychiatric specialists on the lasting injury suffered by rape victims. Rape is not a mere physical attack— it is destructive of the human personality. The remainder of the victim's life may be gravely affected, and this in turn may have a serious detrimental effect upon her husband and any children she may have. I therefore wholly agree with Mr. Justice White's conclusion as far as it goes—that short of homicide, rape is the "ultimate violation of the self." Victims may recover from the physical damage of knife or bullet wounds, or a beating with fists or a club, but recovery from such a gross assault on the human personality is not healed by medicine or surgery. To speak blandly, as the plurality does, of rape victims which are "unharmed," or, as the concurrence, to classify the human outrage of rape in terms of "excessively brutal," versus "moderately brutal," takes too little account of the profound suffering the crime imposes upon the victims and their loved ones.
>
> Despite its strong condemnation of rape, the Court reaches the inexplicable conclusion that the "death penalty is an excessive penalty" for the perpetrator (Coker) of this heinous offense.

As pointed out by one of the dissenting Justices in the *Coker* decision, Chief Justice Warren Burger, the result of the case is that the death penalty may be imposed only on the conviction of murder. Burger also pointed out that the Court's conclusion in that case was very disturbing. He stated:

> the clear implication of today's holding appears to be that the death penalty may be properly imposed only as to crimes resulting

in death of the victim. This case casts serious doubt upon the unconstitutional validity of statutes imposing the death penalty for a variety of conduct which, though dangerous, may not necessarily result in any immediate death, e.g., treason, airplane hijacking and kidnapping. In that respect, today's holding does even more harm than is initially apparent. We cannot avoid judicial notice that crimes such as airplane hijacking, and mass terrorist activity can constitute a serious and increasing danger to the safety of the public. It would be unfortunate indeed if the effect of today's holding were to inhibit States and the Federal Government from experimenting with various remedies—including possibly imposition of the death penalty—to prevent and deter such crimes.

Burger further stated that some of the Justices of the United States Supreme Court are inclined to interject their own feelings against the death penalty by restricting its implementation through strict limitations of its use. This same attitude has been manifested by some state supreme court justices in the strict interpretation of the *Witherspoon* case. As previously mentioned, *Witherspoon* dealt with the alleged undue exclusion of prospective jurors, and the question of whether the facts of a particular case fell within the special circumstances permitting the death penalty to be imposed.

Subsequent Death Penalty Legislation

Since the Coker decision was handed down, the U.S. Supreme Court has invalidated the death penalty in two other landmark cases, establishing new approaches to death penalty limitations. In the case of *Godfrey* v. *Georgia*, 446 US 420 (1980), the U.S. Supreme Court held that the sentence of death amounted to cruel and unusual punishment when pronounced on the defendant Godfrey, even though two murders had been committed. The Court quoted the Georgia statute providing that the death penalty could be invoked where the offense of murder was "outrageously or wantonly vile, horrible or inhuman." The Court held that to fall within that category, the evidence must demonstrate that the offender committed the murder through torture, depravity of mind or an aggravated battery before killing the victim. In the *Godfrey* case, the facts reflect that the defendant shot both victims in the head with a shot gun and that they died instantly. There was no evidence of serious suffering by the victims that would justify the death penalty under the Georgia statute. There were dissenting Justices in that case that felt that the killings by the defendant did fall within the statute as being outrageously or wantonly vile, horrible and inhuman.

In the case of *Enmund* v. *Florida,* 73 L. Ed 2d (1982), the facts reveal that Enmund and two other defendants entered into a conspiracy to rob a victim of money. The three went to the home of the victim Kersey and two of the robbers approached Kersey to commit the crime. Kersey resisted and called for help. His wife came to the rescue and wounded one of the robbers. In retaliation the robbers killed both Kersey and his wife. During this time Enmund was sitting in the get away car. After the killing the three left the scene of the crime, but were later identified, arrested and tried on a charge of first degree murder. In accordance with the Florida statute providing that "the killing of a human being while engaged in the perpetration of or in the attempt to perpetrate the offense of robbery is murder in the first degree even though there is no intent to kill, and for which upon conviction the death penalty may be imposed."

All three defendants were convicted of first degree murder and sentenced to death. Enmund appealed the death sentence on the grounds that the death penalty under the circumstances was in violation of the cruel and unusual punishment clause of the Eighth Amendment of the U.S. Constitution. Enmund alleged that he did not participate in the actual killing, and had no intent to kill during the robbery, and as such the death penalty as applied was disproportionate to the crime he committed. The U.S. Supreme Court agreed with Enmund that the death penalty in his instance was cruel and unusual punishment. The Court stated:

> We have no doubt that robbery is a serious crime deserving serious punishment. It is not, however, a crime so grievous an affront to humanity that the only adequate response may be the penalty of death. It does not compare with murder, which does involve the unjustified taking of human life. Although it may be accompanied by another crime, robbery by definition does not include the death of another person. The murderer kills; the robber if no more than that, does not. Life is over for the victim of the murderer; for the robbery victim, life is not beyond repair. As we said of the crime of rape in the *Coker* case, we have the abiding conviction that the death penalty, which is unique in its severity and irrevocability, is an excessive penalty for the robber who, as such, does not take human life.

The dissenting Justices in the *Enmund* case felt that the death penalty was not disproportionate to the crime of felony murder, even though Enmund did not actually kill or intend to kill the victims. They pointed out that Enmund planned the robbery and assisted in carrying it out by going with the other two defendants to the victim's home and sat in the get away car to aid in the escape after the robbery. As such, he was as guilty of murder as the other two defendants.

The majority of the Justices in the *Enmund* case did not rule out all death penalty sentences in which a co-conspirator did not actually do the killing, but as stated by one of the dissenting Justices:

to invoke the death penalty in such instances there must be proving of intent at the time that the robbery was planned. This could be most difficult as intent is a state of mind and proving the state of mind when a robbery was planned is difficult. Imposing the intent phase in such cases does preclude the death penalty being imposed in most instances.

Attention is called to the fact that even though an appellate court reverses the death penalty, the offender is not necessarily set free. In most instances the sentence will be reduced from the death penalty to life imprisonment without the possibility of parole, or to life imprisonment only depending on the statutes of the particular state. A life sentence without the possibility of parole may also be changed to life imprisonment by a governor at any time. Under a life sentence, most offenders are eligible for parole after serving a term of approximately twelve years. That does not mean that the offender will be paroled after that period of time, but an offender sentenced for life usually does not serve until death.

Executive Clemency

To this point in our study of the procedures in the justice system, we have been dealing exclusively with the judicial branch of the government. We now turn to a procedure frequently referred to as *executive clemency* because it involves the granting of favors to offenders by the executive branch of the government. Simply defined, clemency is an act of mercy or leniency; as it relates to executive clemency, it is the granting of a *reprieve, commutation, or pardon.* The right of the executive branch to grant clemency has its origin in common law. As we have seen, in common law when a criminal law was broken it was a violation of the king's peace. Only the king could grant a favor or act of mercy to one who had broken that peace. As the colonies were formed, the right to grant clemency was permitted to the governors of the colonies. As our state governments were formed, the right of clemency was granted to the governor of the state. It was also granted to the President of the United States if a federal law was involved.

The purpose of executive clemency was spelled out in the case of *Ex Parte Grossman,* 267 US 87 (1925), in which the United States Supreme Court stated:

> Executive clemency exists to afford relief from undue harshness or evident mistake in the operation or enforcement of the criminal law. The administration of justice by the courts is not necessarily always wise or certainly considerate of circumstances which may

properly mitigate guilt. To afford a remedy, it has always been thought essential in popular governments, as well as in monarchies, to vest in some other authority than the courts power to ameliorate or avoid particular criminal judgments. It is a check entrusted to the executive for special cases.

An offender has no constitutional right to have any executive clemency granted. As stated, clemency is an act of mercy that may be bestowed on an offender if the appropriate executive body sees fit to grant that mercy.

Reprieves

A reprieve is merely a delay or postponement in carrying out a sentence. Unless some other act of clemency is granted, the sentence must eventually be carried out. In most instances, the reprieve is a delay in carrying out an execution when the death penalty has been imposed. The usual reasons for granting a reprieve are either to permit further appeals to be taken or to endeavor to discover additional evidence that might make the sentence, particularly the death penalty, inapplicable in the case.

Commutations

The lessening of the punishment imposed by the original sentence is a commutation. Commutations may be either a reduction of the time to be served or a reduction in the severity of the original sentence. For example, an original sentence may have been the death penalty, but a governor has the right to commute the sentence to one of life imprisonment without the possibility of parole, or even life imprisonment with the possibility of parole. Successive governors may grant a commutation beyond that granted by a prior governor. In one case, for example, the offender was convicted of murdering a police officer and was given the death penalty. A governor commuted the sentence to life imprisonment without the possibility of parole. A subsequent governor further commuted the sentence to life imprisonment with the possibility of parole. Thereafter, a third governor granted the offender a pardon. Commutation has been also granted to parolees to shorten the period of time that must be spent on parole.

Pardon

A pardon has been described as an act of grace. Pardon is of ancient origin. The Bible tells of how the Jews learned to expect the pardon of a popular prisoner each Passover time. Frequently in Great Britain, during the mid-1200s, persons who had been convicted of homicide were granted pardons when it was learned that the act was committed by accident, in self-defense, or while of unsound mind. During the 1600s and early 1700s pardons were given to able-bodied prisoners on whom the death penalty had been imposed, in order that they might be sent to the American colonies as cheap laborers. Today pardons are granted as a form of forgiveness and as an aid to the rehabilitation process. It is the policy of the governors of many states to grant pardons to deserving prisoners at Christmas time. However, pardoning is not confined to that time of year.

Who May Pardons Be Given To? A pardon may be granted under one of three circumstances. First, it may be given to one convicted of a crime that he or she did not commit. Second, a pardon may be granted to one for some meritorious reason, such as going to the aid of a guard who is being attacked. Third, pardons are also given to convicted felons who, after being released from custody, have led law-abiding lives for a pre-scribed period of time and make application for a pardon. A pardon under these circumstances is usually accompanied with a certificate of rehabilitation or a letter of good conduct. Such a pardon is frequently referred to as a *full pardon* as distinguished from a *conditional pardon.* As previously noted, a convicted felon loses certain civil rights. In most states the offender loses the right to hold public office, the right to serve on a jury, and the right to contract. The right to vote may even be lost in some states, and the convicted felon may be subjected to impeachment as a witness. A full pardon will restore most of these rights. In a few states the rights are restored automatically on completion of the sentence.

In the early history of the United States most pardons were given under certain conditions or restrictions and were called conditional pardons. This pardon was the forerunner of our parole system. The con-ditions were very similar to those imposed on a parolee today and were given as an aid to rehabilitation. Even today in some states all pardons are conditional for a period of time, except those granted to innocent per-sons who were previously convicted. If the conditions are violated, a pardon could be revoked, but a full or an unconditional pardon may not be revoked.

Authority to Grant Pardons. The right to grant a pardon is usually within the authority of the governor, but a few states provide that a pardon may be granted only by a council or board established for that purpose. In those states where a board is responsible for granting a pardon, the governor is usually a member of that board, and some states hold that the pardon may not be granted by the board unless the gover-nor also votes to grant the pardon. In a few states the governor is not even a member of the board. In other states the governor has unrestricted power to grant a pardon. The governor in others may not grant a pardon without the consent of some other body, such as the Supreme Court, if the offender has been convicted previously of a felony.

Though the pardon idealistically wipes the slate clean, does it really place the offender in a state of status quo, as if the crime had never been committed? May a person who has received a pardon answer a question in an application for employment, concerning having been convicted of a felony, with a negative answer? Generally, in most states, there is no concrete answer to this second question. Many persons believe that if a pardon is to have real significance, the pardoned offender should be able to answer such a question negatively. Others hold that there has been a conviction and a sentence served, and there is no way that the conviction and sentence can be erased by a pardon. The pardon is merely a forgiveness and a restoration of civil rights and does not create an air of innocence. A full pardon does not always wipe the entire slate clean. In many states even though a full pardon is received the pardoned offender may not possess a gun if a gun was used in the crime for which he or she was convicted and later pardoned. The pardon may not automatically restore the license to practice certain professions, nor does it automatically restore a person to an office held before being convicted. In most states a prior conviction of a felony may cause an increase in the sentence received on a subsequent conviction. Generally a pardon does not prohibit the prior conviction from being used to increase the sentence on a second conviction.

In most instances, a pardon may not be granted until an offender has been convicted and sentenced on a felony charge. But in a few states, and in the federal government, an offender may be granted a pardon prior to any formal charges being brought. Thus, the pardon bars any prosecutive action against the offender for the particular offense involved. The Constitution of the United States, in Article II, Section 2, provides that the President of the United States "shall have power to grant reprieves and pardons for offenses against the United States, except in cases of impeachment." This provision permits the President of the United States to grant a pardon to an offender even though the offender has not been formally charged with an offense. (See *Murphy* v. *Ford,* 350 Fed Suppl 1372 [1975].)

Amnesty

A pardon that is granted to a class or group of persons is known as *amnesty,* and generally is granted for political reasons. In most instances amnesty is given to groups of individuals who have evaded military service during a military conflict. The amnesty may impose certain restrictions that must be complied with in order to receive forgiveness. For example, a draft evader may be required to perform social or charitable work for a prescribed time. The purpose of the amnesty is to alleviate tensions among certain factions of society who may have had moral and/or political reservations regarding the military conflict that they avoided. It may also serve as an appeasement to those who may have been in sympathy with the evasion. Presumedly the amnesty does not have to be accepted by all members of the group if they do not feel that they can comply with the restrictions imposed. However those who do comply may receive the amnesty.

Because of the nature of amnesty, it is granted usually by the President of the United States, and is granted in most instances prior to any convictions. Unless prohibited by state law, there is no reason why a governor could not grant amnesty to a group, such as demonstrators who had broken only state laws.

Review Questions

1. What was the original philosophy behind punishment?
2. State the theory behind deterrence as a form of punishment.
3. What has handicapped the effectiveness of deterrence?
4. Why is rehabilitation, when possible, the most idealistic purpose of punishment?
5. List five major handicaps to a rehabilitation program.
6. Name the three types of correctional institutions.
7. List three grants of executive clemency and explain the significance of each.
8. How does a pardon differ from amnesty? In what way are they alike?

Local Procedure

1. Are pardons granted by the governor or by some other body?
2. If pardons are granted by the governor, are there any restrictions?
3. May a pardon be granted before a conviction and sentence?
4. May the death penalty be imposed in this state?

EXTRADITION, WRITS, AND JUVENILE JUSTICE

seventeen

Extradition

From a sequential standpoint *extradition* should have been included in the discussion on arrest, but in view of the technicalities involved in this subject, it was believed that its discussion would be more understandable if delayed until this time. Extradition is the procedure followed in returning an accused from one state or foreign country to the state where the crime was committed, for the purposes of prosecution. The extradition proceedings may be international or interstate. Interstate extradition is referred to by some legal writers as *rendition*.

Interstate Extradition

Interstate extradition is based upon Article IV, Section 2, of the United States Constitution. This section provides that: "A person charged in any state with treason, felony, or other crime, who shall flee from justice, and be found in another state, shall on demand of the executive authority of the state from which he fled, be delivered up, to be removed to the state having jurisdiction over the crime." Because of certain deficiencies of this provision in covering all phases of extradition, most states have adopted the *Uniform Criminal Extradition Act*. Prior to the Act's adoption it was necessary to prove that an accused had actually fled from the state in which the crime was committed to avoid prosecution. The Act makes it unnecessary to prove that the accused fled from justice. The mere presence of the accused in another state is all that is necessary. Prior to the adoption of the Act, if an accused was found in another state to which he had not voluntarily gone, he could not be extradited. For example, in one case a fugitive was wanted for robbery in Utah but fled to Oklahoma. While in Oklahoma the offender committed a bank robbery and was sentenced to serve a federal sentence in the penitentiary in Leavenworth, Kansas. Utah attempted to extradite the fugitive from Kansas after the completion of the bank robbery sentence. It was held that since the fugitive did not voluntarily flee to Kansas, he could not be extradited. The adoption of the Act permits extradition from any state even though the accused did not voluntarily go to that state. An accused may be extradited on either a misdemeanor or a felony charge. However, because of the expense and procedure involved, fugitives are seldom extradited on a misdemeanor charge.

Requirements for Extradition.   In order to extradite an accused there must be a warrant of arrest outstanding against that individual, based on an accusatory pleading filed in the county in which the crime took place. After determining that the accused is in another state, the prosecuting

338

attorney of the county in which the crime was committed will make an application to the governor of his or her state. The application is a request for the governor to make a demand on the governor of the state where the accused is located for the return of the fugitive to the *demanding state* for prosecution. The application must reflect the name of the fugitive, the crime charged, the approximate time and date of the offense, the circumstances surrounding the commission of the crime, and the state and location where it is believed that the fugitive is located. It must also be alleged that the fugitive was in the demanding state at the time that the crime was committed. The application, along with copies of the accusatory pleading and a warrant, will be submitted to the governor of the demanding state. On approval of the application for extradition, the governor of the demanding state will appoint an officer to deliver the extradition papers to the governor of the state in which the fugitive is located, with a demand that the fugitive be returned to the demanding state for prosecution. The state in which the fugitive is located is generally referred to as the *asylum state.*

Acting on the Extradition Request.   On receipt of the papers the governor will review them in an effort to determine if the fugitive should be surrendered to the demanding state. The governor may request the attorney general, or any prosecuting attorney of his state, to conduct an investigation to assist in making the determination. The investigation may include an inquiry to determine that the person sought is actually the one charged in the demanding state; the offender's identity must be certainly established. An inquiry may be made by the asylum state to make certain that the accused has been substantially charged in the demanding state. This is a determination of whether or not a complaint has been filed or an indictment returned, and a warrant of arrest issued. The governor of the asylum state may wish to be satisfied that the accused sought was in the demanding state at the time the crime was committed, and that he or she then left the demanding state. If the investigation concludes that the fugitive should be surrendered, the governor will issue a governor's warrant of arrest directing some officer to place the fugitive under arrest. After the arrest is made, the fugitive will be taken before a local magistrate who will set a date for an extradition hearing. If the offense for which the fugitive is being extradited is a bailable offense in the demanding state, the local magistrate may set bail in order that the fugitive may post bail and be free from custody pending the extradition hearing. The hearing is usually set within a few days after the arrest. During the hearing two major facts will be taken into consideration. First, is the fugitive in custody the person named in the accusatory pleading of the demanding state? Second, was the fugitive in the demanding state at the time the crime was committed? If the magistrate has any reservations about either

340

of these items, a request may be made that the demanding state present further evidence to prove the identity and whereabouts of the fugitive. The fugitive is entitled to the assistance of counsel at the hearing and to present evidence in his or her own behalf. If the magistrate is satisfied that the fugitive at the hearing is the one named in the accusatory pleading and was in the demanding state at the time that the crime was committed, the fugitive will be turned over to the custody of an officer of the demanding state for return to that state. Evidence of the fugitive's guilt or innocence is not pertinent at the hearing and will not be presented. After returning to the demanding state the fugitive may be prosecuted on any charge, not just the one named in the extradition proceedings. In fact the fugitive does not even have to be prosecuted on that charge if the prosecuting attorney wishes to substitute a different charge.

The Fugitive Already Arrested.   Not all fugitives wanted in another state are first arrested on a governor's warrant. Frequently an individual is arrested on a minor local charge, after which it will be determined that there is an outstanding warrant of arrest for that individual in another state. The laws of most states permit a temporary detention of the arrested person until extradition proceedings can be instituted. Many times extradition proceedings are waived under these circumstances. If the person in custody waives the right to extradition proceedings, the waiver will eliminate the application to the governor of the demanding state and the other extradition formalities previously described. Upon agreeing to waive extradition, the arrested person is taken before a local magistrate where consent to be returned to the demanding state will be given. Usually the consent is given in writing. The magistrate will then order the arrested person's return to the demanding state.

Refusal to Extradite.   Although the United States Constitution provides that a person charged with a crime who has fled a state shall upon demand be "delivered up" to the demanding state, there have been times when a governor of an asylum state has refused to honor this constitutional provision. Both the United States Supreme Court and many state courts have held that the governor of an asylum state has the duty to abide by the demand, but there is no authority that can compel the governor to extradite a person wanted for prosecution. It has been held, however, that the governor of the asylum state must, within a reasonable time, either abide by the demand or refuse to extradite. The action cannot just be postponed indefinitely. The demanding state is entitled to know whether the fugitive is to be returned or not. (See *State of South Dakota* v. *Brown,* 144 Cal. Rptr. 758 [1978].) It has also been held that the asylum state has no right to question the merits or motives of the demanding state. The guilt or innocence of the offender is the sole responsibility of the demanding state.

In one case the supreme court of an asylum state ordered a local court to investigate the conditions of the prison in the demanding state from which the offender escaped before the asylum state would authorize the extradition of the offender. However the U.S. Supreme Court held in the case of *Pacileo* v. *Walker*, 449 US 86 (1981) that the state supreme court had exceeded its authority. The facts of the *Pacileo* case reflect that Walker, the defendant, escaped from an Arkansas prison, and was later apprehended in California. The governor of Arkansas requested that Walker be extradited to Arkansas to serve the remainder of his sentence. The governor of California signed the extradition papers, but the California Supreme Court ordered a local court to investigate the conditions of the Arkansas prison system to determine if conditions in the Arkansas prison system violated the cruel and unusual punishment clause of the Eighth Amendment to the U.S. Constitution. The local sheriff who was charged with the responsibility of making the investigation contended that the courts of the asylum state did not have the authority to investigate the prison conditions of the demanding state. The sheriff's contention was appealed to the U.S. Supreme Court. The U.S. Supreme Court held that once the governor of the asylum state signs the extradition papers, the courts of that state may consider only whether or not the extradition documents of the demanding state and asylum state are in order. Any further inquiry is beyond the local court's authority. The U.S. Supreme Court held that this issue had been previously decided in other cases and further stated:

> We [the U.S. Supreme Court] think that the Supreme Court of California ignored the teachings of these cases when it directed one of its own trial courts of general jurisdiction to conduct an inquiry into the present conditions of the Arkansas penal system. Once the Governor of California issued the warrant for arrest and rendition in response to the request of the Governor of Arkansas, claims as to the constitutional defects in the Arkansas penal system should be heard in the courts of Arkansas and not those of California.

Federal Law Against Unlawful Flight

Interstate extradition proceedings are not to be confused with the procedure followed under the federal *Unlawful Flight to Avoid Prosecution Statute*. In the 1930s gangsters began to plague local law enforcement officers by going into a community and committing a series of serious crimes and immediately fleeing for parts unknown. These officers were often handicapped in their efforts to locate the gangsters because many times they would flee to another state. Because of the seriousness of the situation, Congress passed the Unlawful Flight to Avoid Prosecution Statute. This Statute permits the federal government, through the Federal Bureau of Investigation (FBI), to assist in locating and arresting badly wanted fugitives. When a fugitive is identified as having left the state where a crime was committed, the local prosecuting attorney can have a local warrant of arrest issued. The United States Attorney for that district is then requested to file a complaint charging the fugitive with the violation of the Unlawful Flight Statute. A warrant is issued on the federal complaint giving the Federal Bureau of Investigation the authority to locate and arrest the fugitive. In most instances the local prosecuting attorney must agree to handle extradition proceedings, as the Statute was passed to assist in locating and arresting the fugitive and not for return to the demanding state. Originally the Statute permitted assistance in only a few major crimes; however, the Statute now permits assistance to be given for any felony violation.

International Extradition

International extradition is based entirely on treaties with certain countries; these treaties specify the crimes for which an accused may be extradited. In most instances, political crimes are excluded. If a fugitive is extradited from a foreign country, he or she may be prosecuted only on the extradition charge. This prevents countries from extraditing a political fugitive under the pretext of a specified crime and then instigating prosecution for an alleged attempt to overthrow a government or for another political or unspecified crime. International extradition is handled in the United States through the United States Department of State. Instead of the governor of the demanding state directly contacting the officials in the asylum country, the governor will forward the demand for extradition to the Secretary of State. The Secretary of State will submit the demand to the officials of the asylum country, requesting that the fugitive be surrendered to officials of the United States in order that he or she be returned to this country for prosecution. If those officials decide that extradition is in order, the fugitive will be surrendered to this country. As in the case of the governor who does not honor the constitutional provision on interstate extradition, there is little that can be done to compel a foreign country to extradite a person wanted in this country, with the exceptions of registering a protest or breaking a treaty. In most instances, however, the asylum country honors the demand. Treaties differ somewhat between countries. Some treaties provide that any person may be extradited for the specified crimes; other treaties exempt citizens of that particular country. This provision could hamper extradition, as many countries recognize dual citizenship. The lack of a treaty between two countries does not prevent one of them from surrendering a wanted fugitive to the other. Under these circumstances, the fugitive may be prosecuted for any crime unless the two countries agree otherwise.

Writs

A writ defies simple definition. Legally, a writ is defined as a mandatory precept, under seal, issued by a court, and commanding the person to whom it is addressed to do or not do some act. One might think of a writ as a written order issued by a court directing some other court officer to do or not do a particular act. There are a number of writs that may be issued by a court, but only the more frequently encountered writs will be discussed here.

Writ of Habeas Corpus

The writ of habeas corpus has been termed the *great writ* because its purpose is to obtain the prompt release of one who is being unlawfully detained. The right to this writ is embodied in the Constitution of the United States and in the laws of all the states. The statutes of the states read similar to the following: every person unlawfully imprisoned or restrained of liberty, under any pretense whatever, may request a writ of habeas corpus to inquire into the cause of the imprisonment or restraint. The person who believes that he or she is being unlawfully imprisoned, or someone in that person's behalf, may petition the appropriate court to have a writ of habeas corpus issued. Generally a writ of habeas corpus may be issued by a judge of the superior court or its equivalent, or by a justice of an appellate court. In most states the judge of the inferior court has no authority to issue a writ of habeas corpus.

The petition must state the place of confinement, the officer or person doing the confining, and the facts why the petitioner feels unlawfully imprisoned. If the reason is valid, the writ will be issued and served on the person holding the prisoner, commanding that the prisoner be brought before the issuing court for a hearing to determine if there is sufficient cause to confine the prisoner. A copy of the writ is furnished to the local prosecuting attorney in order that evidence may be presented endeavoring to prove the legality of the imprisonment. But the burden of proof is on the imprisoned person to prove by a preponderance of evidence that the imprisonment is unlawful. If the offense for which the person is imprisoned is a bailable one, the person is entitled to post bail pending the habeas corpus hearing.

If, after hearing the evidence presented by the prisoner and the prosecuting attorney, the judge concludes that the prisoner is being unlawfully detained, an order for the prisoner to be set free will be issued. The prisoner may not be charged further on that offense unless additional evidence is developed showing reasonable cause for an arrest and commitment by a legal process. If the judge concludes that the im-

344

prisonment was lawful, the prisoner will remain in custody to await the appropriate judicial processes.

The early use of the writ of habeas corpus was limited to obtaining the immediate release of one unlawfully restrained. But in recent years the use of this writ has been broadened materially to make it applicable in a number of situations. For example, if an offender believes that the bail set for release is excessive, a writ of habeas corpus may be filed in an effort to get a reduction in bail. Also, if a convicted person believes that the sentence is excessive, this writ may be filed to have a determination made on the sentence being excessive. This writ has also been used to determine the effectiveness of counsel. One of the more extensive uses made of the writ in recent years has resulted from some appellate court decisions, particularly those of the United States Supreme Court, that affect the rights of one convicted. For example, the *Witherspoon* decision held that a prospective juror could not be challenged for cause just because the juror had reservations against the death penalty. This decision caused writs of habeas corpus to be filed by all of those convicted and given the death penalty in trials in which prospective jurors had been excused for cause as being against the death penalty. These writs of habeas corpus requested that the sentence of death be reduced to life imprisonment. This was possible since the United States Supreme Court made the *Witherspoon* decision retroactive. When a decision is made retroactive, it is effective even though a trial is completed and the appeal period has passed. If a decision is not made retroactive, only those offenders whose trial or appeal has not been completed may take advantage of the decision.

Writ of Certiorari

This writ is issued by an appellate court to permit the review of a decision or judgment by a lower court. This writ is often issued when other means of appeal are not possible. The writ of certiorari is often granted by a state supreme court to review a lower court's decision in order to establish guidelines to be followed in future cases by either trial judges or lower appellate courts. This is particularly true if there is some doubt concerning a law or procedure. This writ is automatically issued in most jurisdictions to review a case when the death penalty is imposed to determine if the facts warrant a conviction and the imposition of the death penalty. The United States Supreme Court frequently issues this writ to review the decision of a state appellate court when there may be a possible denial of a United States constitutional guarantee. The *Coker* decision is a good example. As stated, Coker was convicted of forceful rape and sentenced to death in a trial court in Georgia. The Georgia Supreme Court affirmed both the conviction and the death penalty. The United States Supreme Court granted Coker a writ of certiorari in order to determine if the death penalty was excessive for the conviction of rape and, thus, a violation of the Eighth Amendment.

Writ of Prohibition

Such a writ is issued by an appellate court to restrain a judicial action or judgment of a lower court. The writ may prohibit a lower court from trying a case over which the lower court has no jurisdiction. In one case the writ was issued to restrain a lower court from submitting question-naires to members of a grand jury in order to determine their ages and incomes after a defendant claimed that poor persons and younger people were being excluded from grand juries. The appellate court held that "In ordering the questionnaires, the trial court abused its discretion by com-pelling disclosure of the panelists' personal affairs without any showing of plausible justification on the part of the accused." (See *People* v. *Superior Court of Nevada County*, 133 Cal Rptr 732 [1974].)

Writ of Mandamus

The purpose of the writ of mandamus (or mandate) is to compel the performance of a duty by a lower court. This writ may be issued to a lower court compelling the dismissal of a case that has not been brought to trial within the prescribed time limit. The writ may also be issued to compel the return of property that was not contraband when the property was seized under a void search warrant. In addition, it may be issued to compel a lower court to grant a change in venue.

Juvenile Justice

Since the handling of the juvenile offender is a complete course of study in itself, the subject of juvenile justice will not be delved into deeply, but a few passing remarks are in order. There are times when a juvenile commits a serious crime, and is tried as an adult. If not prosecuted as an adult, the juvenile offender will be processed through a juvenile or family court. In most states this is not a separate court but only a branch of another court.

Procedures of the Juvenile Hearing

The proceedings are considered as *civil hearings* and not criminal trials. As such, many of the proceedings of a criminal trial are not followed in the juvenile hearings. The purpose of the hearing is to determine whether or not a juvenile offender should be declared a delinquent and what action should be taken to correct or treat his or her condition. If as a result of the juvenile hearing the judge declares the juvenile offender to be a delinquent, the juvenile may be committed to some institution for correctional processing, or be placed on probation for a prescribed period of time. The hearings are usually informal, private affairs and are often held in the judge's chambers. The evidence against the offender is, in many instances, presented by the arresting officer or a probation officer, and in most states the prosecuting attorney rarely makes an appearance unless the case is an exceptional one or particularly complicated.

In the past, since juvenile hearings were considered civil in nature and not criminal, it was felt that the constitutional guarantees, such as the right to the assistance of counsel, the right against self-incrimination, and right of confrontation with witnesses were not applicable in juvenile hearings. But in the case of *In re Gault,* 387 US 1 (1967), the United States Supreme Court held that a written notice had to be given to the juvenile and parents or guardian, prior to a juvenile delinquency hearing, so that a sufficient defense could be prepared. The juvenile and parents were to be advised of the right to the assistance of counsel, and, if they could not afford counsel, that one would be provided for them. The Court also held that the juvenile was entitled to be confronted with any adverse witnesses, and that he or she was entitled to the guarantee against self-incrimination. In relation to the right against self-incrimination the Court stated:

> . . . Against the application to juveniles of the right to silence, it is argued that juvenile proceedings are "civil" and not "criminal," and therefore the privilege should not apply. It is true that the statement of the privilege in the Fifth Amendment, which is applicable to the States by reason of the Fourteenth Amendment, is that no person "shall be compelled in any criminal case to be a witness against himself." However, it is also clear that the availability of the privilege does not turn upon the type of proceeding in which its protection is invoked, but upon the nature of the statement or admission and exposure which it invites. The privilege may, for example, be claimed in a civil or administrative proceeding, if the statement is or may be inculpatory.
>
> It would be entirely unrealistic to carve out of the Fifth Amendment all statements by juveniles on the ground that these cannot lead to "criminal" involvement. In the first place, juvenile proceedings to determine "delinquency," which may lead to commitment to a state institution, must be regarded as criminal for purposes of the privilege against self-incrimination. To hold otherwise would be to disregard substance because of the feeble enticement of the "civil" label-of-convenience which has been attached to juvenile proceedings. Indeed, in over half of the States

juveniles may be placed in or transferred to adult penal institutions after having been found "delinquent" by a juvenile court. For this purpose, at least, commitment is a deprivation of liberty. It is incarceration against one's will, whether it is called "criminal" or "civil." And our Constitution guarantees that no person shall be compelled to be a witness against himself when he is threatened with deprivation of his liberty—a command which this Court has broadly applied and generously implemented in accordance with the teaching of the history of the privilege and its great office in mankind's battle for freedom.

Grounds for Declaring Delinquency

The United States Supreme Court has also held that a judge must be convinced of the delinquency of a juvenile beyond a reasonable doubt before the juvenile may be declared a delinquent. The Court stated in the case of *In re Winship:*

> We turn to the question whether juveniles, like adults, are constitutionally entitled to proof beyond a reasonable doubt when they are charged with violation of a criminal law. The same considerations which demand extreme caution in factfinding to protect the innocent adult apply as well to the innocent child. . . .
>
> We conclude, as we concluded regarding the essential due process safeguards applied in *Gault,* that the observance of the standard of proof beyond a reasonable doubt will not compel the States to abandon or displace any of the substantive benefits of the juvenile process. . . .
>
> In sum, the constitutional safeguard of proof beyond a reasonable doubt is as much required during the adjudicatory stage of delinquency proceedings as are those constitutional safeguards applied in *Gault*—notice of charges, right to counsel, the rights of confrontation and examination, and the privilege against self-incrimination.

Although the United State Supreme Court has held that a juvenile is to be granted certain constitutional guarantees, not all the rights included in the Bill of Rights must be afforded to the juvenile, in order that there be a compliance with the due process of law clause of the Fourteenth Amendment. This Court held in the case of *McKeiver* v. *Pennsylvania,* 403 US 528 (1971), that a juvenile is not entitled to have a delinquency hearing held before a jury. The Court stated:

> The Court has refrained, in the cases heretofore decided, from taking the easy way with a flat holding that all rights constitutionally assured for the adult accused are to be imposed upon the state juvenile proceeding. . . .

It is clear to us that the Supreme Court has properly attempted to strike a judicious balance by injecting procedural orderliness into juvenile court system. It is seeking to reverse the trend whereby the child receives the worst of both worlds.

There is a possibility, at least, that the jury trial, if required as a matter of constitutional precept, will remake the juvenile proceeding into a fully adversary process and will put an effective end to what has been the idealistic prospect of an intimate, informal protective proceeding.

Review Questions

1. What is extradition?
2. Upon what is international extradition based?
3. Upon what is interstate extradition based?
4. In relation to prosecution how do international and interstate extradition differ?
5. In what way did the Uniform Criminal Extradition Act correct certain weaknesses in the extradition procedure?
6. Briefly outline the procedure that must be followed in extraditing an offender.
7. What is the purpose of each of the following writs:
   a. habeas corpus
   b. certiorari
   c. prohibition
   d. mandamus
8. What rights are granted to a juvenile before he or she may be declared a delinquent, as provided in the *Gault* decision?
9. According to the United States Supreme Court must a juvenile hearing be held before a jury?

Local Procedure

1. Has the state adopted the Uniform Criminal Extradition Act?

Appendix

In order that the reader may better understand the procedures followed from an arrest through sentencing, the following chart has been prepared. It reflects in general the steps taken when an arrest has been made without a warrant on a felony charge. An outline of the general procedure that is followed in a criminal trial is also included. Depending upon the jurisdiction, there may be some slight deviation from the procedures set forth in this appendix.

General procedure followed after an arrest without a warrant on a felony charge:

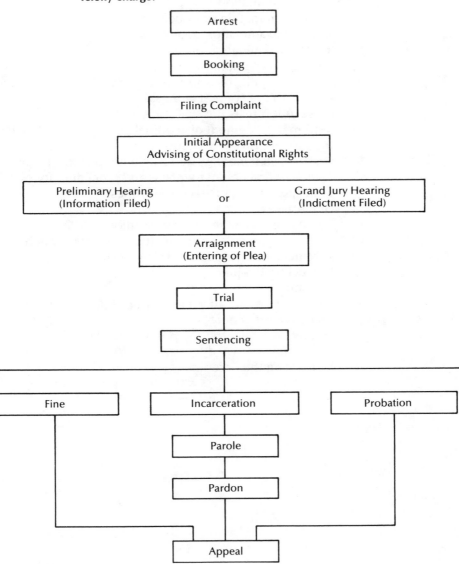

Outline of Trial Procedure

1. Selection of jury
2. Swearing in of jury (trial technically begins at this time)
3. Reading of charge and plea
4. Opening statement by prosecuting attorney
5. Opening statement by defense (this may be waived entirely or until prosecution rests)
6. Calling of first prosecution witness and administration of the oath
7. Direct examination
8. Cross-examination (may be waived)
9. Redirect examination (may be waived)
10. Recross-examination (may be waived)
11. Calling of additional prosecution witnesses, administration of oath, direct examination, and other procedure as in case of first witness
12. Prosecution rests
13. Motion for judgment of acquittal by defense (if denied, then the following procedure)
14. Opening statement by defense (if not previously given)
15. Calling of first defense witness and procedure followed as in case of first prosecution witness
16. Defense rests
17. Rebuttal presentation by prosecution
18. Closing arguments by prosecution and then by defense
19. Rebuttal closing argument by prosecution
20. Instructing the jury
21. Deliberation
22. Return of verdict (if guilty verdict returned, then the following procedure)
23. Request for new trial by defense (if denied, then the following)
24. Sentencing the defendant

cases

353